12/08

brazeal

Conflict and Stability in the German Democratic Republic

Why did the German Democratic Republic last for so long – longer, in fact, than the Weimar Republic and the Third Reich combined? This book looks at various political, social, and economic conflicts at the grass roots of the GDR in an attempt to answer this question and account for regime stability. A local study, it examines opposition and discontent in Saalfeld, an important industrial and agricultural district. Based on previously inaccessible primary sources as well as on interviews with local residents, the book offers a novel explanation for the durability of the regime by looking at how authorities tried to achieve harmony and consensus through negotiation and compromise. At the same time, it shows how official policies created deep-seated social cleavages that promoted stability by hindering East Germans from presenting a united front to authorities when mounting opposition or pressing for change. All of this provides an indirect answer to perhaps the major question of the postwar period: Why did the Cold War last as long as it did?

Andrew I. Port is an assistant professor of History at Wayne State University in Detroit. He earned a Ph.D. in history from Harvard University and a B.A. in history from Yale University. He has published articles in *Social History* and the *Frankfurter Allgemeine Zeitung*, as well as chapters in several edited volumes.

Contents

...so sind die Vorgänge und die Geschichte eines Dorfes und die eines Reiches im Wesentlichen dieselben; und man kann am Einen wie am Anderen die Menschheit studieren und kennen lernen.

...the events and history of a village and of a kingdom are essentially the same; and we can study and learn to know humanity just as well in the one as in the other.

–Arthur Schopenhauer

Illustrations and Tables

Illustrations

Tables

Acknowledgments

This book began the night the Berlin Wall fell. I had graduated from college several months earlier and moved to West Berlin to study history at the Free University, and I was spending the evening chatting with friends in a café when the news suddenly broke on the radio. That very night, and over the next two years, I traveled as often as I could to the eastern half of Germany, where I tried to learn from East Germans as much as possible about what their lives had been like under "real-existing socialism." This personal experience largely explains why I decided to attend graduate school and become a trained historian, and why I later chose to write a dissertation on the history of the German Demo-cratic Republic (GDR). The following study is a substantially revised version of that dissertation, which I wrote at Harvard University under the superb direc-tion of Charles Maier, David Blackbourn, and – on loan, so to speak, from the Friedrich Schiller University in Jena, Germany – Lutz Niethammer. Their own work and ways of thinking about history have long served as an inspiration and model, and I thank them wholeheartedly for their many years of support and guidance.

I have incurred a number of additional debts, intellectual and otherwise, over the past decade and a half, and it is with great pleasure that I now acknowledge them as well – beginning with the "otherwise." The Alexander von Humboldt Foundation, the Krupp Foundation, and the Minda de Gunzburg Center for European Studies at Harvard University provided generous funding and other support during the two years that I spent in Germany carrying out initial research for this project. A fellowship in the humanities from the Mrs. Giles Whiting Foundation relieved me of my teaching duties for a year, which allowed me to write a substantial part of what follows. Another significant por-tion was written at the Zentrum für Zeithistorische Forschung (ZZF, or Center for Contemporary Historical Research) in Potsdam, Germany, where I spent three months as a visiting scholar. More recently, the Department of History and the College of Liberal Arts and Sciences at Wayne State University provided me with a summer research grant that allowed me to carry out a number of important revisions, as well as a generous subsidy that assured publication of this book.

Over the course of this project, I have received advice, encouragement, and constructive criticism from colleagues on both sides of the Atlantic: Arnd Bauerkämper, Volker Berghahn, Richard Bessel, John Connelly, Christoph Conrad, Richard Gray, Siegfried Grundmann, Peter Hübner, Konrad Jarausch, Jürgen John, Rainer Karlsch, Jürgen Kocka, Jeff Kopstein, Charles Lansing, Sigrid Meuschel, Jörg Roesler, Helmut Smith, Helke Stadtland, Gale Stokes, Rüdiger Stutz, Dorothee Wierling, and Stefan Wolle. Klaus Tenfelde and Hans-Ulrich Wehler kindly gave me the opportunity to present some of my early findings in the colloquium on modern social history that they used to conduct jointly at the University of Bielefeld. I am also grateful for the insightful feedback that I received from the participants in the study group on modern Germany run by David Blackbourn and Peter Burgard at Harvard University. During the earliest phase of my research, Hartmut Zimmermann spent many hours sharing with me his vast knowledge about the GDR (and his seemingly endless supply of tea). I am deeply saddened that he did not live to see the appearance of this book.

Two other scholars deserve special mention as well. Henry Turner, who served as my undergraduate thesis adviser, first introduced me to the art of history. He has since maintained a keen interest in my subsequent development as a historian, helped me in more ways than I can imagine, and become a cherished mentor and friend. The same is true of Peter Bender, whose wisdom, fair-mindedness, and *humanitas* continue to awe me now as much as they did when I first met him almost two decades ago. There were few in the West who knew the GDR as intimately as Peter; fewer still have shown as much sustained interest in my project as he.

During the two years I spent in Thuringia carrying out research, I was extremely fortunate to have Lutz Niethammer – who first suggested Saalfeld for a case study about the GDR – as my academic host. He and the participants in his colloquium on modern German history at the Friedrich Schiller University not only provided generous advice and feedback, but also graciously listened to my anecdotes about the often humorous (and sometimes maddening) experiences I had in the archives and in the field. That was especially true of Rüdiger Stutz and his family, who warmly welcomed me into their home. My good fortune continued upon returning to the United States, where I spent several years as a resident Fellow at Harvard's Center for European Studies. I am especially grateful to the directors at the time, Stanley Hoffmann and Charles Maier, who created an intellectually invigorating space for interdisciplinary discussion, as well as to Abby Collins and Annette Schlagenhauff, who offered their friendship along with their administrative support. Konrad Jarausch, Christoph Kleßmann, and above all Peter Hübner were equally gracious hosts at the ZZF in Potsdam, whose staff has produced some of the most innovative and exciting research to appear on the GDR in recent years. A word of thanks as well to my colleagues at Wayne State University, my new academic home. Under the skilled stewardship of Marc Kruman, the Department of History has provided a nurturing environment that made completion of this study possible.

Some of the material in this book has previously appeared elsewhere. Chapter 2 is a revised version of "When Workers Rumbled: The Wismut Upheaval of August 1951 in East Germany," *Social History* 22 (1997): 145–73. Sections of Chapters 5 and 7 were originally published in "The 'Grumble *Gesellschaft*': Industrial Defiance and Worker Protest in Early East Germany," in Peter Hübner and Klaus Tenfelde, eds., *Arbeiter in der SBZ–DDR* (Klartext: Essen, 1999), 787–810.[1] I would like to thank the publishers, Taylor and Francis (http://www.tandf.co.uk) and Ludger Claßen of the Klartext Verlagsgesellschaft mbH, respectively, for their kind permission to use that material here. I am also grateful to Gerhard Werner, the former director of the Stadtmuseum in Saalfeld, for permission to use his map of the district; Claudia Streitberger, who also works at the museum, helped me find and obtain permission to use photographs of Saalfeld from the postwar period. Wilfried Peper kindly granted me access to the Maxhütte Archiv in Unterwellenborn, and Katrin Beger of the Thüringisches Staatsarchiv Rudolstadt went out of her way to assist me in locating an abundance of useful material. The other archivists in the former East German archives also merit mention: Many of them taught me more about the way in which the GDR functioned than any document I came across.

Lew Bateman, my editor at Cambridge University Press, first expressed interest in this project almost a decade ago. I am indebted to him for the support and encouragement he has offered ever since. His colleagues Jessica Cepelak and Helen Wheeler did a wonderful job of shepherding the manuscript through the production process while patiently answering all of my questions; I could not have asked for a more conscientious copy editor than Helen Greenberg. I would also like to thank the two anonymous referees for the considerable time and effort they put into carefully reading and commenting on the original manuscript. Their insightful observations helped improve the final product immeasurably.

For many years, a number of friends have listened to me talk at length about a place many of them had never heard of before: Katrin Brockmann, Kevin Cramer, Charitini Douvaldzi, Frieda Fuchs, Ivo Georgiev, Michel Goyer, Lutz Kirschner, Rowena Olegario, Jonathan Rosenberg, Anna Stavrakopoulou, and Jens Trefflich. I thank them for their patience and good cheer. Three others deserve special words of gratitude: Beate Bender, who first kindled my interest in Germany and all things German; Sonja Vandenrath, who rescued me from the archives and, in so doing, introduced me to all of the wonderful charms

---

[1] To avoid any possible confusion: Several sections of this article also appeared – in somewhat altered form and without quotation or acknowledgment – in Corey Ross, *Constructing Socialism at the Grass Roots: The Transformation of East Germany, 1945–1965* (Houndsmill, UK, 2000), 7, 95–7, 99–100, 167. According to an e-mail that I received from Ross on February 26, 2004, the approximately one dozen disturbing parallels in wording and content were the unintentional result of "naiveté" and "carelessness."

xiv

that Europe has to offer; and Mark Baker, the one person who made graduate school not only stimulating but also downright fun. I would also like to thank my parents, Lois and Bob Sansky, whose financial support made my studies possible from the very beginning.

My greatest debt belongs to my wife, Sylvia Taschka, to whom I lovingly dedicate this book. Not every historian is lucky enough to have another historian as a partner – especially one as patient, probing, and perspicacious. Unlike Sylvia, who diligently read every word (several times), our daughter, Hannah – who arrived several months before the galleys – was largely spared the many hours her father spent typing away in a dark and lonely study. Her sparkling eyes, like those of her mother, now make all of my days that much brighter.

Nuremberg, Germany, July 2006

Abbreviations

BV	Belegschaftsversammlung, Betriebsversammlung
CDU	Christlich–Demokratische Union Deutschlands
DA	*Deutschland Archiv*
DDR	Deutsche Demokratische Republik
DFD	Demokratischer Frauenbund Deutschlands
EOS	Erweiterte Oberschule
FDGB	Freier Deutscher Gewerkschaftsbund
FDJ	Freie Deutsche Jugend
GDR	German Democratic Republic
Gen.	Genosse
Gew.	Gewerkschaft
GG	*Geschichte und Gesellschaft*
GO	Grundorganisation
GST	Gesellschaft für Sport und Technik
HaNaGe	Handel-Nahrung-Genuss
HO	Handelsorganisation
IB	Informationsbericht
IG	Industriegewerkschaft
ILWCH	*International Labor and Working-Class History*
IM	Inoffizielle Mitarbeiter
JHK	*Jahrbuch für Historische Kommunismusforschung*
KD	Kreisdienststelle
KG	Kommanditgesellschaft
KL	Kreisleitung
KOM	Kraftomnibus
KPD	Kommunistische Partei Deutschlands
KPKK	Kreisparteikontrollkommission
Kr.	Kreis
KR	Kreisrat
KrA-S	Kreisarchiv Saalfeld
KV	Kreisverwaltung, Kreisvorstand
KVP	Kasernierte Volkspolizei
LDPD	Liberal–Demokratische Partei Deutschlands
LEB	Landeseigene Betriebe
LPG	Landwirtschaftliche Produktionsgenossenschaft
LPKK	Landesparteikontrollkommission
LS	Leitungssitzung
LV	Landesverwaltung
Maxh.	Maxhütte
MB	Maschinen-Betrieb
MEW	Mitteldeutsches Elektromotorenwerk
Mitgl.	Mitglied
MTS	Maschinen–Traktoren–Station
MV	Mitgliederversammlung
MxA-U	Maxhütte Archiv Unterwellenborn

n.d.	no date
NDPD	National–Demokratische Partei Deutschlands
Niederschr.	Niederschrift
NÖS	Neues Ökonomisches System
n.p.	no place
NSDAP	Nationalsozialistische Deutsche Arbeiterpartei
NVA	Nationale Volksarmee
PB	Produktionsberatung
PO	Parteiorganisation
Prot.	Protokoll
PV	Produktionsversammlung
SAG	Sowjetische Aktiengesellschaft
SAPMO-BA	Stiftung Archiv der Parteien und Massenorganisationen der DDR im Bundesarchiv Berlin
SED	Sozialistische Einheitspartei Deutschlands
Sekr.	Sekretariat
Sitz.	Sitzung
Slf	Saalfeld
SMAD	Sowjetische Militäradministration in Deutschland
SPD	Sozialdemokratische Partei Deutschlands
SStA-C	Sächsisches Staatsarchiv Chemnitz
StA-S	Stadtarchiv Saalfeld
SV	Sozialversicherung
TAN	Technisch begründete Arbeitsnorm
ThHStA-W	Thüringisches Hauptstaatsarchiv Weimar
ThStA-R	Thüringisches Staatsarchiv Rudolstadt
Thür.	Thüringen
TSW	Thüringer Schokoladenwerk
UACZ	Unternehmensarchiv der Carl Zeiss Jena GmBH
VdgB	Verein der gegenseitigen Bauernhilfe
VEB	Volkseigener Betrieb
VfZ	*Vierteljahrshefte für Zeitgeschichte*
VPKA	Volkspolizeikreisamt
WA	Wohnungsamt
Wema	Werkzeugmaschinenfabrik
WL	Werkleiter, Werkleitung
ZAWG	Zentralarbeiterwohnungsbaugenossenschaft
ZfG	*Zeitschrift für Geschichtswissenschaft*
ZPKK	Zentralparteikontrollkommission

Note on the Text

The original German titles have been provided for all documents cited in the footnotes, which use the British dating system. If the document had no title, a short descriptive phrase is provided in English. Many of the document folders from the Maxhütte factory archive had no call number at the time they were consulted. The names and dates written on the covers of those folders have been provided instead.

Those wanting further documentation and examples in support of the individual points made in this book should consult the original dissertation upon which it is based: "Conflict and Stability in the German Democratic Republic: A Study in Accommodation and Working-Class Fragmentation, 1945–1971" (Ph.D. diss., Harvard University, 2000).

All translations from the original sources are by the author unless otherwise indicated.

Conflict and Stability in the German Democratic Republic

Introduction: The Puzzle of Stability

All good history writing begins at the end. However artfully it may be disguised, however unthinkingly it may be assumed, the end of the story is there at the beginning. Where the end is judged to lie in time, what its character is, how it is defined – in taking these decisions about any piece of work, historians necessarily make their judgement about the general significance of their particular theme or period.

—Timothy Mason[1]

When exactly did the story of the German Democratic Republic (GDR) end? On November 9, 1989, the day the Berlin Wall fell? On October 3, 1990, the day the two postwar German states were officially unified? Or could it be argued that its story still continues and will only come to an end when the scars of division finally heal and the many social, cultural, and economic disparities between the eastern and western halves of the new Federal Republic are finally overcome? Whatever the answer to this difficult question, and for reasons that will become readily apparent, the following study of the GDR chooses an entirely different endpoint: 1971, the year that Erich Honecker succeeded Walter Ulbricht as head of the East German Socialist Unity Party (SED). Even if one dismisses the bold suggestion that Ulbricht was one of the "most successful German statesmen" of the twentieth century, the GDR was in many respects a success story the year he fell from power.[2] The economy and

---

[1] Timothy Mason, *Social Policy in the Third Reich: The Working Class and the "National Community,"* ed. Jane Caplan, trans. John Broadwin (Providence, RI, 1993), 1.

[2] Quotation from Sebastian Haffner, *Zur Zeitgeschichte: 36 Essays* (Munich, 1982), 122. For contemporary assessments of the GDR's development under Ulbricht, see, e.g., Joachim Nawrocki, *Das geplante Wunder: Leben und Wirtschaften im anderen Deutschland* (Hamburg, 1967). On the fall of Ulbricht, see Monika Kaiser, *Machtwechsel von Ulbricht zu Honecker: Funktionsmechanismen der SED Diktatur in Konfliktsituationen, 1962 bis 1972* (Berlin, 1997); Peter Przybylski, *Tatort Politbüro* (Berlin, 1991). On tensions in divided Germany and the challenges of reunification, see Mike Dennis and Eva Kolinsky, eds., *United and Divided: Germany since 1990* (New York, 2004).

infrastructure had largely been rebuilt following wartime ravaging, and the living standard of those who had chosen to remain had improved considerably since the end of the Second World War. Though still behind its West German rival, the GDR had the strongest economy in the Soviet bloc and was on the verge of gaining widespread international recognition beyond the iron curtain.[3] But most important, and for the purposes of this study, the GDR still *existed* in 1971.

Since the opening of the archives more than a decade ago, many investigations of the GDR have understandably focused on the dysfunctional nature and ultimate collapse of the postwar socialist state in light of the dramatic events of 1989.[4] The following examination tries, instead, to account for regime stability by focusing on its early decades – and, in so doing, avoids the sort of teleological approach that has characterized so many studies of the Weimar Republic. The implicit point of departure for much recent work on the GDR was that it was similarly doomed to fail, that its history was a "decline by installments" – an "*Untergang auf Raten*."[5] Yet the East German regime lasted for more than forty years, i.e., considerably longer than the Weimar Republic and the Third Reich combined. In fact, one of the most striking aspects of the GDR was its remarkable stability: From the outside, it appeared to be one of the most stable states in Eastern Europe and its population among the most docile. After the well-known mass uprising of June 1953 and before the fall of 1989, there were no major challenges to the regime from below – even though, as this study will show, many of the same social, economic, and political grievances that had led to the earlier upheaval remained pervasive. What, then, despite overwhelming evidence of widespread discontent, held East Germany together and accounted for so many years of domestic stability? This is a puzzle, and it is the question that has driven the following investigation: an attempt to explain the longevity of the GDR and, by extension, the Soviet bloc as a whole.

Coercion and consent, as Mary Fulbrook has pointed out, are two of the most common explanations used to account for the stability of a given political system. Both reflect traditional assumptions about successful forms of domination

---

[3] Good overviews of the GDR during the Ulbricht era include Christoph Kleßmann, *Die doppelte Staatsgründung: Deutsche Geschichte, 1945–1955* (Bonn, 1991); idem, *Zwei Staaten, eine Nation: Deutsche Geschichte, 1955–1970* (Bonn, 1997); Dietrich Staritz, *Geschichte der DDR* (Frankfurt am Main, 1996); Klaus Schroeder, *Der SED–Staat: Geschichte und Strukturen der DDR* (Munich, 1998); Hermann Weber, *Geschichte der DDR* (Erfstadt, 2004).

[4] For an overview of the vast literature on the collapse, see Beate Ihme-Tuchel, *Die DDR* (Darmstadt, 2002), 73–89; Corey Ross, *The East German Dictatorship: Problems and Perspectives in the Interpretation of the GDR* (London, 2002), 126–48.

[5] See Armin Mitter and Stefan Wolle, *Untergang auf Raten: Unbekannte Kapitel der DDR–Geschichte* (Munich, 1993). Wolle has similarly suggested elsewhere that the GDR went through forty "last years." See his *Die heile Welt der Diktatur: Alltag und Herrschaft in der DDR, 1971–1989* (Berlin, 1998), 244. Along similar lines, see Rolf Steininger, *17. Juni 1953: Der Anfang vom langen Ende der DDR* (Munich, 2003). For a critical assessment of the teleological approach to the Weimar period, see Detlev Peukert, *The Weimar Republic: The Crisis of Classical Modernity*, trans. Richard Deveson (New York, 1992), xii.

and authority: that they hinge on the ability of those in power to ensure obedience, either by using – or threatening to use – force to discourage and penalize deviant behavior, or by convincing those who are ruled to believe in the legitimacy and advantages of an existing political order.[6] With respect to the GDR, one of the most popular arguments along these lines holds that the Berlin Wall, the state security apparatus – the infamous Stasi – and, above all, Soviet tanks and bayonets were the keys to quiescence and acquiescence. The collapse of East Germany was a foregone conclusion, the argument goes, once backing had been withdrawn from Moscow and the threat of repression had more or less vanished: "In the end it was tanks and nothing but tanks that held Stalin's empire together thirty-six years after his death."[7] Such claims are sometimes complemented by another popular explanation that focuses on national character and revisits the myth of the "unpolitical" or "passive" German: an obedient subject conditioned by history and without civic courage. The GDR, according to this view, was "typically German," a state where "the sins of the oppressors were . . . complemented by the sins of the oppressed."[8]

A more subtle approach to this question argues that the ruling SED managed to maintain stability because of the various and supposedly successful ways in which it sought to legitimize its rule and thus win over large segments of East German society. The regime's antifascist rhetoric and the promise of a future socialist utopia devoid of inequality, insecurity, and social conflict supposedly resonated, for example, with the workers and farmers in whose name the party claimed to rule. And the specific policies adopted to that end – above all the vast array of social benefits that allegedly assured East Germans affordable housing, inexpensive goods, and a modicum of social and economic security – all helped to ensure stability by procuring some degree of loyalty toward the regime. So, too, did wide-ranging job security as well as the supposedly unprecedented opportunities for education, professional advancement, and social mobility made available to members of previously disadvantaged social groups.[9]

The various strands of this argument have at least one important element in common: the belief that large numbers of East Germans came to support or at least accept the regime. This was "the glue . . . that held the state together," according to one study that claims, moreover, that the "system functioned" for

---

[6] Mary Fulbrook, *Anatomy of a Dictatorship: Inside the GDR, 1949–1989* (Oxford, 1995), 271–4.

[7] Hannes Schwenger, "Immer wieder Panzer," *Der Tagesspiegel*, June 26, 2000. For a now classic statement on the stabilizing role played by repression, see Mitter and Wolle, *Untergang*.

[8] Fulbrook, *Anatomy*, 11. For claims about supposedly apolitical East Germans, see Sigrid Meuschel, *Legitimation und Parteiherrschaft in der DDR: Zum Paradox von Stabilität und Revolution in der DDR, 1945–1989* (Frankfurt am Main, 1992), 15–22. On the extent to which East Germans supposedly followed the "special path" of their forebears, see, e.g., Jürgen Kocka, "Ein deutscher Sonderweg: Überlegungen zur Sozialgeschichte der DDR," *APuZ* B40 (1994): 34–45; Stefan Wolle, "Die DDR in der deutschen Geschichte," *Geschichte in Wissenschaft und Unterricht* 50 (1999): 396–411.

[9] See the essays in Christoph Boyer and Peter Skyba, eds., *Repression und Wohlstandsversprechen: Zur Stabilisierung von Parteiherrschaft in der DDR und der CSSR* (Dresden, 1999).

more than four decades "because of the involvement and active participation of the majority of the population."[10] Others have remained highly skeptical of this and similar claims that such acceptance lay in widespread support for the regime's humanitarian rhetoric and goals[11] – or that the stability of the GDR rested on the energetic involvement of most East Germans. As Mark Allinson has argued, most "failed to identify with their state" and "did not particularly support their political system...." Yet they were "by and large prepared to accept [their] lot for the foreseeable and perhaps unforeseeable future." All of this translated into pervasive "apathy," which supposedly lay at the heart of the regime's "stable instability."[12] In a sense, this argument represents a throwback to the idea of a "niche society" originally formulated in the early 1980s by Günter Gaus, the Federal Republic's first official diplomatic representative beyond the Wall. The concept, which came to represent "the dominant Western view of political stability" in the GDR before its collapse, refers to what Gaus identified at the time as a widespread "withdrawal into the private sphere" and a single-minded preoccupation with the satisfaction of personal needs.[13]

Another nuanced interpretation looks at the sites of everyday conflict and emphasizes the way in which the regime – and especially its representatives at the local level – endeavored to hammer out conciliatory arrangements and avoid confrontations with ordinary East Germans. This frequently involved giving in to their demands, turning a blind eye to noncompliance and insubordination, or negotiating some sort of settlement that often involved partial concessions – all in an assiduous attempt to maintain harmony at the grass roots, i.e., in the factories and communes where most conflict played out.[14] Yet those who have contributed most to a better understanding of this important process have not always drawn an explicit connection to long-term regime stability. In fact, some scholars even claim that such practices were themselves exactly what led to the downfall and collapse of the GDR. In a valuable study of East German industrial relations, for example, Jeff Kopstein suggests that the official leniency that came in response to widespread worker intransigence hindered the introduction of essential reforms that might have helped salvage the economy. The result was an economic decline that proved ultimately explosive.[15]

[10] Jeannette Z. Madarász, *Conflict and Compromise in East Germany, 1971–1989: A Precarious Stability* (Houndmills, UK, 2003), 4, 8–9.

[11] See, e.g., Rolf Henrich, *Der vormundschaftliche Staat: Vom Versagen des real existierenden Sozialismus* (Reinbek bei Hamburg, 1989).

[12] Mark Allinson, *Politics and Popular Opinion in East Germany, 1945–68* (Manchester, 2000), 163–7.

[13] See Günter Gaus, *Wo Deutschland liegt: Eine Ortsbestimmung* (Munich, 1987), 115–69; Ross, *Dictatorship*, 102.

[14] The seminal work on East German factory relations is Peter Hübner, *Konsens, Konflikt und Kompromiß: Soziale Arbeiterinteressen und Sozialpolitik in der SBZ/DDR, 1945–1970* (Berlin, 1995).

[15] See Jeffrey Kopstein, *The Politics of Economic Decline in East Germany, 1945–1989* (Chapel Hill, NC, 1997).

This important argument draws attention to a fundamental paradox: Many of the factors that may have accounted for the stability of the GDR were in themselves potentially destabilizing, at least in the long run. The tendency to give in to worker demands may have ensured momentary tranquility on the shop floor. But at the same time, it indirectly contributed to chronic material shortages and other economic deficiencies that only heightened the discontent and dissatisfaction with the regime. The same was arguably true of those strategies aimed at winning popular support and legitimizing the rule of the SED – especially when reality failed to correspond to rhetoric. The regime's self-styled antifascist legacy may have struck a positive chord with those East Germans who welcomed a break with their country's recent and catastrophic past: According to Sigrid Meuschel, such rhetoric "promoted and strengthened" belief in the legitimacy of the regime. But how widespread were the feelings of guilt and gratitude that supposedly hindered the novelist Christa Wolf and other intellectuals of her generation from criticizing leading Communist figures who had spent the war in concentration camps or in exile?[16] More to the point, if most East Germans perceived a distinct disjunction between what the regime preached and what it practiced, could this not have been a potential source of even greater disaffection and resentment – and, by extension, instability?

The GDR's much vaunted social welfare policies and egalitarian rhetoric prompt similar questions. Rehearsing a familiar set of arguments, Konrad Jarausch has suggested that the "pervasiveness of...public popularity" lay in the "tangible social benefits" and other "non-compulsive sources of regime support," e.g., subsidized foodstuffs, low-cost housing, cheap transportation, and free kindergartens for working mothers. He argues, moreover, that the supposed "leveling of [social] distinctions" and the "remarkable homogeneity" of East German society "created a greater sense of equality that also helped reinforce popular loyalty" – a claim also made by others with regard to the Nazi dictatorship.[17] Since the headlong integration of the GDR into the Federal Republic's market economy, all of this has clearly become a nostalgic source of longing

---

[16] Meuschel, *Legitimation*, 29–40.

[17] Konrad Jarausch, "The Totalitarian Temptation: Ordinary Germans, Dictatorship and Democracy" (working paper, Center for European Studies, Harvard University, Cambridge, MA, November 1999). In a published version of this paper, Jarausch writes that their "actual performance in providing tolerable lives...helped keep [the East German and Nazi dictatorships] in power." See "Totalitarian Temptation," in Konrad Jarausch and Michael Geyer, *Shattered Past: Reconstructing German Histories* (Princeton, NJ, 2003), 162. On the supposed popularity of the regime, also see Heinz Niemann, *Meinungsforschung in der DDR: Die geheimen Berichte des Instituts für Meinungsforschung an das Politbüro der SED* (Cologne, 1993); Walter Friedrich, "Regierte die SED ständig gegen die Mehrheit des Volkes?" in Jochen Cerny, Dietmar Keller, and Manfred Neuhaus, eds., *Ansichten zur Geschichte der DDR*, vol. 5 (Bonn, 1994), 123–47. On the Nazi period, see Ralf Dahrendorf, *Gesellschaft und Demokratie in Deutschland* (Munich, 1965); David Schoenbaum, *Hitler's Social Revolution: Class and Status in Nazi Germany, 1933–1939* (New York, 1980).

for many former East Germans.[18] But how did they actually feel at the time, i.e., when the SED still ruled and the GDR still existed? Did the regime really deliver the goods and fulfill its lofty promises? And what were the potential consequences for stability if it did not?

Repression and obedience, legitimacy and loyalty, withdrawal and apathy, conciliation and compromise: These are some of the main explanations for the longevity of the GDR. Were they mutually exclusive or did they somehow work together – at different times and in fluctuating degrees – to ensure the stability of the regime? Or has something crucial been left out of the equation? What about the peculiarities of the GDR within the Soviet bloc, e.g., its strong prewar industrial base; the unswerving commitment of high-level Communist functionaries fiercely dedicated to preserving the antifascist state and its principles; the parameters of the Cold War and Moscow's steadfast attachment to what was arguably its most important and staunchest ally in the strategic buffer zone that it had created in Eastern Europe after 1945; the undeniable benefits of economic ties to West Germany during the latter years of its history? All of this clearly played an important role in shoring up the regime.[19]

To get at this and other essential issues, the following investigation looks at the GDR through the lens of Saalfeld, a provincial administrative district located on the eastern edge of the Thuringian forest near the Bavarian border. The reasons for the choice of Saalfeld, as well as the benefits and limitations of any case study, are addressed in greater detail later. But one of the most obvious and important advantages to this approach is that it allows for an intimate and immediate exploration of significant trends and developments at the grass roots that reflect and help account for larger social and political processes – in this case, the stability and longevity of a postwar socialist state. More specifically, an examination of the GDR from below sheds light on the way in which the regime actually functioned, or failed to function, on an everyday level. It reveals the behavior of ordinary East Germans and offers important insights into the way in which they reacted to high-level policies and directives, as well as to more general developments in a wide variety of areas: from the onerous political and participatory demands placed on them by the party and state, for example, to the daily struggle for scarce goods and services. Such an approach also provides a better understanding of their everyday concerns and attitudes, the often difficult choices they had to make, and their main sources

---

[18] See, e.g., the essays in Stefan Bollinger and Fritz Vilmar, eds., *Die DDR war anders: Eine kritische Würdigung ihrer sozialkulturellen Einrichtungen* (Berlin, 2002). Also see Thomas Goll and Thomas Leuerer, eds., *Ostalgie als Erinnerungskultur? Symposium zu Lied und Politik in der DDR* (Baden-Baden, 2004); Thomas Ahbe, *Ostalgie: Zum Umgang mit der DDR–Vergangenheit in den 1990er Jahren* (Erfurt, 2005).

[19] See Christoph Kleßmann, "Rethinking the Second German Dictatorship," in Konrad Jarausch, ed., *Dictatorship as Experience: Towards a Socio-Cultural History of the GDR* (New York, 1999), 365–6; Catherine Epstein, *The Last Revolutionaries: German Communists and Their Century* (Cambridge, MA, 2003).

of discontent. The last are especially important because they gave rise to a wide range of tensions and conflicts at the workplace and in the community that posed a latent threat to domestic tranquility. How such discontent manifested itself and how officials responded to open displays of discord consequently constitute a major focus of the following study, for they arguably provide an important key to understanding the long-term stability of Saalfeld and the GDR as a whole.

All of this inexorably leads to the thorny issue of nonconformist and oppositional activity in the GDR, another central theme of this investigation. Its motivation and sources, the question of who participated, how widespread such participation was and what it meant to those involved, how this changed over time, and the very definition and nature of such behavior, have all been the subject of considerable controversy. A number of scholars and commentators have, on the one hand, tended to downplay or minimize both the extent and effect of popular resistance and opposition to the dictates of the regime, largely limiting it to the activities of a small group of dedicated dissidents fundamentally opposed to the party and state on moral and political grounds. According to one of these dissidents, "Whoever condemns the former leadership should remember that they were covered by the groveling of ninety-eight percent of the people."[20] This and similar claims that most East Germans not only shied away from conflict but also remained either actively or passively loyal to the regime stand in stark contrast to the findings of other studies that have painstakingly detailed both the breadth and depth of oppositional behavior, which supposedly "ran like a red thread" from the earliest years of the GDR to its final collapse.[21]

Much of this debate ultimately hinges on what one considers to be defiant activity as well as on the definitions one chooses to characterize various forms of social, economic, and political behavior that ran counter to official norms and expectations – from refusals to satisfy so-called sociopolitical obligations, for example, to outright forms of protest aimed at toppling the regime. These are issues that we will return to over the course of the following investigation. But even if the empirical evidence suggests that disobedient behavior was indeed far more widespread than Western observers traditionally assumed – which was

---

[20] Cited in Ross, *Dictatorship*, 106. Also see Ehrhart Neubert, *Geschichte der Opposition in der DDR, 1949–1989* (Bonn, 1997).

[21] Quotation from Hans-Joachim Veen, "Warum dieses Lexikon?" in Hans-Joachim Veen and others, eds., *Lexikon: Opposition und Widerstand in der SED–Diktatur* (Berlin, 2000), 14. On the supposedly widespread nature of resistance, also see Mitter and Wolle, *Untergang*; Karl Wilhelm Fricke, *Politik und Justiz in der DDR: Zur Geschichte der politischen Verfolgung, 1945–1968: Berichte und Dokumentation* (Cologne, 1979); idem, *Opposition und Widerstand in der DDR* (Cologne, 1984); Gary Bruce, *Resistance with the People: Repression and Resistance in Eastern Germany, 1945–1955* (Lanham, MD, 2003). For an overview of the literature on resistance, see Ross, *Dictatorship*, 97–125. On political opposition specifically in Thuringia, see Ehrhart Neubert and Thomas Auerbach, *"Es kann anders werden": Opposition und Widerstand in Thüringen, 1945–1989* (Cologne, 2005).

certainly the case in Saalfeld – an important question still remains: What role did all of this play in weakening or shoring up the SED regime? Did it slowly "chip away" at and help undermine the long-term viability of the GDR, or was it a mere distraction with no tangible effects, a safety valve that allowed East Germans to vent their anger and frustration so that they could otherwise toe the line in a way that ultimately helped stabilize the regime?[22] Or did it somehow contribute to stability in an entirely different manner: by alerting officials to potential trouble spots and allowing them to calibrate responses aimed at defusing important sources of discontent and conflict – be it through terror and repression or the adoption of more nuanced methods that involved an ongoing and increasingly refined process of give-and-take between the so-called rulers and ruled?

The following chapters will explore all of these questions in greater depth. But whatever their relationship to the central issue of longevity, the varied patterns and possibilities of popular defiance and official response raise fundamental issues about the very character of the East German regime as well as state–society relations under Soviet-style socialism. This, too, has been a major source of scholarly discussion, and one that focuses on the nature of domination and authority in the GDR, as well as on the extent to which the SED was able to control the so-called masses and reshape society as it wished. Most agree that these were its desired goals, yet the debate pits those who argue that the party more or less managed to realize its total claims and achieve complete domination in almost all areas of society against those who emphasize the supposed "limits" of the dictatorship.[23] In essence, the dispute boils down to a deceptively simple question: Was the GDR totalitarian in reality as well as in theory?

Those who believe it was tend to concentrate on the formal structures of socialist rule, on the various instruments of state repression, and on the general absence of political pluralism, free elections, independent representative bodies, guaranteed civil rights, and the rule of law – in other words, on all of those features that clearly made the GDR a dictatorship. According to Klaus Schroeder, who has no qualms about characterizing East Germany as a totalitarian state, the central leadership enjoyed "all-embracing and unlimited, i.e., total, power."[24] Others have been somewhat less blunt, employing instead a variety of euphemisms that take into account the supposedly more salutary

[22] See Jeffrey Kopstein, "Chipping Away at the State: Workers' Resistance and the Demise of East Germany," *World Politics* 48 (1996): 391–423; Neubert, *Geschichte*, 24.

[23] See the essays in Richard Bessel and Ralph Jessen, eds., *Die Grenzen der Diktatur: Staat und Gesellschaft in der DDR* (Göttingen, 1996); Thomas Lindenberger, ed., *Herrschaft und Eigen–Sinn in der Diktatur: Studien zur Gesellschaftsgeschichte der DDR* (Cologne, 1999).

[24] Schroeder, *SED–Staat*, 633. Also see Klaus Schroeder, "Einleitung: Die DDR als politische Gesellschaft," in Klaus Schroeder, ed., *Geschichte und Transformation des SED–Staates: Beiträge und Analysen* (Berlin, 1994), 11–26; Eckhard Jesse, "War die DDR totalitär?" *APuZ* B40 (1994): 12–23.

aspects of the regime but that, in the end – as Ilko-Sascha Kowalczuk has pointed out – make largely similar claims about the extensive degree of party and state control.[25]

Without denying the basic autocratic attributes of the GDR, a number of scholars have increasingly cast doubt on such characterizations. They ground their criticism on archivally based investigations that look at life in East Germany at the grass roots and that, in so doing, supposedly get at the reality that existed behind the façade of dictatorship. What almost all of these investigations have in common are their attempts to demonstrate that the intentions and goals of the regime did not automatically translate into actual practice. In fact, outcomes were supposedly often at odds with official desires for a variety of reasons: the weight of traditional social structures, mentalities, and milieus, for example, or the supposedly immanent contradictions of the socialist project.[26] Just as important and along similar lines, critics of the totalitarian model highlight the everyday possibilities of autonomous action and agency on the part of ordinary East Germans, i.e., the ways in which their behavior militated against official demands and dictates as well as the ways in which they successfully looked out for their own interests and needs – what Alf Lüdtke has aptly described as *Eigen–Sinn*.[27] In short, this approach emphasizes the distinct limits to the SED's total claims in all areas of public and private life as well as its ability to direct and reshape society.

Such arguments fly in the face of controversial claims put forth by Sigrid Meuschel, a sociologist who argues that the destruction of independent social institutions and regulatory mechanisms in the GDR (e.g., unions and associations as well as the market and media) led to the gradual "withering away" of East German society. What this meant, in more concrete terms, was the far-reaching elimination of societal autonomy vis-à-vis the party and state – one important reason, in her view, for the very stability of the regime as well as the power of its leadership. Another, according to Meuschel, was the extensive eradication of material differences that supposedly led, very much in line with official ideology and aims, to the creation of a homogeneous, classless society. Her point is not that social inequality completely disappeared in the GDR or

---

[25] See, e.g., Meuschel, *Legitimation*; Jürgen Kocka, "Eine durchherrschte Gesellschaft," in Hartmut Kaelble, Jürgen Kocka, and Hartmut Zwahr, eds., *Sozialgeschichte der DDR* (Stuttgart, 1994), 547–53; Konrad Jarausch, "Realer Sozialismus als Fürsorgediktatur: Zur begrifflichen Einordnung der DDR," *APuZ* B20 (1998): 33–46. Also see Torsten Diedrich and Hans Ehlert, "'Moderne Diktatur' – 'Erziehungsdiktatur' – 'Fürsorgediktatur' oder was sonst? Das Herrschaftssystem der DDR und der Versuch seiner Definition," *Potsdamer Bulletin für Zeithistorische Studien* 12 (1998): 17–25. Kowalczuk's comments are cited in Lindenberger, *Herrschaft*, 19.

[26] See Ralph Jessen, "Die Gesellschaft im Staatssozialismus: Probleme einer Sozialgeschichte der DDR," *GG* 21 (1995): 96–110.

[27] On the concept of *Eigen–Sinn*, see Alf Lüdtke, *Eigen–Sinn: Fabrikalltag, Arbeitererfahrungen und Politik vom Kaiserreich bis in den Faschismus* (Hamburg, 1993). For ways in which it has been applied to the GDR, see the essays in Lindenberger, *Herrschaft*.

that conflicts of interest entirely ceased to exist. Yet the main "line of antag-onism" in East Germany was supposedly the one that ran between state and society, between "them" and "us." The absence of any possibilities allowing for the public articulation of competing interests – as well as the inability and failure of individuals to "join together in integrated and ... functioning groups" that could advance their own particular agendas – meant, however, that such conflicts and tensions remained largely dormant.[28]

Where does the following investigation of Saalfeld fit into these debates? It clearly sides with those who reject sweeping assertions about the unlimited power of the party and state – and especially about the extent to which the regime managed to put its policies into practice. Like other recent studies, it also questions assumptions about the absence of significant social distinctions in the GDR and the creation of a classless society largely devoid of conflict.[29] Yet it goes a step further by attempting to draw a direct connection between such arguments and the reasons underlying the very longevity of the East German regime. To that end – and unlike most previous work on the GDR, which focuses almost exclusively on the vertical relationship between state and society – it look as well at the horizontal relations *among* East Germans themselves. That is not to suggest that the interaction between the so-called rulers and ruled – and especially between the grass-roots representatives of the regime and those immediately under their charge – played no role in accounting for the general absence of significant challenges to the SED from below. In fact, that very relationship, as well as its intimate connection to the fundamental issue of stability, will be a recurring theme in the chapters that follow. Yet a central contention of this study is that it represented only one side of the proverbial coin. How ordinary East Germans interacted among themselves, how official policies shaped that interaction, and what all of this meant for the long-term stability and viability of the GDR were the other.

Before exploring those issues, the actual subjects of the following investiga-tion as well as the reasons for the choice of Saalfeld need to be addressed. The primary focus will be on industrial workers and farmers, the two largest

---

[28] See Sigrid Meuschel, "Überlegungen zu einer Herrschafts- und Gesellschaftsgeschichte der DDR," *GG* 19 (1993): 5–14; also see Meuschel, *Legitimation*, 9–15.

[29] See Johannes Huinik, Karl-Ulrich Mayer, and Martin Diewald, eds., *Kollektiv und Eigensinn: Lebensläufe in der DDR und danach* (Berlin, 1995); Heike Solga, *Auf dem Weg in eine klassenlose Gesellschaft? Klassenlagen und Mobilität zwischen Generationen in der DDR* (Berlin, 1995); Michael Vester, Michael Hofmann, and Irene Zierke, eds., *Soziale Milieus in Ostdeutschland: Gesellschaftliche Strukturen zwischen Zerfall und Neubildung* (Cologne, 1995); Detlef Pollack, "Die konstitutive Widersprüchlichkeit der DDR: Oder: War die DDR–Gesellschaft homogen?" *GG* 24 (1998): 27–45; Winfried Thaa and others, *Gesellschaftliche Differenzierung und Legitimitätsverfall des DDR–Sozialismus: Das Ende des anderen Wegs in der Moderne* (Tübingen, 1992); Lothar Mertens, ed., *Soziale Ungleichheit in der DDR: Zu einem tabuisierten Strukturmerkmal der SED–Diktatur* (Berlin, 2002); Madarász, *Conflict*.

TABLE 1. *Social Structure of the Saalfeld District (ca. 1952)*

Social Group	% of Population
Industrial workers (*Arbeiter*)	47.8
Farmers (*Bauern*)	20.7
White-collar employees (*Angestellte*)	3.5
Craftsmen (*Handwerker*)	1.5
Tradespeople (*Gewerbetreibende*)	1.0
Intelligentsia	0.5
Other (*Sonstige*)	25.0

Source: ThStA Rudolstadt, BDVP 21/025, Kreis Saalfeld Analyse, n.d.

social groups in Saalfeld and the GDR, and the ones in whose name the party claimed to rule (Table 1).[30] Raw numbers and ideological pride of place do not alone sufficiently justify a focus on these two social groups, however. After all, those involved in the service sector, white-collar employees (*Angestellte*), and craftsmen, as well as highly trained specialists and other professionals who performed nonmanual work (the so-called intelligentsia), may have played an equally important role in accounting for stability. Although they made up only a relatively small percentage of the population that lived and labored in Saalfeld, their behavior and actions will, in fact, also be taken into consideration. So, too, will the potential significance of gender, age, and political affiliation. Yet industrial workers and farmers – and especially their relationship to the regime itself and to other social groups, as well as among themselves – will take center stage.[31] The fact that they were at the forefront of the first large-scale upheaval in the history of the GDR, the fact that they subsequently failed to launch another major challenge to the party and state, and the fact that they played a largely subordinate role in the popular protest movement that ushered in the final collapse of the regime are all important reasons for this focus.[32]

---

[30] According to official ideology, there were only two classes in the GDR (workers and collective farmers) and one so-called stratum (the intelligentsia). For a succinct overview, see Peter Ludz and Ursula Ludz, "Sozialstruktur," in Hartmut Zimmermann, ed., *DDR Handbuch*, vol. 1, 3rd ed. (Cologne, 1985), 1218–26.

[31] It should be emphasized at the outset that the aim of this study is not to offer a systematic description of the various social groups and milieus that made up East German society. The terms *workers* and *farmers* are used to refer very generally to those Saalfelders who earned their income through manual labor, regardless of skill level, social background, economic sector, etc. Such distinctions within the workforce will be duly noted and explored when they help to explain the larger issue of regime stability. On the social structure of the GDR, see the literature in footnote 29 as well as Rainer Geißler, *Die Sozialstruktur Deutschlands: Ein Studienbuch zur Entwicklung im geteilten und vereinten Deutschland* (Opladen, 1992).

[32] See Chapter 3 and the Conclusion on the role of workers and farmers in 1953 and 1989.

But why Saalfeld?[33] David Crew rightly pointed out in one of the first local studies in the field of German social history that "many researchers will be tempted to search out the 'typical' or 'representative' community [but] it may be argued that no community is strictly 'typical' of more than a rather limited number of cases."[34] Saalfeld itself was not necessarily typical of the GDR as a whole, but it was not radically different from other places either. Like every town, district, and region, it had certain peculiarities, of course – above all, its proximity to the West German border. Moreover, its inhabitants did not enjoy the same privileges as those who lived in major cities and regions deemed politically and economically more essential. The extent to which this influenced developments there or made them significantly different from those in other areas obviously deserves careful consideration – as do the findings of other investigations that have looked at East Germany and other socialist states. As John Connelly has persuasively demonstrated, great diversity did exist in the Soviet bloc as a result of national traditions and experiences.[35] But if the same types of grievances and patterns of behavior, the same types of conflicts and outcomes, as well as the same types of responses by local authorities continued to appear in different factories and communes across Saalfeld and throughout the period examined in this study, then the findings of this study arguably say a great deal about the postwar Communist experience as a whole – especially since the same basic systemic structures existed throughout the socialist world. An understanding of stability in that world provides an indirect answer to perhaps *the* major question of the postwar period: Why did the Cold War last as long as it did?

Given that this investigation focuses on the issue of stability, it might nevertheless have made more sense to focus on a city or district that had at one point been at the forefront of instability: East Berlin in 1953, for example, or Leipzig in 1989. Saalfeld was no sleepy provincial community, however: It was an important industrial and agricultural district that had a turbulent history of labor struggle both before and after 1945. In fact, a major but little-known upheaval involving rioting uranium miners took place there in August 1951 – the first in the GDR and yet another of the district's peculiarities.[36] The point is that Saalfelders were not previously known for their obedient serenity, but would, like those who lived elsewhere in East Germany, remain largely quiescent during the many decades of Communist rule. Explaining that puzzle lies at the heart of this study.

---

[33] And why 1971, the year of a major *political* caesura, as the endpoint for a social history about regime stability? Two main factors influenced this decision: (1) the sheer bulk of archival material, even for a small administrative district like Saalfeld (that very bulk was, in fact, an important reason for the choice of Saalfeld), and (2) the increasingly opaque and formulaic character of the primary source material beginning in the late 1950s after the abrupt end of destalinization and especially after the construction of the Berlin Wall in 1961.

[34] David Crew, *Town in the Ruhr: A Social History of Bochum, 1860–1914* (New York, 1979), 7.

[35] John Connelly, *Captive University: The Sovietization of East German, Czech, and Polish Higher Education, 1945–1956* (Chapel Hill, NC, 2000).

[36] See Chapter 2.

FIGURE 1. Aerial view of the town of Saalfeld. © Bildarchiv des Stadtmuseums Saalfeld.

A Brief History of Saalfeld

Familiar to military buffs because of a minor Napoleonic battle that took place there in 1806, Saalfeld was best known to many East Germans because of the *Feengrotten* ("fairy grottos"), a series of underground caverns with impressive stalactite formations open to tourists. The district achieved additional notoriety after the Second World War thanks to the "Max needs water" campaign of 1949, a highly publicized effort by the official East German youth organization to build a water pipeline from the Saale River to the Maxhütte steel mill – the district's largest and most important factory as well as the site of the only functioning blast furnace in the Soviet zone of occupation.[37]

At a time when many eyes in Germany focused at least momentarily on this provincial backwater located almost midway between Munich and Berlin, native Saalfelders could themselves look back on a long if not particularly distinguished history that stretched back more than a millennium. Although

[37] The following overview of Saalfeld's history is based primarily on Gerhard Werner, *Geschichte der Stadt Saalfeld*, vols. 3 and 4 (Bamberg, 1997, 1998); Richard Künstler and others, *Unser Heimatkreis: Saalfeld (Saale)* (Pößneck, 1955). On the history of Thuringia during the modern era, see Ulrich Hess, *Geschichte Thüringens, 1866–1914*, ed. Volker Wahl (Weimar, 1991); Reinhard Jonscher, *Kleine thüringische Geschichte: Vom Thüringer Reich bis 1945* (Jena, 1993); Detlev Heiden and Gunther Mai, eds., *Nationalsozialismus in Thüringen* (Weimar, 1995); Werner Bramke and Ulrich Heß, eds., *Sachsen und Mitteldeutschland: Politische, wirtschaftliche und soziale Wandlungen im 20. Jahrhundert* (Weimar, 1995); Wolfgang Mühlfriedel, *Die Industrialisierung in Thüringen: Grundzüge der gewerblichen Entwicklung in Thüringen von 1800 bis 1945* (Erfurt, 2001).

the earliest known settlement dated from the late ninth century, the first major community was established in 1180 and would later develop into an important commercial center during the early modern period – thanks in large part to the growth of copper and silver mining in the surrounding hinterland. Like much of Central Europe, however, Saalfeld fell on hard times following the havoc and destruction of the Thirty Years' War. Several of its medieval buildings still survive, and it briefly became the residence of the Saxe-Coburg-Saalfeld dynasty, from which Queen Victoria and Prince Albert would later descend. Yet, the district entered into a sustained period of economic decline that lasted until the mid-nineteenth century. A sewing machine factory was opened in 1860, but Saalfeld's industrial takeoff really began a decade later following the arrival of the first train in 1871 and the construction of the first blast furnace in the village of Unterwellenborn – the future site of the Maxhütte – the following year.

Other industry soon followed and largely settled in the nearby town of Saalfeld itself, from which the surrounding district took its name in 1868. As a result of brisk industrial development, the population of the administrative capital jumped from approximately 6,000 in the early 1870s to almost 23,000 on the eve of the Second World War. By that time, the district's diverse manufacturing base had grown to include steel production and machine-building, iron and slate mining, printing and graphics, as well as chocolate and optics (what would later become a branch of the renowned Zeiss optical firm, whose main headquarters were located in nearby Jena, opened on the eve of the First World War). The agrarian sector remained vital as well during this period. But unlike the northern half of eastern Germany, there were few large estates in Saalfeld; most of its agricultural holdings were small to middle-sized as a result, and tended to concentrate on the breeding of pigs and cattle as well as the production of wheat, vegetables, and fruit. The district's prewar economic activities remained essentially the same after 1945.

Like elsewhere in Germany, economic modernization led to the rapid growth of an industrial working class in Saalfeld. Local metalworkers established their first union in 1875 and staged their first wage-related strike a decade later at a local sewing-machine factory. A branch of the German Social Democratic Party (SPD) was founded in the town of Saalfeld in March 1889, and SPD candidates regularly received between 50 and 70 percent of the vote in all of the national parliamentary elections that took place over the next thirty years. A vibrant working-class culture took shape as well at the time, especially during the final decade of the nineteenth century: The SPD set up two local newspapers and a library, as well as its own printing press, and workers established their own singing group, bicycle club, and gymnastics association.[38] The first May Day celebration took place in Saalfeld in 1892 and attracted several hundred revelers – despite a warning issued one year earlier by a group

---

[38] On working-class culture during this period, see, e.g., Vernon Lidtke, *The Alternative Culture: Socialist Labor in Imperial Germany* (New York, 1985); Lynn Abrams, *Workers' Culture in Imperial Germany: Leisure and Recreation in the Rhineland and Westphalia* (London, 1992).

of leading industrialists that threatened those who participated with immediate redundancy. The relationship between factory owners and workers deteriorated considerably over the next two decades, culminating in a wave of industrial unrest that lasted for more than half a year in 1906, several months in 1907, and then again in brief spurts in 1911 and 1912.

Developments in Saalfeld during the First World War, the Weimar Republic, and the Third Reich were not radically different from those elsewhere in the industrial provinces of Germany at the time. Following the revolution of 1918, a series of industrial strikes and political demonstrations punctuated the early years of the new republic. The SPD consistently remained the single strongest party until the statewide elections of the early 1930s, when the National Socialists scored their first major successes. Founded a decade earlier in March 1924, the local branch of the NSDAP still had fewer than 70 members on the eve of the Great Depression – a number that would grow by almost 1,000 a month after the appointment of Adolf Hitler as chancellor in January 1933. Among their staunchest adversaries in Saalfeld was a small but dedicated group of radical working-class militants that had established a local chapter of the German Communist Party (KPD) in the summer of 1919.[39] Despite the rapid buildup of a thriving Communist subculture – including the requisite youth organization and paramilitary formation – the KPD's electoral support remained modest in comparison to that of the SPD and did not exceed 10 percent until the early 1930s. This was not unusual for Thuringia, a social-democratic stronghold since the late nineteenth century (and the birthplace of the German labor movement). Nor was it unusual that the Nazis performed better in Saalfeld than in most regions outside of Thuringia, where the first National Socialists had already entered a governing coalition in 1929.[40]

The basic contours of the Nazi dictatorship more or less took shape in Saalfeld within two years after the so-called seizure of power at the national level. All non–National Socialist political parties, trade unions, and organizations were disbanded or dissolved and their property seized; the local administrative and security apparatus was thoroughly purged and filled with Nazi loyalists; active members of the defunct left-wing parties were arrested and imprisoned or forced to go underground.[41] Fewer than two dozen Jews resided in the town of Saalfeld at the time the Nazis took control, yet the local press duly issued a call in March 1933 demanding that local residents boycott all Jewish stores and businesses. A large anti-Semitic demonstration took place in the main square five years later on November 10, 1938, the day following Crystal Night; shortly thereafter, a visiting political dignitary delivered

---

[39] On the history of the German Communist movement, see, e.g., Eric Weitz, *Creating German Communism, 1890–1990: From Popular Protests to Socialist State* (Princeton, NJ, 1997); also see Hermann Weber, *Kommunismus in Deutschland, 1918–1945* (Darmstadt, 1983).

[40] See the essays in Heiden, *Nationalsozialismus*.

[41] On political persecution in Saalfeld during the Third Reich, see the memoirs written by local Communist functionaries in ThStA-R, KR Slf 944, 945; also see StA-S, Erlebnisbericht von Gen. Robert Stephan, 11.12.74.

a rabid speech in which he openly called for a "final solution of the Jewish question."

The late 1930s not only witnessed growing anti-Semitic agitation in Saalfeld but also signs of increasing militarization: It became a garrison town in 1936, the manufacture of armaments began a year later, and several local factories continued to produce military devices throughout the Second World War. The first forced laborers arrived in early 1940 and were used – along with an increasing number of local women after the declaration of total war in 1943 – to make up for mounting labor shortages in the industrial sector. The population nevertheless rose considerably during the last two years of the war as large numbers of evacuees began to flow into Saalfeld. The resulting housing deficit – along with escalating shortages of everyday goods and the introduction of strict rationing – brought increasing hardship to those still living in the district. Yet, the residents of Saalfeld were largely spared the horrors and destruction of the war until its final days. That is where our story begins.[42]

---

[42] As a result of a major administrative reform carried out across the GDR in 1952, the Saalfeld district lost about half of its population and territory. In the redrawn district, approximately 60,000 individuals lived in sixty-three towns and villages stretched over 334 square kilometers; about half of its residents resided in the town of Saalfeld itself. See *125 Jahre Landkreis Saalfeld, 1868–1993* (n.p., n.d.). For consistency, the developments discussed in Part I only consider those areas that would later belong to the truncated district.

FIGURE 2. Map of the Saalfeld district (after the administrative reform of 1952).

PART I

UPHEAVAL (1945–1953)

I

Creating a "New Order"

The war finally reached Saalfeld in all its fury on the morning of April 9, 1945, less than one month before the official end of hostilities. By dusk, American fighter planes had dropped more than 1,000 bombs on the district's main industrial town, completely destroying the railroad station and severely damaging a large number of nearby factories and dwellings. Approximately 200 persons died as a result of the attack, including 38 unfortunate souls who had vainly sought refuge in an air-raid shelter located near the Saale Gate, a medieval structure that visitors still pass today on their way from the train station to the town center. Such a trek would have been impossible during the final month of the war: Several days after the massive aerial assault, the last remaining members of the Wehrmacht blew up the majestic stone bridge that spanned the Saale River connecting the eastern and western halves of the city – just before fleeing themselves, along with the National Socialist mayor of Saalfeld, who had voiced approval of this last desperate measure.[1]

Later that day the first American troops entered the town, along with a large number of returning Saalfelders who had sought shelter that week in the surrounding forests and iron ore tunnels that had long played a vital role in the economic life of the region. The "liberators" would not stay long, however:

---

[1] On the last days of the war and the ensuing American occupation, see Gerhard Werner, *Geschichte der Stadt Saalfeld*, vol. 4 (Bamberg, 1998), 41–50; Hermann Kreutzer, "Die Besetzung Saalfelds durch die Amerikaner 1945: Kommunal- und Regionalverwaltung in der 'Stunde Null,'" in Dietrich Grille and August-Wilhelm Kaiser, eds., *Kultur und Geschichte Thüringens: Landeskundliches Jahrbuch für Deutschlands Mitte* 8–9 (1988–9): 28–45; StA-S, Erlebnisbericht von Gen. Robert Stephan, 12.11.74. On the occupation period more generally, see Norman Naimark, *The Russians in Germany: A History of the Soviet Zone of Occupation, 1945–1949* (Cambridge, MA, 1995); Dietrich Staritz, *Die Gründung der DDR: Von der sowjetischen Besatzungsherrschaft zum sozialistischen Staat*, 3rd ed. (Munich, 1995); Wolfgang Zank, *Wirtschaft und Arbeit in Ostdeutschland: Probleme des Wiederaufbaus in der sowjetischen Besatzungszone Deutschlands* (Munich, 1987); Thomas Großbölting and Hans-Ulrich Thamer, eds., *Die Errichtung der Diktatur: Transformationsprozesse in der Sowjetischen Besatzungszone und in der frühen DDR* (Munster, 2003).

FIGURE 3. Saalfeld's main bridge was destroyed by the retreating Wehrmacht during the final days of the war. More than three dozen people were killed in an air-raid shelter located under the Saale Gate, which stands behind the bridge to the right. © Bildarchiv des Stadtmuseums Saalfeld.

Under the terms of an earlier Allied agreement that assigned Saalfeld and the rest of Thuringia to the Soviet zone of occupation, the American forces completely evacuated the city on the night of June 30. According to one eyewitness account, their sudden and unannounced departure came as a complete surprise to the residents of Saalfeld – including a sleepy, scantily clad, and somewhat bewildered young German woman discovered early the next morning in the Roter Hirsch Hotel, which had served as the headquarters of the occupying forces during their brief ten-week stay.

The departure of the "Amis" did not come as a shock to one small group of Saalfelders, however: Alerted to the impending change several weeks earlier, local Communists had prepared for the arrival of their Soviet "friends" by hanging red banners and welcoming signs along the main streets. The half-dozen men who had surreptitiously reestablished the local chapter of the German Communist Party in a garden shed in mid-April had all held prominent positions in the local KPD before the Nazi seizure of power twelve years earlier. Despite their illegal underground activities and intermittent imprisonment during the Third Reich, they had somehow managed to survive the Nazi dictatorship – only to be unceremoniously treated by the first units of the Soviet army that entered the town on July 2: Using the butts of their rifles, the soldiers forced the welcoming committee to load a printing press from the town hall onto a waiting truck – Saalfeld's first reparations payment to the Soviet Union.[2]

Denazification and the Seizure of Power

Relations between local Communists and the Soviet occupiers improved considerably after this first embarrassing encounter. The local party cell was officially recognized shortly thereafter, and joint efforts immediately got under way to purge the local administrative apparatus of "fascist elements" and replace them with politically reliable antifascists. The first steps in that direction had already occurred during the American occupation with the arrest and imprisonment of prominent Nazis who had not fled or committed suicide. The most important changes took place at the highest levels of the local bureaucracy: After consulting with a local Catholic priest, the U.S. commander appointed a skilled foundry worker as interim mayor of the town and the director of the Knoch Sewing Machine Factory as *Landrat*, the highest civil administrator in the district. Both men were relieved of their positions shortly after the arrival of the Soviets, who decided to replace them with seemingly more reliable functionaries from the two working-class parties. The local Soviet commandant explained that this was not a "dismissal in the normal sense of the word" but rather a "necessity" in line with the creation of a "new order."[3]

The Social Democrats had reconstituted themselves in June, and two of the SPD's founding members – Paul Möbus and Hugo Liedloff – would go on to serve as the first mayors of Saalfeld under Soviet occupation. Both were skilled workers who had fought during the First World War and then entered local politics and engaged in union activities during the Weimar era. Later persecuted by the Nazis, both served lengthy prison sentences during the Third Reich: Liedloff, who became the mayor of Saalfeld following Möbus's premature death in December 1945, had spent time in the nearby Buchenwald concentration camp two years earlier.[4] Both men not only had similar backgrounds, then, but also strong antifascist credentials. The Soviet decision to appoint Social Democrats and not members of the KPD – as well as a later decision to replace Hermann Kißauer, a member of the Communist Party and the first *Landrat* under Soviet occupation, with another founding member of the postwar SPD – were not entirely surprising given the comparative strength of the two local working-class parties at the time: In April 1946, the month that the SPD and KPD officially united in the Soviet zone of occupation to form the new Socialist Unity

---

[2] On reparations in the Soviet zone, see Rainer Karlsch, *Allein bezahlt? Die Reparationsleistungen der SBZ/DDR, 1945–1953* (Berlin, 1993); Naimark, *Russians*, 141–204.

[3] StA-S, Personalakte Paul Möbus.

[4] StA-S, Personalakte Hugo Liedloff and Personalakte Paul Möbus. On the reestablishment of the SPD in the East after the war, see Albrecht Kaden, *Einheit oder Freiheit: Die Wiedergründung der SPD 1945/46* (Hannover, 1964).

Party, the Social Democrats in Saalfeld were, in terms of membership numbers and in keeping with prewar tradition, almost twice as strong as the KPD.[5]

This political constellation, not uncommon in the eastern half of the occupied country, soon proved intolerable for the German Communists and their Soviet patrons. A systematic purge consequently got under way in 1950 aimed at eliminating from public life large numbers of former Social Democrats who were allegedly hostile to the new regime.[6] The purge had already begun a year earlier in Saalfeld with the arrest of leading Social Democrats in the spring of 1949. This included three of the founding members of the postwar SPD as well as its former chairman, Paul Kreutzer, his son, and his daughter-in-law, a stenographer who held no political functions at the time. A military tribunal subsequently found them guilty of "counterrevolutionary activities" and, in August 1949, meted out prison sentences of up to twenty-five years.[7] Henceforth, only politically reliable SED members would occupy key positions in the local administrative apparatus. In the summer of 1949, for example, Hugo Liedloff was replaced as mayor by a former member of the KPD.[8]

The creation of a "new order" in Saalfeld and the rest of eastern Germany did not only involve the persecution of Social Democrats, of course: It also entailed efforts to arrest, punish, and remove former Nazis and war criminals from responsible positions in the public and private sectors.[9] During the earliest phase of denazification, American occupation officials had summarily arrested prominent Nazis still living in Saalfeld, often basing their decisions on information provided by local antifascists. A more systematic approach got under way in May 1945 with the compulsory registration of all former members of the NSDAP and its sister organizations, who were required to fill out so-called *Fragebögen* (questionnaires) detailing their activities during the Third Reich.

---

[5] ThStA-R IV/4/10/355, analysis of the town of Saalfeld, n.d.

[6] On the creation of the SED and the purge of former Social Democrats, see Beatrix Bouvier, *Ausgeschaltet: Sozialdemokraten in der sowjetischen Besatzungszone und in der DDR, 1945–1953* (Bonn, 1996); Harold Hurwitz, *Die Stalinisierung der SED: Zum Verlust von Freiräumen und sozialdemokratischer Identität in den Vorständen, 1946–1949* (Opladen, 1997); Andreas Malycha, *Die SED: Geschichte ihrer Stalinisierung, 1946–1953* (Paderborn, 2000). For a comparative study of party purges at the time, see Hermann Weber and Ulrich Mählert, eds., *Terror: Stalinistische Parteisäuberungen, 1936–1953* (Paderborn, 1998).

[7] See Karl Wilhelm Fricke, *Politik und Justiz in der DDR: Zur Geschichte der politischen Verfolgung, 1945–1968: Berichte und Dokumentation* (Cologne, 1979), 119–20; Hans-Joachim Veen and others, eds., *Lexikon: Opposition und Widerstand in der SED–Diktatur* (Berlin, 2000), 230.

[8] After subsequently serving as director of the fairy grottos, he later worked as a private mechanic in Saalfeld. See AdsD, Ostbüro 00523j, report, 22.5.53.

[9] See Helga Welsh, *Revolutionärer Wandel oder Befehl? Entnazifizierungs- und Personalpolitik in Thüringen und Sachsen, 1945–1948* (Munich, 1989); Rainer Eckert, Alexander von Plato, and Jörn Schütrumpf, eds., *Wendezeiten – Zeitenwende: Zur "Entnazifizierung" und "Entstalinisierung"* (Hamburg, 1991); Ruth-Kristin Rössler, ed., *Die Entnazifizierungspolitik der KPD/SED, 1945–1948: Dokumente und Materialien* (Goldbach, 1994); Olaf Kappelt, *Die Entnazifizierung in der SBZ sowie die Rolle und der Einfluss ehemaliger Nationalsozialisten in der DDR als ein soziologisches Phänomen* (Hamburg, 1997); Timothy Vogt, *Denazification in Soviet-Occupied Germany: Brandenburg, 1945–1948* (Cambridge, MA, 2000).

Civilian and Soviet occupation authorities would partially base many of their later decisions on these documents, which the Americans handed over to the *Landrat* before departing.[10]

Like their predecessors in Saalfeld, the Soviets concentrated their initial efforts on arresting the more notorious and better-known Nazis and Nazi sympathizers.[11] At the same time, they launched a sweeping program aimed at purging former party members from all ranks of government and industry. Hugo Liedloff, the chief of police at the time, reported that local security forces had been completely "cleansed" by the fall of 1945: By the end of the year, in fact, most members of the criminal police were either in the KPD or SPD. And by 1946, only three of the sixty-two mayors in the district had earlier been members of the NSDAP: More than half now belonged to the SED.[12]

The results in other areas were much more uneven. By December 1946, approximately three-quarters of those who had worked in the town and district administrations and who had been members of the NSDAP or one of its affiliated organizations had lost their positions. Many were forced to perform penitential manual labor to atone for their earlier activities, but approximately one-third were later rehabilitated and thus allowed to return to their posts: Almost all had since joined the SED or one of the quiescent middle-class block parties formed after the war. The purge of the education sector was somewhat more exhaustive, but by the early 1950s, slightly more than one-fifth of all teachers in the town of Saalfeld had earlier been members of the Nazi party.[13]

How was this possible? The final phase of denazification, which began in late 1946 and lasted until March 1948, constituted a last-ditch attempt to purge any remaining Nazis from public life and positions of influence. But as in the western zones, Soviet authorities now placed greater emphasis on distinguishing between the so-called active and nominal, i.e., between Nazi zealots, militarists, and war criminals, on the one hand, and those, on the other, who had only played a minor role during the Third Reich and who were now supposedly willing to contribute to the "restoration of a peaceful and democratic Germany."[14] The distinction was made most clear in the Soviet

[10] Kreutzer, "Besetzung," 41.

[11] See, e.g., StA-S, Kreisamt 52, Aufstellung über die beim Landesrat in der Zeit vom 15.5.–1.9.45 entlassenen, beurlaubten und in Haft befindlichen Beamten, Angestellten und Arbeiter, n.d.

[12] See the reports and correspondence in StA-S 5804; ThStA-R, Kreisantifablock (R230) 39.

[13] See the statistics and reports in ThStA-R, KR 282, 474; ThStA-R IV/4/10/355, analysis of the town of Saalfeld, n.d.; ThStA-R, Kreisantifablock (R230) 1, Liste der voraussichtlich politisch tragbaren Lehrkräfte, n.d. On the denazification of the education sector elsewhere, see Charles Lansing, "Brandenburg an der Havel's Teachers, 1933 to 1953: German *Lehrer* Under Two Dictatorships" (Ph.D. diss., Yale University, 2004), 152–70; also see, with caution, Chapter 1 of John Rodden, *Repainting the Little Red Schoolhouse: A History of Eastern German Education, 1945–1995* (Oxford, 2002).

[14] Wolfgang Meinicke, "Die Entnazifizierung in der sowjetischen Besatzungszone, 1945 bis 1948," in Eckert et al., *Wendezeiten*, 47; also see Naimark, *Russians*, 66, 456–7. On denazification in the West, see, e.g., Lutz Niethammer, *Die Mitläuferfabrik: Die Entnazifizierung am Beispiel Bayerns* (Berlin, 1982).

Military Administration (SMAD) Directive 24 and Order 201, which established so-called cleansing committees (*Säuberungsausschüsse*) and denazification commissions (*Entnazifizierungskommissionen*) staffed by local antifascists
in charge of carrying out the final purge. By the time the denazification program in the eastern zone officially came to an end, the Saalfeld denazification
commission had reviewed 828 cases at sixty-six public meetings: Two-thirds of
those investigated because of their activities during the Third Reich were fully
acquitted. Of the 270 individuals found guilty, approximately one-third were
merely placed on probation for up to four years. The vast majority of those
convicted either lost their businesses or were forced to suspend their previous
economic activities for up to three years. Only a small handful of public administrative personnel (less than two dozen) was either demoted or fired, and only
six individuals were subsequently placed in detention for further investigation.[15]

The results of denazification in Saalfeld were, then, imperfect at best. This
was generally true of Thuringia as a whole – the eastern province where, according to SED leader Walter Ulbricht, "National Socialism ran the deepest."[16]
That very fact helped explain the surprisingly lenient treatment of many former Nazis in the region. For example, the above-average percentage of NSDAP
members in the Thuringian administrative apparatus made it exceedingly difficult and highly impractical to eliminate them entirely: Their technical expertise
and know-how were not only important elements in ensuring that the local and
state bureaucracies would continue to function smoothly, but also essential to
postwar reconstruction efforts more generally.

Such leniency occasionally led to hefty disputes with those rank-and-file SED
members who demanded a more thorough purge – as in the case of one former Nazi and wartime economic official who became the new technical director of the Maxhütte steel mill in 1949. Partly because of such protests, and
partly because of tense relations with other officials at the factory, he eventually decided to flee to the West in late 1950.[17] Fearing the further loss of such
indispensable technical experts, the Thuringian SED launched an investigation
in which it not only emphasized the necessity of forming a temporary alliance
with the old (i.e., prewar) intelligentsia, but also publicly denounced the "sectarian tendencies" of those members who openly opposed the party's efforts to
win over individuals desperately needed because of their technical skills.[18]

As this suggests, pragmatic concerns sometimes prevented the party from
complying with demands from below for more radical policies supposedly in
tune with orthodox Communist ideology. But there was another important
justification for such leniency: A more thorough purge would have unfairly

---

[15] See ThStA-R, KR 947, Statistischer Schlussbericht, 3.17.48; ThStA-R, KR 282, Prot., 9.25.47.
[16] Naimark, *Russians*, 172.
[17] See ThStA-R, Maxh. 616, Niederschr. über die Partei-Aktiv-Sitz., 13.1.49; AdsD, Ostbüro 0072e
(02379), Personelles der Maxh., 7.2.49.
[18] See the series of reports and analyses in ThStA-R IV/4/10/238; ThStA-R, Maxh. 390, correspondence, 13.11.50.

penalized those individuals who had not enthusiastically supported the regime but who had joined the party for purely practical reasons, e.g., in order to keep their jobs. As one official nevertheless pointed out in a trenchant critique of the local denazification program, "Today all former party members claim to have been nominal, or to have entered the party because of pressure or economic reasons." He went on to describe the case of one man who had joined the NSDAP in 1932 but who still held a leading administrative position because of his technical expertise: "The authorities have had two and a half years to find another specialist. Even a bear learns to dance: Why can't an antifascist [master] this special subject?" He concluded that the "decisions made by the denazification commission are ridiculous. One only has to hear the Nazis talking among themselves: They view it all as a comedy."[19]

The failure to weed out more Nazis also reflected the general unwillingness of many local residents to provide authorities with sufficient "incriminating material."[20] Such evidence was sometimes willfully ignored, however, as in the case of Erich Klabes. Born in 1917 near the town of Wittenberg, Klabes entered the Waffen SS in the mid-1930s and later served as a sergeant in the Second World War until he lost his arm during the Wehrmacht campaign in Poland. After his active service came to an end, Klabes retrained as a clerk and then joined the German National Democratic Party after the war (established in 1948, the NDPD was intended to attract and help integrate nominal Nazis and craftsmen into the new political system).[21] He served as district chairman of the NDPD in Torgau from 1952 to 1957 before being reassigned to Saalfeld, where he assumed the same function. A television report about Klabes's temporary appointment as mayor of Saalfeld in the mid-1960s prompted heated discussions among workers at a nearby chemical factory in Rudolstadt, where he had been employed throughout much of the war: They wanted to know how a man who had been in the SS, who had purportedly helped blow up Saalfeld's main bridge in April 1945, and whose wife had allegedly shown photographs of him standing next to hanged prisoners in Buchenwald could hold such an important position. His lengthy service as a Stasi informant who went by the code name of "Claus" and his willingness since the early 1950s to report on former Nazis in the NDPD had obviously played an important role, apparently making it easier for officials to turn a blind eye to his tarnished past.[22]

Erich Klabes was an exception in many respects, yet his biography supports more recent claims that the old scholarly consensus about denazification – that it was much more far-reaching in the Soviet zone than in the West – was

[19] ThStA-R IV/4/10/289, Kritik zur Entnazifizierung, n.d.

[20] See, e.g., ThStA-R, KR Slf 939, Meldung (21.12.47–10.1.48); ThStA-R, KR Slf 282, Prot. der Arbeitstagung in Weimar, 19.1.48, 20.1.48; ThStA-R, KR Slf 943, correspondence, 12.3.48.

[21] Unlike that of the other block parties, little has been written about the history of the NDPD; see Siegfried Suckut, "Geschichte und Funktion der Blockparteien in der SBZ/DDR," in Rainer Eppelmann, Bernd Faulenbach, and Ulrich Mählert, eds., *Bilanz und Perspektiven der DDR–Forschung* (Paderborn, 2003), 98.

[22] See BStU ASt-G, KD Slf, X778/60.

inaccurate.[23] More to the point, his story clearly underscores the incomplete nature of political cleansing in the East – by design or by default. As we shall see in the next section, that was equally true of those policies intended to create a "new order" east of the Elbe by fundamentally transforming property relations in the countryside.

Reforming the Countryside

German Communists and their political rivals may not have seen eye to eye on most issues, but they did agree on the need for land reform – even if their overall conceptions differed significantly. Like their patrons in Moscow, the former wished to eliminate the Prussian Junkers and other large landowners supposedly responsible, at least in part, for the rise of German fascism and militarism. To that end, occupation authorities announced in early September 1945 that all estates larger than 100 hectares were to be confiscated without compensation. Nazi activists and war criminals were to be deprived of their property as well, but politically untainted middle-sized farmers with more than twenty hectares – misleadingly referred to as *Großbauern* – were allowed to retain their holdings. Hoping to gain support among a traditionally hostile constituency, the Communists planned to redistribute the expropriated land among those who owned little property, tenant farmers, and agricultural laborers. Thousands of refugees from the former eastern territories – who flowed nonstop into the district over the next three years and who, as a result, would make up a quarter of its population by mid-1948 – were to receive land as well so that they could begin a new life as so-called new farmers (*Neubauern*).[24]

---

[23] See Kappelt, *Entnazifizierung*; Vogt, *Denazification*. On the incomplete nature of political cleansing in the West, see Norbert Frei, *Vergangenheitspolitik: Die Anfänge der Bundesrepublik und die NS-Vergangenheit* (Munich, 1996).

[24] As of July 1, 1948, 33,004 of the 127,171 persons living in the district were refugees. See ThStA-R, KR Slf 2026. On the land reform program, see Arnd Bauerkämper, ed., *"Junkerland in Bauernhand"? Durchführung, Auswirkungen und Stellenwert der Bodenreform in der Sowjetischen Besatzungszone* (Stuttgart, 1996); idem, *Ländliche Gesellschaft in der kommunistischen Diktatur: Zwangsmodernisierung und Tradition in Brandenburg, 1945–1963* (Cologne, 2002), 51–122, 223–60; Naimark, *Russians*, 150–62; Hans Franzky and Astrid Franzky, *Die Enteignungsmaßnahmen auf dem Gebiet der Landwirtschaft von der Bodenreform bis zur Kollektivierung in der ehemaligen SBZ/DDR* (Hannover, 1991); Ulrich Kluge, Winfrid Halder, and Katja Schlenker, eds., *Zwischen Bodenreform und Kollektivierung: Vor- und Frühgeschichte der "sozialistischen Landwirtschaft" in der SBZ/DDR vom Kriegsende bis in die fünfziger Jahre* (Stuttgart, 2001); Corey Ross, *Constructing Socialism at the Grass-Roots: The Transformation of East Germany, 1945–65* (Houndsmill, UK, 2000), 17–30; Boris Spix, *Die Bodenreform in Brandenburg, 1945–1947: Konstruktion einer Gesellschaft am Beispiel der Kreise West- und Ostprignitz* (Munster, 1997); Damian van Melis, ed., *Sozialismus auf dem platten Land: Mecklenburg–Vorpommern, 1945–1952* (Schwerin, 1999); Barbara Schier, *Alltagsleben im "sozialistischen Dorf": Merxleben und seine LPG im Spannungsfeld der SED-Agrarpolitik, 1945–1990* (Munster, 2001), 45–53; Jonathan Osmond, "Kontinuität und Konflikt in der Landwirtschaft der SBZ/DDR zur Zeit der Bodenreform und der Vergenossenschaftlichung, 1945–1961," in Richard Bessel and Ralph Jessen, eds., *Die Grenzen der Diktatur: Staat und Gesellschaft in der DDR* (Göttingen, 1996), 137–69.

When the Communist leader Wilhelm Pieck officially launched the land reform program in early September 1945 by declaring "Junker lands in farmer hands," he clearly did not have Saalfeld in mind: Unlike the flatter regions located in the northern half of the Soviet zone, there were few large landholdings in the district.[25] As a result, the yield of sequestered land was relatively low, and by mid-1948, authorities had confiscated only about 10 percent of all arable farmland in the district. This included approximately 5,800 hectares taken from twenty-six private estates as well as from three dozen Nazi activists and war criminals.[26] More than 2,300 individuals subsequently received approximately 85 percent of the expropriated land, with each recipient obtaining an average of two to three hectares. The main beneficiaries were farmers with little property as well as refugees: While the former obtained the most land overall, the latter received the most hectares per individual.[27]

What effect did this have on local land distribution? On the eve of the reform, large estates with more than fifty hectares accounted for one-quarter of all farmland within the district; by late 1947, these units had all but disappeared. Just as important, the number of small proprietors with less than five hectares had more than doubled; they remained the largest group of landowners in terms of raw numbers but still held less than 20 percent of all landed property in Saalfeld. The number of middle-sized farmers with twenty to fifty hectares stayed more or less constant, but their share of land increased from 30 to more than 40 percent because of provisions allowing them to purchase confiscated property. As a result, more than 80 percent of the land remained in the hands of a small minority of farmers (approximately 16 percent), which clearly suggested the limited effect of the reform program in Saalfeld. Local officials had nevertheless achieved their primary goals: All large estates had been dismantled, a number of Nazis had been expropriated, and almost twice as many individuals now owned small parcels of land.[28]

This accomplishment was all the more impressive given the considerable resistance to land reform, which got off to an extremely slow start in Saalfeld. Authorities attributed the low level of engagement on the part of those farmers who stood to benefit most from the reform to twelve years of National Socialist rule, arguing that many had simply become "unaccustomed" to "active involvement" in public life. But there were other important reasons as well for their restrained response: Many farmers remained highly skeptical about the new law and "just couldn't believe that the property of the large landowners was simply expropriated." Many also doubted that farms with five hectares

[25] This was true of Thuringia as a whole for geographical reasons as well as because of reforms introduced after the First World War. See Helga Welsh, "Thüringen," in Martin Broszat and Hermann Weber, eds., *SBZ Handbuch* (Munich, 1990), 169.
[26] See the statistics and reports in ThHStA-W, KR Slf 62, 86, 88, 96.
[27] Almost 1,000 hectares were also given to the state, local communities, and public agencies. See the statistics in ThHStA-W, KR Slf 86, 88.
[28] See ThHStA-W, KR Slf 703, Liste der Güter über 100 ha Gesamtfläche, n.d.; ThHStA-W, KR Slf 86, Aufstellung der im Kr. Slf aufgeteilten Güter/Wirtschaften, 5.9.46. More generally, see the statistics in ThHStA-W, KR Slf 88.

or less could be productive. High-level authorities summarily dismissed such "rumors" or attributed them to the machinations of *Großbauern*, yet similar concerns were shared by local officials preoccupied with ensuring adequate production levels.[29]

Angered by the slow progress made in Saalfeld early on, Soviet officers exerted increasing pressure on local authorities to accelerate the program: "The land reform... should have already been completed long ago," they lectured as early as mid-November 1945. "If things continue like they have up to now, some of those in responsible positions will suffer a miserable fate.... The happiness of the entire country depends on how well the farmers cultivate the earth." While generally agreeing on the need to distribute land to those in need, local officials nevertheless emphasized the considerable difficulties they faced: There was an important difference, they reminded the Soviets, "if an officer of the Red Army or a civilian appears. In the latter case, the farmers always have all sorts of excuses." Occupation officials nevertheless demanded strict adherence to expropriation guidelines, and were most disturbed by the apparent leniency shown toward several large landowners and former members of the NSDAP still living in the district. Those in charge of the reform usually defended their decisions by arguing that the individuals in question had not incriminated themselves politically during the Third Reich or that their neighbors were not in favor of expropriation: When asked, for example, why one family in the village of Kleingeschwenda had been allowed to retain part of its estate – even though the head of the household had owned more than 100 hectares and had joined the NSDAP in 1937 – the *Landrat* explained that their neighbors had had no complaints about these people and "knew them to be industrious workers." Because they had not been politically active during the Nazi period, he continued, even the members of the local land reform commission wanted them to keep some of their land: "But if it is now demanded that the land be divided, it will be divided."[30]

That membership in the NSDAP was not necessarily indicative of pernicious behavior during the Third Reich was a reasonable objection – and one that had also played an important role during the spotty denazification campaign. Yet the attempt to distinguish between active and nominal Nazis clearly led to some questionable decisions by local officials: Protesting the planned seizure of one farmer's holdings in the village of Langenschade, for example, the members of the district land reform commission suggested that his mistreatment of Russian prisoners of war had not been "so serious as to warrant

29 ThHStA-W, KR Slf 62, Bericht über die Durchführung der Bodenreform im Landkr. Slf, 2.1.46, and Bericht Nr. 6 über die Landwirtschaft im Kr. Slf: Durchführung der Bodenreform, n.d. As we shall see in Chapter 3, such concerns were well founded and would prompt the SED to introduce agricultural collectivization in the following decade.

30 See the reports in ThHStA-W, KR Slf 62. For a firsthand account of the tensions with local Soviet officials by a former member of the Saalfeld land reform committee, see Rolf Becker and Claus Bremer, eds., *Immer noch Kommunist? Erinnerungen von Paul Elflein* (Hamburg, 1978), 112–19.

expropriation."[31] Small wonder, then, that only three dozen Nazis lost their landed property in Saalfeld – or that many former NSDAP functionaries (*Ortsgruppenleiter*) would continue to occupy positions of leadership in local villages well into the 1950s.[32]

Such forbearance angered not only the Soviets but also a number of local antifascists, who vehemently criticized officials for not imposing harsher penalties on tainted individuals. After the release of one farmer from prison four days after his property had been confiscated, the land reform committee in Beulwitz wrote a scathing letter of denunciation to the *Landrat*. Branding him an active Nazi who had supposedly persecuted his neighbors and mistreated foreign workers during the war, they called the decision a "slap in the face" to antifascists, who can "differentiate very well between the decent Nazis and such rascals." The letter concluded with a telling allusion to the German revolution of 1918–19:

> We have a right to be liberated finally from such elements . . . [and will] no longer tolerate this type [of Nazi brood] within our community. . . . Our patience is at an end. We won't let power be taken away from us again, but will instead make a thorough sweep of things. . . . That's how the voles (*Wühlmäuse*) started again in 1918–1923. We were too lenient that time. That can't be allowed to repeat itself. Away with these people; they'll be the first to stab us in the back. . . . [33]

Those penalized by the land reform were often just as vehement in their defense – as in the case of an arrested Nazi functionary in Dorfilm whose son argued for the return of his family's land by naming neighbors who were allowed to keep their property, even though they had supposedly been "much more active" than his father. This was a "screaming injustice," he charged, and suggested that outside authorities trust the judgment of those most familiar with local circumstances, i.e., those who lived in the village. According to the *Landrat*, local antifascists all supported his appeal and had decided to reverse the decision "out of consideration for public opinion." He further implied that the entire affair had been caused by the allegations of an individual motivated by "selfish reasons." Higher-level officials later concluded that the accusations had been improperly investigated and that the entire procedure had been conducted unlawfully: Bowing to these arguments, the state reversed the decision and turned over the land to the son.[34]

The effort to weed out reactionaries from the countryside undoubtedly led to a number of arbitrary arrests and confiscations. Yet the willingness of authorities to modify some decisions clearly suggested that the rule of law was not entirely moribund during the early years of Communist rule. If these and similar cases attested to the readiness of some upright individuals to support those

---

[31] ThHStA-W, KR Slf 96, correspondence, 11.5.46.

[32] See the detailed analyses of the district's villages in ThStA-R IV/4/10/353–5.

[33] See ThHStA-W, KR Slf 62, Bericht der Dorfkommission Beulwitz, 28.12.45; ThHStA-W, KR Slf 96, Prot. der Enteignung von Nazivermögen (Beulwitz), 28.11.45.

[34] See the correspondence related to this and similar cases in ThHStA-W, KR Slf 103.

who had been penalized unfairly, they illustrated at the same time the gusto with which others denounced their neighbors. Some were obviously motivated by a desire to expose treacherous or criminal behavior during the Third Reich. Yet others were clearly more interested in using the land reform program to advance their own material interests or settle old scores, usually by claiming that their adversary had been a virulent Nazi or had made disparaging comments about the Russians. In one conflict that lasted several years, a farmer in Wickersdorf claimed that a local clique of former Nazi activists had not only discriminated against him because of his political background – he was, in his own words, the "one and only antifascist" in the village – but had also manipulated the land redistribution to their own advantage.[35]

A subsequent investigation found that the farmer's allegations were overblown, yet they raise an important question about the extent to which politics played a role in the redistribution of land: More specifically, did membership in the SED improve one's chances of acquiring property? According to available statistics, party members – when compared to membership levels in the countryside – were disproportionately represented in terms of both the number of recipients and the amount of land received. This was especially true in those villages where the SED dominated the local land reform committees, which might help explain why more than half of all the so-called new farmers belonged to the party.[36] A high-level SED official from the region would later complain, in fact, about opportunists who had only joined in order to improve their chances of receiving land – and then quit once their holdings had been secured. Authorities concluded that such mistakes had resulted from the "rapid realization" of the reform program, but they rejected requests to dispossess these simulants and redistribute their land to "genuine" antifascists: Clearly averse to alienating those who had already benefited from the reform, they suggested instead that district officials increase political agitation in the countryside in order to win greater support for the party.[37]

The apparent absence of enthusiasm shown by many new farmers for the SED was only one important reason why many were not "one hundred percent worthy" of the land they had been given: Their lack of any previous agricultural experience was clearly another – a serious shortcoming compounded by a variety of severe material shortages that hurt the performance of *all* farmers in Saalfeld during the immediate postwar years.[38] Realizing that heightened political agitation alone would not make up for the absence of enough stalls, machinery, seed, livestock, and housing, authorities prudently decided to introduce more tangible measures aimed at alleviating the desperate situation.

[35] Surviving records indicate, in fact, that none of the members of the village land reform committee had been in the NSDAP. See the documents related to this case in ThStA-R IV/4/10/301, 303; ThHStA-W, KR Slf 62, 477.

[36] See the statistics in ThHStA-W, KR Slf 88; ThStA-R IV/4/10/91.

[37] ThStA-R IV/4/10/301, correspondence between SED KV–Eisenach and SED LV–Thür., August 1947; ThHStA-W, KR Slf 62, report by Kommission S., n.d.

[38] See Arnd Bauerkämper, "Die Neubauern in der SBZ/DDR 1945–1952: Bodenreform und politisch induzierter Wandel der ländlichen Gesellschaft," in Bessel and Jessen, *Grenzen*, 108–36.

To that end, they distributed a variety of scarce agricultural resources, offered credit at low interest rates, and set up Associations for Mutual Farmers Assistance (VdgB) designed to help those who were struggling most.

The most important measure came in the fall of 1947, however, with the pronouncement of SMAD Order 209, which called on state and local officials to supply new farmers with sufficient housing and other requisite buildings. Acute material and labor shortages notwithstanding, Saalfeld made greater progress than most of its neighboring districts, and by the time the building program ended in the early 1950s, 174 new farmsteads had been built at a cost of 2.6 million marks. This success was due, at least in part, to the voluntary efforts of urban industrial workers, who reportedly did more than many of the new farmers themselves: "They are of the opinion that they were expelled from their homeland and have lost everything, so the state should provide them with all they lost. In some cases, worker units helped construct the farms and the new farmers just looked on."[39] Their astounding sense of entitlement was just as remarkable as the workers' admirable show of solidarity, which was all the more impressive given the disastrous housing situation in the district's industrial centers at the time.

Housing Shortages and Forced Requisitioning

Wartime destruction, the arrival of the Soviets, and the influx of large numbers of refugees from the East combined to make urban housing shortages one of the most pressing and intractable problems of the immediate postwar period. Despite significant regional differences across Germany, Saalfeld was no exception in this regard: According to Mayor Liedloff, an additional 2,800 apartments were needed in order to alleviate the desperate situation, which was marked by both overcrowding and homelessness. He blamed the crisis in part on the National Socialists, who had seriously neglected the construction of living quarters because of their militaristic policies: Almost all available building material had been used to erect barracks during the war, which meant that no new civilian housing had been built in the town since 1942. To make matters worse, Allied bombing during the last month of the war had destroyed 146 apartments and damaged several hundred others, leaving more than 200 families without a roof over their heads. In addition, more than 40 percent of all living quarters were in urgent need of repair.[40]

---

[39] ThII IStA-W, KR Slf 375, Niederschr. über Besprechung, 6.4.48, and correspondence, 17.9.48. On the implementation of and many difficulties involved in carrying out Order 209 in Saalfeld, also see the reports and correspondence in ThHStA-W, KR Slf 62, 88, 94, 95, 374, 375, 475, 481, 536, 2094; ThStA-R IV/4/10/301, 302, 314.

[40] StA-S, Allg. Verw. 178, Tätigkeitsbericht vom BM Hugo Liedloff, August 1946. Also see the statistics in StA-S, Sekr. des BM 2092. On housing shortages more generally, see Hannsjörg Buck, *Mit hohem Anspruch gescheitert: Die Wohnungspolitik der DDR* (Munster, 2004); Karl Christian Führer, "Managing Scarcity: The German Housing Shortage and the Controlled Economy, 1914–1990," *German History* 13 (1995): 326–54.

The grave challenges posed by insufficient housing throughout occupied Germany prompted the Allied Control Commission to issue an important decree in early March 1946 that called for the creation of local housing committees in all cities, towns, and villages. Charged with overseeing the distribution of available lodging, these new bodies were required to register all units according to size and occupancy, draw up lists that divided housing applicants into three categories according to urgency, and assign the needy to supposedly underoccupied quarters. Authorities in the Soviet zone instructed local officials to apply socioeconomic and political criteria when making distribution decisions, which meant that large families and refugees, invalids and the handicapped, so-called victims of fascism, skilled workers, and members of the intelligentsia were all given priority. Officials were also given the power to remove Nazi activists and war criminals from their homes by force in order to make room for those in need.[41]

Working together with the district housing office, the local committees in Saalfeld devoted most of their initial energy to the district's most pressing challenge: finding accommodation for the large number of newly arrived refugees – more than 33,000 by mid-1948: "The housing office has the duty to find humane quarters for all of those who lost their homeland and everything else they had because of Hitler's criminal war . . . and to give them a feeling of equality with older residents."[42] This was, on a number of levels, easier said than done. Most refugees were provided at first with temporary lodging in hotels, pubs, barracks, and other large public buildings; 600 even found refuge in the modest town castle for three months in 1946. But shortages of eating utensils, furniture, and clean linen made living conditions in these overcrowded, makeshift shelters extremely unhygienic.[43] The vast majority were subsequently placed in furnished rooms located in underoccupied units, or in homes that had previously belonged to Nazi activists, war criminals, and other individuals forcibly removed from their dwellings. Steadfast resistance on the part of many local residents averse to taking in lodgers or vacating their premises made this process extremely difficult. As a result, and under increasing pressure from the local Soviet commandant as well as from state authorities in Weimar, assignments to private quarters usually took place by "forceful means" – leading to anger and resentment as well as to considerable tensions between natives and newcomers.[44]

The difficulty of finding accommodations for the district's newest arrivals was exacerbated by the simultaneous need to secure housing for those employed at the Maxhütte steel mill, considered at the time to be one of the most important

---

[41] See Johannes Frerich and Martin Frey, *Handbuch der Geschichte der Sozialpolitik in Deutschland: Sozialpolitik in der DDR*, vol. 2 (Munich, 1993), 56.

[42] StA-S, Sekr. des BM 2092, Tätigkeitsbericht des WA Slf für die Zeit vom 1.5.45–31.7.46.

[43] See, e.g., StA-S, Abt. Wohnungspolitik 5948, correspondence, 16.4.47.

[44] See the reports in StA-S, Abt. Wohnungspolitik 5948 (quotation from Tätigkeitsbericht, October 1947); also see the minutes of the public meetings held in 1948 in ThStA-R, KR Slf 850.

production sites in the entire Soviet zone. Providing adequate lodging for both groups proved to be a delicate balancing act, in fact, with priorities continually shifting from one to the other – which only added to the general confusion.[45] When making distribution decisions, the Maxhütte itself usually gave preference to skilled workers and technical specialists; the unskilled and semiskilled were accordingly given low priority. As a result, factory functionaries were forced to lodge large numbers of workers – especially male youths – in overcrowded and unsanitary public buildings, where living conditions were often abominable:

We then visited a barrack located in the male living quarters. The room . . . was occupied by seven men and made an extremely dirty and dilapidated impression. The bed frames were partly broken, the straw sacks unimaginably dirty; one of the occupants told us that they only had two blankets and that one was used as a sheet and the other as a cover. . . . These blankets have been used continuously since October of last year [1948] and are completely filthy since the workers – because of apathy or ease – sleep in their work clothes. . . . The rooms as well as the windows – at least those that were not broken or replaced with cardboard – were dirty. The floor was thick with dust. . . . The room is heated by a small iron stove, which was broken because of overuse. . . . The conditions described here were the same in other rooms as well. . . . The whole place is lighted at night by a 25 watt bulb whose filaments can hardly be seen because of the layers of filth . . . [I]t was not clear where the occupants go the bathroom. . . . These older workers and . . . youths live in an unimaginable condition of filth as well as mental and physical lethargy, and it seems that nobody is concerned about them.[46]

Officials endeavored to build additional housing and enlarge existing quarters in response to such alarming reports. Several projects got under way in the late 1940s, thanks to substantial financial support from the state: Clearly attesting to its privileged position in the Soviet zone, the Maxhütte received 2 million of the 9 million marks earmarked by Thuringian authorities for state housing projects in early 1949, for example. Such efforts were seriously hampered, however, by severe material and labor shortages, as well as by poor planning and bureaucratic obstacles. As a result, more than 700 steel workers continued to live that year in mass shelters located far away from the factory. Several dozen leading functionaries still had no lodging whatsoever at the time.[47]

To assure an adequate labor supply as well as "healthy work morale," officials at the steel mill were most concerned about providing staff members with decent housing in the immediate vicinity of the factory: "The German worker needs a certain degree of orderliness and domesticity . . . and he who has nothing to lose doesn't have the same interest in work as one who has a real apartment and a sense of order."[48] With that in mind, district authorities set up organized

45 See, e.g., the correspondence from June and July 1947 in MxA-U, BGL 58 and WL B150.
46 MxA-U, BGL 62, report to Fritz Selbmann, 12.2.49.
47 See MxA-U, WL B129, Prot. der WL–Besprechungen, 23.3.49, 3.6.49.
48 MxA-U, WL B150, Niederschr. über die Besprechung der Unterbringung von Maxhüttearbeitern, 22.10.47.

competitions that awarded monetary premiums to those functionaries who managed to locate the most housing; at the same time, they equated failure with sabotage and threatened to punish those who failed to meet official targets.[49] Despite such pressure tactics and despite repeated extensions of official deadlines, the competitions failed to produce the desired results – usually because of tenacious resistance on the part of local residents who refused to take in lodgers or exchange their apartments with supposedly more needy individuals.[50]

Authorities nevertheless managed to secure lodging for almost 1,000 families in the immediate vicinity of the steel mill between 1949 and 1951 alone – thanks in large part to special housing laws that permitted forcible evacuations when efforts to reach amicable agreements with local residents failed to satisfy the Maxhütte's voracious needs.[51] Those who refused to comply sometimes turned to party, state, and housing officials for support, but such appeals usually fell on deaf ears: As one resolute member of the district's Antifascist Committee put it, transfers were "absolutely essential," regardless of whether or not they suited those adversely affected.[52] Subsequent refusals to vacate usually led to forced expulsion by armed members of the so-called People's Police; authorities also brought pressure to bear on stubborn individuals by threatening to withhold their ration cards. The Soviets not only encouraged such drastic measures but also sometimes carried them out themselves. In September 1947, for example, the district commandant ordered the evacuation of "everyone not tied to the plant" from nearby villages and personally intervened when tenants refused to vacate their homes – a decision that ultimately affected forty families in nearby Grosskamsdorf alone. This was no isolated episode: Two months earlier, several hundred families had been forcibly evicted from villas located in the fashionable Feldherrnhügel district overlooking the town of Saalfeld in order to make room for ranking Soviet personnel.[53]

Thanks to such tactics, and despite continuing resistance by the local population, authorities were eventually able to find housing for most of those considered economically and politically most vital.[54] Steel workers, eastern refugees, and Soviet troops were not, however, the only privileged groups to benefit from the thousands of inspections, transfers, and forced evictions that took place in Saalfeld during the first years following the end of the war. In the summer of 1949, for example, officials carried out a series of expulsions in the district's southernmost villages in order to make room for security personnel stationed

---

[49] On resistance to such pressure, see MxA-U, BGL 50, report, 13.5.49.
[50] See StA-S, Abt. Wohnungspolitik 5947, reports, 15.6.49, 2.3.50.
[51] See the reports in MxA-U, WL B60 and B150; also see MxA-U, WL B17, Aufstellung über Wohnungen, die nach 1945 erstellt worden sind, n.d.
[52] MxA-U, WL B150, Niederschr. über die Besprechung der Unterbringung von Maxhüttearbeitern, 22.10.47.
[53] See StA-S, Abt. Wohnungspolitik 5948, Tätigkeitsberichte, July–August 1947; ThHStA-W, KR Slf 784, Prot. des Wohnungsausschusses, 11.9.47; MxA-U, B150, Prot. der Besprechung der Unterbringung von Maxhüttearbeitern, 22.10.47.
[54] See the reports in MxA-U, WL B150 and BGL 50.

on the East German–West German border; as we shall see in the next chapter, a similar campaign would be launched a year later following the arrival of large numbers of uranium miners.[55] They, along with the many technicians, engineers, teachers, and doctors who also descended upon Saalfeld at the time, would "completely suck up all remaining living space" by the early 1950s.[56] The priority given to these groups meant, of course, that little room was left over for less privileged individuals urgently in need of lodging as well; in fact, only a "small fraction" of the 1,700 other registered housing cases could be resolved by the early part of the decade. As the head of the town housing committee concluded at the time, there was not just a "housing plight" in Saalfeld: There was a "housing misery."[57]

That held equally true for another basic necessity made scarce by the serious dislocations caused by the war: adequate food supplies. In response to this major challenge, authorities swiftly adopted the unpopular expedient of mandatory requisitioning, which obliged East German farmers to hand over a sizable portion of their yield to the state, according to quotas that varied by product and region as well as by the size of an individual holding. Originally introduced by the Soviets to provide for the maintenance of occupation troops, this practice was continued by German authorities in order to safeguard the supply of foodstuffs throughout the zone.[58]

Less enthusiastic about giving than receiving, most farmers in Saalfeld chafed at compulsory deliveries, which soon became one of the most important sources of friction and discontent in the countryside. They usually complained that their production quotas were either unduly high or that they could not be filled because of poor harvests, energy and material shortages, or damage caused by wild boars and Soviet troops trampling across their fields.[59] District officials conceded that such problems frequently accounted for low fulfillment rates and occasionally appealed to their superiors in support of individual requests for lower quotas. Such pleas were usually in vain, however, and the pressure from above to meet district quotas largely accounted for the subsequent intransigence of many local functionaries themselves.[60]

The latter consequently devised a number of strategies to encourage deliveries and boost production, which regularly fell below expected figures.[61] This included a constant flurry of agitation and "education" in the countryside, as

---

[55] See the reports in StA-S, Abt. Wohnungspolitik 5946–8.
[56] StA-S, Sekr. des BM 2254, Allg. Wohnraumüberprüfung im Stadtgebiet Slf, 11.2.52.
[57] StA-S, Abt. Wohnungspolitik 5943, Rechenschaftsbericht des WA, 4.10.51; StA-S, Abt. Wohnungspolitik 5947, Rechenschaftsbericht des Wohnungsausschusses für das Jahr 1949, 31.1.50; StA-S, Abt. Wohnungspolitik 5946, Hauptausschuss-Sitz., 12.12.52.
[58] See Naimark, *Russians*, 156–66. On supply difficulties throughout Germany at this time, see, e.g., Rainer Gries, *Die Rationen-Gesellschaft: Versorgungskampf und Vergleichsmentalität: Leipzig, München und Köln nach dem Kriege* (Munster, 1991).
[59] See the reports in ThHStA-W, KR Slf 101, 374; ThStA-R IV/4/10/314, 317; KrA-S 14390, 23741.
[60] See the reports in KrA-S 23739, 23741; ThStA-R IV/4/10/99, 314, 317.
[61] See the statistics in KrA-S 23739.

well as the launching of periodic agricultural competitions in which participating landowners received monetary premiums and other material rewards
for honoring their production pledges or performing special tasks.[62] As an
additional incentive and in an attempt to discourage black-market activities –
the scourge of the immediate postwar period throughout occupied Germany –
farmers were also permitted to sell their surplus goods on the open market:
"We hope to ensure that excess products are made available to the working
population [so] that their nutrition improves and they are able to produce
more industrial goods."[63]

These inducements were generally less successful than authorities had hoped.
Black marketeering continued apace in Saalfeld because farmers could usually
obtain higher prices through illicit bartering than they could by selling their
goods to the state or on the open market; the premium system similarly failed
to motivate farmers, and many simply refused to participate in production
competitions.[64] In response to such refusals, as well as to the consistent failure of most farmers to meet their quotas, authorities applied various forms of
pressure against those who had fallen in arrears. They sent threatening letters
and imposed heavy fines, for example, or dispatched members of the People's
Police and agricultural inspectors to local villages in order to determine the
cause of poor deliveries – a practice that sometimes led to verbal altercations
and even brawls. The SED District Secretariat, the locus of local political
power, vowed to introduce harsh punishments in cases supposedly involving
"irregular" activities and "malevolence": The series of confiscations, interrogations, arrests, trials, and prison sentences meted out in Saalfeld during the
late 1940s and early 1950s clearly attested to the seriousness of that threat.[65]

Reconstruction and Restructuring

Personnel purges, a sufficient food supply, and adequate housing were not the
only practical concerns of the immediate postwar period; another was the rapid
revival of industrial production. And as with denazification and land reform,
developments in this area were considered equally essential to the construction
of a "new order" in the Soviet zone. The first steps got under way in Saalfeld
in the spring of 1945 with the initial repair of those factories most seriously
damaged during the aerial bombardment of early April. Small-scale production began in a number of firms the following month, but the most important
development took place in February 1946, when the Maxhütte, the site of the

---

[62] See, e.g., KrA-S 23741, Jahresbericht 1948.
[63] ThStA-R IV/4/10/317, Prot. der Sitz. der landwirtschaftlichen Sachbearbeiter, 14.8.48.
[64] See, e.g., the reports in ThStA-R IV/4/10/99, 100, 103, 314, 317; KrA-S 3925, 23741; ThHStA-W,
KR Slf 374.
[65] ThStA-R IV/4/10/99, Ablieferung, 18.12.52. On the repressive measures taken against local
farmers at this time, see the reports in ThHStA-W, KR Slf 475; KrA-S 23739; ThStA-R
IV/4/10/100, 314. Also see ThStA-R, BDVP Gera 21/212, Lageanalyse, 25.1.53; ThHStA-W,
KR Slf 233, Strafverfahren gegenüber Klein- und Mittelbauern, 7.5.53.

FIGURE 4. The Maxhütte steel mill, located in the village of Unterwellenborn, was the district's largest factory and the site of the only functioning blast furnace in the Soviet zone of occupation. © Bildarchiv des Stadtmuseums Saalfeld.

only functioning blast furnace in the entire Soviet zone, resumed iron and steel production – making it by far the most important factory in the district.

Originally founded in the early 1870s at the time of Saalfeld's industrial takeoff, the Maxhütte was acquired by the infamous Flick Concern in 1929 following a lengthy wage dispute misleadingly described by one East German scholar as the firm's "first and last strike."[66] Under the direction of Friedrich Flick's son, it became a major armaments manufacturer during the Third Reich and later employed hundreds of forced laborers during the war – a practice continued, incidentally, under the postwar Communist regime. In accordance with SMAD Orders 124 and 126, the Soviets seized Flick's sizable holdings in the East as part of their effort to remove active Nazis and militarists from public life – and, of course, to ensure reparation payments to the USSR. To that end, the Maxhütte itself became one of approximately 200 sequestered firms that were transformed in mid-1946 into so-called Soviet stock companies (SAGs) owned and administered by the occupying power; the steel mill was handed over to the state of Thuringia several months later, however, and in July 1948 it officially became a People's Factory (*Volkseigener Betrieb*, or VEB) – the clumsy East German term for all state-run enterprises.

By the end of the 1940s, all of the oldest, largest, and most lucrative businesses in the district had been transformed into VEBs owned and administered

---

[66] Ulrich Hartmann, *Geschichte der Arbeiterbewegung im VEB Maxhütte Unterwellenborn, 1945–1949* (master's thesis, Allgemeinbildende Polytechnische Oberschule Jena, 1966), 2; also see the histories of the steel mill in MxA-U, WL B13, B14.

by the state.[67] Among the most prominent of these was the Mauxion chocolate factory, founded on the outskirts of the town of Saalfeld in 1901 by the sons of a French confectioner and later acquired by Ernst Hüther, an aspiring business-man from the region. Thanks to Hüther's impressive entrepreneurial skills, the factory flourished during the First World War, enabling its new proprietor to become a leading figure in communal politics as well as a major industrial and real estate magnate. His holdings, which were all seized after the war, included Saalfeld's most distinguished hotel and restaurant, the Roter Hirsch am Markt and the Gaststätte zum Loch. Hüther died in 1944 amid speculation that he had had ties to the July 20 conspiracy to assassinate Adolf Hitler, and his private villa, the Haus Bergfried (built on a fifty-acre estate in the early 1920s), was later given to the Maxhütte as a sanatorium for staff members.[68] The choco-late factory itself, the heart of Hüther's vast empire and an armaments supplier during the war, became a VEB in July 1948 and was renamed Rotstern (red star) six years later: By that time, there were only fourteen private firms left in the entire town. With fewer than 400 workers and employees, they represented only a tiny fraction of the district's economic activity.[69]

The seizure and subsequent nationalization of key industries and major facto-ries represented only one part of the postwar effort to construct a new economic order in the Soviet zone; the introduction of centralized planning, the bedrock of the socialist economic system, was another.[70] And to ensure satisfaction of the almighty plan targets now determined on high, officials were determined to boost productivity levels by creating material incentives that would stimu-late the performance of industrial workers. To that end, authorities embraced the so-called performance principle (*Leistungsprinzip*), which linked individ-ual income to quantitative performance. The most important practical mea-sure promoting this principle was SMAD Order 234 of October 1947, which called for the systematic expansion of *Leistungslohn*, or piecework wages: By making income dependent on the fulfillment of assigned production quotas or *norms*, piecework tied individual earnings to output by rewarding high – and penalizing low – production levels. Despite the allure of higher wages, workers in Saalfeld and throughout the eastern zone showed little initial interest in this

[67] See the reports on SMAD Orders 124 and 126 in ThHStA-W, KR Slf 79, 83, 84, 243, 244, 287, 289, 290, 291, 295, 391, 505, 2116. Also see the extensive lists in ThStA-R IV/4/10/289, 292.

[68] On Ernst Hüther and the history of Mauxion, see Walter Schwädke, *Schokoladenfabrik Mauxion m.b.H Saalfeld Saale* (Berlin, 1931), 5–8; Gerhard Werner, *Geschichte der Stadt Saalfeld*, vol. 3 (Bamberg, 1997), 75, 134–5, 154; Werner, *Geschichte* (vol. 4), 67, 69; ThStA-R IV/4/10/289, Überschrift über die Kriegsfertigungsproduktion der Schokoladenfabrik Mauxion in der Zeit von Ende 1939 bis Frühjahr 1945, 14.1.48. On rumors that Hüther had links to the July 20 conspiracy, see Kreutzer, "Besetzung," 43.

[69] KrA-S 14780, Analyse der Stadt Slf/Saale, 30.8.58.

[70] On Communist central planning, see the classic study by János Kornai, *The Socialist System: The Political Economy of Communism* (Princeton, NJ, 1992). On the GDR in particular, see Peter Caldwell, *Dictatorship, State Planning, and Social Theory in the German Democratic Republic* (New York, 2003).

system: In the fall of 1948, for example, only one-quarter of all workers at the Maxhütte had agreed to accept piecework earnings.[71]

There were several important reasons why the wage scheme was so unpopular. In the first place, many workers apparently feared that it would lead to substantial wage decreases. Since the nineteenth century, the German workers' movement had traditionally fought against piecework, which was viewed as an exploitative measure used to squeeze out higher performance levels while maintaining low wages. After the war, most workers remained impervious to official claims that socialist forms of factory ownership had rendered obsolete this old form of capitalist exploitation; in fact, the familiar slogan "Piecework is death" (*Akkord ist Mord*) was once again heard on shop floors across the eastern half of Germany.[72] There was also little incentive to boost earnings at a time when official currency had little value because of shortages and rationing. For that reason, many workers devoted much of their energy to bartering on the black market, trading with farmers in the countryside, or cultivating small parcels of land themselves, all of which helped account for the inordinately high levels of factory absenteeism reported during the immediate postwar years.

Attitudes toward piecework temporarily changed following the introduction of a so-called progressive system in September 1948, and by the end of the year, the percentage of piecework earners at the Maxhütte had jumped to more than 60 percent.[73] The new system was so popular because it allowed workers to increase their wages substantially by rewarding performance levels with unlimited, progressively increasing premiums. As a result, some workers at the steel mill were able to boost their earnings by more than 25 percent during the last three months of 1948. But the strategy to win acceptance of piecework had worked only too well: Wage costs soared as workers flocked to piecework throughout the eastern zone, yet the expected increases in productivity failed to materialize. One important reason for this was that production quotas had been set too low by factory officials concerned about maintaining harmony on the shop floor.[74] Arguing that the progressive system had had disastrous

[71] MxA-U, BGL 28, Entwicklung der Löhne und Gehälter, 28.6.47, 12.10.48. On the introduction of and resistance to piecework wages, see Peter Hübner, *Konsens, Konflikt und Kompromiß: Soziale Arbeiterinteressen und Sozialpolitik in der SBZ/DDR, 1945–1970* (Berlin, 1995), 16–57; Jeffrey Kopstein, *The Politics of Economic Decline in East Germany, 1945–1989* (Chapel Hill, NC, 1997), 17–45; Axel Bust-Bartels, *Herrschaft und Widerstand in den DDR-Betrieben: Leistungsentlohnung, Arbeitsbedingungen, innerbetriebliche Konflikte und technologische Entwicklung* (Frankfurt am Main, 1980), 28–49; Jörg Roesler, "Vom Akkordlohn zum Leistungslohn," *ZfG* 32 (1984): 778–95; Klaus Ewers, "Einführung der Leistungsentlohnung und verdeckter Lohnkampf in den volkseigenen Betrieben der SBZ (1947–1949)," *DA* 13 (1980): 612–33. For a contemporary discussion of piecework wages in the GDR and the performance principle, see Harry Matthes, *Das Leistungsprinzip als Grundlage der Entlohnung in der volkseigenen Wirtschaft* (Berlin, 1954).

[72] For such claims in Saalfeld, see ThStA-R IV/4/10/247, IB der SED–KL Slf, 5.2.54.

[73] MxA-U, BGL 98, Bericht der Abt. Lohn und Tarif für das Jahr 1949, January 1950.

[74] See MxA-U, Betriebsdirektion: Personalfragen, 1950–4, Bericht der Personalleitung, 22.1.49; MxA-U, BGL 384.

effects on firm profitability, Soviet officials decided to rescind the measure in late December. Within three months, the number of workers earning piecework wages at the steel mill and throughout the occupation zone had sunk again to previous levels.[75]

To avoid future wage distortions, local functionaries were now given the difficult task of stimulating interest in piecework while at the same time establishing "technically determined" norms (TANs) that were supposedly more realistic (i.e., stricter) than earlier ones. Despite worker discontent about the decision to abolish progressive piecework, officials at the Maxhütte were able to report success on the first score, if not the second: With a participation rate exceeding 70 percent by December, piecework had more or less prevailed there by late 1949, and would climb to over 80 percent at the steel mill and at other local VEBs by the end of the following decade.[76] Several factors helped account for this turnabout. In the first place, the base rates of piecework wages were set at a higher level than those of hourly wages. Just as important, the increasing availability of goods gave monetary income greater importance. So, too, did the creation of state-run stores (*Handelsorganisationen*, or HOs) in October 1948: By offering access to scarce goods at elevated prices, the HOs gave workers new incentive to earn higher wages.[77]

But the most important development leading to greater worker acceptance of piecework was arguably the informal institutionalization of the "soft" norm, which allowed for substantial increases in earnings because it could be easily filled – and overfulfilled. Because efforts to introduce more stringent quotas continued to meet with undisguised hostility, factory officials tended to set low norms in an effort to keep the peace. This flew in the face of vigorous high-level efforts aimed at raising productivity by instituting stricter quotas: In the summer of 1949, for example, leading SED and union officials called for norm hikes of up to 25 percent in the metallurgical industry.[78] Later that year, the Maxhütte claimed to have increased average quotas by 40 percent above December 1948 levels, strongly suggesting just how soft earlier norms had been. But despite such optimistic reports, most norms were still weak and would remain so, largely because workers at the steel mill attempted "to create difficulties and raise objections whenever new norms [were] set."[79] The chairman of the factory

---

[75] MxA-U, BGL 98, Bericht der Abt. Lohn und Tarif für das Jahr 1949, January 1950. For similar figures and developments throughout the GDR, see the studies by Hübner, Kopstein, and Bust-Barthels in footnote 71.

[76] See MxA-U, BGL 21, Prot. der Sitz. der Lohnausschüsse und Lohnverrechner der VESTA angeschlossener Betriebe, 5.12.49; ThStA-R, FDGB BV Gera 851/208, correspondence, 20.8.58. For similar figures in other factories, see the reports in ThStA-R, FDGB BV Gera 855/210.

[77] At Zeiss, for example, piecework earnings were on average 125 percent higher than hourly wages. See ThStA-R IV/7/231/1167, IB der SED–GO Zeiss, 25.7.49. Also see Hübner, *Konsens*, 40.

[78] See Hübner, *Konsens*, 43.

[79] MxA-U, BGL 62, report, 11.4.49. On similar resistance in other factories, see MxA-U, WL B79, Prot. der Versammlung der BG-Funktionäre der LEB im Kr. Slf, 26.9.47.

union committee (*Betriebsgewerkschaftsleitung*, or BGL) similarly complained that most norms were not yet TANs because officials there did not work with enough "resolution"; even department heads and party members had expressed hostility to norm adjustments and demanded phony quotas. Despite reports of approximately 3,000 supposedly voluntary increases in 1950 and 1951 alone, average norm fulfillment at the steel mill hovered at around 125 percent, a figure that would remain steady over the next two years.[80]

Subsequent efforts to introduce more realistic quotas would play a significant role during the statewide upheaval of June 1953, as we shall see in Chapter 3. The next major demonstration of worker opposition to official economic policy came two years earlier, however, with the introduction of so-called collective factory labor contracts (*Betriebskollektivverträge*, or BKVs) in the spring of 1951. To secure acceptance of production quotas and base wage levels, workers were now required to discuss publicly and then agree in writing to plan figures set forth in each BKV, which were based on model contracts hammered out by ministerial and high-level union officials for each economic sector. In turn, factory directors and union officials were required to make a variety of pledges with regard to bonuses, working conditions, job-related training, and vacation time, as well as a variety of other social and cultural benefits.

Despite this official attempt to give workers the impression that they had an important say in the running of their factory, the first contracts met with widespread resistance in Saalfeld and throughout the GDR.[81] The most important objections concerned base wages (which were generally considered too low given the purportedly high cost of living), the elimination of overtime bonuses for work performed on Sundays, reduced sick pay benefits, and the decision to pay only 90 percent of hourly base wages during production disturbances beyond worker control. Another major complaint at the time – and one that would resurface regularly over the next two decades – focused on what many considered to be unfair pay differentials among workers, which were clearly set forth in each contract.[82]

Protracted shop-floor negotiations continued in Saalfeld throughout the summer, past anticipated deadlines. Party, management, and union functionaries were forced to meet several times with staff members in those factories and

---

[80] See MxA-U, BGL 26, correspondence, 22.12.50; MxA-U, BGL 62, Bericht über den FDGB Instrukteureinsatz, 29.12.50.

[81] See Hübner, *Konsens*, 179–87; Axel Bust-Bartels, "Der Arbeiteraufstand am 17. Juni 1953: Ursachen, Verlauf und gesellschaftspolitische Ziele," *APuZ* B25 (1980): 24–54.

[82] To attract workers to those sectors and industries deemed most essential to economic revival, base wages were set at a significantly higher level in sectors such as mining, metallurgy, and machine building. In addition, they were determined within each factory according to the difficulty, responsibility, and requisite training associated with a given worker's task. Finally, districts in the GDR were assigned to one of several territorial categories, each with a different tariff scheme reflecting size and economic importance. For various complaints about the BKV, see the reports from the spring and summer of 1951 in MxA-U, BGL 125, 170; ThStA-R IV/4/10/90, 245; ThStA-R, FDGB KV Slf 3540, 7595.

departments where opposition was most pronounced in order to address criticism and respond to demands for revision. The following description of one meeting at the Maxhütte gives some indication of the tenor of these discussions: "The gathering, which took place in [an atmosphere] devoid of all understanding, degenerated into deliberate nastiness and ridicule. Not one point in the contract won acceptance." Arguing that the BKV draft represented a "curtailment of worker rights," those in attendance claimed that it was a "blow" against the laboring classes. Similar complaints were voiced in other factories: "Things can't always come at the expense of the little man ... we're all in the same boat and are giving our all to rebuild Germany." To the dismay of those on high, many union officials as well as rank-and-file SED members also joined in the fray instead of setting a "positive example" for their colleagues.[83]

High-level party and union officials were quick to politicize such behavior by suggesting that "class enemies" or party members with "social democratic" tendencies had been responsible for fomenting opposition to the BKV. The SED district leadership found other scapegoats as well: Factory party cells were criticized for not assuming a "leading role" in the preparation and discussion of the new contracts, for example.[84] But despite such censure and despite the hefty opposition they faced on the shop floor, factory officials throughout the district eventually secured acceptance of the first BKV – primarily through compromise and cajolery. While many of the more contentious provisions remained in the final documents, officials made some partial concessions or promised to secure revision of the more controversial stipulations. To that end, the chairman of the Maxhütte BGL drove to Berlin to meet with high-level metal union officials after a particularly rancorous meeting at the rolling mill. His efforts were largely in vain, however, and one week later, he reported that the atmosphere in the department was still "very tense." The following weekend, an entire shift of young workers called in sick to protest against the contractual elimination of Sunday bonuses.[85] Such collective demonstrations were atypical, however, and most protest remained limited to grumbling or a stubborn refusal to sign the contract. The clash over the BKV nevertheless foreshadowed a violent upheaval that would take place in Saalfeld later that summer – and one that would earn the district the dubious distinction of hosting "the first major strike in the GDR...."[86]

Whatever the limitations of denazification and land reform, and notwithstanding the obstacles that hindered official efforts aimed at spurring industrial and agricultural productivity, the main structures of the postwar socialist

[83] See MxA-U, BGL 170, Prot. der BV in der Technischen Kontrollorg., 13.6.51, and Prot. der BV in der Werksküche, 13.6.51; ThStA-R IV/4/10/245, IB der SED–KL Slf, 27.6.51. On developments at the VEB Zeiss, see UACZ, Bestand BACZ 06246.

[84] See, e.g., ThStA-R IV/4/10/241, IB der SED–KL Slf, 8.10.51.

[85] MxA-U, BGL 264, Bericht der AGL–Walzwerk, 26.9.51.

[86] A young woman living in Saalfeld wrote these words in a private letter intercepted by the Stasi. See BStU ASt-G AS 21/74, vol. 1, copy of letter, 17.8.51.

system had largely been established in Saalfeld by the early 1950s. With the backing of Soviet authorities, local Communists had successfully secured public positions of influence throughout the district and carried out a series of major reforms aimed at creating an entirely new political, economic, and social order. Widespread resistance to many of these measures – along with official efforts aimed at coping with the existential challenges produced by wartime destruction – nevertheless created an explosive atmosphere marked by severe tensions among local residents, as well as between them and local representatives of the regime. As we shall see in the next two chapters, these frictions effectively set the stage for two major disturbances that would shake the district and shock authorities in the late summer of 1951 and then again in June 1953.

2

The GDR's "First Strike"

The growing antagonism of the Cold War led to the creation of the German Democratic Republic on October 7, 1949, and officials in Saalfeld duly organized a number of ceremonies throughout the district to celebrate the momentous event. Despite continuing disputes over forced requisitioning and piecework wages, local farmers and industrial workers purportedly "expressed their solidarity" with the new state by publicly pledging to perform "extraordinary acts of production." A major rally held at the town marketplace on October 13 capped off the weeklong festivities: According to celebratory newspaper accounts, no fewer than 10,000 residents were in attendance.[1]

Another demonstration would take place there less than two years later, however – and one that strongly suggested the ephemeral nature of whatever elation had earlier existed. Prompted by the arrest of several uranium miners who had recently moved to the district, the new gathering culminated in the storming of the local prison and police precinct as panic-stricken officials climbed out of windows, onto rooftops, and down trees in order to avoid the swinging picks of rampaging miners who refused to return to the pits until their *Kumpels*, or mates, were set free. Some 3,000 miners and civilians were reportedly involved in this incident.

An unfamiliar chapter in the history of the GDR, the upheaval and its aftermath shed light on some of the more serious social and economic tensions underlying East German society during its formative years, as well as on the ways in which socialist authorities dealt with protest and open conflict in an attempt to maintain (or restore) stability. Because of previous archival constraints, we know very little about large-scale demonstrations in the GDR apart from the uprising of June 17, 1953, when hundreds of thousands of East Germans took to the streets to protest against the policies of the ruling SED in the first statewide insurrection in the Soviet bloc.

[1] Gerhard Werner, *Geschichte der Stadt Saalfeld*, vol. 4 (Bamberg, 1998), 71.

46

The early years of the GDR were clearly a highly volatile period, and this volatility was connected in large part to the introduction of key aspects of the Soviet system. The single-minded economic policies of the Stalinist period – including the almost exclusive emphasis placed on coal and steel production in the first Five-Year Plan (launched in January 1951) – alienated many in Saalfeld and contributed considerably to the climate of growing discontent by leading to serious shortages of basic goods, high prices, and appalling working conditions. So, too, did the increasingly weighty costs of remilitarization engendered by the burgeoning Cold War struggle. It is within this context that one must consider the upheaval of 1951 as well as the more serious – though in Saalfeld considerably less dramatic – mass uprising that would take place almost two years later.

The Events of August 16, 1951

In their feverish attempt to develop atomic weapons after the Second World War, Soviet officials made the exploitation of uranium discovered in eastern German territory in the 1940s a major component of their reparations program. The Wismut Aktiengesellschaft, a Soviet stock company placed under the direct control of officials in Moscow, was formed in 1947 to supervise extraction of this strategically valuable material. In order to win volunteers for the new mines, occupation and East German authorities launched massive recruitment campaigns beginning in the latter part of the decade. Given the disastrous economic situation and the poor supply of basic provisions following defeat, it was not surprising that inducements of high wages and an elevated standard of living succeeded in attracting labor, especially among returning prisoners of war as well as uprooted refugees from the former eastern territories.

These efforts apparently failed to attract enough volunteers to satisfy the voracious demands of Wismut, however, for authorities also resorted to forced labor recruitment, making use of a decree promulgated in January 1946 by the Allied Control Council that permitted the coercion of German labor for reparation payments. Former Nazi activists, political prisoners, and even convicts were among those forced in this way to work for Wismut. In addition, firms were required to submit lists of men whose jobs could be performed by women, youths, and the handicapped; pressure, including threats of redundancy or the canceling of food ration cards, was then placed upon these workers to sign up. According to the notes of a lecture held in the late 1950s at the Technical University in Dresden, Wismut officials often resorted to "forceful measures" during this early phase of uranium mining in order to maintain "order and discipline" and "improve" the attitude of reluctant miners toward their work.[2]

---

[2] SStA-C W V/9/10. On the difficulties of finding workers and on recruitment strategies in the Saalfeld region, see the reports in ThStA-R IV/2/6/823–4. On the early history and organization of Wismut, see Rainer Karlsch and Zbynek Zeman, *Urangeheimnisse: Das Erzgebirge im Brennpunkt der Weltpolitik, 1933–1960* (Berlin, 2003); Rainer Karlsch and Harm Schröter, eds.,

Mining, which was centered in the Ore Mountains of western Saxony, spread to southeastern Thuringia and the environs of Saalfeld in the spring of 1950. The swift transfer of large numbers of miners and administrative personnel to this region had dramatic demographic effects: The population of the area's most important mining site, Dittrichshütte, jumped from 300 to 3,000 by the end of 1952.[3] Almost overnight, this sleepy, isolated hamlet, nestled high in the hills of the Thuringian forest at an altitude of nearly 2,000 feet, turned into a bustling center of intensive mining activity. Serious frictions came in the wake of this large, rapid population increase: Heavy drinking, fighting, and vandalism, especially among young male miners, created an atmosphere reminiscent of the nineteenth-century American Wild West. Their rowdy behavior not only led to frequent, sometimes violent run-ins with police officials called upon to intervene, but also produced strained relations with local residents, many of whom treated the "intruders" with open contempt.[4]

The miners' conduct was not the only cause of resentment, however: They represented an added burden to what was already one of the most explosive social problems in this region, namely, the severe housing shortage made acute by the need to find lodging for refugees from the East as well as for those employed at the Maxhütte.[5] To help relieve the desperate situation created by this demographic shakeup, many local residents were forced to share or sometimes even abandon their living quarters in order to make room for uranium workers, who would number more than 5,000 by the winter of 1952.[6]

The lodging with which miners were provided was generally poor; sanitary and hygienic conditions were often substandard. Many were forced to live close together in barracks, schools, or factory halls. Insufficient bathing facilities and shortages of fresh water, linen, and eating utensils were not uncommon. Miners placed in private quarters complained about high rents and hostile landlords: "Nobody wants to take in a Wismut worker, or else they [the miners] are assigned the lowest quality apartments or quarters." One SED official reported

---

"Strahlende Vergangenheit": Studien zur Geschichte des Uranbergbaus der Wismut (St. Katharinen, 1996); Ralf Engeln, Uransklaven oder Sonnensucher? Die sowjetische AG Wismut in der SBZ/DDR, 1946–1953 (Essen, 2001); Norman Naimark, The Russians in Germany: A History of the Soviet Zone of Occupation, 1945–1949 (Cambridge, MA, 1995), 235–48; Reimar Paul, Das Wismut Erbe: Geschichte und Folgen des Uranbergbaus in Thüringen und Sachsen (Göttingen, 1991), 11–61. Also see the two anonymous reports published in West Germany in 1950 or 1951 by individuals intimately familiar with the workings of Wismut: Sopade Informationsdienst, Der Uranbergbau in der Sowjetzone, Denkschrift #27 (Hannover, n.d.); Der Uranbergbau in der sowjetischen Besatzungszone (n.p., n.d.).

[3] ThStA-R IV/2/6/823, report, 20.1.53. The population of the Aue district in Saxony similarly doubled from 110,000 to 212,000 between 1946 and 1951. See Naimark, Russians, 241.

[4] See the reports by local police, party, and state officials in ThHStA-W, LBdVP 5/29; ThStA-R IV/2/6/821–3. Also see the excerpts from interviews with Wismut miners and mining personnel in Sopade, Uranbergbau, 69–82; Paul, Erbe, 131–78.

[5] See Chapter 1.

[6] ThHStA-W, KR Slf 2264, report, 27.2.52.

that "the mates had to live in ice-cold rooms without any family contact," which suggested at least one reason for the high rates of sexual disease and prostitution reported in the region.[7] Relations with local women as well as frequent visits to the pubs apparently offered miners an escape from their cramped lodgings.

The wretched conditions in the pits must have stimulated alcohol consumption as well. Working close together in poorly ventilated spaces underground, most Wismut miners received low-quality tools and inadequate protective clothing. While some worked up to their knees in water because of poor drainage, others ran the risk of developing pneumoconiosis because they were often forced to drill without water in order to speed up production. Accidents, linked in part to poor security measures, were not uncommon. Daily exposure to radioactive material caused stiffness in the joints and heart pains; long-term exposure was, of course, fatal. According to a confidential report submitted in 1965 by Erich Apel, the chairman of the State Planning Commission, over 6,000 Wismut miners had suffered from vocational ailments since 1952: 2,500 accidents had occurred in 1964 alone, of which 27 were described as serious and 10 as fatal. These figures give some idea of what conditions must have been like in the mines during the early years of Wismut, when conditions were even more primitive. As one former miner later recalled, "Health and labor protection played no role. Ore was all that mattered."[8]

The combination, then, of compulsory recruitment, deplorable working and living conditions, social ostracism, and heavy alcohol consumption created serious tensions throughout the mining regions and promoted rowdy, aggressive behavior on the part of many Wismut workers.[9] Frictions increased considerably in southeastern Thuringia during the summer of 1951, linked primarily to the sudden transfer of 2,000 miners to the Dittrichshütte–Saalfeld region in mid-June. It was later reported that "some of these mates had gone for days without lodging and had to sleep wherever they could." Aggression levels rose and a series of brawls took place in mid-August between Wismut miners and members of the local Free German Youth (FDJ).[10]

7 ThHStA-W, LBdVP 5/29, Prot. der Sitz., 25.8.51; ThStA-R IV/4/10/93, Prot. der Sekretariatssitz. der SED–KL Slf, 1.2.52. On the high rates of sexual disease, see ThHStA-W AIV/2/3–230, Bericht über die Durchführung des Sonderarbeitsplanes, November 1951.
8 East German authorities were already aware of the health risks associated with uranium mining in the late 1940s. See SAPMO–BA, Büro Ulbricht, J IV/2/202–55, report, 1.10.65; Naimark, *Russians*, 242; Paul, *Erbe*, 141.
9 Similar social tensions generally accompanied the rapid industrialization and urbanization of mining regions, where tiny villages often metamorphosed into major towns overnight. See Klaus Tenfelde, *Sozialgeschichte der Bergarbeiterschaft an der Ruhr im 19. Jahrhundert*, 2nd ed. (Bonn, 1981), 328. On miners and alcohol consumption, see Franz-Josef Brüggemeier, *Leben vor Ort: Ruhrbergleute und Ruhrbergbau, 1889–1919* (Munich, 1983), 143–7.
10 See ThHStA-W, BdMP 1296, Außendienstbericht, 4.6.51; ThStA-R IV/4/10/299, Bericht über den Aufruhr seitens der Wismutarbeiter, 20.8.51; also see the bulletins, teletypes, and police reports from August 1951 in ThHStA-W, LBdVP 5/29.

During the early evening hours of August 16, another fight broke out, this time between two drunken miners in the marketplace in Saalfeld.[11] The police were summoned after one of them injured a civilian with a broken bottle, and the three high-ranking officers sent to investigate arrested one of the workers (the other apparently slipped away into the crowd). Police reports allege that the miner forcefully tried to resist arrest on the way to the precinct, which was housed in the former Roter Hirsch Hotel located directly across the square. He was carried into the precinct after one of the officers rendered him unconscious with a blow to the chin. A small group of miners, recognizable by their rubber pit uniforms and blackened faces, began to gather in front of the station house to protest against the arrest. The crowd grew as miners who had witnessed the incident gathered their mates from the local pubs (August 16 had been payday in Dittrichshütte). Protests and demands for the worker's release led to the arrest of four other miners who, according to police reports, were particularly abusive and inflammatory: They called for the forceful freeing of the miner, demanded that the arresting officers immediately be brought to justice, and encouraged the others not to return to the mines until their colleagues had been released.

Efforts by local state and party officials to disperse the growing crowd, which by this time included a "significant part...of the local population," were in vain.[12] The reports emphasize that two women were especially active in inciting the crowd to thrash the police and free the miners by force. Small groups forced their way into the station house several times to demand the release of the workers, but each time the police cleared the building. The new

---

[11] The following depiction of the events that took place in the marketplace is based primarily on (1) reports submitted by the local police; (2) investigative analyses by party, state, and high-level police officials; (3) the protocols of Stasi interrogations of witnesses and arrested miners; and (4) private letters written by local residents shortly after the events and later intercepted by the state security service. Apart from obvious reservations about any eyewitness accounts, a number of difficulties concerning the reliability of these sources should be emphasized. In the first place, the police reports are highly biased: Because they were submitted to the officers' superiors, they served, in part, to justify and defend the measures taken. In addition, their wording is sometimes remarkably similar, suggesting that some were directly copied from others or that the officers had discussed the events among themselves. The protocols of the Stasi interrogations should also be treated circumspectly: The stilted language suggests that they were little more than forced confessions. The private letters by local residents provide a nonofficial account that serves as a control factor of sorts. Also see the eyewitness report in Christoph Kleßmann and Georg Wagner, eds., *Das gespaltene Land: Leben in Deutschland, 1945 bis 1990: Texte und Dokumente* (Munich, 1993), 388–9. In addition to Andrew Port, "When workers rumbled: the Wismut upheaval of August 1951 in East Germany," *Social History* 22 (1997): 145–73 (this chapter is a revised version of that article), the upheaval has received treatment in Heidi Roth and Torsten Diedrich, "'Wir sind Kumpel – uns kann keiner': Der 17. Juni 1953 in der SAG–Wismut," in Karlsch and Schröter, *Strahlende Vergangenheit*, 233–5; Gary Bruce, *Resistance with the People: Repression and Resistance in Eastern Germany, 1945–1955* (Lanham, MD, 2003), 141–4; Ehrhart Neubert and Thomas Auerbach, *"Es kann anders werden": Opposition und Widerstand in Thüringen, 1945–1989* (Cologne, 2005), 47–8.

[12] ThHStA-W, LBdVP 5/29, Stellungnahme zu dem Vorkommnis, 10.10.51.

shift of miners did not drive to Dittrichshütte at 10 P.M.; instead, empty cars were sent to bring those getting off work back to the marketplace. Fearing that the situation was getting out of hand, the local police appealed to the Soviets for assistance. The latter refused to intervene, however, citing "international considerations."[13] Regional police authorities in Weimar were then contacted by telephone for reinforcements and instructions. After consultation with high-level state security officials, they ordered the immediate release of the arrested miners and forbade the use of firearms under any circumstances.

The subsequent freeing of the four workers failed to placate those assembled in front of the precinct. Calls went up from the crowd demanding the release of other miners who, it was claimed, were still imprisoned. Assurances by the police that there were no more in the building were met with skepticism, as were those of a delegation of miners allowed to inspect the station house. The throng demonstrated its disbelief by showering the façade with a cascade of stones that miners had, in the meantime, brought by the truckload from Dittrichshütte. At around 11 P.M., approximately 100 individuals climbed into the building through the large, now broken panes of glass on the street floor and searched in vain for other miners. Having found none, a much larger group then proceeded to the city prison located directly behind the town hall across the square. According to police reports, this group was led by one of the more voluble Wismut women, the same one who had allegedly incited the first stoning of the precinct by throwing a beer bottle through one of the windows. Using a tree as a lever, the crowd lifted the prison door from its hinges, threatened to hang the guards, and freed the two other miners whom they found inside. The group then returned to the marketplace and claimed that the imprisoned men had been beaten so badly by the police "that they were not able to move on their own" – an announcement that heightened tensions considerably.[14]

Shortly after the storming of the prison, a motorized police unit sent by the East German chief of police, Karl Maron, abruptly sped into the marketplace. The surprised crowd encircled these reinforcements and dragged two of the policemen from their motorcycles: Punched and kicked, one of them suffered a serious concussion after a miner smashed his protective helmet with a pickaxe. Directly after this melee, at some point between midnight and 1 A.M., some 50 to 150 miners and civilians stormed the precinct. They climbed in through the windows on the ground floor, shouting, "Beat them to death, string them up. . . ." An official who had just arrived from Weimar reported that the mob "broke down the doors with their sticks, axes, and picks, and searched for

---

[13] Ibid. One Soviet officer did address the crowd around midnight, however, threatening to "clear the square with the help of Soviet troops." See BA-P, HVdVP 11/8, Bericht über den Vorfall in Slf, 18.8.51. On similar reticence by the Soviets during the early stage of the June 1953 uprising, see, e.g., Volker Koop, *Der 17. Juni 1953: Legende und Wirklichkeit* (Berlin, 2003), 340–2.

[14] BStU ASt-G, Ref. XI 16/52, Bde. 1–9, Urteil des Landesgerichts Thür., 19.5.52.

members of the People's Police." Fearing for their lives, most of the officers abandoned the building by climbing out of windows and then down trees or onto the roof. The chief of police later wrote that he had ordered the evacuation in order to avoid a "bloodbath."[15]

At least five officers were nonetheless injured, two of them seriously. Approximately 1,000 windows were smashed; dozens of typewriters, doors, locks, desks, and lamps were damaged. Several weapons, a variety of confiscated goods, and some of the officers' personal belongings were stolen. Files from the criminal division were thrown into the marketplace, doused with gasoline, and set aflame. The rampage lasted until about 1:30 A.M., when, "intoxicated by their victory and show of strength, the [miners] climbed into their [company] cars and drove away singing and shouting...."[16] According to the police, approximately 3,000 persons had gathered in the marketplace that evening: Of these, about one-third were Wismut miners.

Underlying Causes

The dynamics of the uproar in Saalfeld were more or less straightforward: Events gathered momentum as large segments of the crowd, emboldened by drink and incensed by rumors of police brutality, took increasingly violent action, spurred on by several of the more voluble participants and, inadvertently, by the intervention of outside police officials.[17] In many respects, the upheaval was a throwback to the sort of social protest more closely associated with early modern than twentieth-century Europe, where peaceful demonstrations and union-led strikes had by and large come to replace more violent and less organized forms of collective action. The events in Saalfeld possessed many salient characteristics of more traditional forms of popular protest such as the classic food riot: Violent, localized, and more or less spontaneous, the uproar involved direct action, with women playing a loud and prominent role. Stone throwing, threats of hanging, and record burning were traditions reaching back to the peasant uprisings of the Late Middle Ages – and would be repeated two years later in other East German towns and cities during the large-scale disturbances of June 1953. The upheaval apparently lacked long-term organization, despite later claims by officials, and concluded with a "ritual sacking of the wrongdoer's dwelling."[18]

---

[15] ThHStA-W, LBdVP 5/29, report, 18.8.51, and Bericht über die Vorkommnisse, 28.8.51.

[16] ThHStA-W, LBdVP 5/29, Bericht über den Aufruhr, 18.8.51.

[17] On the dynamics of urban crowd behavior, see, e.g., Anthony Oberschall, *Social Conflict and Social Movements* (Englewood Cliffs, NJ, 1973), 324–45.

[18] Louise Tilly and Charles Tilly, eds., *Class Conflict and Collective Action* (Beverly Hills, CA, 1981), 20. On the distinction between preindustrial and more modern forms of social protest, see George Rudé, *The Crowd in History: A Study of Popular Disturbances in France and England, 1730–1848* (New York, 1964). Also see Jürgen Kocka and Ralph Jessen, "Die abnehmende Gewaltsamkeit sozialer Proteste: Vom 18. zum 20. Jahrhundert," in Peter-Alexis Albrecht and Otto Backes, eds., *Verdeckte Gewalt* (Frankfurt am Main, 1990), 33–57.

Why did miners lash out at the police with such vehemence? And why did their protest find expression in this more traditional form? While it is difficult to establish a direct causal connection, the upheaval can in one sense be interpreted as a release of the tensions that had gradually been mounting in Saalfeld and the surrounding region over the past year. During discussions with state and party officials held immediately after and during the months following the incident, miners emphasized in particular their miserable housing situation, insufficient provisioning, low wages, and poor transportation to and from the mines.[19] The grievances aired at these meetings strongly suggested that many had taken advantage of the escalating situation in the marketplace to vent their anger and frustration against a visible representative of state authority.

One important reason for the form of the miners' protest was, of course, the absence of institutionalized mechanisms allowing for effective redress of their complaints. A comment by one police official made this clear: "The Wismut workers are indignant about their social and hygienic care, which has produced rather hefty discussions. They've already approached the factory union committees because of this, but [their members] only make empty promises."[20] That miners had approached union officials with their grievances should be underscored: It suggested that they had at least entertained the hope that this organization would or could fulfill its classic role. But this expectation was frustrated. The mechanisms of conflict regulation that had become a fixture in Europe since the second half of the nineteenth century certainly existed pro forma in East Germany, but most miners did not perceive them as free or effectual. As the Wismut SED leadership itself admitted, many mates were afraid to complain about serious deficiencies "because in some cases, when they made criticisms . . . they were excluded or penalized with respect to wage increases."[21] In the absence of open, institutionalized organs that effectively represented their interests, miners resorted to violence in order to articulate their discontent and call attention to their difficulties.[22]

---

[19] See the reports in ThStA-R IV/2/6/821–3; ThStA-R SED–KL Slf IV/4/10/299. On the difficulty of establishing a direct causal link between tensions and actions, see Heinrich Volkmann and Jürgen Bergmann, eds., *Sozialer Protest: Studien zu traditioneller Resistenz und kollektiver Gewalt in Deutschland vom Vormärz bis zur Reichsgründung* (Opladen, 1984), 16–17.

[20] ThHStA-W, LBdVP 5/29, Prot. der Diskussion, 25.8.51. Union membership was, by East German standards, particularly low among Wismut miners and mining personnel, hovering around 50 percent during this period. See Rainer Karlsch, "Der Aufbau der Uranindustrien in der SBZ/DDR und CSR als Folge der sowjetischen 'Uranlücke,'" *ZfG* 44 (1996): 15. On workers' attitudes toward the unions more generally, see Chapter 6.

[21] ThStA-R IV/4/10/299, Entschließungsentwurf der 2. Objektdelegiertenkonferenz der Objektparteiorg. Kreuzmann, 1952.

[22] Compare the behavior of miners in the Ruhr region of western Germany after the Second World War, where protests against insufficient food supplies prior to the currency reform of 1948 took the form of (generally) nonviolent strikes and mass demonstrations. See Christoph Kleßmann and Peter Friedemann, *Streiks und Hungermärsche im Ruhrgebiet, 1946–1948* (Frankfurt am Main, 1977), 40–5.

That the miners had material cause for complaint was candidly acknowledged in the reports submitted by state and party officials. But socioeconomic factors alone do not account for upheavals like the one in Saalfeld, as criticism of the overly deterministic "tension-release" explanation of popular protest has pointed out.[23] It could be argued in the case of Wismut, for instance, that compulsory labor coupled with wretched living and working conditions might have instead engendered passivity and listlessness on the part of the miners. Just as important, other workers living in this area at the time shared many similar grievances, yet remained relatively docile. Of all the groups in the region, why was it, then, that the Wismut miners resorted to collective action?

Because of the high priority accorded the exploitation of uranium, authorities had promised recruits proper housing and a relatively high standard of living.[24] The reality was often disappointing, however, despite efforts by Soviet and East German authorities to make good on their pledges. It was bruited about after the riot, for instance, that the disturbances had been sparked by an unfavorable labor contract, a rumor clearly related to the serious wage disputes that had erupted several months earlier during negotiation of the first BKV.[25] One miner working in Dittrichshütte complained in November, "I earn a mere 400 marks; they promise a lot here but don't deliver anything; such conditions don't exist in the West...." Using similar arguments, the head of the Wismut personnel office in Frankenhausen refused to contribute to a solidarity fund for workers in West Germany: "I won't contribute anything for the workers striking in Hesse. They receive an hourly wage of 1.80 [marks]. We should strike here instead. My office assistant receives a salary of 250 marks; she should go on strike."[26]

Shortages of consumer goods caused great consternation as well. At least on paper, the daily rations allotted to underground miners in their labor contracts compared favorably to those enjoyed by other heavy laborers in East Germany, averaging nearly twice as much for most foodstuffs. But workers received these special ration cards only if they had completely filled their production quotas, which explains why the miners were so incensed when they could not reach the pits on time because of poor roads and inadequate transportation service. Those who did obtain these or even less favorable ration cards were then often frustrated by the everyday shortages familiar to most East Germans. Their frustration must have been all the greater given the high expectations resulting from the handsome promises made by authorities. It was perhaps no coincidence that the fight that set off the disturbances of August 16 had begun in a store.

[23] See, e.g., Barrington Moore, Jr., *Injustice: The Social Bases of Obedience and Revolt* (White Plains, NY, 1978); Tilly and Tilly, *Conflict*, 13–15; Volkmann and Bergmann, *Sozialer Protest*. Also see E. P. Thompson, "The Moral Economy of the English Crowd in the Eighteenth Century," in *Customs in Common: Studies in Traditional Popular Culture* (New York, 1991), 185–258.

[24] These promises were set down in individual job contracts given to volunteers. There is a sample of a Wismut labor contract from this period in SStA-C W V 1/5/19.

[25] See Chapter 1.

[26] ThStA-R IV/2/6/822, IB der SED–Wismut, 11.9.51, 17.11.51, 19.10.51.

Frustrated material expectations were not the only factor nourishing the miners' sense of injustice, however: Angered by what they perceived to have been excessive use of force by the arresting officers, they demanded immediate retribution in the marketplace. In a sense, this was the "moral" component of the upheaval that legitimized the protest in the eyes of the participants. In fact, the miners' claims that the police had used excessive force were not exaggerated: A doctor from the local hospital reported that one of the arrested workers had "several lumps caused by blunt blows."[27] But it is doubtful that the arrests on that day alone would have prompted the events that transpired; rather, they served in part as a pretext to retaliate for previous run-ins with the police. While most officers in Saalfeld played down the level of friction in their reports, one admitted that August 16 was "a welcome event...for the Wismut workers, who were often called to account by the People's Police because of their behavior...." Relations between miners and police were also soured by the fact that the latter had sometimes been used to capture and bring back runaways.[28] Personal grievances also suggested at least one possible explanation for the active role played by women during the upheaval: Two of those later convicted for their participation had previously been arrested for illegally traveling to the West, for fencing stolen goods, and for allegedly "spreading sexual diseases." That they were already well known to local officials might also explain why they attracted so much attention: They were more easily identifiable.[29]

Though on a lesser scale, violent confrontations between police and miners were not uncommon in the Wismut regions. Many of the uranium workers transferred to Saalfeld in mid-June 1951 had come from Oberschlema, a town in the Ore Mountains that had previously witnessed a series of similarly "wild scenes." Pitched battles had reportedly taken place there at the local train station, for example, where the local police used high-power water hoses to pacify stone-throwing miners.[30] The bravado of many Wismut workers was arguably linked as well to their knowledge of the paramount importance that Soviet and

---

[27] BStU ASt-G, Ref. XII 16/52, Bd. 13, doctor's report, 10.10.51; BA-P, HVdVP 11/20, report, 12.7.51. It is possible that the strong-arm methods used by local police officers were linked to their military training during the Second World War: The supposedly "zealous and impulsive" head of the municipal police division had been a sergeant, the head of the criminal division a noncommissioned officer. On possible connections between military experience and police brutality, see Karin Hartewig, "'Eine sogenannte Neutralität der Beamten gibt es nicht': Sozialer Protest, bürgerliche Gesellschaft und Polizei im Ruhrgebiet (1918–1924)," in Alf Lüdtke, ed., *"Sicherheit" und "Wohlfahrt": Polizei, Gesellschaft und Herrschaft im 19. und 20. Jahrhundert* (Frankfurt am Main, 1992), 319–22.

[28] ThHStA-W, LBdVP 5/29, Stellungnahme zu dem Vorkommnis, 10.10.51. Also see Paul, *Erbe*, 24–6; Sopade, *Uranbergbau*, 29–30. Turnover rates in the mines were high, jumping from 7 percent in 1947 to 44 percent in 1949. See Karlsch, "Aufbau," 14.

[29] Four male miners and at least one civilian later taken in for questioning had also been arrested on earlier occasions. See BStU ASt-G, Ref. XII 16/52, Bde. 5, 11.

[30] See Paul, *Erbe*, 24–6.

East German authorities attached to their labor: "We are Wismut," the mates were known to boast, "we are invulnerable" (*uns kann keiner*).[31]

A combination of factors precipitated the August explosion in Saalfeld, then: The miners' material situation, previous run-ins with the police, and a strong sense of injustice mixed with a heightened sense of self-confidence provided the oil, heavy drinking on payday and strong-arm arrests the spark. Rudimentary forms of solidarity and organization were certainly discernible – the rapid securing of stones and spreading of rumors, the refusal to return to the pits until their mates were released – and provided another important ingredient. Such behavior was fostered by shared experiences inside and outside the pits, by communal living in large quarters, and by past encounters with law enforcement officials.[32] But the degree of organization and solidarity among the miners should not be exaggerated: The protest fizzled out the following day and no further large-scale collective action followed, even though other miners were arrested over the next few weeks.

The social composition of the Wismut labor force helped account for this, at least in part. As recruiting patterns at the time suggest, most of the uranium workers did not stem from a long mining tradition. Detailed biographical information about the dozen individuals (nine men and three women) later convicted by the Thuringian state court for their participation in the upheaval confirms this impression: None of them had a mining background, and eleven of the twelve had joined only within the past two years. "With the building-up of Wismut," party officials later wrote, "a concentrated industrial proletariat not to be found in any other area of the GDR has *come into being*."[33] This was important because it suggested that developed forms of organization and solidarity could not have existed among Wismut miners: Most were newcomers to the profession as well as to the region.[34] Chronic material shortages – which led to the theft of tools and even to fights among workers eager to fill their production quotas – were another important factor hindering the development of solidarity.[35]

In light of the serious tensions that also existed between Wismut workers and the local population, the involvement of so many civilians – displaying what

---

[31] ThStA Weimar, LBdVP 5/29, Bericht über den Aufruhr, 18.8.51.

[32] On the development of working-class organization and solidarity among German miners elsewhere, see Tenfelde, *Sozialgeschichte*, 334–42, 573–97; David Crew, *Town in the Ruhr: A Social History of Bochum, 1860–1914* (New York, 1979), 159–94. More generally, see Ira Katznelson and Aristide Zolberg, eds., *Working-Class Formation: Nineteenth-Century Patterns in Western Europe and the United States* (Princeton, NJ, 1986).

[33] Italics not in the original. ThStA-R IV/2/6/821, Entschließung der außerordentlichen Tagung der SED Gebietsleitung–Wismut, 19.12.54.

[34] Approximately one-half of the more than fifty persons later identified as having taken part in the disturbances had originally come from other parts of Thuringia or eastern Germany; one-fourth were resettlers from the East, and only one-fifth were natives of Saalfeld. These figures are based on questionnaires filled out by the twelve convicted persons, as well as on the lists of participants in BStU ASt-G, Ref. XII 16/52, Bde. 1–16.

[35] See Karlsch, "Aufbau," 16. On the way in which such tensions hindered the formation of extended solidarity networks in East Germany, see Chapter 8.

might be construed as a solidarity of sorts with the demonstrating miners – was somewhat perplexing. The local police dismissed the approximately 2,000 civilians who congregated in the square as "curious bystanders," which undoubtedly many of them were.[36] But that did not explain why so many locals actively participated in the storming of the prison and precinct. In some cases, personal reasons clearly played a role: Two of the women involved were related to one of the arrested miners, for example. Other residents apparently took advantage of the disturbances to express their dissatisfaction with the regime: When a local shopkeeper interrupted a speech held the following day by the Thuringian minister of the interior with shouts of "lying pigs," a watchmaker supposedly responded, "Those are the first sensible words spoken here in Saalfeld for a long time."[37]

But there was perhaps another reason as well for the civilian participation in the upheaval. Relations between the local population and the police were severely strained, in part because of the tensions made acute by the recent transfer of miners: As one officer commented, the uprising was greeted enthusiastically by many local residents because their "housing situation had been crowded by the influx of Wismut workers...."[38] What was the connection? Despite promises of restitution in the form of rent or a new home, many residents simply refused to abandon their property, which often led to forced eviction by the local police – a drastic measure that understandably created deep-seated resentment.[39] In a symbolic sense, then, the civilian population of Saalfeld joined the miners in turning the tables on the People's Police, invading its sphere just as theirs had been invaded during the long series of confiscations and forced evictions that had taken place during the immediate postwar years.

A Political Protest?

As we have seen, state and party authorities reacted with considerable reserve at the time of the uproar: The use of firearms was forbidden, and the miners' demands for the release of the prisoners were met. While police officials in

---

[36] ThHStA-W, LBdVP 5/29, Bericht über den Aufruhr, 18.8.51. Little information is available about the civilian participants, apart from a list of fourteen individuals identified in the marketplace: These included the mother and sister of one of the arrested miners, a shopkeeper, a jeweler, a baker's apprentice, a haulage contractor, an artist, a clerk, a publican, a steelworker, and the head of security at a local factory. See BStU ASt-G, Ref. XII 16/52, Bde. 11, 15. On apparent solidarity between miners and civilians during the June 1953 uprising, see Heidi Roth, *Der 17. Juni 1953 in Sachsen* (Cologne, 1999), 382–94.

[37] ThHStA-W, LBdVP 5/29, Bericht über die Untersuchung über die Ursachen der Vorkommnisse, 25.8.51.

[38] ThHStA-W, LBdVP 5/29, Stellungnahme zu dem Vorkommnis, 10.10.51.

[39] On the forced evictions and sequestrations, see the reports and correspondence in ThHStA-W, BdMP 1295, 1296. On the early history of the People's Police, see Thomas Lindenberger, *Volkspolizei: Herrschaftspraxis und öffentliche Ordnung im SED Staat, 1952–1968* (Cologne, 2003); Richard Bessel, "Police of a 'New Type'? Police and Society in Eastern Germany after 1945," *German History* 10 (1992): 291–301.

Weimar had decided in conjunction with a high-level Stasi colonel not to use weapons because of the presence of so many civilians in the square, the arrested miners were supposedly let go because of the "hopelessness" of the situation (the precinct was understaffed).[40] These decisions also must have taken into account the great importance attached by occupation officials to the uninterrupted mining of uranium. Caught unawares by the developments in Saalfeld, the Soviets themselves clearly wished to avoid at all costs any escalation of the crisis, which might have seriously disrupted uranium production even further. As a Soviet lieutenant major commented to the local chief of police, "it's alright when a pub is smashed up, but it's bad when half of a production shift is cancelled."[41] A bloodbath involving occupation troops would have been particularly inopportune during the FDJ festival for world peace taking place at the time in Berlin.

After the dust had settled and the shards of glass had been swept away, East German authorities nevertheless responded with a number of sticklike measures. Heavily armed reinforcements were sent to the region immediately after the uproar, and as one local civilian wrote to an acquaintance the day after the storming of the precinct, "We're living here almost in a state of siege. The only things missing are tanks and machine guns."[42] Over the next several weeks, several dozen persons were arrested or brought in for questioning by the Stasi: Most were "made aware of the reprehensible nature of their behavior," but were then told that the Ministry of State Security would "treat them magnanimously and let them go" in the hope that they would "agitate the . . . mates against the criminals of August 16 and 17." The alleged ringleaders were not as lucky: In May 1952, the Thuringian state court convicted a dozen participants and handed down prison sentences ranging from eight to fifteen years.[43]

The incident in Saalfeld attracted the attention of the Politburo, the highest organ of the SED and the locus of political power in East Germany. Its members discussed the events in the marketplace at several meetings held in late August and early September 1951, indicating the seriousness with which high-level party officials viewed the disturbances. In mid-November, the Politburo adopted a formal resolution that included an assessment of the situation as well as a number of corrective measures that were to be immediately implemented in the Wismut regions.[44] The first part of the resolution criticized the performance of the local party and unions, arguing that their poor work had made

---

[40] BStU ASt-G, AS 21/74, Bd. 1, correspondence, 17.8.51.

[41] ThHStA-S, LBdVP 5/29, Aktennotiz, 23.8.51.

[42] BStU ASt-G, AS 21/74, Bd. 1, copy of letter, 17.8.51.

[43] BStU ASt-G, Ref. XII 16/52, Bde. 1–16, Abschlußbericht der Aktion Slf, 14.9.51, and Urteil des Landesgerichts Thür., 19.5.52.

[44] The protocols are rather parsimonious: There are neither copies of the reports delivered by those in attendance nor minutes of the discussions. See SAPMO–BA IV/2/2/163–5, Prot. der Sitz. des SED–Politbüros, 28.8.51, 4.9.51, 11.9.51. Also see SAPMO–BA IV/2/2/176, Stellungnahme über die Maßnahmen zur Verbesserung der Parteiarbeit und der Arbeit auf allen Gebieten in der Wismut, 13.11.51.

it possible for Western "agents" to stir up discontent among the miners. As Erich Mückenberger, the head of the Thuringian SED, would later declare, it was clear "that the roots of this event were not material but rather political."[45] Certain "social grievances," as well as poor work on the part of local officials, might have facilitated the work of the agents, but in the end, it was solely the machinations of these bogeymen that had caused the uproar: This was a tortuous dialectical maneuver that would be repeated again after the mass uprising of June 1953.

Griping about poor work by local officials and the intrigues of phantom agents was a typical if rather vacuous reaction by the SED. But the efforts from above to politicize the events nevertheless draw attention to an essential problem concerning the nature of most conflicts in the GDR: the difficulty of separating neatly the political from the socioeconomic in a society as deeply politicized as East Germany. Conflicts often assumed political overtones because of the party's totalitarian claims in all areas of social life. It determined economic policy, and its officials held positions of power in most VEBs. As a result, any worker unrest could perforce be interpreted as agitation against the ruling SED. In the case of Wismut, if miners were dissatisfied with their living and working conditions, against whom else could they vent their anger besides the state, party, and police officials who ran and supervised the mines? But if the preceding analysis concerning the underlying causes of the events in Saalfeld is correct, the uproar should not be considered political in the narrow sense of fundamental opposition to the regime as such. A report by the chief inspector of the Thuringian People's Police inadvertently supports this conclusion: "It is extremely remarkable that the bandits did not damage in the least a single political slogan, poster or picture during the sacking" of the precinct.[46]

This should not suggest that all Wismut miners were somehow unpolitical or indifferent to the East German regime, or that they did not recognize the political dimension of the events in Saalfeld. An anonymous letter sent in March 1952 to the *Landrat* of the neighboring Rudolstadt district vividly made this point:

We've made great mistakes up 'til now by not having gotten rid of all of you a long time ago.... We have explosives [and c]ourage as well, we proved that in Saalfeld. Haven't you up there noticed that the working people don't want to have anything to do with you, that everything is a great big fraud?... You talk about reconstruction. Can we young people ever think of setting up our own little house with a little garden. Which is the desire of all young people. It will soon be seven years that we were liberated by the Russians. Everything is sinfully expensive. And everything a fraud. Is this a life for a German worker, to labor under the rifle of a Russian? Where have the Communists brought us? They're all rogues and criminals. And on top of that this fraud about unity and peace. No people has ever been so lied to and cheated like we in the eastern zone.

---

[45] ThStA-R IV/4/10/93, Prot. der Sitz. der SED Thür. mit den Gen. des Kreissekr. Slf, 8.2.52.
[46] "This attests," he continued, "to the extreme sophistication (*Raffiniertheit*) of the attack." See ThHStA-W, LBdVP 5/29, Vorläufiger Schlußbericht über die Ereignisse in Slf, 19.8.51.

The Russian is happy that he's made it to the Elbe. And you criminals help [him]. When somebody wants to visit his relatives [in the West], he faces the greatest difficulties getting a permit or a passport. That's the reality, as opposed to the speeches made by [Minister President Otto] Grotewohl, who is just as much a Russian vassal as all the others [who were] not elected by the people in a free election with a secret ballot. That's why nobody wants any [elections].... But things are going to change, you can be sure of that. A murderous fratricidal war is coming, like Grotewohl said.... [W]e can already tell you what will be done with you. You'll be ground in a mincing machine and the mush that comes out will be spread onto the fields so that the farmers can harvest even larger potatoes.... At least then you'll have served a purpose. For what we dig out isn't gold or silver or even coal, but filth for uranium for the production of atomic bombs. Then they tell us during our training that that's for peace. Haven't you yet noticed that nobody still believes that?... Haven't you noticed that nobody wants to have anything to do with you politically?... Stop the agitation once and for all. Tell the Russians to scram and to take you with them, that would be the best for you, you Russian vassals [signed] Object 30 near Bürkersdorf and Dittrichshütte, several victims of Stalinism.... [47]

This was only the tip of the iceberg. Several months earlier, an "agent in miners' clothing" had been seen distributing pamphlets at the train station in Saalfeld: "To all German unionists," it read, "German Communists [are] not Communists, but traitors to the working class." There were also stories of miners who physically attacked SED and FDJ functionaries: In Rudolstadt, for example, a Pioneer leader was assaulted late at night by eight drunken miners who supposedly commented, "Here's another one in a Russian shirt," before tearing off his party symbol and striking him on the head with a mining lamp. According to other reports, Wismut workers were frequently overheard singing fascist songs such as the "Horst–Wessel–Lied" or spouting "reactionary" (i.e., National Socialist) propaganda. On September 1 (a symbolic date, the day that Germany had attacked Poland in 1939), the SED District Secretariat in nearby Ilmenau reported that the "mates who live in Rudolstadt had driven home ... after their shift and gathered together; one held a provocative speech which spoke of 'the victorious German army, the Greater German Empire, and the glorification of Adolf Hitler.' They then withdrew in closed formation and sang the fascist song 'Today Germany belongs to us and tomorrow the entire world.'" [48]

Apart from the letter to the *Landrat* and the pamphlets, it is unclear just how political these incidents actually were – and if they were, they certainly suggested a broad political spectrum among Wismut miners. In the first place, attacks by aggressive mates were not limited to SED members. And the singing of fascist songs might have been no more than an antiauthoritarian gesture intended to provoke high-level officials, whose antifascist credentials were an important part of the early legitimization strategy used by the SED to justify its

[47] ThHStA-W AIV/2/3–230, copy of letter, 2.3.52.
[48] See the series of reports from 1951 and 1952 in ThStA-R IV/2/6/822–3. The Pioneers were the East German equivalent of the Cub Scouts.

position of leadership in the GDR.[49] Though it is impossible to determine with any certainty the deeper meaning of such behavior, the incidents nevertheless call attention to the difficulties involved in denazification and reeducation east of the Elbe.[50]

The Creation of a "Privileged Cadre"

Although party and state officials never seem to have wavered (at least on paper) in their belief that Western agents were responsible for the uprising, they nevertheless recognized the socioeconomic factors underlying the alarming series of incidents in the Wismut regions. If earlier efforts by East German authorities to persuade the Soviets to improve the mates' conditions had largely been in vain, the dramatic events in Saalfeld apparently did the trick, for the final part of the Politburo resolution of November 1951 explicitly addressed many of the grievances recently voiced by the miners about their living conditions. It called for the construction of new buildings in the uranium regions and ordered state-run stores to improve the supply of goods available to uranium workers; more special shops open only to them were to be set up as well. The minutes of the meeting at which the resolution was passed shed some light on the role played by occupation officials in this matter: "The Politburo approves the Soviet recommendations.... Comrades Ulbricht and [Paul] Verner are charged with working the Soviet recommendations into the already existing ones."[51]

The Politburo statement included two other important measures that did not directly address the miners' grievances but did aim to reduce tensions in the region. The first called for greater inclusion of Wismut workers in local government bodies, such as communal councils and housing committees. This was meant to ensure the representation and protection of miners' interests and to help integrate them into the local communities. The other measure ordered the setting up of cultural centers, movie theaters, libraries, and the like in order to broaden the variety of cultural activities available to miners: that "the mates sit in pubs and run the risk of succumbing to alcohol ... should prick up our ears.... Cultural education plays an important role here. Cabarets aren't enough; one must systematically organize the highest quality theater and

---

[49] See Manfred Agethe, Eckhard Jesse, and Ehrhart Neubert, eds., *Der Missbrauchte Antifaschismus: DDR–Staatsdoktrin und Lebenslüge der Deutschen Linken* (Freiburg, 2002); Sigrid Meuschel, *Legitimation und Parteiherrschaft in der DDR: Zum Paradox von Stabilität und Revolution in der DDR, 1945–1989* (Frankfurt am Main, 1992), 29–122.

[50] It was reported at this time that members of the local FDJ also sang fascist songs. See ThStA-R, FDJ–KL Slf 128, correspondence, n.d.

[51] According to notes taken by East German President Wilhelm Pieck at a meeting with high-level occupation officials at their headquarters in Berlin–Karlshorst, Soviet authorities had ordered these measures earlier that month. See SAPMO–BA IV/2/2/176, Prot. der Sitz. des SED–Politbüros and Stellungnahme, 13.11.51; Rolf Badstübner and Wilfried Loth, eds., *Wilhelm Pieck – Aufzeichnungen zur Deutschlandpolitik, 1945–1953* (Berlin, 1994), 378–9. On earlier efforts to persuade the Soviets to improve the conditions of the miners, see Naimark, *Russians*, 241–7.

cultural groups."[52] Though clearly intended as an alternative to the local pub, these efforts to raise the miners' "cultural level" must also be seen in a larger context, of course, i.e., the traditional effort of the German working-class movement to "improve" workers by encouraging them to pursue more "respectable" cultural activities.[53]

Adopting new policies to improve the lot of Wismut workers was one thing, carrying them out quite another. To that end, a number of state and party commissions were established to supervise the implementation of the Politburo's measures, and their reports offer a good indication of the extent to which the resolution was actually realized: It was, in a word, modest at best.[54]

Not surprisingly, the construction of new housing was given top priority. One week after the adoption of the Politburo resolution, Soviet officials drew up two detailed inventories for building projects that were to be carried out over the course of 1952: In addition to street and road repairs, 5,000 apartments, 1,500 private homes for members of the intelligentsia, and dozens of schools, clubhouses, mess halls, stores, bathhouses, athletic fields, hospitals, clinics, and sanitaria were envisioned.Walter Ulbricht and several government officials agreed at a meeting held later that month that the State Planning Commission would allocate 150 million marks to these projects. All of that sounded promising, but most reports emphasized just how little headway was made.[55]

Attempts to improve the supply of basic goods were also less than successful. New Wismut stores were opened in some areas, but severe shortages continued as before. As Erich Mückenberger angrily pointed out six months after the upheaval, there was still "no appreciable difference in the supply of Wismut workers with daily goods. . . . The network of stores has not been expanded." Difficulties with the distribution of wages and ration cards remained serious as well: "Workers have to wait on line for hours to receive their pay. As a result, some colleagues arrive at work one shift earlier, wait on line for their money, and then drive to their shift, so that they're on the go for sixteen to twenty hours."[56]

Analyses of the efforts made to improve the array of cultural activities were equally gloomy. A number of new cultural centers were set up, yet most investigators complained of limited success in drawing miners away from the pubs. Mückenberger lamented in February 1952, for example, that only seven miners in the Saalfeld district had theater subscriptions: "the social make-up of the concert-going public . . . does not correspond to our goals." Who was to blame? One party official admonished the district extension school for not organizing

[52] ThHStA-W, BdMP 1295, Schlußwort des Ministerpräsidenten, n.d.
[53] See the literature cited in footnote 38 of the Introduction.
[54] See the reports in ThStA-R IV/2/6/821–3; ThStA-R IV/4/10/299; ThHStA-W AIV/2/3–230.
[55] See ThHStA-W, BdMP 1295, Förderung und Entwicklung der Grundstoffindustrie im Lande Thür., 11.3.52; ThStA-R IV/2/6/823, report, 20.1.53. See the Soviet plans and the minutes of this meeting in SAPMO–BA, Nachlass Walter Ulbricht NY4182–987.
[56] ThHStA-W AIV/2/3–230, Analyse über den gegenwärtigen Stand der Partei- und Massenarbeit im Kr. Slf, 14.2.52.

any talks on political themes of special interest to the miners; along similar lines, he criticized the town's Cultural League for holding recent lectures on topics such as "How did primitive man live?" or "How can we prolong our lives?"[57] These may not necessarily have been topics that would have gotten the miners running, but they were probably more enticing than the sorts of events that most party officials had in mind. Wismut SED functionaries cobbled together the following list of cultural offerings to serve as a model program: plays by Goethe, Schiller, Lessing, and Shakespeare, operas by Verdi and Smetana, symphony concerts, ballet evenings, and literary matinees.[58] Efforts to bring high culture to Wismut workers may have been noble, but they were not particularly realistic.

Attempts to increase the participation of miners in local government were also disappointing, in part because of resistance by local residents – such as one mayor who rejected the inclusion of miners on the village council because they were not "morally... irreproachable." Such views may have helped explain why not a single Wismut worker took part in the communal government in Dittrichshütte, even though natives represented barely 10 percent of the population.[59] That said, the apathy of the miners themselves apparently played an important role as well: More than 100 miners were represented on various administrative bodies in the Saalfeld district by the fall of 1952, but officials were quick to point out that their involvement was often "perfunctory."[60]

In short, then, the measures aimed at improving the lot of the Wismut miners were implemented unevenly, to say the least. This drew heavy criticism from high-level SED officials, who characteristically blamed local party and state functionaries. The latter were quick to point out that they were hardly in a position to speed up the plodding pace of the reform measures, in large part because of the financial and material constraints imposed by the lackluster economy.[61] This scenario, typical of the difficult situation in which many low-level officials found themselves, has aptly been characterized as the *whipping boy syndrome*: Under great pressure from their superiors, these chided officials were often unable to satisfy the demands placed upon them from above – or

57 ThStA-R IV/4/10/93, Prot. der Sitz. der SED Thür. mit den Gen. des Kreissekr. Slf, 8.2.52.

58 SAPMO–BA, Nachlass Walter Ulbricht NY4182–987, Entwurf eines Perspektivplanes für die kulturelle Massenarbeit im Jahr 1952. The inclusion of the national classics reflected the early "antifascist-democratic" phase of East German cultural policy, which embraced the humanistic traditions of so-called bourgeois German culture. See Manfred Jäger, *Kulturpolitik in der DDR, 1945–1990* (Cologne, 1995), 19. Also see the interview with the former SED Central Committee secretary for education and culture, "Ludwig Haber," in Lutz Niethammer, Alexander von Plato, and Dorothee Wierling, *Die Volkseigene Erfahrung: Eine Archäologie des Lebens in der Industrieprovinz der DDR* (Berlin, 1991), 208–20.

59 ThStA-R IV/2/6/821, Förderung und Entwicklung der Grundstoffindustrie im Lande Thür., 11.3.52.

60 ThStA-R IV/4/10/299, Plan zur Entfaltung der Masseninitiative der Bergarbeiter und Bevölkerung von Slf, 1.10.52; ThHStA-W AIV/2/3–230, Analyse über den gegenwärtigen Stand der Partei- und Massenarbeit im Kr. Slf, 14.2.52.

61 SAPMO–BA IV/2/2/101, Stenographische Niederschr. der 8. Tagung des ZK der SED, February 1952; ThHStA-W IV/L/2/3–069, Auswertung der Sekretariatssitz. der SED–KL Slf, 14.2.52.

from below – because of the insufficient means at their disposal. But the hands of high-level GDR officials were tied as well by unyielding Soviet demands for uranium. The rapid extraction of this strategic mineral had priority – even at the cost of domestic peace. Not even the storming of the precinct in Saalfeld led to a slackening of the pace: 1,500 new miners were transferred to Dittrichshütte three months later, in November 1951.[62]

In response to these challenges, the regime continued to promote the interests of some groups at the cost of others. The seizure of houses, land, and other private property continued in full force after the upheaval, further alienating large sectors of the civilian population.[63] The impression that uranium workers enjoyed preferential treatment in terms of supplies and earnings continued to fuel tensions and resentment as well, leading in some cases to brawls between miners and local residents: "Many simply ignore the fact," the Thuringian minister president commented with an equanimity that bordered on folly, "that the miners have a right to the best care because of their outstanding production performance."[64]

The success of these initial efforts to improve the miners' living conditions may have been imperfect, and tensions may have remained high after the disturbances of August 16, but there were no further explosions of this magnitude until the statewide uprising of June 1953.[65] What accounted for this relative stability? In the first place, the conciliatory efforts by East German officials to introduce corrective measures in response to their grievances must have made a positive impression on the miners. More to the point, and despite sluggish progress early on, all of this marked an important turnabout in their treatment and in their material position: Over the course of the 1950s, they would become a caste of "privileged cadre workers"[66] – a development that can, in all likelihood, be traced back to the events that took place on August 16 in the marketplace in Saalfeld.

---

[62] ThStA-R IV/2/6/822, IB der SED–Wismut, 17.11.51. On the whipping boy syndrome, see Niethammer, *Volkseigene Erfahrung*, 450–77.

[63] A large number of pubs and hotels were also taken over by Wismut. See ThHStA-W, BdMP 1296, Bericht aus der Arbeit der Kommission zur Bearbeitung von Fragen der Grundstoffindustrie, 14.2.52. To justify the revocation of one proprietor's license, local police even designed a plan to stage a fight in his hotel involving Wismut miners. See SAPMO-BA IV/2/5/1022, Plan für eine Aktion gegen den Besitzer des Hotel "Zapfes" mit dem Ziel, diesem die Konzession zu entziehen und das Hotel zu einem Kulturhaus für die Wismutarbeiter auszubauen, 7.9.51.

[64] ThStA-R IV/2/6/821, Förderung und Entwicklung der Grundstoffindustrie im Lande Thür., 11.3.52. On brawls between miners and civilians, see the reports in ThStA-R IV/2/6/822–3.

[65] Serious confrontations between miners and police continued well into the 1950s in Saxony and eastern Thuringia. See the reports from 1953–4 in the journal *Informationsbüro West*. On the behavior of Wismut miners on June 17, 1953, see Roth and Diedrich, "Kumpel," 228–59; Roth, *Sachsen*, 364–94.

[66] Lutz Niethammer, "Erfahrungen und Strukturen: Prologomena zu einer Geschichte der Gesellschaft der DDR," in Hartmut Kaelble, Jürgen Kocka, and Hartmut Zwahr, eds., *Sozialgeschichte der DDR* (Stuttgart, 1994), 101. Similar improvements in the living and working conditions of Czech uranium miners were undoubtedly linked to the events in Saalfeld as well. On developments in Czechoslovakia, see Karlsch and Zeman, *Urangeheimnisse*, 121–2.

But that was not the only explanation, of course. The disturbance apparently functioned as a cathartic discharge of sorts that helped relieve some of the tension that had been building up in the area for over a year. The series of new arrests might have triggered renewed unrest, but they seem instead to have had a sobering effect: By removing the alleged ringleaders, officials apparently neutralized those individuals most likely to spark new disturbances. Just as important, the building of barracks and other large living quarters now surrounded by fences and watch towers facilitated more careful supervision of miners; the Soviets also tried to improve security by distributing special identification cards and by ordering a general increase in the proportion of police to civilians in all of the Wismut regions.[67]

All in all, these carrots and sticks achieved their ultimate goal of maintaining peace in the region so that mining could proceed on schedule. To that end, high-ranking party and state officials also adopted plans to remove so-called "asocial elements" from the Wismut regions – supposedly dangerous individuals who, because of their "amoral" behavior, posed a serious threat to stability. This action provides a disturbing coda to this little-known chapter in the history of the early GDR.

"Outcast Elements"

On December 15, 1951, Walter Ulbricht met with the Soviet managing director of Wismut and local party secretaries, as well as with high-level representatives from the state governments and the People's Police. It was announced that all persons who had recently moved to the Wismut regions from the West were to be expelled, and that all individuals who were not working for Wismut but who had moved to the area over the past two years were to be investigated.[68] On the day that this meeting took place, the East German Ministry of the Interior ordered the drawing up of a list of "outcast elements" (*deklassierte Elemente*) who were to be removed from the area as well. These were to include "persons with criminal records linked to theft, economic crime, robbery, murder or disturbance of the peace, [persons] who have no earned income since completion of their sentence or who have performed no socially useful work for more than three months... persons without permanent domicile or employment," and prostitutes. These measures had been decided upon one month earlier at a meeting between East German President Wilhelm Pieck and Soviet officials.[69]

The expulsions were to proceed in the following orderly manner: First, local police were to obtain each individual's criminal record as well as character

---

[67] BA-P, HVdVP 11/20, Bericht der wichtigsten Maßnahmen zur Verbesserung der polizeilichen Arbeit in den Bergbaukreisen, 10.12.51. Also see Paul, *Erbe*, 36–8, 142; Sopade, *Uranbergbau*, 23–31; Badstübner and Loth, *Pieck*, 378–9.

[68] SAPMO–BA, Nachlass Walter Ulbricht NY4182–987, Prot. der erweiterten Sekretariatssitz. der SED–Wismut, 15.12.51.

[69] See BA-P, HVdVP 11/20, Durchführung von Maßnahmen zur verstärkten Säuberung der Wismutgebiete von deklassierten Elementen, 15.12.51; Badstübner and Loth, *Pieck*, 378.

sketches by the local mayor or *Landrat*. They were then to invite the person to the district police office and order him or her to leave the district within eight days: "The individual to be expelled is to confirm this notification with his signature." If the person – who was allowed to choose his or her new domicile, as long as it lay at least fifty kilometers away from the Wismut regions – refused, the expulsion was to be carried out "by force without attracting any [public] notice." A letter sent in early March 1952 from a high-level police official to a member of the Soviet Control Commission described how this operation proceeded in practice:

[A] large number of those persons to be expelled rejects the order in the absence of pressure. In order to bring about the departure, food ration cards are blocked or lodgings are confiscated by communal authorities on the planned departure date. The affected persons respond in various ways to the notification of expulsion. Some accept [it] without voicing any opposition. Others, primarily women, stage sobbing scenes and declare categorically that this is a crime against humanity....[70]

All in all, the action did not involve large numbers of persons due to bureaucratic infighting. By June 1953, only sixty-four individuals from the entire Saalfeld district had been arrested or expelled, and at least seven had returned after their removal – an important reminder that the East German repressive apparatus was still in its infancy during the formative years of the GDR.[71] Local authorities in other regions steadfastly refused to accept those who were banished, frequently using housing shortages as an excuse. One such case involved a woman with tuberculosis who was expelled in late 1952 and sent to no fewer than four towns before finally being forced to return to Saalfeld.[72]

It is noteworthy that three-quarters of all the persons affected by these measures were women, many of whom were expelled for allegedly practicing prostitution or spreading sexual disease. That high levels of both phenomena were reported in the Wismut regions was not surprising, given that so many miners were either single or separated from their families. What is striking, however, is the language used by officials in their internal reports. In the first place, many of these women were designated as "HWG," a bureaucratic term referring to their "frequently changing sexual partners" (*häufig wechselnde Geschlechtspartner*). Along similar lines, the women who had received so much attention during the events in the marketplace in Saalfeld were repeatedly described as "harlots" and the one who had supposedly led the storming of the prison as an "incorrigible

[70] BA-P, HVdVP 11/20, Durchführung von Maßnahmen zur verstärkten Säuberung der Wismut-gebiete von deklassierten Elementen, 15.12.51; BA-P, HVdVP 11/21, correspondence, 31.3.52.

[71] See Richard Bessel, "Grenzen des Polizeistaates: Polizei und Gesellschaft in der SBZ und frühen DDR, 1945–1953," in Richard Bessel and Ralph Jessen, eds., *Die Grenzen der Diktatur: Staat und Gesellschaft in der DDR* (Göttingen, 1996), 224–52.

[72] On this and similar cases as well as on the numbers involved in this "action," see BA-P, HVdVP 11/21–22. Also see Rainer Potratz, "'... zur Entfernung deklassierter Elemente...': Die Ausweisungen aus den Uranbergbaukreisen 1952–1954," in Karlsch and Schröter, *Strahlende Vergangenheit*, 209–27.

whore." These women were, in fact, the only persons arrested the morning after the events in the marketplace; a local newspaper account of the incident that appeared a week after the upheaval even disclosed their names and addresses.[73]

This deprecatory language, the singling out of women, and the emphasis placed on their supposedly baleful influence revealed prevailing male attitudes toward women, especially the more emancipated ones. More generally, the language used by officials with regard to both women and "asocials" suggested that East German authorities had clear ideas as to what constituted correct social and sexual behavior. The measures taken to deal with supposedly deviant individuals clearly revealed, moreover, the lengths to which they were willing to go in order to enforce social – and not merely purely political – norms.[74]

The removals from the Wismut regions served as a trial run for a more far-reaching purge that would take place eighteen months after the August 1951 upheaval, when politically unreliable persons were forcibly relocated from the five-kilometer border zone abutting the West German frontier. Unofficially referred to as Operation Vermin, this action, which took place in May 1952, affected dozens of individuals and families in the Saalfeld district alone.[75] Forced population transfers had punctuated the first half of the twentieth century and were, by this point, nothing novel. In the GDR itself, refugees from the East had been shipped from one town to the next in the late 1940s, and those living in underoccupied houses or apartments were regularly evicted at this time as well. But the eugenic terminology used by officials nevertheless brings to mind a number of disturbing associations. In December 1937, the Prussian minister of the interior had issued a decree similar in wording to the one drawn up by East German authorities in December 1951: "Such persons shall be deemed asocial who . . . by virtue of petty repeated infringements of the law, are not prepared to comply with the order that is a fundamental condition of a National Socialist state, e.g., beggars, vagrants, prostitutes, drunkards, . . . persons with

---

73 See BA-P, HVdVP 11/21, Abschlußbericht bez. der deklassierten Elemente, 16.12.52; ThI IStA-W, LBdVP 5/29, Prot. der Diskussion, 25.8.51; BStU ASt-G, AS 21/74, Bd. 1, correspondence, 17.8.51. The article about the upheaval appeared in *Das Volk*, August 24, 1951, Saalfeld edition.

74 There are a number of important studies about postwar attitudes toward women and sexual relations in the GDR. These include Dagmar Herzog, *Sex and Fascism: Memory and Morality in Twentieth-Century Germany* (Princeton, NJ, 2005); Elizabeth Heineman, *What Difference Does a Husband Make? Women and Marital Status in Nazi and Postwar Germany* (Berkeley, CA, 1999); Uta Poiger, *Jazz, Rock, and Rebels: Cold War Politics and American Culture in a Divided Germany* (Berkeley, CA, 2000). Also see Chapter 8. On attitudes toward and treatment of so-called asocials, see Sven Korzilius, *"Asoziale" und "Parasiten" im Recht der SBZ/DDR: Randgruppen im Sozialismus zwischen Repression und Ausgrenzung* (Cologne, 2005).

75 See the reports in ThStA-R, Rat des Bez. 2.1/3. Also see Manfred Wagner, *"Beseitigung des Ungeziefers": Zwangsaussiedlungen in den thüringischen Landkreisen Saalfeld, Schleiz und Lobenstein, 1952 und 1961: Analysen und Dokumente* (Erfurt, 2001); Inge Bennewitz and Rainer Potratz, *Zwangsaussiedlungen an der innerdeutschen Grenze: Analysen und Dokumente* (Berlin, 1994); Norbert Moczarski, "Quellen über die Vorbereitung und Durchführung der Zwangsaussiedlungen zu Beginn der 50er und 60er Jahre in Südthüringen," *Archivmitteilungen* 42 (1993): 135–41; Armin Mitter and Stefan Wolle, *Untergang auf Raten: Unbekannte Kapitel der DDR–Geschichte* (Munich, 1993), 29–31.

sexually transmitted diseases ... the work-shy, work evaders. ..."[76] One should, of course, avoid heavy-handed comparisons between the GDR and the Third Reich: "Asocial" individuals in the Wismut regions were allowed to choose another domicile; under the Nazis, they often wound up in concentration camps. But the forced removals, as well as the language used by East German state and party officials, nevertheless underscore the necessity of considering the GDR in a larger historical context.

The upheaval in Saalfeld was a spectacular but rare event. That it was discussed at the highest party and state levels attested to this fact. Yet the tensions brought about by the buildup of Wismut and the ensuing explosion draw attention to many of the underlying social strains that plagued much of eastern Germany during the immediate postwar years. The arrival of uranium miners in southeastern Thuringia exacerbated many of these difficulties and, as a result, further rent a community already saturated with conflict: It intensified the daily struggles over scarce goods such as housing and provisions, heightened frictions between civilians and the People's Police, and brought about new manifestations of the resentment and social ostracism already familiar to the other recent newcomers, namely, the refugees from the East who had been forced to abandon their homes after the war.[77]

The events in the marketplace in Saalfeld also illustrated the extent to which the dictates of high politics linked to the escalation of the Cold War had priority over domestic peace in the GDR. At the same time, they reflected the way in which growing militarization was causing serious social frictions in East Germany. As in the Federal Republic, remilitarization met with widespread disapproval at the grass roots, in part because of the diversion of scarce resources away from basic consumer goods and supplies east of the Elbe.[78] Many of these tensions would resurface two years later during the more serious statewide

---

[76] Detlev Peukert, *Inside Nazi Germany: Conformity, Opposition, and Racism in Everyday Life*, trans. Richard Deveson (New Haven, CT, 1987), 211. Also see Michael Burleigh and Wolfgang Wippermann, *The Racial State: Germany, 1933–1945* (Cambridge, 1991), esp. Chapter 6.

[77] On the difficulties experienced by local refugees, see ThHStA-W, KR Slf 850. More generally, see Michael Schwartz, *Vertriebene und "Umsiedlerpolitik": Integrationskonflikte in den deutschen Nachkriegs-Gesellschaften und die Assimilationsstrategien in der SBZ/DDR 1945 bis 1961* (Munich, 2004); Philipp Ther, *Deutsche und polnische Vertriebene: Gesellschaft und Vertriebenenpolitik in der SBZ und in Polen, 1945–1956* (Göttingen, 1998); Manfred Wille, ed., *50 Jahre Flucht und Vertreibung: Gemeinsamkeiten und Unterschiede bei der Aufnahme und Integration der Vertriebenen in die Gesellschaften der Westzonen/Bundesrepublik und der SBZ/DDR* (Magdeburg, 1997).

[78] Leaflets protesting remilitarization were found, for example, at the local train station. See ThStA-R, BDVP Gera 21/212, Lageanalyse, 31.12.52. Strong pacifist tendencies after the war, as well as the added demands remilitarization represented in terms of paramilitary participation in the GDR, were other important factors; this is discussed in Chapter 5. On resistance to remilitarization in the Federal Republic, see, e.g., Hans Karl Rupp, *Außerparlamentarische Opposition in der Ära Adenauer: Der Kampf gegen die Atombewaffnung in den fünfziger Jahren* (Cologne, 1970); David Clay Large, *Germans to the Front: West German Rearmament in the Adenauer Era* (Chapel Hill, NC, 1996).

uprising of 1953, an episode that might have been avoided had officials in Berlin and Moscow paid greater attention to the warning signals set off by the disturbances in Saalfeld. As Erich Mückenberger cautioned in February 1952, there was "nothing worse for the party than when it's taken by surprise by things it doesn't suspect."[79] These words would soon come back to haunt him and his comrades in the SED, as we shall see in the next chapter.

That said, the carrots of social pacification introduced by authorities after the upheaval in Saalfeld deserve emphasis because they demonstrate that repression was not the only – or even the principal – way in which socialist functionaries responded to protest or open conflict. This should in no way minimize the arrests that followed the disturbances, the draconian sentences later handed down to many of the participants, or the series of expulsions from the Wismut regions. But the many discussions held with miners after the events in the marketplace, as well as the determined efforts by officials to respond to their grievances, suggest the need for a more nuanced way of characterizing the way in which they dealt with protest and conflict, especially when workers were involved. Repression and the *threat* of repression certainly played an important role. But the introduction of corrective measures constituted an equally essential part of the way in which authorities responded to unwelcome developments that posed a threat to regime stability. If the efforts to bring about change and rectify deficiencies were usually less than successful, this failure lay more in the constraints and shortcomings of state socialism and its rigid planned economy than in a lack of will on the part of harried officials regularly taken to task by demanding superiors.

[79] ThStA-R IV/4/10/93, Prot. der Sitz. der SED Thür. mit den Gen. des Kreissekr. Slf, 8.2.52.

3

The Revolution *Manquée* of June 1953

Less than one year after the Wismut upheaval, the SED announced with great fanfare at its Second Party Conference in Berlin that political and economic conditions had finally reached a stage allowing for the systematic "construction of socialism." That meant, in more concrete terms, the acceleration of earlier socialist reforms as well as the introduction of new policies that would help complete the process of Sovietization begun in the late 1940s: Agricultural collectivization, a massive buildup of paramilitary forces, and greater state centralization were all on the official agenda adopted in the summer of 1952. Over the next ten months, authorities introduced a series of widely unpopular financial measures to pay for these costly programs: State subsidies for social benefits were significantly reduced, and the prices of many staple goods were increased. In addition, food ration cards were taken away from the self-employed, who were now forced to purchase high-priced wares at state-run stores. Their property and income taxes were also raised to crippling levels, reflecting the SED's desire to purge the GDR of all remaining "elements of capitalism."[1]

[1] The literature on the June 1953 uprising is vast. A good place to start still is the classic account by Arnulf Baring, *Uprising in East Germany: June 17, 1953*, trans. Gerald Onn (Ithaca, NY, 1972). The most important recent studies include Torsten Diedrich, *Der 17. Juni 1953 in der DDR: Bewaffnete Gewalt gegen das Volk* (Berlin, 1991); idem, *Waffen gegen das Volk: Der 17. Juni in der DDR* (Munich, 2003); Manfred Hagen, *DDR – Juni '53: Die erste Volkserhebung im Stalinismus* (Stuttgart, 1992); Ilko-Sascha Kowalczuk, Armin Mitter, and Stefan Wolle, eds., *Der Tag X, 17. Juni 1953: Die "Innere Staatsgründung" der DDR als Ergebnis der Krise, 1952–1954* (Berlin, 1995); Heidi Roth, *Der 17. Juni 1953 in Sachsen* (Cologne, 1999); Hubertus Knabe, *17. Juni 1953: Ein deutscher Aufstand* (Munich, 2003); Ilko-Sascha Kowalczuk, *17.6.1953: Volksaufstand in der DDR: Ursachen – Abläufe – Folgen* (Bremen, 2003); Hans-Joachim Veen, ed., *Die abgeschnittene Revolution: Der 17. Juni in der deutschen Geschichte* (Cologne, 2004). Useful overviews of the historiography include Jonathan Sperber, "17 June 1953: Revisiting a German Revolution," *German History* 22 (2004): 619–43; Ilko-Sascha Kowalczuk, "Der 17. Juni 1953," in Rainer Eppelmann, Bernd Faulenbach, and Ulrich Mählert, eds., *Bilanz und Perspektiven der DDR-Forschung* (Paderborn, 2003), 160–6; Beate Ihme-Tuchel, *Die DDR* (Darmstadt, 2002), 22–42. For the official SED version of the events, see *Geschichte der Sozialistischen Einheitspartei Deutschlands: Abriß* (Berlin, 1978), 288–98.

These and other measures only served to alienate large segments of East German society. The Second Party Conference reaffirmed the emphasis on investment in heavy industry at the cost of other sectors, for example, leading to further neglect of consumer items and housing – a situation exacerbated by the increasing diversion of scarce resources to the military, by the disastrous economic consequences of the campaign against the middle classes, and by a poor harvest in 1952.[2] The tensions created by these policies were compounded by forced collectivization in the countryside, large-scale military recruitment, and a fresh wave of political and economic repression: Abetted by a new criminal law directed against individuals who had supposedly committed offenses against state property, the "heightening of class warfare" announced at the conference led to economic sanctions and the instrumental use of political justice against "enemy agents," members of the middle classes, and those farmers who refused to join a collective. Security officials also cracked down at the time on the churches, focusing in particular on members of the religious Youth Congregations (*Junge Gemeinden*).

These divisive and combative policies not only failed to solve the financial predicament created by the forced construction of socialism, but also placed even greater strains on the economy by prompting large numbers of East Germans to flee to the West. Their number increased from approximately 86,000 in the first half of 1952 to almost 200,000 during the first half of the following year. In Saalfeld itself, approximately 300 persons fled between January and June 1953: One-third were between ages eighteen and thirty-five, and more than half of those gainfully employed were industrial workers.[3]

In a last-ditch effort to stem the worsening financial crisis, party officials decreed in mid-May 1953 that the production quotas of all industrial workers were to be raised by an average of at least 10 percent by June 30 – just in time to celebrate Walter Ulbricht's sixtieth birthday. The party hoped that these "voluntary" norm increases would be economically beneficial for at least two reasons: They would spur an increase in worker productivity, and they would reduce state expenditures by lowering labor costs. Yet the effort to combat soaring wages, which had largely resulted from the institutionalization of soft norms in the late 1940s, meant, in effect, that the SED would now face a struggle on almost all social fronts. Beginning in late May, the campaign to raise production quotas created serious unrest in factories throughout the GDR, leading some workers to lay down their tools in protest.[4]

---

[2] On military spending at this time, see Diedrich, *Waffen*, 13–30; Bruno Thoß, *Volksarmee schaffen – ohne Geschrei: Studien zu den Anfängen einer "verdeckten Aufrüstung" in der SBZ/DDR, 1947–1952* (Munich, 1999).

[3] ThStA-R, DVP 21/222, Vertrauliche Verschlußsache, n.d. For GDR figures, see Henrik Bispinck, "'Republikflucht': Flucht und Ausreise als Problem für die DDR–Führung," in Dierk Hoffmann, Michael Schwartz, and Hermann Wentker, eds., *Vor dem Mauerbau: Politik und Gesellschaft der DDR der fünfziger Jahre* (Munich, 2003), 291, 306–9.

[4] See Armin Mitter and Stefan Wolle, *Untergang auf Raten: Unbekannte Kapitel der DDR–Geschichte* (Munich, 1993), 62–87. See Chapter 1 on the institutionalization of soft norms.

Three months after Joseph Stalin's death in early March 1953, his successors summoned top East German party and state officials to Moscow for emergency discussions. Troubled about the deteriorating situation in the GDR, reflected most seriously in the alarming rates of migration to the Federal Republic, the Soviets ordered their German allies to slacken the pace of the forced transition to socialism. They were told to pay greater attention to the production of consumer goods, halt forced collectivization in the countryside, and ease the repressive measures taken against the middle classes and the churches.[5] One week later, on June 11, the Politburo published a communiqué in *Neues Deutschland*, the official party newspaper, which admitted that the SED leadership had recently made a "series of mistakes." It also unveiled a more moderate policy, subsequently referred to as the New Course, which reversed almost all of the repressive and unpopular measures adopted since the 1952 party congress – with the exception of the norm hike announced one month earlier.

Industrial workers across the GDR perceived the party's decision to offer olive branches to every other major social group except themselves as a slap in the face. And on June 16, thousands of construction workers in East Berlin went on strike and marched through the streets of the capital in protest against the norm increases. A conciliatory announcement by the minister for heavy industry that afternoon – that the government had just decided to rescind the norm hikes – came too late, for the protest and strike movement had already begun to escalate. So, too, had worker demands, which now included calls for a general strike, the immediate resignation of the government, and free elections. Word of the events in East Berlin spread quickly, thanks in part to broadcasts by the American radio station RIAS. The following day, hundreds of thousands of East German workers throughout the GDR joined in the protest by laying down their tools and taking to the streets; strike committees subsequently formed in many factories and drafted a wide array of political and economic demands. In a throwback to the events that had taken place in Saalfeld two years earlier, a number of demonstrations culminated in the violent storming of local prisons as well as party, state, and union offices, prompting the deployment of Soviet troops and the newly created East German Barracks Police (KVP) to quell the disturbances.

The March on Saalfeld

In the early morning hours of June 17, security officials at the Maxhütte steel mill arrested a worker employed at a nearby construction site after he and an accomplice had supposedly tried to persuade a police officer to give them

---

[5] Less than two weeks later, Czech and Hungarian leaders were also called to Moscow, where they were given similar orders. For general developments that year, see Christoph Kleßman and Bernd Stöver, eds., *1953 – Krisenjahr des Kalten Krieges in Europa* (Cologne, 1999).

his uniform and weapon.[6] After learning during the ensuing interrogation that "something serious" had taken place in the capital, factory police contacted the first secretary of the SED factory organization, the director of the Maxhütte, and state security officials in order to decide on appropriate measures. As word of the imprisonment rapidly spread, hundreds of construction workers lay down their tools later that morning and "banded together" to protest against the arrest. They mixed demands for the immediate release of their colleague with political slogans critical of the government: "resign already.... We're sick and tired of the regime ... only workers are oppressed" here. In addition, they complained that union functionaries only made empty promises and that they had no real power to represent workers' interests.

At some point in the early afternoon, approximately 1,000 construction workers decided to march to the Maxhütte to encourage the steel workers to join their strike. Security forces made no attempt to hinder them from entering the factory compound, later explaining that any resistance would have been "absurd" (the police had only enough ammunition to defend the factory for a half hour, again suggesting the embryonic state of the security apparatus during this early period).[7] The workers wandered through the halls of the factory, where they were "decisively turned back" – not only by management officials but also by the steel workers themselves, who supposedly exhorted the demonstrators to leave the factory "or else wind up in the ... blast furnace."[8]

Loyal party cadres dispatched by the SED District Secretariat successfully steered the construction workers into the factory's dining hall with promises to negotiate but quickly lost control of the gathering. According to reports, an unknown "agent provocateur" dressed in a suit and carrying a black briefcase addressed the crowd and announced that he was an old Communist "but wanted nothing to do with [current] conditions" in the GDR. Together with a half dozen workers, he elaborated a series of political and economic demands similar to those advanced that day by strikers elsewhere in East Germany: a

---

[6] These workers were employed by the Bau-Union Jena, one of many construction firms involved in a series of special building projects throughout the GDR at the time; many of their workers participated elsewhere in the disturbances of June 17. See Baring, *Uprising*, 56–7. The following description of the events in Saalfeld is, unless otherwise noted, based primarily on the reports in ThStA-R, BPKK IV/2/4/617, 619–22, 626; ThStA-R, BdVP 21/026, 21/093; ThStA-R, FDGB BV Gera 911/226; MxA-U, BGL 285. On events elsewhere in Thuringia, see Ehrhart Neubert and Thomas Auerbach, *"Es kann anders werden": Opposition und Widerstand in Thüringen, 1945–1989* (Cologne, 2005), 57–69.

[7] On the helplessness of police officials elsewhere in the GDR, see Knabe, *Aufstand*, 313–33.

[8] Workers in the blast-furnace department had themselves telephoned members of the factory union committee earlier that day and threatened to strike "just like in Berlin" if an official did not come immediately to the shop floor and address their grievances. They asked whether or not the norm hikes had really been reversed, complained about the way in which piecework wages were determined, and called for higher earnings, demanding that the salaries earned by high-level management officials and members of the intelligentsia be reduced instead. There were no reports of labor disruption in any other department. See MxA-U, BGL 285, Über die Ereignisse in der Maxh., 19.6.53.

40 percent price decrease in state-run stores, the abolition of piecework, free elections, German unification, the withdrawal of Soviet troops, the redrawing of the Oder–Neisse frontier with Poland, the release of all political prisoners, amnesty for all participants in the strike, and the immediate resignation of the government – "since we little ones will also be punished, the big ones should be as well."[9]

Having failed to convince staff members at the Maxhütte to lay down their tools, the construction workers left the factory and marched through the village of Unterwellenborn, shouting, "We don't need any People's Police, we don't need any People's Army, down with the government." After enjoining workers at other nearby construction sites to join their demonstration, they returned to the steel mill carrying pickaxes and gathered in front of the main administrative building, where they demanded in vain that the factory director announce a general strike over the public address system.[10] Police officials armed with rubber truncheons, pistols, and carbines quickly arrived on the scene, occupied the building, and exhorted the workers to disperse. Apparently intimidated by this show of force, the construction workers decided to leave the steel mill and march four miles due west to the town of Saalfeld, where they planned to protest in the marketplace for higher wages and lower prices.

Party functionaries at the Maxhütte notified police officials at 3:30 P.M. that some 600 workers had set out on foot for the city. Several workers and functionaries from the steel mill were sent along to help security officials later identify and arrest the alleged ringleaders. After checking with local Soviet authorities and the SED District Secretariat, the head of the district police declared a state of emergency and occupied key strategic points throughout the city. Dispatched Soviet troops and police officials waited for the procession on a bridge located behind the main train station, but a violent confrontation failed to materialize: The already diminished crowd of 300 construction workers that eventually arrived at the outskirts of the city quickly dwindled further. A truckload of agitators sent by Maxhütte party officials mixed with the remaining protesters and managed to disperse the crowd by 7 P.M.

There were no other serious disturbances in the district on June 17. Apart from a few workers at the steel mill who had shown open support for the strikers, "not a minute of production" was lost and no "absurd demands" were made. In fact, their "model" behavior on June 17 was later emphasized repeatedly in official SED pronouncements. The only other reported incident took place at the VEB Zeiss optical factory, located near the bridge where the occupation troops awaited the construction workers. At a series of meetings organized by the departmental union committees, staff members advanced a number of economic demands, including a 40 percent price decrease and the abolition of night shifts. In addition, women in the prism department called for free elections, German unification, and the release of all political and wartime

[9] On similar demands throughout the GDR, see, e.g., Knabe, *Aufstand*, 108–231.
[10] ThStA-R, BDVP Gera 21/093, Berichterstattung zu den Ereignissen, 2.7.53.

prisoners. The demands were written down in petitions signed by dozens of rank-and-file SED members but were not accompanied by any serious production disturbances.[11]

Later that evening, several run-ins took place in the marketplace between the People's Police and construction workers and youths who refused to obey the curfew imposed by the state of emergency; at least four individuals were arrested but then immediately released. Over the next several days, tensions remained high at construction sites in Unterwellenborn and in the town of Saalfeld: Agitators were forced to hold discussions, for example, with several workers who threatened to go on strike again to secure the release of imprisoned colleagues. Yet no further mass demonstrations or major upheavals were reported in the district that summer. The storm had left Saalfeld as suddenly as it had come.

Popular Reactions

The disturbances in Saalfeld were far less dramatic than those that took place that day in many other areas of the GDR. In a sense, the district had already had its "June 17" two years earlier in the summer of 1951; many residents would, in fact, later conflate the two episodes.[12] This was not altogether surprising, given that the behavior of the Wismut miners was repeated by workers in many other cities and towns during the late afternoon of June 17, when the more radical, turbulent phase of the uprising began.[13] In Saalfeld itself, both protests began with demands for the release of arrested colleagues. On both occasions, members of the People's Police exhibited extreme caution and tried at all costs to avoid direct confrontation with the protesters. Flickers of protest continued to flare up in the months immediately following the two incidents, though on a far smaller scale. Finally, as we shall see, high-level East German officials responded similarly to both upheavals – not only by placing the blame on enemy agents and the West, by heightening security measures, and by arresting alleged ringleaders, but also by meeting with workers and by introducing a series of corrective measures that sought to address many of their material grievances.

There were, however, important differences. The 1953 protest in Saalfeld was, for one thing, more overtly political than the Wismut upheaval: From the very beginning, the construction workers – like their counterparts in Berlin and elsewhere – mixed calls for major economic reform with far-reaching political demands. In an attempt to characterize the nature of the uprising, some scholars nevertheless continue to perpetuate old, often polemical debates about the goals

[11] ThStA-R IV/7/231/1162, Referat, 17.11.53.
[12] See the article commemorating the August 1951 upheaval in *Ostthüringer Zeitung*, August 16, 1996, Saalfeld edition.
[13] See Knabe, *Aufstand*, 151–62. On the behavior of Wismut miners on June 17, see the literature cited in Chapter 2, footnote 65.

of the participants by accentuating *either* the political *or* the socioeconomic demands of the participants – as if the two could be so easily separated in a state where the ruling party had infiltrated all areas of public life.[14]

During the days and weeks following the upheaval, factory personnel and higher-level functionaries met with industrial workers and other local residents to get a better sense of their grievances as well as the prevailing climate of opinion; following the lead of those in Berlin, they also took this opportunity to express regret for recent "mistakes" made by the regime. Workers' comments at these meetings revealed the extent to which social, economic, and political discontent was intertwined – even if most discussions in the factories did, admittedly, focus on everyday economic grievances; these included calls for higher wages and lower prices, improved housing and supplies, and better working conditions. There were also scattered calls at the time for higher pensions and rations, as well as a "domestic day" off each month (the so-called *Haushaltstag*) for *all* women, not just a select few.[15]

This was, in short, a time for workers in Saalfeld and throughout the GDR to vent their pent-up grievances, and they did so with gusto. As one explained, the recent events had given them "some courage."[16] Yet, given the wave of intense political repression during the months preceding the uprising as well as the series of arrests that followed the upheaval, most workers – stripped of their anonymity in these smaller gatherings – were obviously careful not to make hostile political remarks for fear of imprisonment or other sanctions. The consequent emphasis on social and economic issues should not suggest, however, that they were necessarily considered more significant or that the political demands propounded on June 17 had merely been "implanted" by Western radio broadcasts.[17] Those workers who did make overt political statements after the upheaval generally called for free elections and a more open political system, or argued that East German leaders had lost the trust of the masses and that they should thus resign or be punished for the mistakes they had made. In

---

[14] See the exchange between Torsten Diedrich, "Zwischen Arbeitererhebung und gescheiterter Revolution in der DDR: Retrospektive zum Stand der zeitgeschichtlichen Aufarbeitung des 17. Juni 1953," in *JHK* (Berlin, 1994), 288–305, and Ilko-Sascha Kowalczuk, "Die Ereignisse von 1953 in der DDR: Anmerkung zu einer 'Retrospektive zum Stand der zeitgeschichtlichen Aufarbeitung des 17. Juni 1953,'" in *JHK* (Berlin, 1996), 181–6. Also see Diedrich, *Waffen*, 136–46, as well as the balanced comments on this debate in Mary Fulbrook, *Anatomy of a Dictatorship: Inside the GDR, 1949–1989* (Oxford, 1995), 178–9.

[15] Following the Second Party Congress, the number of those entitled to a paid domestic day, which was intended to give working women more time to attend to their household duties, was significantly reduced. More generally, see Carola Sachse, *Der Hausarbeitstag: Gerechtigkeit und Gleichberechtigung in Ost und West, 1939–1994* (Göttingen, 2002).

[16] ThStA-R, FDGB BV Gera 854/209, Prot. der BV in der Wema, 26.6.53. On the many complaints voiced at the time, see the reports in ThStA-R, FDGB BV Gera 911/226. Also see ThStA-R IV/2/4/619, Bericht über die Entwicklung des faschistischen Abenteuers im Bez. Gera, 30.6.53; ThStA-R IV/4/10/246, IB der SED–KL Slf, 3.8.53; MxA-U, BGL 304, Bericht über Normenarbeit, 27.6.53; ThStA-R, FDGB BV Gera 855/210, report, 22.6.53.

[17] Compare Hans Bentzien, *Was geschah am 17. Juni? Vorgeschichte – Verlauf – Hintergründe* (Berlin, 2003), 121–8.

fact, many openly criticized the SED – "as the party of the working class" – for not representing the interests of the laboring masses more faithfully. Much of this anger was directed at Walter Ulbricht, who was branded a "scoundrel and a swine . . . not a representative of workers (*Arbeitervertreter*) but rather a crusher of workers (*Arbeiterzertreter*)" – the "initiator of all these severe measures." Similar charges were leveled against union officials, who were condemned as spineless "appendages" of the SED and criticized for not having done enough to advance the social and economic interests of those whom they were supposed to represent.[18]

Notwithstanding these and similar criticisms, a number of Saalfelders nevertheless distanced themselves from the more destructive behavior and perceived excesses of striking workers in other parts of the GDR. As one man at the VEB Abus crane factory remarked, "we shouldn't senselessly destroy what we built up with our own hands." He added, however, that factory functionaries were themselves responsible for the recent disturbances: "They're only interested in their salaries and show no concern for worker affairs."[19] These comments, made by a refugee from the East who had previously distinguished himself on the shop floor as a so-called best worker, underscore the difficulty of compartmentalizing East Germans into simple categories of loyal or subversive. At the same time, they remind us that criticism of the regime and desire for reform were not necessarily linked to a categorical rejection of the East German state as such, particularly among those who had actively helped reconstruct Germany as well as their own lives after the war.[20]

Comments made by rank-and-file party members in support of the strikers' demands or critical of the SED's recent policies similarly suggest the danger of drawing another simple dichotomy, i.e., between those East Germans who belonged to the party and the rest of society. The behavior on June 17 of one member of the Factory Party Secretariat at Zeiss vividly illustrated this point: Though lauded by the SED for his "model" defense of the optical firm that day as a member of its factory combat unit, he was simultaneously censured for signing – along with twenty-five other party members – a resolution calling for a series of urgent economic reforms.[21] Although there were no reports of

---

[18] See ThStA-R IV/2/4/621, report, n.d.; ThStA-R IV/2/4/625, KPKK Analyse über das Verhalten einzelner Mitglieder unserer Partei während der Vorgänge am 17.6.53, n.d.; ThStA-R, FDGB BV Gera 854/209, IB der BGL–Wema, 24.6.53; ThStA-R IV/4/10/246, IB der SED–KL Slf, 3.8.53.

[19] ThStA-R IV/2/4/622, Stellungnahmen von einzelnen Gen. und Parteilosen, 22.6.53. Jonathan Sperber suggests that many intellectuals, for their part, remained aloof from the disturbances because of their tendency to associate mass protest and violence with the fascist era. See Sperber, "Revisiting," 632.

[20] See the interviews with members of the so-called *Aufbau* generation in Lutz Niethammer, Alexander von Plato, and Dorothee Wierling, *Die Volkseigene Erfahrung: Eine Archäologie des Lebens in der Industrieprovinz der DDR* (Berlin, 1991).

[21] Despite his comments in late June that the party had never paid attention to popular criticism and that rascals (*Halunken*) occupied the highest positions of authority, he was chosen later that decade to replace the factory's even more recalcitrant union committee chairman. See ThStA-R IV/2/4/625, correspondence, 24.6.53; ThStA-R IV/7/231/1162, Referat, 17.11.53. The union shakeup at Zeiss is discussed in Chapter 6; on factory combat units, see Chapter 5.

SED members actively taking part in or supporting the physical disturbances that took place in Saalfeld, a number of comrades were nevertheless scolded either for failing to help secure factories and other key strategic points or for not responding vigorously enough to hostile discussions. Not even the District Party Secretariat remained immune to censure: Three members were expelled later that summer for supposedly having displayed "cowardly behavior" on June 17.[22]

A Sense of Injustice

Even if high-level East German officials were taken unawares by the events of June 1953,[23] the protest by local construction workers should not have come as a complete surprise to authorities in Saalfeld. Alarm signals had already been set off six months earlier during union elections, when workers in this sector reelected only 3 percent of the rank-and-file leadership. The poor results prompted an immediate inquiry, and at a series of talks with investigators, workers complained that union functionaries did not tend to their needs; they pointed in particular to poor security measures at the workplace, insufficient provisioning by state-run stores, and inadequate distribution of protective clothing. In further meetings held one day after the march on Saalfeld, construction workers similarly complained about low pay and poor conditions in their overcrowded, "humble" barracks, as well as empty promises by union and management officials to supply them with scarce goods.[24] Wismut miners and local construction workers not only acted similarly in 1951 and 1953, but also voiced strikingly similar complaints.

On the day of the strike itself, construction workers focused above all on the recent norm hikes, complaining that they had been unfairly introduced in a "dictatorial" manner by shop-floor functionaries who had failed to explain why the increases were necessary. Workers at other factories in the district voiced similar complaints about the compulsory introduction of higher norms, and during the wave of self-criticism that followed the outburst of June 17, local officials acknowledged that many of the supposedly voluntary increases had, in fact, been achieved by forceful means – or, at the very least, by the exertion of what was euphemistically referred to as "moral pressure."[25]

---

[22] ThStA-R IV/2/4/617, Einschätzung über die Sitz. der SED–KL mit dem Kreisparteiaktiv, 13.8.53; ThStA-R IV/2/4/620, report, 18.12.53.

[23] See, e.g., Rudolf Herrnstadt, *Das Herrnstadt-Dokument: Das Politbüro der SED und die Geschichte des 17. Juni 1953*, ed. Nadja Stulz-Herrnstadt (Reinbek bei Hamburg, 1990).

[24] ThStA-R IV/2/4/622, report, n.d. The Bau-Union's district board had already submitted a similar report to higher-level union officials in Gera several months earlier. A subsequent resolution called for timely elimination of the existing deficiencies, but officials admitted that very little had been done. See ThStA-R IV/4/10/100, Prot. der Sekretariatssitz. der SED–KL Slf, 30.1.53.

[25] See ThStA-R IV/2/4/622, Telefonische Durchsage der SED–KL Slf, 17.6.53; ThStA-R IV/2/4/619, Bericht über die Entwicklung des faschistischen Abenteuers im Bez. Gera, 30.6.53.

Such methods were subsequently condemned as "sledge-hammer policies" (*Holzhammerpolitik*) by high-level officials. But even prior to the outburst of mid-June, some factory functionaries had realized that the recent drive to raise production quotas had created bad blood among workers, many of whom characteristically refused to raise their production quotas voluntarily and thus continued to work with the same phony norms. Officials at Zeiss and at the Maxhütte admitted, in fact, that their own efforts to introduce more stringent "technically determined" quotas had largely been lackluster, just as they had been prior to the spring of 1953 – which suggests at least one reason why workers there might have refrained from joining the strike.[26]

Even if the methods used to raise norms had been unduly confrontational in at least some firms, the high-level decision to increase quotas had not been entirely unreasonable. Since the struggle over piecework in the late 1940s, most quotas had been set at levels that could easily be satisfied, with average norm fulfillment hovering between 120 and 150 percent during the period immediately preceding the announced hike. As late as early June, officials at the local washing-machine factory had reported that almost 40 percent of their piece-work earners were still achieving fulfillment rates of up to 200 percent. There had been, in other words, ample room to modify many of these soft norms and still allow workers to overfulfill their quotas by a sizable margin.[27]

Yet, according to most investigations of the uprising, income suffered because of the norm increases introduced in the spring of 1953 (as well as because of production bottlenecks created by the SED's recent economic policies); some workers in Saalfeld made similar claims during the series of discussions that took place immediately after the upheaval. It is not clear, however, that this had necessarily been the case for all or even most workers: According to one analysis from June 26, most firms in the region had not, in fact, experienced wage decreases following the recent norm hikes. Several weeks before the upheaval, the washing machine factory reported that wages had even increased *despite* the norm adjustments.[28]

How was this possible despite official reports that production quotas had risen an average of 10 to 15 percent in Saalfeld? It is possible, of course, that these statistics were falsified in an attempt to forestall high-level censure. But there was another equally plausible explanation: Workers employed a wide

[26] See ThStA-R, FDGB BV Gera 854/209, Prot. der Sitz. der WL, BPO, BGL im Waschmaschinenwerk, 26.5.53; ThStA-R, FDGB BV Gera 851/208, Prot. der Sitz. der BGL–Zeiss, 8.7.53; ThStA-R IV/7/231/1163, Prot. der Funktionärberatung, 17.4.53; ThStA-R, Maxh. 385, Arbeitsplan der BPO für Mai 1953, 2.5.53.

[27] ThStA-R, FDGB BV Gera 854/209, Prot. der Sitz. der WL, BPO, BGL im Waschmaschinenwerk, 26.5.53 (the Max Schaede washing machine factory became a VEB after 1945). The point about norms is also made in Baring, *Uprising*.

[28] See ThStA-R IV/2/4/619, Analyse über die politische und ökonomische Situation im Bez. Gera vor und während der Ereignisse am 17. und 18. Juni 1953, 27.6.53; ThStA-R, FDGB BV Gera 854/209, Prot. der Sitz. der WL, BPO, BGL im Waschmaschinenwerk, 26.5.53. Some workers at the Maxhütte enjoyed wage increases as well; see the reports in MxA-U, BGL 384.

variety of tricks to adjust their output and thus secure norms that could easily be satisfied, with the holding back of labor reserves being the most popular method by far. One party official at the VEB Wema machine-building factory reported in April 1953, for example, that several workers had earned an hourly wage of 0.91 mark during a TAN investigation, but that these same individuals actually received 1.76 marks on payday and even 2.40 marks *after* new norms had been adopted. When approached about this discrepancy, they cheekily asked officials, "Do you think we're so dumb that we work like we normally do when a person in charge of TAN is watching?"[29]

If the recent increases had not necessarily had any measurable effect on gross income, what had made the 1953 decision so unpalatable, then, apart from the supposedly bureaucratic way in which the norm hike was carried out? And why was there no similar unrest in 1949 following the highly unpopular decision to abolish progressive piecework wages – and then add insult to injury by ordering even higher production quotas?[30] In the first place, the campaign to raise norms in the late 1940s was carried out far less rigorously than the one launched in the spring of 1953; in addition, it affected fewer workers because the proportion of Saalfelders who earned piecework wages was significantly lower at the time (only 40 percent in 1949).[31] More important, the 1953 hike followed a recent price increase; as a result, real wages – if not necessarily gross income – *did* decrease significantly. As workers at the VEB Wema argued one week after the uprising, if consumer goods had been cheaper, "the norm question would not have become so acute."[32]

The SED's decision to raise prices after the Second Party Congress could not have come at a worse time: Staple goods were becoming increasingly scarce because of a recent harvest failure, as well as because of the increasing emphasis placed on investment in heavy industry and the military. The supply situation had certainly improved by the early 1950s, especially when compared to the immediate postwar period, yet district officials still noted serious shortages of basic foodstuffs and consumer durables – especially in the months following the SED's fateful decision to construct socialism. The chairman of the Liberal Democratic Party (or LDPD, one of the East German middle-class block parties) reported in November 1952, for example, that "wild scenes of cursing and even fisticuffs are not uncommon when there's butter, etc." in the state-run stores.[33]

The combination of unpopular policies and unpleasant material developments had created, in short, unprecedented levels of unrest and discontent in Saalfeld and throughout the rest of the GDR. As a result, the decision to rescind

[29] ThStA-R IV/7/231/1163, Prot. der Funktionärberatung, 17.4.53. The VEB Wema was a merger of several local machine-building factories founded in the late nineteenth century.
[30] See Chapter 1.
[31] ThHStA-W, KR Slf 559, Kurzanalyse Volkswirtschaftsplan 1951 (Entwurf), 28.1.52.
[32] ThStA-R, FDGB BV Gera 854/209, IB in der Mittagspause, 23.6.53.
[33] See the reports from 1953 in ThHStA-W, KR Slf 2101; ADL, BV Gera 33105. For an assessment by the local branch of the Christian Democratic Union of tensions in Saalfeld on the eve of the upheaval, see the reports in ACDP III-045-165-3.

the price hikes on June 11 and then reverse the norm increases on June 16 had simply come too late to assuage irate workers: Tensions had already reached dangerous levels and events now took on a dynamic of their own – especially with critics of the regime heartened and its most ardent supporters left uncertain following the news of Stalin's death and the announcement of a New Course.[34] That said, the strangling effects of high prices and scarcity – as well as the pressure to raise productivity levels – may have become more intense on the eve of the uprising. But this alone did not necessarily explain why workers finally took to the streets en masse. The "sudden relaxation after a year of economic excess and political repression" did not necessarily do so either.[35]

What actually did trigger the disturbances of June 1953 was the decision to abrogate almost all of the unpopular measures introduced over the past ten months *except* for the one that had solely affected production workers alone: the norm hike. The party's retreat on all other fronts, along with the admission that it had made serious mistakes, must have emboldened workers to go on the offensive. But even more important than this sign of official weakness was the SED's decision to offer olive branches to all other social groups – except the one in whose name it claimed to rule. East German workers saw this as a slap in the face and as an affront to their sense of justice.[36]

There is little archival evidence of workers explicitly making this connection, yet the timing of the strike wave itself strongly supports this conclusion. Most scholars agree that an article in the June 16 issue of the official union newspaper *Die Tribüne* reaffirming the norm hikes as "completely correct" was the spark that ignited the demonstrations in East Berlin.[37] Yet, it was not so much the norm policy itself and its consequences (which, as we have seen, were not necessarily that dramatic) as the decision *not* to rescind the hike along with all of the other onerous measures that caused such anger. This is a subtle but important distinction – and one that helps explain something else that took place in Saalfeld at this time as well.

The SED's conscious omission served to intensify the widespread sense of social injustice deeply felt by many local residents, especially regarding the supposedly superior treatment of other individuals and groups. In so doing, it prompted an outpouring of outrage about privilege and social differentiation that runs like a thread through almost all of the discussions that took place in Saalfeld at the time – just as it had during the first factory labor contract negotiations of 1951 and then again after the arrival of Wismut. One of the greatest sources of anger this time was the privileged position of the Maxhütte,

---

[34] On the state of popular opinion at the time, see Knabe, *Aufstand*, 85–97; Mitter and Wolle, *Untergang*, 62–96.

[35] Compare Sperber, "Revisiting," 627.

[36] On the role played by feelings of injustice more generally, see Barrington Moore, *Injustice: The Social Bases of Obedience and Revolt* (White Plains, NY, 1978).

[37] See, e.g., Dietrich Staritz, *Geschichte der DDR, 1949–1985* (Frankfurt am Main, 1985), 84. On the norm issue more generally, see Jörg Roesler, *Der 17. Juni 1953 – Aufstand gegen die Norm?* (Berlin, 2003).

however (by the spring of 1953, most of the uranium miners had already left the region). Complaints focused on the greater supply of scarce goods made available to staff members at the steel mill, as well as on special work permits that gave them exclusive access to the Maxhütte's own state-run store. Such resentment had long been brewing in Saalfeld: "The 'little' man is excluded from these privileges. Many believe that these special allotments should be a privilege for all working people. But only a few benefit from them."[38]

There was certainly good reason for such resentment. In response to the deteriorating supply situation ushered in by the Second Party Congress, the District Council (the highest state organ at the local level) focused almost exclusively on how to improve provisioning at the Maxhütte and in nearby villages inhabited mainly by steel workers. Scarce industrial goods sent from Berlin were exclusively earmarked for the region around Unterwellenborn as well, as were limited staples such as margarine, butter, oil, and sugar – all of which were largely unavailable to the remaining population: "[I]f we're lucky," workers at the washing-machine factory complained, "we get light bulbs and lemons every once in a while...."[39] Not surprisingly, calls for better treatment of nonprivileged firms and regions became one of the central demands voiced in Saalfeld after the uprising. Along similar lines, and echoing complaints first made during the BKV negotiations of 1951, many Saalfelders also criticized the "unjustifiable" variations in wages and rations awarded to workers based on the economic importance of their job or sector. This not only led to the creation of "first-, second-, and third-class workers," they complained, but also produced a great deal of "discord" among colleagues themselves.[40]

The Limits of Solidarity

Widespread resentment about privilege may have created an atmosphere conducive to unrest, but it arguably helped account for the limited extent of the upheaval as well. Most studies have understandably concentrated on the strikes and demonstrations that took place on June 16 and 17, and a major debate has focused on whether or not the disturbances constituted a "people's uprising" or merely a "workers' uprising." Recent research has clearly demonstrated that broad sectors of the population – and not just industrial workers – were actively involved in the dramatic events that transpired in the GDR that spring.[41] Yet

---

[38] ADL, BV Gera 33105. For similar complaints, see ThStA-R IV/4/10/246, IB der SED–KL Slf, 3.8.53. On divisions and resentment elsewhere, see Gareth Pritchard, *The Making of the GDR, 1945–53: From Antifascism to Stalinism* (Manchester, UK, 2000), 217–20.

[39] KrA-S 3926, Bericht über die Warenbereitstellung im III. Quartal, 25.11.53; ThStA-R, FDGB BV Gera 854/209, Prot. der BV im Waschmaschinenwerk, 2.6.53.

[40] See ThStA-R, FDGB BV Gera 854/209, Prot. der BV im Waschmaschinenwerk, 2.6.53, 22.6.53; ThStA-R, FDGB BV Gera 709/178, Situationsbericht, 10.7.53.

[41] Compare, e.g., the older study by Baring, *Uprising*, with Hagen, *Volkserhebung*; Mitter and Wolle, *Untergang*, 27–162. On protests outside of the GDR's main industrial centers, also see Knabe, *Aufstand*, 232–42; Diedrich, *Waffen*, 147–55.

the fact remains that the overwhelming majority of East Germans did not participate in the more overt forms of protest: According to recent estimates, approximately 900,000 individuals were somehow involved, i.e., roughly 11 percent of the working population.[42] Even if one includes those who merely gathered together to discuss their grievances, the participants still remained in the minority. This was clearly the case in Saalfeld, where, apart from the construction workers in Unterwellenborn, not a single factory struck on June 17.[43]

What accounted for the general passivity of most workers in the district? In those areas that experienced serious disturbances, there was usually at least one major factory or large group of workers that emboldened others to strike: Acting as a trailblazer of sorts, they forcibly entered other factories and tried to encourage workers there to join their protest. As Torsten Diedrich has observed, "Mutual encouragement to act against the policies of the SED . . . had immense importance" that day. But because workers at the Maxhütte failed to join the march on Saalfeld, and because the construction workers themselves were halted at the outskirts of the city, there was no "rousing example" in the town itself, where most of the district's factories were located.[44]

As discussions held after the uprising made clear, those workers who failed to strike or demonstrate on June 17 were not necessarily unsympathetic to the demands or grievances voiced by the more active participants. Yet, the fact remains that the vast majority of industrial workers did not take to the streets to demonstrate against the regime and its recent policies. In fact, what took place in Saalfeld – or, rather, what failed to take place – was typical of most cities and towns throughout East Germany: Disturbances of widely varying magnitude were reported in almost 700 locales, yet slightly less than 600 factories went on strike in the entire GDR.[45] That clearly underscores the mass nature of the uprising. But while most investigations have understandably focused on the more spectacular events, one must also ask why only certain groups of workers joined in the protest, why there were so few examples of concerted strike action, why the demonstrations petered out so quickly, and why some regions experienced no disturbances at all.[46] The rapid deployment of security forces and Soviet troops, as well as the subsequent capitulation of party and state officials to many of the strikers' demands, provide important answers to these questions. But the course of events in Saalfeld – particularly in Unterwellenborn, the center of strike activity in the

[42] Diedrich, *Gewalt*, 288.

[43] ThStA-R IV/2/4/617, Analyse der BPKK Gera, 7.8.53. A similar point is made in Pritchard, *Making*, 210–11.

[44] Diedrich, *Gewalt*, 97, 112.

[45] For a list of the locales where demonstrations took place, see Kowalczuk, *Volksaufstand*, 284–93.

[46] The only known cases involving some degree of coordination and cooperation among striking workers employed at different factories took place in the region around Bitterfeld and in the city of Görlitz. See Roth, *Sachsen*, 245–320.

district – also underscored the important way in which the types of social divisions discussed earlier served to hinder coordinated and sustained forms of protest.

As we have seen, the striking construction workers failed to persuade those at the Maxhütte to join their demonstration, but met instead with an "unequivocal rebuff and had to beat a hasty retreat...."[47] This was significant because it suggested not only a notable absence of working-class solidarity, but also the success authorities had had in winning over certain privileged groups – thanks to the preferential treatment of those deemed most essential to the economy. While it is difficult to establish a direct causal connection, the superior material position of the steel workers apparently made them largely impervious to the overtures of their striking colleagues. In fact, many were even dispatched to another steel mill in a neighboring district to help officials there calm down their own disgruntled workers.

Those employed at the Maxhütte certainly shared many of the grievances expressed at the time by other Saalfelders, as discussions held with them following the disturbances made abundantly clear. Yet they were far better off than almost all other workers in the district – and not only with respect to provisioning. Since 1949, government and management officials had responded to many of their most pressing complaints by investing millions of marks in social and cultural benefits, as well as in improved shop-floor facilities. As a result, staff members at the Maxhütte had exclusive access to their own hospital and pharmacy, vacation resort and sanatorium, sports field, theater, library, nursery, shoe-repair shop, and seamstress service. More than 200,000 marks were invested annually to improve worker safety, and in 1953, almost all departments received new bathing facilities and relaxation rooms. Six weeks prior to the upheaval, lunch rations in the new dining hall – built that year at a cost of 1 million marks – were doubled: Workers now enjoyed subsidized lunches consisting of 140 grams of meat, 20 grams of fat, and 20 grams of sugar – at a time when others in Saalfeld were having difficulty finding any butter or sugar at all. Given the privileged treatment of those employed at the steel mill, their unwillingness to participate in the upheaval was not particularly puzzling. While it is not clear that authorities purposefully pursued such policies in a conscious attempt to divide workers, this certainly seems to have been the effect.

The material situation of those at the steel mill contrasted most sharply with that of those in the construction industry, suggesting at least one reason why it was the latter who struck on June 17: Because they lived and labored in close proximity to the Maxhütte – for which they were building apartments and other structures at the time – their indignation and frustration must have been all the greater. Their bitter complaints about their own abominable living and working conditions, as well as their demands that they be given access to the same type of priority provisioning enjoyed by those at the Maxhütte,

---

47 ThStA-R IV/2/4/621, Bericht des 1. Sekretärs der SED BPO–Maxh., 24.6.53.

clearly support these conclusions.[48] There were a number of other reasons, of course, why construction workers, of all groups in the district, were most active during the upheaval – not least of which was the fact that their colleagues in East Berlin had initiated the disturbances. In a show of solidarity with those in the capital, construction workers had led a large number of strikes throughout the GDR, in fact. As with the Wismut miners, similar everyday experiences, as well as communal living in barracks and other large quarters, must have promoted at least a rudimentary sense of cohesion among these hardy young men, emboldened not only by the great importance attached to their work but also by the severe labor shortages that plagued this key industry. Their own sense of solidarity nevertheless failed to extend beyond their own ranks.

Official Responses

High-level officials responded to the June uprising much as they had to the events of August 1951, i.e., by combining sticks and carrots. Over the next several months, security forces arrested thousands of individuals throughout the GDR. The main "troublemakers" in Saalfeld itself had either been photographed or recognized at the Maxhütte, and by June 23, 129 individuals found themselves in jail. Most were male workers, young, and politically unaffiliated – as were most of those arrested throughout the GDR. Unlike the Wismut upheaval, local women had not played a leading – or at least a visible – role.[49]

Repression was not the only response, however. In a move reminiscent of the way in which they had responded to the Wismut disturbances two years earlier, central authorities adopted a series of corrective measures over the next several months: They not only followed through on the reforms announced in early June, but also strove to eliminate many of the social and economic sources of discontent that had come to light during and immediately after the uprising. Greater stress was now placed on the production of consumer goods; production quotas as well as official prices returned to previous levels. The lowest base wages were raised in all economic sectors that August, and many of the social benefits eliminated earlier that year were reintroduced.[50]

Local officials made a number of significant overtures as well. Union functionaries at the Maxhütte promised workers that they would now serve more diligently as their spokesmen, for example, and would try to win support for their demands – "as long as they [were] justified" – at the highest levels of government. As evidence of the positive changes that were to come, they announced

---

[48] ThStA-R, FDGB BV Gera 911/226, Situationsberichte, 26.6.53, 21.7.53. On the superior provisioning of and various amenities at the Maxhütte, see MxA-U, BGL 236, 281, 396.

[49] The gendered aspect of the uprising has received little scholarly attention: see Sperber, "Revisiting," 632–3. For lists of those arrested, see ThStA-R, BDVP Gera 21/026, Berichterstattung über die Festgenommenen, 23.6.53; ThStA-R, FDGB BV Gera 911/226, report, n.d.; ThStA-R, BDVP Gera 21/026, Haftlisten, 5.6.54, 19.6.53; ThStA-R IV/4/10/247, IB der SED–KL Slf, 16.6.54.

[50] See, e.g., Staritz, *Geschichte*, 87–95; Christoph Kleßmann, *Die doppelte Staatsgründung: Deutsche Geschichte, 1945–1955* (Bonn, 1991), 277–82.

that the umbrella East German union organization (FDGB) had already persuaded the government to pay time and a half for all shift work performed on Sundays – a major demand since the BKV negotiations of 1951.[51] Officials also tried to reduce tensions by prohibiting the further use of force to solve the district's acute housing situation, instead devoting greater energy and resources to the construction of new units. Possibly in response to threats that they would "have another June 17 on their hands here in Saalfeld" if the desperate living situation were not quickly remedied, local SED officials announced that 600 million marks would now be spent on repairs as well as on the construction of new apartments.[52]

It should come as little surprise that district authorities paid special attention to ameliorating conditions at local construction sites. Living quarters were currently being improved, FDGB officials noted optimistically on June 22, and the "colleagues are amazed at how fast the union has brought about a change in conditions."[53] A series of emergency programs were introduced later that summer to enhance provisioning, assure the timely delivery of production materials, and eliminate supposedly unfair wage differentials among construction workers. Similar promises to correct deficiencies and reduce preferential treatment were made in other factories as well.[54] In late June, union officials began to prepare staff members at the Maxhütte for the pending changes:

...we've already spoken about this, and it would be wrong if we didn't say something about it again today: We receive too many special allotments. We don't need to have so much margarine, butter, cheese, etc. One has to be fair to the general public. If we receive a half pound, that's enough, and that way other workers can also get a quarter pound.... If we simply don't have enough, then that which is available...must be distributed to all working individuals.[55]

While many in Saalfeld apparently greeted these reforms, others remained highly skeptical that the policy revisions would lead to any real change – or suspected that they represented little more than a return to the status quo ante. This did not mean that local residents were not pleased about the announced corrections, leaders of the Christian Democratic Union (CDU) assured members of the other block parties, but that they simply wanted an honest "rendering of the facts." The SED's decision to suspend the recent political repression nevertheless brought a temporary sigh of relief, and many residents supposedly welcomed the chance to "speak freely again." But, as one party member at the

---

[51] MxA-U, BGL 316, Prot. der PV im Hochofen, 15.7.53.
[52] Quotation from ThStA-R IV/4/10/105, Vorlage, 21.8.53. Also see ThStA-R IV/4/10/104, Anwendung von Zwangsmaßnahmen durch die WA, 17.7.53; ThStA-R, FDGB BV Gera 854/209, Prot. der BV in der Wema, 26.6.53. See Chapter 10 on the housing situation in Saalfeld after 1953.
[53] ThStA-R, FDGB BV Gera 911/226, Situationsbericht, 22.6.53.
[54] See, e.g., ThStA-R, FDGB BV Gera 911/226, Monatsbericht, 11.8.53, and Berichterstattung für den Monat August, 10.9.53; ThStA-R, FDGB BV Gera 855/210, Prot. der Sitz. der BGL–Hebezeugwerk, 3.7.53; ThStA-R, FDGB BV Gera 854/209, Prot. der BV in der Waschmaschinenfabrik, 22.6.53.
[55] ThStA-R, Maxh. 385, Prot. der BV im Kalkwerk Öpitz, 30.6.53.

Maxhütte bitterly remarked, nothing could be done to make amends for the time that "innocent people" had spent in jail.[56]

Collectivization and Class Conflict

Similar sentiments were expressed at the time in the countryside, where the SED's decision to change course in the summer of 1952 and promote collectivized farming had created a situation no less explosive than that in the industrial centers of the GDR. The shift to collectivization was an essential component of the drive to construct socialism, and ideological, political, and economic considerations had all played a role in this policy turnabout. In the first place, officials saw it as a way to strengthen the party's rural position by undermining the supposed influence of larger and wealthier farmers, the so-called *Großbauern*. The campaign reflected, at the same time, the growing realization that the small holdings created during the land reform campaign were not economically viable. By constructing larger units held and worked in common, officials hoped to stimulate agricultural productivity by allowing for the introduction of more modern and more efficient farming methods; this would not only increase rural earnings and improve living standards, they argued, but also help ensure fulfillment of the unpopular production quotas imposed by the state.[57]

As elsewhere, the campaign to form agricultural collectives (LPGs) began in Saalfeld with the delegation to the countryside of agitators, who focused their "educational activities" on one region at a time. At local assemblies and in discussions with individual farmers, these trained emissaries – primarily low-level functionaries, rank-and-file SED members, and industrial workers delegated by local factories – stressed the alleged economic and political advantages of collectivization and promised considerable state aid to those communities willing to join the movement.[58] But despite their efforts – or, in some cases, because

---

[56] Christian youths who had been expelled from a local secondary school were allowed to return, and one reinstated teacher even received a bouquet of flowers from her pupils. See ThStA-R, BDVP Gera 21/026, Erstellung einer Analyse über die Ausschreitungen am 17.6.53 im Bez. Gera (Entwurf), 26.6.53; ThStA-R, FDGB BV Gera 854/209, Prot. der BV in der Wema, 26.6.53; ThStA-R IV/4/10/246, IB der SED–KL Slf, 3.8.53, 27.11.53; ACDP III-045–071/2, report, July 1953; ThStA-R IV/2/4/626, Analyse über das Verhalten einzelner Mitglieder unserer Partei während der Vorgänge am 17.6.53, n.d.

[57] On the decision to introduce collective farming as well as the campaign against large farmers, see Arnd Bauerkämper, *Ländliche Gesellschaft in der kommunistischen Diktatur: Zwangsmodernisierung und Tradition in Brandenburg, 1945–1963* (Cologne, 2002), 159–93; Corey Ross, *Constructing Socialism at the Grass-Roots: The Transformation of East Germany, 1945–65* (Houndsmill, UK, 2000), 30–2, 60–70; Joachim Piskol, "Zum Beginn der Kollektivierung der Landwirtschaft im Sommer 1952," *Beiträge zur Geschichte der Arbeiterbewegung* 37 (1995): 19–26; idem, "Zur sozialökonomischen Entwicklung der Großbauern in der DDR, 1945–1960," *ZfG* 39 (1991): 419–33.

[58] See, e.g., ThStA-R IV/4/10/306, Bericht über den Stand der Entwicklung der LPG im Kr. Slf, n.d., and Hilfe und Unterstützung der Partei, der Massenorg., sowie des Staatsapparates, 9.10.52; also see the reports in ThStA-R IV/4/10/98–100, 103.

of them (many farmers purportedly refused to join the LPG because they felt "hounded") – officials complained early on about slow progress: Only two collectives had been formed in the entire district by the end of 1952, in Marktgolitz and Probstzella.

Both villages were located in the southernmost portion of the district – right in the heart of the regional slate industry, whose distinctive products still adorn the rooftops of many homes in the area. The industrial character of these communities, their social and political constellations, and their close proximity to the border help explain why they became the first LPGs in Saalfeld. Unlike most villages in the district, both could boast of relatively large SED organizations that had built on established working-class traditions: Industrial workers constituted the largest social group in both villages, in fact, and many owned small parcels of land themselves. Their own willingness to enter a collective, as well as their constant presence and agitation, must have persuaded others to join. Probstzella itself was an important border crossing, and many leading members of the community had fled to the West in the late 1940s and early 1950s; this included a large number of former National Socialists, the head of the local Hitler Youth, and Franz Itting, a well-known entrepreneur and the head of the local SPD before 1933. That was important because the absence of such potentially disruptive individuals must have made the task of the agitators somewhat easier. Finally, the very fact that these two communities were located on the West German frontier suggested another reason why officials were so determined to establish LPGs there: They were meant to serve as socialist beacons for those beyond the border.[59]

Under a steady stream of pressure, the number of collectives jumped to ten in early March 1953 and then to thirty-five by mid-June. But this meant that there were still LPGs in only about half of the district's villages on the eve of the 1953 disturbances. Most farmers in Saalfeld refused to become members, and their tenacious resistance proved to be one of the greatest impediments to collectivization. While many simply told the agitators to leave them in peace, the more aggressive ones physically drove the unwelcome visitors from their farms. Those who were more willing to engage in discussion offered a variety of reasons for their refusal to join: They were satisfied with their individual accomplishments; they did not need an LPG because "God has helped us up to now and he'll continue to help us"; they themselves wanted to become members but their wives or parents were opposed; they feared they would wind up like Russian farmers, who "own nothing anymore and have to go around dressed in rags"; or they wanted to wait and see what the advantages were. In response to this last objection, officials organized trips to model LPGs located elsewhere in the GDR in order to convince farmers of the many benefits that collectivization supposedly offered. This strategy sometimes backfired, however: When one group visited an LPG in Saxony, the first farmer they encountered told them that "if I had remained alone, I'd already be finished with my fields and harvest."

[59] On the background and social makeup of these villages, see ThStA-R IV/4/10/354–5.

Such incidents only served to fortify the reservations of those skeptics so jealous of their independence.[60]

A number of farmers also refused to join because of official restrictions that excluded *Großbauern* from membership in the LPG: The collectives would not be viable without them, the argument went, because they held the largest and most productive property. Many villagers depended on them as well for heavy machinery and other forms of assistance. This reliance was, of course, one of the most important reasons for their official exclusion from the LPGs: The SED hoped to isolate large landowners and weaken their rural influence in order to shore up the party's own power in the countryside. Such ostracism was part of the "class struggle" that had begun in earnest after the Second Party Congress, and one of the regime's primary tasks was now to eliminate *kulak* privileges, "break the[ir] resistance," and "smash" their attempts to reestablish their former positions of power.[61] This meant, in practice, their removal from leading positions in rural organizations, as well as their exclusion from all forms of state aid; it also involved increasing harassment and arrest for alleged sabotage or a failure to fill production quotas. A number of village functionaries were fired or arrested as well at the time because they had supposedly cooperated with or were related to this "class enemy."[62]

Authorities justified such repressive measures by pointing to the purported hostility of the *Großbauern* and their alleged accomplices to the regime.[63] Yet, many showed greater interest in the LPGs than their less well-to-do neighbors; in fact, the greatest resistance to collectivization came from those middle-sized farmers who had held their property prior to the land reform of the mid-1940s. To the further dismay of district officials, low-level functionaries could find little evidence linking actual acts of sabotage to large landowners. Although this failure was summarily dismissed as another sign of "conciliatory behavior" (*Versöhnlertum*) on the part of the regime's rural representatives, it further suggested just how little support existed for the crusade against the *Großbauern*.[64] So, too, did the reelection of more than two dozen of them to local VdgB committees in 1953: Many small landowners, authorities concluded, were

[60] See the reports in ThStA-R IV/4/10/98–100, 235, 236, 306, 309, 314. On similar resistance elsewhere in the GDR, see Jens Schöne, "'Wir sind dafür, dass über diese Fragen keine Berichterstattung erfolgt': Die Kollektivierung der Landwirtschaft in der DDR 1952/1953," in Falco Werkentin, ed., *Der Aufbau der "Grundlagen des Sozialismus" in der DDR, 1952–1953* (Berlin, 2002), 71–94.

[61] ThStA-R IV/4/10/101, Bericht über die Arbeit der SED–PO im Staatsapparat der KV, 4.2.53; KrA-S 2368, Prot. der Sitz. des KR, 2.5.53. Also see the reports in ThStA-R IV/4/10/98, 102, 103, 309.

[62] See, e.g., KrA-S 2368, Prot. der Sitz. des KR, 2.5.53; also see the reports in ThStA-R IV/4/10/96, 99, 100, 235, 246, 306.

[63] See, e.g., ThStA-R IV/4/10/99, Vorlage zur Vorbereitung des Kongresses der werktätigen Bauern, 10.12.52; KrA-S 2368, Prot. der Sitz. des KR, 5.2.53.

[64] ThStA-R IV/4/10/101, Bericht über die Arbeit der SED–PO im Staatsapparat der KV, 4.2.53. On the willingness of large farmers to join the LPG as well as on the resistance to collectivization by middle-sized farmers, see the reports in ThStA-R IV/4/10/309.

simply unable to liberate themselves from the influence of these "reactionary elements."[65]

Given the widespread resistance to class struggle and collectivization, it was not surprising that storm clouds also appeared on Saalfeld's rural horizon during the June 1953 tempest. Emboldened by the policy changes announced by the Politburo in its June 9 communiqué as well as by a series of conciliatory statements by local officials, a number of farmers made use of a clause found in all LPG statutes that allowed them to withdraw voluntarily.[66] The exodus, which had already begun in some villages during the week prior to the upheaval, gathered speed after June 17 and continued through the summer and fall. Three LPGs dissolved themselves entirely in mid-July, and another two would follow suit by late November. By the end of the year, more than 40 percent of all collective farmers in Saalfeld had withdrawn. Except for several dozen SED members and a handful of new farmers, the vast majority were landowners who had held their property before 1945.[67]

Similar to those industrial workers angered by the manner in which the recent norm hike had been introduced, many justified their decision by pointing to the coercive way in which they had been persuaded to join the collectives in the first place: "Ah, we can finally breathe again," one farmer rejoiced, 'We can disband the LPG and no longer have to be afraid we'll be locked up." Even the *Landrat* admitted in a confidential report that "inadmissible" pressure had been applied after the Second Party Conference.[68] That may have been true, but compulsion alone did not necessarily account for the wave of withdrawals; after all, actual experience might have convinced local landowners of the many advantages touted by functionaries. In fact, the economic performance of many LPGs had been decidedly weak, a "miscarriage from the start."[69] While some farmers complained about low profitability or argued that the supposed benefits

---

[65] ThStA-R IV/4/10/100, Bericht über die Tätigkeit zur Verstärkung der Klassenwachsamkeit auf dem Dorfe, 25.2.53. On the measures taken against large landowners as well as on their reelection to local governing bodies, see ThStA-R IV/4/10/99, Vorbereitung des Kongresses der werktätigen Bauern, 18.12.52; ThStA-R IV/4/10/306, Monatsbericht der Abt. Landwirtschaft, n.d.

[66] See, e.g., KrA-S 15581, Statut der LPG "Heller Weg" (Punkt 11), 28.5.53. The possibility of withdrawing from a collective had also been assured by the head of the SED District Sekretariat. See ThStA-R IV/4/10/104, Prot. der Sekretariatssitz. der SED KL–Slf and Situationsbericht der LPG, 10.7.53.

[67] See the statistics in ThStA-R IV/4/10/108, 306. The fact that the new farmers had received so much state support might explain why they were apparently less hostile to the regime and its policies. That said, and despite considerable assistance, dozens had already returned their land prior to the collectivization campaign: In the absence of any prior agricultural experience, they had simply not been up to the challenge of farming. See ThStA-R IV/4/10/91, Analyse über die Durchführung der Bodenreform im Kr., 24.9.51. More generally, see Arnd Bauerkämper, "Die Neubauern in der SBZ/DDR 1945–1952: Bodenreform und politisch induzierter Wandel der ländlichen Gesellschaft," in Richard Bessel and Ralph Jessen, eds., *Die Grenzen der Diktatur: Staat und Gesellschaft in der DDR* (Göttingen, 1996), 108–36.

[68] ThStA-R IV/4/10/306, Lage der LPG im Kreisgebiet, 18.7.53; ThStA-R IV/4/10/108, report, 13.11.53. On LPG withdrawals more generally, see the other reports in these files as well as those in ThStA-R IV/2/4/105, 236, 622, 625.

[69] KrA-S 3925, Situationsbericht über die LPG, 11.6.53.

of collectivization had failed to materialize, others claimed that they were now much worse off than they had been before joining.[70] District officials blamed this on inadequate material assistance as well as on the failure of local functionaries and agronomists to provide sufficient guidance. As a result, many collectives suffered from poor organization, shabby bookkeeping, and severe supply shortages.[71]

Authorities were quick to point out the economic success of those LPGs that had supposedly worked in a "strictly collective" manner, yet individual farming continued to predominate in most villages. This reflected the strong predilection of many local landowners to labor independently, which was why they so fiercely opposed the physical consolidation of private holdings required for reasons of efficiency.[72] Collective work was hindered as well by the internal tensions that apparently wracked many LPGs at the time: Frequent allegations that fellow members enjoyed a distinct advantage – because they supposedly received more state aid, for instance, or because they enjoyed lower production quotas – only served to fuel existing disagreements, e.g., over the distribution of the harvest or over the purported failure of many landowners to assist their colleagues or do their share of the work.

Such frictions came to a head in the village of Kleingeschwenda and ultimately led to the dissolution of its LPG in the fall of 1953. Small proprietors there claimed that they had been forced to work for their larger and wealthier neighbors, whose own family members had supposedly stopped toiling themselves soon after the LPG had been set up. They similarly maintained that these "*kulaks*" – who supposedly formed an incestuous "clique" on the LPG's managing board – had greater access to feed and manure and had threatened to "beat to death" those who trespassed on their fields. In response to such charges, one of the larger farmers told officials, "We stick together and work for ourselves first … the little ones should figure out how to manage, they should also stick together."[73] That was obviously grist to the mill of local authorities, who characteristically attributed the breakup of many LPGs to the alleged machinations of large landowners and other "foes" of the regime.[74]

Many local farmers were equally upset about the preference supposedly given to landowners living in nearby villages: They received more state aid and superior provisioning, it was claimed, as well as lower production norms and higher prices for their deliveries. Along similar lines, some villages claimed

---

[70] ThStA-R IV/4/10/306, Lage der LPG im Kreisgebiet, 18.7.53; ThStA-R IV/4/10/106, Prot. der Sekretariatssitz. der SED–KL Slf, 4.9.53.

[71] See the reports in KrA-S 2368, 3925.

[72] See the reports in ThStA-R IV/4/10/104, 106, 246, 316.

[73] See the reports in ThStA-R IV/4/10/236; ThStA-R IV/4/10/106, Prot. der Sekretariatssitz. der SED–KL Slf, 4.9.53. On tensions in other LPGs, see, e.g., KrA-S 3925, Situationsbericht über die LPG, 11.6.53; ThStA-R IV/4/10/316, Prot. der Bauernberatung in Wickersdorf, 9.7.53, and Prot. der Landparteiaktivtagung, 15.9.53; ThStA-R IV/4/10/105, report, 7.8.53; ThStA-R IV/4/10/108, report, 13.11.53.

[74] See, e.g., ThStA-R IV/2/4/622, Durchsage der SED–KL Slf, 14.6.53; ThStA-R IV/4/10/108, report, 13.11.53.

to be at an unfair disadvantage in the production competitions set up by officials to stimulate agricultural performance. In fact, the fight for rewards and
bonuses even prompted struggles among LPGs over access to machinery that
was in short supply. Widespread hostility between farmers who had joined a
collective and those who had decided to remain on their own compounded
existing frictions, leading to mutual harassment, name-calling, and a general
refusal to cooperate. Such tensions only worsened during the summer following the June upheaval, when livestock belonging to several LPGs were found
poisoned.[75]

Whether or not some farmers or villages really enjoyed an unfair advantage
was less important than the fact that this was widely perceived to be the case.
This rent many communities in Saalfeld, turned farmers against one another,
and, in so doing, prevented the creation of solidarity networks that might have
been more effective in rebuffing the demands of the party and state. The fact
that farmers quit their collectives and dissolved the LPGs in droves after June
17 spoke volumes about the way in which the policies of the regime effectively
atomized East German society, unwittingly or not. This is an important point
that we will return to in Part II.

Apart from the wave of withdrawals and dissolutions, there were no other
serious signs of mass unrest.[76] The mayor of Breternitz wrote on June 20, for
example, that all of the villagers "behave[d] peacefully," continued to perform
their work, and rejected the recent destruction as "senseless." Officials elsewhere submitted reports that were similarly formulaic, but duly noted the outrage many farmers felt about the unpopular demands imposed on them by the
regime.[77] In fact, many eagerly took advantage of the opportunity to express
their strong misgivings about the SED and its recent agricultural policies at a
series of public gatherings organized and attended by district officials over the
course of the summer. The already familiar complaints about mandatory deliveries, insufficient state aid, and severe shortages of consumer goods and staples
all surfaced at these meetings: Production quotas were too high, and the payment they received for their products was too low. Farmers also demanded to
know how they could ever satisfy their norms when the supply of seed, manure,
tools, and other forms of material assistance was so inadequate – or, given their
low incomes, how they could ever purchase expensive industrial wares. That
was, they hastened to add, when and if such goods were available at all.[78]

75 See, e.g., KrA-S 3925, Situationsbericht über die LPG, 11.6.53; ThStA-R IV/4/10/316, Prot. der
   Bauernberatung in Arnsgereuth, 21.7.53; ThStA-R IV/4/10/236, Bericht über die Genossenschaft
   Kleingeschwenda, 4.9.53; ThStA-R IV/4/10/306, Bericht über die Unterstützung der LPG'en im
   Kr. Slf durch den Staatsapparat, 15.12.53; ACDP III-045–181/2, Planbericht, July 1953.
76 That was not the case in other regions of the GDR. On rural protests elsewhere, see Knabe,
   Aufstand, 232–42; Diedrich, *Waffen*, 147–52; Mitter and Wolle, *Untergang*, 126–31.
77 See the reports in KrA-S 14390.
78 On the various complaints voiced at this time, see the minutes of meetings held with local
   farmers in ThStA-R IV/4/10/316. Also see ThStA-R IV/2/4/622, Durchsage der SED–KL Slf,
   13.6.53; ThStA-R IV/4/10/246, IB der SED–KL Slf, 3.8.53.

Others lamented the failure of so-called factory sponsors (*Patenbetriebe*) to make good on their pledges to support the LPGs by sending workers and necessary materials – or complained about the often shoddy assistance provided by local machine-and-tractor stations (MTSs), which regularly failed to honor contractual obligations or sent workers who either were poorly trained or used old and defective machinery. The severe damage caused by wild boars and the failure of authorities to deal with this problem – despite frequent appeals for assistance – were additional sources of discontent. So, too, were the insurmountable difficulties created by severe labor shortages in the countryside: Landowners complained in particular about the steady loss of youths who were recruited by the East German paramilitary – or who left in droves to earn higher wages in urban factories.[79] In short, and for all of these reasons, they were either unwilling or unable to satisfy their production quotas.

Authorities took these criticisms seriously and responded by adopting a series of corrective measures soon after the June 17 upheaval: They lowered delivery quotas, for example, admitting that they had often exceeded the economic capabilities of many local landowners. In a similar attempt to assuage angry farmers and forestall future unrest, they also promised more state aid for the LPGs in the form of higher credit and more adequate agricultural supplies; the MTSs were to be equipped with better tractors and other essential machinery as well. Distancing itself from the recent wave of repression, the SED also agreed to return confiscated properties to those farmers who had earlier lost their land because of poor deliveries, tax evasion, or flight to the West: By August, district officials had returned a dozen of these holdings to their former owners.[80]

While many of Saalfeld's rural residents looked favorably on these policy revisions, others felt that authorities had not gone far enough. One farmer in the village of Volksmanndorf complained, moreover, that the decision to lower delivery quotas had simply come much too late:

[T]he agricultural sector has become so damaged in the meantime that this decree ... can in no way make up for the resulting harm. He demanded that the guilty be punished. The world had never witnessed what the government has done here.... One can't even buy scythes or nails, which had earlier been available in every small shop.... The farmers have no trust in the government and won't have any in the future.[81]

In equally aggressive tones, farmers in the village of Weischwitz called for new elections, rejected the modified production quotas, and threatened not to deliver any hay or vegetables that year. Landowners elsewhere in the district apparently believed that they were no longer required to make punctual deliveries or even sell their products to the state. Despite concerted efforts to combat this "misreading" of the recent measures through increased "education," authorities

---

79 See ThStA-R IV/4/10/316, Prot. der Bauernberatungen, 9.7.53, 16.7.53, 21.7.53, 24.7.53, 27.7.53; KrA-S 14390, correspondence, 20.6.53, 27.6.53; ThStA-R IV/2/4/622, report, 20.6.53; ThStA-R IV/4/10/246, IB der SED–KL Slf, 3.8.53.

80 See the minutes and reports in ThStA-R IV/4/10/316.

81 ThStA-R IV/4/10/316, Prot. der Bauernberatung in Volksmanndorf, 15.7.53.

continued to complain about poor deliveries over the next several months and concluded that many local farmers were doing all that they could to avoid meeting their quotas.[82]

As we shall see in Part II, official endeavors to counter such resistance and boost productivity – not only in the countryside but also in the People's Factories – would remain a constant struggle in Saalfeld over the next two decades. Moreover, and despite the important series of conciliatory reforms adopted by the SED, many of the same social, economic, and political grievances voiced during the 1953 disturbances would continue to resurface regularly during this period as well. The supply situation would certainly improve considerably, especially when compared to the so-called hunger years of the late 1940s and early 1950s, but periodic shortages of even the most basic foodstuffs would continue to recur with alarming regularity. Inadequate housing, poor working conditions, supposedly low incomes, and high prices would all remain serious points of contention as well. So, too, would the preferential treatment of certain groups, which would continue to raise the ire of many Saalfelders and lead to frequent complaints about supposedly unjust variations in income and differential access to scarce commodities.

Yet the 1953 uprising, the first of its kind in the Soviet bloc, was also the last of its kind in the GDR – another turning point in German history that failed to turn.[83] Never again, not even during the mass demonstrations that led to the demise of the regime in the fall of 1989, would large numbers of Saalfelders and other East Germans engage in a demonstrable show of force against the party and state. Taking a more thematic approach, the remainder of this study will try to explain why the proverbial dog remained so silent during the long night leading up to the collapse of the regime, i.e., why there was so little large-scale collective action in Saalfeld – and, by extension, in East Germany as a whole – during the remaining years of the GDR.

---

[82] See, e.g., KrA-S 14390, correspondence, 10.7.53; ThStA-R IV/4/10/306, Lage der LPG im Kreisgebiet, 18.7.53; ThStA-R IV/4/10/246, IB der SED–KL Slf, 28.10.53.

[83] This clever turn of phrase was first used to describe the failed revolution of 1848; see A. J. P. Taylor, *The Course of German History: A Survey of the Development of Germany since 1815* (London, 1945).

PART II

THE CALM AFTER THE STORM (1953–1971)

4

The Limits of Repression

The period from 1945 to 1953 was clearly a tumultuous time in the history of Saalfeld and eastern Germany as a whole. But in many respects, the two decades that followed the June uprising were as well, beginning with the so-called destalinization campaign launched by Soviet Premier Nikita Khrushchev in early 1956. This brief political thaw sparked a vigorous and relatively open debate in the GDR about the possibility and necessity of internal reforms that would make East Germany a more viable state. It was soon cut short, however, by popular upheavals in Poland and Hungary and rapidly gave way to a major crackdown against those who had earlier called for change. A new crisis began in the winter of 1958, triggered this time by Khrushchev's unilateral threat to alter the postwar status of Berlin. Faced with the growing possibility that the most popular exit route to the West was about to be closed – and following a high-level decision to step up collectivization in the countryside once again – East Germans swarmed to the Federal Republic in unprecedented numbers. High-level officials responded to this massive flight by adopting an extraordinary measure that grabbed international headlines in August 1961: the construction of a concrete and barbed wire barrier around the western sectors of the city.

Now apparently secure in the shadow of the infamous Berlin Wall, the East German leadership adopted a new series of policies aimed at stabilizing the regime and shoring up the flagging economy: It launched a major production campaign that fall, introduced military conscription several months later, and unveiled a far-reaching economic reform program during the mid-1960s. Despite some initial success, the so-called New Economic System (NÖS) proved unable to reverse many of the alarming trends of the previous decade. This failure, along with growing tensions between Walter Ulbricht and the Soviet leadership over Western efforts to normalize relations between the two German states, led to the fall of the feisty Saxon in the spring of 1971. With the appointment of Erich Honecker as head of the SED, one era came to an end in the GDR and another began – one that would culminate in the collapse of the regime in 1989.[1]

The years from June 1953 to the changing of the political guard in 1971 were undoubtedly turbulent, then, and the changes that took place throughout the GDR did not leave Saalfeld unscathed. The collectivization campaign transformed production relations in the countryside, the Berlin crisis prompted a significant exodus to the West, and the NÖS led to a major restructuring of the local industrial sector. While these and other important developments fueled new conflicts and tensions, many of the old sources of popular discontent continued to strain relations between local representatives of the regime and those who lived and labored in Saalfeld – as well as *among* the district's inhabitants themselves. There was no repeat performance of the twin disturbances of the early 1950s, however, and the ones that gripped the GDR's neighbors in the Soviet bloc – Poland and Hungary in 1956, Czechoslovakia in 1968, and Poland once again in 1970 – had no corollary in Saalfeld or anywhere else in East Germany. And as one scholar once wrote in a different historical context, "In an era of upheaval, it is continuity and stability that need explanation."[2]

One of the most common explanations for the stability of the regime after 1953 – especially from those scholars who emphasize its supposedly totalitarian nature – focuses on state-sanctioned repression and the growing climate of fear that this engendered.[3] Such apprehension was clearly related to the brutal suppression of the June uprising as well as to the subsequent buildup of the GDR's repressive apparatus. The latter involved a substantial growth in the number of Stasi personnel, as well as the development of increasingly refined methods of terror and surveillance – all part of a concerted attempt to enhance an underdeveloped system of control that had failed so miserably in 1951 and 1953.[4]

---

[1] For overviews of the post-1953 period, see footnote 3 of the Introduction.

[2] Charles Maier, *Recasting Bourgeois Europe: Stabilization in France, Germany, and Italy in the Decade after World War I* (Princeton, NJ, 1988), 3.

[3] For a representative statement of such claims, see Rainer Eckert, "Opposition und Repression in der DDR vom Mauerbau bis zur Biermann–Ausbürgerung (1961–1976)," *Archiv für Sozialgeschichte* 39 (1999): 355–90; Armin Mitter and Stefan Wolle, *Untergang auf Raten: Unbekannte Kapitel der DDR–Geschichte* (Munich, 1993); Klaus Schroeder, *Der SED–Staat: Geschichte und Strukturen der DDR* (Munich, 1998). For a critical examination of such assertions, see Mary Fulbrook, *Anatomy of a Dictatorship: Inside the GDR, 1949–1989* (Oxford, 1995), 8–13.

[4] On the post-1953 security buildup, see Mitter and Wolle, *Untergang*, 143–62. Since the opening of the archives, hundreds of books and articles have appeared on the Stasi. A good place to start is Siegfried Suckut and Jürgen Weber, eds., *Stasi–Akten zwischen Politik und Zeitgeschichte: Eine Zwischenbilanz* (Munich, 2003). Also see Joachim Gauck, *Die Stasi–Akten: Das unheimliche Erbe der DDR* (Reinbek bei Hamburg, 1991); David Gill and Ulrich Schröter, *Das Ministerium für Staatssicherheit: Anatomie des Mielke–Imperiums* (Berlin, 1991); Manfred Schell, *Stasi und kein Ende: Die Personen und Fakten* (Bonn, 1991); David Childs, *The Stasi: The East German Intelligence and Security Service* (Houndmills, UK, 1996); Jens Gieske, *Mielke–Konzern: Die Geschichte der Stasi, 1945–1990* (Stuttgart, 2001); Mike Dennis, *The Stasi: Myth and Reality* (Harlow, UK, 2003); Clemens Vollnhals, "Das Ministerium für Staatssicherheit: Ein Instrument

Yet fear and repression were nothing new in the eastern half of Germany: They had been in evidence since the immediate postwar period, when large numbers of politically motivated, often arbitrary arrests by Soviet officials and German Communists seemed to confirm years of National Socialist propaganda about the "Bolshevik hordes" – while also bringing to mind some of the more repressive aspects of the Nazi dictatorship itself.[5] The wave of persecution that followed the Second Party Conference of 1952 and then the June 1953 upheaval not only confirmed such impressions but also heightened the anxiety of a populace already predisposed to fear – and arguably set the tone for the remaining decades of the GDR. That authorities were both willing and able to employ terrorist methods against real or imagined enemies became, in short, abundantly clear early on. The extent to which this accounted for the subsequent stability of the regime nevertheless remains an open question.

A Siege Mentality

If their speeches and reports are taken at face value, local officials and ideologues apparently believed that formidable adversaries were lurking around every corner, insidiously trying to undermine whatever progress East German society was making on its march toward a socialist utopia. The members of this subversive fifth column – variously referred to as *class enemies, hostile elements, Western agents, spies,* and *social democrats* – supposedly employed a variety of resourceful tactics to that end: industrial sabotage, for example, or passing on industrial and technological secrets to the West. Referring to one alleged case of espionage at the local steel mill, the director of the Maxhütte claimed in 1955 that American imperialists hoped to use such information to ruin the East German economy and prove to West Germans that the GDR could not succeed because it was run by "simple workers who aren't capable of leading a state."[6] This was an important reason why authorities were so concerned about setting up reliable security forces at major factories, and why they remained especially wary of those individuals who had relatives in the Federal Republic or who maintained any form of contact with persons living in the West.[7]

Local officials were equally convinced that the Western powers and their alleged dupes were trying to foment domestic unrest in Saalfeld in a variety

---

totalitärer Herrschaftsausübung," in Hartmut Kaelble, Jürgen Kocka, and Hartmut Zwahr, eds., *Sozialgeschichte der DDR* (Stuttgart, 1994), 498–518. For a useful overview of the literature, see Jens Gieske, "Die Geschichte der Staatssicherheit," in Rainer Eppelmann, Bernd Faulenbach, and Ulrich Mählert, eds., *Bilanz und Perspektiven der DDR-Forschung* (Paderborn, 2003), 117–25.

[5] On arrests during the immediate postwar years, see Norman Naimark, *The Russians in Germany: A History of the Soviet Zone of Occupation, 1945–1949* (Cambridge, MA, 1995), 353–97; Peter Erler, Wilfried Otto, and Lutz Priess, "Sowjetische Internierungslager in der SBZ/DDR, 1945 bis 1950," *Beiträge zur Geschichte der Arbeiterbewegung* 32 (1990): 723–34.

[6] MxA-U, BGL 430, Prot. der Sitz. der AGL–Verw., 22.6.55; ThStA-R IV/4/10/250, IB der SED–KL Slf, 6.7.55.

[7] See, e.g., the Stasi reports and analyses in BStU ASt-G, KD Slf 0552.

of other cunning ways, e.g., by spreading political jokes, by fabricating false rumors, or by circulating incendiary leaflets. They were supposedly most active during politically volatile periods as well as on the eve of upcoming elections: In 1958, for example, the members of the SED District Secretariat characteristically suspected that a recent wave of sexual harassment had been a conscious tactic intended to prevent women from voting.[8] Official evidence might have been slim, and many of their suspicions clearly suggested the sort of siege mentality that prevailed in the GDR. It would nevertheless be wrong to dismiss such claims as little more than simple paranoia: Even if *Tag X* – a foreign plot that had supposedly led to the 1953 upheaval – was merely a figment of an overactive Communist imagination, it was nevertheless true that the Western media had actively tried to sway public opinion through radio broadcasts, that the U.S. Central Intelligence Agency had launched a program in the early 1950s to smuggle in hostile propaganda across the border via balloon, and that the SPD's Eastern Office (*Ostbüro*) had assiduously collected information about the district and maintained contacts with local residents hostile to the regime.[9]

Possible evidence of industrial sabotage in Saalfeld suggests the need for similar caution before dismissing official allegations about enemy activity. In early 1956, for instance, functionaries at the VEB Rotstern noted that many customers had recently found a variety of foreign objects in their chocolate products, including thumbtacks, nails, and pencils. Officials admitted that this might have been the result of carelessness or dirtiness on the shop floor, but it was also possible that "such things were purposely thrown into the raw material.... We don't have any real evidence for the time being, but the two anonymous letters recently sent to our Stasi demonstrate that there are hostile forces in our factory." Several years later, the Party Secretariat reported production disturbances caused by foreign objects found in factory machinery: The fact that this had occurred "each time" that members of an investigative committee had visited the firm suggested to them that this was not a mere coincidence.[10]

That was certainly possible, of course. But such traditional methods of worker protest were neither peculiar to East Germany nor necessarily indicative of active political opposition. Moreover, many incidents of suspected sabotage turned out to be little more than the result of objective factors such as old machinery: One state security investigation concluded that the inordinately

---

[8] ThStA-R IV/4/10/257, IB der SED–KL Slf, 17.10.58. On the oppositional activities attributed to enemy agents, also see the police reports in ThStA-R, BDVP Gera 21/212 and 21/250, as well as the Stasi reports in BStU ASt-G, KD Slf 0552. On sexual harassment, see Chapter 8.

[9] On the balloon action, see Evan Thomas, *The Very Best Men: Four Who Dared: The Early Years of the CIA* (New York, 1995), 61. Also see the reports in AdsD, Ostbüro 0072e (02379), 0073f (02401), 0523j. On the belief that the GDR was under constant siege by Western agents, see the revealing interviews with former Stasi officials in Christina Wilkening, *Staat im Staate: Auskünfte ehemaliger Stasi-Mitarbeiter* (Berlin, 1990).

[10] ThStA-R IV/4/10/251 and 259, IB der SED–KL Slf, 12.4.56, 30.5.59; ThStA-R IV/7/226/1137, IB der SED GO–Rotstern, 28.3.56. For reports of sabotage in factories throughout the district, see BStU ASt-G, KD Slf 0552.

high waste quotas at Zeiss were linked to poor training and inadequate experience – and not to subversive wrecking practices or conscious intervention by regime opponents, as previously assumed. The discovery of more concrete evidence – such as a note found in the Maxhütte that read "Friends: by sabotaging reconstruction, you help us, the friends of the Yanks" – nevertheless kept such fears alive, grist for the mills of those who called for greater security measures in the VEB and elsewhere.[11] That was also true of anonymous threats sent to factory officials: "My dear colleague Sch[noot]," began a menacing New Year's greeting sent to the director of the Thälmann graphics factory in 1954, "You don't give a hoot. Now you sit on your high horse. But things could change of course. You'd better watch out. Or the workers might explode and shout." A series of anonymous threats were also made that year by individuals (or an individual) who identified themselves as the "Black Hand."[12]

Evidence nevertheless suggests that there were far fewer active opponents and enemies in Saalfeld than authorities imagined – and even fewer who were working on behalf of Western imperialists. These terms were, in fact, red herrings, i.e., labels used to designate and thereby discredit various manifestations of discontent. Negative comments, work stoppages and other economic "crimes," nonconformist, disobedient, and supposedly immoral behavior – all of this was somehow attributed to the cunning intrigues of those actively opposed to and committed to undermining the regime.[13] After all, it was easier to assign blame to the machinations of these bogeymen than to accept the fact that widespread discontent reflected genuine dissatisfaction with unpopular policies and unwelcome developments in the GDR.

Punitive Measures

Whether justifiable or not, concerns about the ubiquitous class enemy often prompted local officials to report suspicious behavior or signs of unrest to state security officials or the People's Police for further investigation.[14] But many

[11] See BStU ASt-G, KD Slf 0552, Halbjahresanalyse II. Halbjahr 1965, 17.12.65; ThStA-R IV/4/10/238, Bericht des Vorsitzenden der LPKK Thür. über die Überprüfung der Maxh. im Auftrag der ZPKK, 11.50, and report, 13.11.50.

[12] *"Mein lieber Kollege S., Dir ist alles ganz schnuppe, Du sitzt jetzt auf dem großen Pferd, vielleicht kommt's wieder mal umgekehrt. Nimm Dich nur in Acht, daß nicht einmal um Euch alles kracht."* ThStA-R IV/4/10/247 and 248, IB der SED–KL Slf, 11.1.54, 13.10.54.

[13] See, e.g., ThStA-R IV/4/10/243, Bericht der KPKK Slf an die ZPKK über feindliche Einflüsse und hemmende Faktoren bei der Entwicklung der sozialistischen Umgestaltung der Landwirtschaft, 16.2.60.

[14] See, e.g., the information reports in ThStA-R IV/4/10/246 (28.10.53), 247 (29.1.54, 9.2.54, 11.2.54), 249 (28.4.55), 254 (6.6.57), 256 (19.6.58), 263 (18.11.60); ThStA-R IV/A-4/10/092 (11.10.63). Available evidence makes it difficult to determine just how often the Stasi or People's Police were alerted to such instances: While a number of reports include a notation that the names of the person or persons involved were passed on, many simply recount the incident or record the "hostile" remark without providing any names, making it unclear whether such cases were later pursued. It is also difficult to tell whether or not reported cases ultimately led to repressive or disciplinary measures.

also chose to deal with such cases by instead imposing penalties themselves: an official reprimand or public scolding, for example, a cut in premiums, a ban on further training, promotion, or travel abroad, transfer to the production floor in the case of white-collar workers and members of the intelligentsia. The chosen punishment usually depended on the severity of the offence and the disposition or mood of the officials involved, as well as on the past record of the wrongdoer and his or her willingness to recant or show penance.[15] But as a rule, officials were usually reluctant to dismiss individuals from their position unless they had committed a particularly grievous offense.

Concerns about labor shortages were only one important consideration in this regard.[16] In March 1951, a representative from the SED Central Committee reproved officials at the Maxhütte for having recently fired too many staff members "unfairly" and argued that this would only drive them into the arms of the enemy; he suggested that they try, instead, to "help" those who had made mistakes rather than simply letting them go.[17] Factory officials throughout Saalfeld tended to act accordingly over the next two decades. In the winter of 1961, for example, SED functionaries issued an official reprimand (*Rüge*) to the director of a local transportation company and decided to suspend him from his post as well as from further study because of "behavior inimical to the party": "We don't want to destroy him," one visiting official remarked, and expressed hope that the man would learn from his past mistakes and become a "useful" party functionary in the future. Earlier that year, officials at the VEB Rotstern had dealt in a similar fashion with a former FDJ secretary who had embezzled funds in order to finance a trip to West Berlin. Adopting almost the same words ("Comrade W. is young, we don't want to destroy him completely") as well as a similar form of punishment (an official reprimand and a two-year suspension from studies), the Factory Party Secretariat decided to give him a second chance and allow him to prove himself by working on the production floor.[18]

Occasional, offhand complaints about the many shortcomings and deficiencies of the East German regime usually met with similar leniency and rarely brought negative repercussions. This undoubtedly reflected the high frequency

---

[15] In the fall of 1953, for example, one factory union committee took two workers to task for having accepted American care packages during a recent trip to West Berlin; this was considered a punishable offense. After a vote on whether or not to fire them ended in a tie, its members consulted with the Factory Party Secretariat as well as district metal union officials, and finally decided to dismiss the one colleague who had stubbornly defended his behavior and refused to admit his mistake. The other was kept on after expressing regret for his actions: The fact that he was considered to be a talented worker who performed well on the job appeared to have played a role as well. See ThStA-R, FDGB BV Gera 855/210, Prot. der Sitz. der BGL–Abus, 25.9.53.

[16] On the role played by labor shortages, see Chapter 7.

[17] MxA-U, Kaderabt.: Abwanderung nach dem Westen (Berichte, 1949–57), Prot. der Arbeitsbesprechung in der Personalleitung, 16.3.51.

[18] ThStA-R IV/7/220/1003, Prot. der MV der SED GO–Kraftverkehr, 21.11.61, 15.12.61; ThStA-R IV/7/226/1136, Prot. der MV der SED GO–Rotstern, 14.1.61.

of such criticism (a theme discussed at greater length in the chapters that follow): After all, authorities could have ill afforded to lock up or severely penalize every individual who, at one time or other, had openly expressed dissatisfaction with unpopular developments in the GDR. But there were other reasons as well why officials tended to tolerate widespread grumbling. In the first place, it served as a relatively innocuous but important and therapeutic safety valve that helped to defuse tension in Saalfeld by allowing those who lived there to let off steam. This, in turn, gave local authorities some sense of prevailing popular opinion and enabled them – in theory, if not always in practice – to respond to some of the more serious sources of discontent. Finally, their own reports suggested that many functionaries shared or at least understood the frustrations and grievances of those under their immediate charge, something that must have made them even more reluctant to introduce disciplinary measures. What officials chose to include – and exclude – in their "public opinion" reports often reflected, in fact, their own concerns and desires for change; moreover, many apparently thought of these reports as a way in which to influence higher-level policy decisions.[19]

A particularly open and critical analysis submitted in the mid-1950s by party officials at the Zeiss optical firm vividly illustrated this last point. The report began by describing a number of highly unpopular and arbitrary acts by state officials, including those related to the difficult procedure involved in procuring travel visas for short trips to the Federal Republic or even to other states within the eastern bloc. It then detailed a Kafkaesque case involving the mother-in-law of one worker who had sent a package of clothes to her grandchildren living in the West. After the parcel was returned with a stamp that read "commercial goods ... cannot be sent in duplicate," she decided to send two packages that were also returned with the same stamp:

It is especially in such cases that one no longer knows what to do or say as a party member.... As a result, nobody wants to agitate anymore [apart from] a few conscientious party members, of which there are few left in our factories.... I can only imagine what these people write to their relatives in West Germany[:] evil "Eastern Zone" ... I ask myself if those working at the post office or in customs don't have enough tact or knowledge about human nature to differentiate between commercial goods and gifts. Admittedly, no measures are carried out in our GDR without good reason, regardless of whether it's permission for a visa or the sending of packages; but one must be able to distinguish, one doesn't need to be more bureaucratic than bureaucratic. If we continue as we have up to now, we shouldn't be amazed if more and more people turn away from us and if trust continues to decrease.... One high school student had the opportunity to work during vacation to earn some money. During a break he sat with construction workers and heard how they talk among themselves. It's shocking to hear how rotten the mood is among construction workers. They are forced after the end of the workday to work somewhere for private people on Saturdays and Sundays, just to

[19] Also see the arguments in Mario Keßler and Thomas Klein, "Repression and Tolerance as Methods of Rule in Communist Societies," in Konrad Jarausch, ed., *Dictatorship as Experience: Towards a Socio-Cultural History of the GDR* (New York, 1999), 117–19.

support their families. I'm writing this report in this way so that the leadership doesn't continue to believe that everything's in order, and I'd like to point out that responses to the complaints I've passed on ... are just as important as all other questions. ... [20]

The fact that many of the same complaints continued to surface over and over again clearly suggests the limited effect of such sympathetic reports. But the latter nevertheless helped explain, at least in part, the surprising reluctance of many local officials to take punitive action against those who griped.

The point is not that purportedly hostile or negative remarks about the regime had no consequences whatsoever. Incriminated individuals were often taken to task in front of their peers or called in for private discussions with officials and asked to account for their comments. Those who refused to recant, or whose remarks were considered so egregious that no amount of contrition could make amends for their alleged offence, almost always faced one of the penalties mentioned earlier. [21] And even if critical comments did not automatically lead to punitive measures, they often left a black mark on the individual's record: In 1960, for example, party officials at the VEB Wema noted during a discussion about the difficulties they were having with one of the rank-and-file members that he had remarked on the third anniversary of the June 17 uprising that the government should be dismissed. East German authorities clearly had long memories (kept fresh by the recording of such remarks in the individual's personnel file) and frequently kept close tabs on those known for their poor political attitude. This could, at some future point, hurt their chances for promotion, job-related studies, or a choice vacation spot – as in the case of one foreman at Zeiss not promoted because of his earlier refusal to sign a public declaration in support of official policies. [22]

Local officials were apparently least tolerant of grumbling during potentially explosive periods: The number of politically motivated arrests increased right after the construction of the Wall, for instance, including that of a man accused of nothing more serious than ridiculing the Pioneers (the East German equivalent of the Cub Scouts). [23] But even if captious comments alone did not usually have severe consequences except during extraordinary situations, officials did tend to deal summarily at all times with various types of behavior perceived as either clearly oppositional in nature or seriously detrimental to the social and economic well-being of the GDR. This included overt forms of political protest (e.g., the distribution of oppositional pamphlets), attempted flight to the West, confirmed cases of industrial or agricultural sabotage, and economic

---

[20] ThStA-R IV/7/231/1167, IB der SED GO–Zeiss, n.d. For a similar story involving obtuse customs officials and savvy SED functionaries, see Peter Bender, "Die DDR von unten gesehen: Eindrücke in den sechziger Jahren," in Gisela Helwig, ed., *Rückblicke auf die DDR: Festschrift für Ilse Spittmann-Rühle* (Cologne, 1995), 8.

[21] See, e.g., ThStA-R IV/7/231/1163, Prot. der MV der SED GO–Zeiss, 14.11.53; ThStA-R IV/A-7/230/498, IB der SED GO–Wema, 23.12.64.

[22] See ThStA-R IV/7/230/1157, Prot. der Sitz. der SED–BPL Wema, 1.12.60; ThStA-R IV/7/231/1165, Prot. der LS der SED GO–Zeiss, 3.2.56.

[23] ThStA-R IV/4/10/243, IB der KPKK Slf, 15.9.61.

"crimes" – all of which generally led to arrest and imprisonment. The last category included willful acts, such as industrial theft or refusal to deliver agricultural products, as well as unintentional or careless mistakes that adversely affected the economy.[24]

Officials were most responsive, however, to reports of hostile cliques of individuals that were supposedly conspiring against the East German state, and authorities even claimed to have uncovered several such conspiracies during the late 1940s and early 1950s: the celebrated Kreutzer case of 1948, for example, or the discovery several years later of an alleged espionage ring at the Maxhütte.[25] Yet these were the exceptions, and there were very few reports and very little evidence after 1953 of alleged cabals systematically engaged in activities inimical to the regime. As the local Stasi admitted in 1965, "We still have few successes [uncovering] underground conspiratorial activities or destructive activities directed against the economy and the state apparatus. . . . [O]perative measures are not taken because there are no known grounds for suspicion of hostile activity." This was perhaps why they saw fit to concentrate their efforts instead on the "hostile activity" of seemingly innocuous groups such as the local stamp club. Based on their reports and analyses from the 1960s, in fact, the Stasi apparently believed that local youths ("beatniks") posed the greatest domestic threat to regime stability.[26]

Apart from youth gangs and the occasional conspiratorial faction, most of the Stasi's activities in Saalfeld focused on suspect *individuals*. Investigations of their behavior – known as *operative procedures* – were usually systematic attempts to gather incriminating information that would justify arrest and allow for a crackdown on alleged oppositional activity.[27] According to available evidence, local security officials launched almost fifty such inquiries between 1963

---

[24] On arrests and imprisonment related to alleged economic crimes and other oppositional activities (such as flight to the West), see, e.g., the reports in ThStA-R IV/4/10/238; MxA-U, Kaderabt.: Abwanderung nach dem Westen (Berichte, 1949–57); BStU ASt G, KD Slf 0552; ThStA-R, BDVP Gera 21/212.

[25] See Chapter 1.

[26] See BStU ASt-G, KD Slf 0552, Lagebericht II. Halbjahr, 4.1.65, and Gesamteinschätzung der politisch-operativen Lage im I. Halbjahr 1962, 4.7.62. On the persecution of East German youths, see Marc-Dietrich Ohse, *Jugend nach dem Mauerbau: Anpassung, Protest und Eigensinn (DDR, 1961–1974)* (Berlin, 2003); Gabrielle Schnell, *Jugend im Visier der Stasi* (Potsdam, 2001); Patrik von zur Mühlen, *Der "Eisenberger Kreis": Jugendwiderstand und Verfolgung in der DDR, 1953–1958* (Bonn, 1995); Dorothee Wierling, "Die Jugend als innerer Feind: Konflikte in der Erziehungsdiktatur der sechziger Jahre," in Kaelble, Kocka, and Zwahr, *Sozialgeschichte*, 404–25; Mark Fenemore, "The limits of repression and reform: youth policy in the early 1960s," in Patrick Major and Jonathan Osmond, eds., *The Workers' and Peasants' State: Communism and Society in East Germany under Ulbricht, 1945–71* (Manchester, UK, 2002), 171–89; Thomas Auerbach, "Jugend im Blickfeld der Staatssicherheit," in Clemens Vollnhals and Jürgen Weber, eds., *Der Schein der Normalität: Alltag und Herrschaft in der SED–Diktatur* (Munich, 2002), 201–17. More generally, see Ulrich Hermann, ed., *Protestierende Jugend: Jugendopposition und politischer Protest in der deutschen Nachkriegsgeschichte* (Weinheim, 2002).

[27] On the terminology used by the Stasi, see Siegfried Suckut, ed., *Das Wörterbuch der Staatssicherheit: Definitionen zur "politisch-operativen Arbeit"* (Berlin, 1996).

and 1965. The overwhelming majority focused on alleged instances of espionage or oral and written "rabble-rousing" (*Hetze*), and by late 1965, approximately 40 percent of these cases had ended with a verdict of "unconfirmed."[28] Only five had led to arrest – not a particularly high figure, given the number of those who lived and worked in Saalfeld. This included one case at the Maxhütte that clearly revealed the lengths to which security officials would sometimes go in order to combat adversarial activity. Following reports that swastikas and other "inflammatory remarks" were being etched in bathroom stalls at the steel mill, they posted an assistant

near the toilets who secretly photographed everyone who used them. They were then regularly examined by special members of the People's Police to see if new scribbling had appeared. These measures allowed us to narrow down the number of possible culprits to eight people. In addition, the criminal division had the walls of the toilets painted with chemicals that left traces of the swastika scratches on the culprit's clothing, which could then be seen using a special treatment.

The culprit in Operation Scribbler was a transportation worker who subsequently received a two-year prison sentence.[29] Yet, as the low arrest figures from this period clearly suggest, clandestine investigations did not necessarily lead to incarceration. In fact, the local Stasi often exhibited remarkable caution before taking punitive action: Just months before Operation Scribbler, they had justified a decision not to pursue reports about death threats made against two "progressive" comrades by arguing that this was not rabble-rousing as defined by the East German criminal law code.[30] Lack of sufficient evidence and a surprising concern for legality could often impede action as well. Several years earlier, the Stasi had similarly refused to arrest a railroad employee in Probstzella who had purportedly told political jokes about the regime and its leaders: Because they could not find conclusive proof, officials explained, they could not prosecute him for conspiratorial activities. The public prosecutor also refused to pursue the case and tried to play down its significance by suggesting that it was all a mere misunderstanding.[31]

What might have accounted for such cautious decisions, and what does this say more generally about the East German repressive apparatus? It implies, in the first place, that the rule of law was not entirely moribund in the GDR – even if it had clearly degenerated into a distorted shadow of its pre-1933 self.[32] At the same time, and without minimizing the undeniable misfortune of those

---

[28] The only surviving statistics for Stasi investigations in Saalfeld during the Ulbricht era are from the early 1960s. See BStU ASt-G, KD Slf 0552.

[29] BStU ASt-G, KD Slf 0023, report, 9.4.63.

[30] BStU ASt-G, KD Slf 0552, Lagebericht III. und IV. Quartale 1962, 21.12.62.

[31] ThStA-R IV/4/10/240, Bericht über den Einsatz der Brigade der BL der SED in Probstzella (Entwurf), 27.5.59.

[32] On the rule of law in Germany, see David Blackbourn, "The Discreet Charm of the Bourgeoisie: Reappraising German History in the Nineteenth Century," in David Blackbourn and Geoff Eley, *The Peculiarities of German History: Bourgeois Society and Politics in Nineteenth-Century Germany* (Oxford, 1987), 190–205.

who suffered at the hands of the Stasi, most Saalfelders clearly had little to fear from security officials – as long as they avoided overt displays of fundamental opposition to the party and state (where the line was drawn remained arbitrary, of course, but most residents apparently developed a sense for this over time; the older ones could, in that respect, draw on their experiences under the Third Reich). While it is difficult to draw firm conclusions in the absence of comprehensive statistics for the entire period, the relatively low number of Stasi investigations and arrests that took place in Saalfeld during the early 1960s should not suggest a dearth of ferment from below: Nonconformist behavior and open criticism of the regime remained widespread after June 1953, as we shall see in the next chapter. Yet local authorities apparently considered everyday grumbling and other expressions of discontent to be relatively harmless and even potentially salubrious – as long as they remained isolated and were not indicative of a more organized attempt to undermine the regime. There was another possible explanation as well: The East German security apparatus expanded significantly after the "shock" of 1953, but there was still only a handful of Stasi personnel in the district through the late 1960s. In other words, the seemingly low number of investigations and arrests may have simply reflected the limited capacity of the local machinery.

For that very reason, and to ensure the exposure of "hostile elements," security officials relied on the assistance of *unofficial collaborators* (IMs), informants who agreed – either voluntarily or under pressure – to provide oral or written reports about friends, family members, acquaintances, neighbors, and colleagues.[33] It is difficult to determine with any accuracy how many informants were working in Saalfeld during the early decades of the regime. But raw numbers say little anyway about the quality of intelligence supplied by IMs: As Stasi officers readily admitted, many – and above all those coerced into informing – furnished little or no useful information. In 1963, for example, the local bureau characteristically broke off contact with one man because of his "negative attitude" and consequent refusal to provide any damaging evidence: "He describes his and our activity as snooping and wants to be left in peace...."[34] Two years later, Stasi officials complained more generally that the web of local informants was simply not large enough to detect "negative activities" and that this situation needed to be rectified, especially because the current recruits generally did little to "fight and expose" dangerous behavior. One report from the early 1970s similarly complained that the "existing unofficial network" still prevented "offensive operative procedures," but nevertheless noted some signs of improvement: "[F]ifty percent ... were begun thanks to clues from unofficial sources."[35]

---

33 See Helmut Müller-Enbergs, *Inoffizieller Mitarbeiter des Ministeriums für Staatssicherheit: Analysen und Dokumente* (Berlin, 1996).
34 BStU ASt-G, KD Slf 0550, Abschlußbericht, 30.1.63.
35 BStU ASt-G, KD Slf 0552, Lagebericht II. Halbjahr 1965, 30.12.65; BStU ASt-G, KD Slf 0023, Analyse über den Stand der operativen Vorgangsarbeit, 22.3.72.

This undoubtedly reflected the beginning of a larger development through-out the GDR, namely, the great increase in the number of IMs – as well as full-time Stasi staff members – in response to official concerns about the potentially destabilizing effects of West German *Ostpolitik*. Whatever the reasons underlying this later development, it is safe to say – based on trends in Saalfeld and elsewhere – that the GDR was not a "nation of spies" under Walter Ulbricht and that the Stasi's popular image as a "ubiquitous and highly efficient intelligence-gathering agency" deserves revision, at least for this earlier period.[36]

In addition to the information provided by IMs, local authorities relied on sporadic and often unsolicited reports by ordinary Saalfelders who were not in regular contact with security officials – much as the similarly understaffed Gestapo had done during the Third Reich.[37] This usually involved accusations against colleagues and acquaintances that were not always strictly political in nature, but were often motivated instead by a desire for personal or professional gain. After unsuccessfully running for election as chair of the district's Women's League (DFD), for example, one woman denounced her rival to high-level officials by claiming that she had been a member of a Nazi organization – while emphasizing, of course, that she herself had always been an antifascist.[38] This and similar charges about behavior during the Third Reich were most common during the first decade after the war and – like similar acts of denunciation – were frequently linked to efforts aimed at obtaining a promotion, for example, or a coveted apartment.[39]

But apart from material considerations, what might have been the motivation of those who informed on persons who had either made negative political statements or otherwise engaged in activities frowned upon by the regime, e.g., shopping in West Berlin, feigning illness, stealing or shirking in the workplace, or even wasting energy at home? Genuine political conviction was one obvious possibility, but personal interest, mutual animosity, and jealousy, as well as the desire to ingratiate oneself with officials or demonstrate one's own loyalty to the regime, often played an important role as well. In a number of cases, a combination of several factors apparently came into play. In 1957, for instance, one woman at the VEB Rotstern complained to factory union officials about

---

[36] For a critical assessment of this view, see Dennis, *Stasi*, 11, 104, 242–6. On West German *Ostpolitik*, see Peter Bender, *Die "Neue Ostpolitik" und ihre Folgen: Vom Mauerbau bis zur Vereinigung* (Munich, 1995); Timothy Garton Ash, *In Europe's Name: Germany and the Divided Continent* (New York, 1993).

[37] See Robert Gellately, *The Gestapo and German Society: Enforcing Racial Policy, 1933–1945* (Oxford, 1990).

[38] ThStA-R IV/4/10/365, correspondence, 14.2.48.

[39] On denunciations related to housing, see Chapter 10. A useful introduction to the topic of denunciation is Sheila Fitzpatrick and Robert Gellately, eds., *Accusatory Practices: Denunciation in Modern European History, 1789–1989* (Chicago, 1997). With respect to the GDR in particular, also see Clemens Vollnhals, "Denunziation und Strafverfolgung im Auftrag der 'Partei': Das Ministerium für Staatssicherheit," in Vollnhals and Weber, *Schein*, 113–56.

colleagues who frequently left the factory during the workday in order to make private purchases: Besides being upset that they were able to acquire goods she could not obtain herself, she was angered by the fact that their poor discipline adversely affected her own performance and earnings.[40]

Many also lashed out at colleagues, friends, and family members when they themselves came under pressure from officials. Unlike confidential or anonymous forms of denunciation, this semipublic defamation usually took place at party, factory, or communal gatherings – as in the case of one party member who defended his own marital infidelity by informing the leaders of his factory cell that "I'm cursed at home for being a Communist and my wife often says: 'You'll be one of the first to be hanged from the trees'" once the SED fell from power. A common variation on this was the *bandwagon* attack, in which a series of individuals took turns criticizing, maligning, and ultimately denouncing one or more colleagues coming under fire from their superiors. This sometimes involved strictly political offenses but was more commonly prompted by discussions about questionable personal behavior, such as alcohol abuse or adultery.[41] The obvious point is that the local repressive apparatus could not have functioned without the willing participation of ordinary Saalfelders themselves – an important point that has been made about the first German dictatorship as well.[42]

According to a popular trope, the East German regime was one large penitentiary: a "state prison," in the words of one scholar, a "mega concentration camp" in those of another.[43] Such characterizations obviously refer first and foremost to the immense difficulties faced by those who wished to flee or simply make short visits abroad.[44] But they are also clear indictments of the repressive nature of the regime.

There is no denying that the GDR was a police state and that those who acted in ways considered to be significantly detrimental to its well-being and stability were commonly subject to various forms of terror, intimidation, and political justice – all part of a concerted effort to curb opposition and create a climate of fear and suspicion. The methods adopted to that end changed over

---

[40] ThStA-R, FDGB KV Slf 3245, Prot. der Sitz. der BGL–Rotstern, 24.7.57. On the motivation of Stasi informants in particular, see Barbara Miller, *Narratives of Guilt and Compliance in Unified Germany: Stasi Informers and their Impact on Society* (London, 1999); Wilkening, *Staat im Staate*; Dennis, *Stasi*, 90–106; Müller-Enbergs, *Mitarbeiter*.

[41] See Andrew Port, "Moralizing 'from Above' and 'from Below': Social Norms, Family Values, and Adultery in the German Democratic Republic" (paper presented at the annual meeting of the German Studies Association, Salt Lake City, UT, October 1998).

[42] See Gellately, *Gestapo*.

[43] For *Staatsknast*, see Stefan Wolle, *Die heile Welt der Diktatur: Alltag und Herrschaft in der DDR, 1971–1989* (Berlin, 1998), 282. For *mega-KZ*, see Hans-Peter Schwarz, "Wenn der Namenspatron ein Massenmörder war," *Die Welt*, January 17, 1992, quoted in Corey Ross, *The East German Dictatorship: Problems and Perspectives in the Interpretation of the GDR* (London, 2002), 16.

[44] This is discussed in Chapter 5.

time. As a result, the mass arrests that took place during the early postwar years gradually gave way during the post-Stalinist era to more refined and arguably less brutal practices aimed at nipping supposedly dangerous forms of dissent and nonconformity in the bud. This shift toward more preventive measures brought in its wake the rapid buildup of a repressive apparatus that involved an enormous increase in the number of security officials and informants, especially during the last two decades of the GDR: These were the years of "complete surveillance" *(flächendeckende Überwachung)*, if such a thing ever existed at all.[45] They nevertheless culminated in a mass protest movement that ended with the collapse of the regime – something that in itself clearly underscores the limits of repression as an explanatory factor when trying to account for regime stability and longevity.[46]

Timothy Mason once argued that "[c]ommon sense suggests that there are limits to the degree to which, or time for which, people ... are prepared to be ruled by fear." Or as Adolf Hitler himself once said, "One cannot rule by force alone."[47] These are both debatable suppositions. Yet the question remains: To what extent did the strong-arm response to the twin upheavals of the early 1950s and the subsequent buildup of state security forces effectively forestall further large-scale eruptions over the next several decades? Traumatic memories of Soviet intervention must have made most Saalfelders more cautious and therefore less willing to take to the streets once again and engage in more collective forms of protest. The very fact that Poland, the only country in the eastern bloc where serious disturbances were never put down by Soviet tanks, was also the only country to have experienced repeated waves of widespread labor unrest strongly supports this hypothesis. The potential for future unrest also diminished considerably with the arrest, imprisonment, or flight of the more active participants, i.e., of those apparently most willing to express their discontent in a forceful manner.[48]

---

[45] On the changing nature of Stasi methods, see, e.g., Keßler and Klein, "Repression"; Dennis, *Stasi*; Gieske, *Mielke–Konzern* (esp. 132–59 on the idea of *flächendeckende Überwachung*); Roger Engelmann, "Funktionswandel der Staatssicherheit," in Christoph Boyer and Peter Skyba, eds., *Repression und Wohlstandsversprechen: Zur Stabilisierung von Parteiherrschaft in der DDR und der CSSR* (Dresden, 1999), 89–97.

[46] Mikhail Gorbachev's policies may have emboldened many East Germans to engage once again in active protest, but as those who participated in the events of 1989 later recollected, the fear of violent reprisals remained a justifiable and constant source of concern. See, e.g., Dirk Philipsen, ed., *We Were the People: Voices from East Germany's Revolutionary Autumn of 1989* (Durham, NC, 1993).

[47] See Tim Mason, "The Containment of the Working Class in Nazi Germany," in Jane Caplan, ed., *Nazism, Fascism and the Working Class* (Cambridge, 1995), 241; quotation by Hitler in James Scott, *Domination and the Arts of Resistance: Hidden Transcripts* (New Haven, CT, 1990), 49. For the claim that terror played only a relatively minor role in accounting for the "staying power" of the Third Reich, see Robert Gellately, *Backing Hitler: Consent and Coercion in Nazi Germany* (Oxford, 2001).

[48] According to one informant who supplied the West German SPD *Ostbüro* with reports about Saalfeld, local workers expressed critical opinions quite openly at production meetings: "They have not allowed themselves to act rashly, however, because June 17 and all its consequences are still too fresh in mind." See AdsD, Ostbüro 00523j, report, 30.10.57.

That said, the SED's decision to reverse a wide range of unpopular policies and then offer carrots of social and economic pacification in 1951 and then again in 1953 must have made many realize at the same time that large-scale protest was an effective way in which to bring about desired change – or, at the very least, elicit official promises of reform. Moreover, the cautious behavior of security officials in August 1951 and June 1953, the need to rely on Soviet troops during the latter incident, and the mere fact that these two events took place at all certainly underscored the limited ability of the East German security apparatus to respond to and defuse – let alone preempt – crisis situations. That was especially true, of course, during its earliest phase – even though the ranks of the Stasi had more than doubled to approximately 10,000 over the course of 1952 alone, making it even larger than an earlier security organization that had to maintain control of a much larger population, i.e., the Gestapo.[49]

Despite an even greater buildup after 1953, the very fact that the two earliest and most vigorous challenges to the SED regime had both taken place at the peak of Stalinist terror nevertheless suggests that neither repression nor the fear of repression could alone stifle popular protest and mass unrest.[50] With that in mind, the remainder of this study will examine those factors that were arguably more important in accounting for so many years of domestic tranquility – as well as the ways in which most Saalfelders increasingly came to express their disquiet and displeasure in a climate of fear.

[49] See Hubertus Knabe, *17. Juni 1953: Ein deutscher Aufstand* (Munich, 2003), 47. On the size of the Gestapo, see Gellately, *Gestapo*, 44–76.

[50] The number of imprisoned East Germans doubled from 30,000 to 60,000 between mid-1952 and mid-1953; see Jonathan Sperber, "17 June 1953: Revisiting a German Revolution," *German History* 22 (2004): 624.

5

Exit, Voice, and Apathy

The year 1961 began on a positive note in Saalfeld. On January 14, the infant East German television network broadcast its first live concert from the Maxhütte's new neoclassical Cultural Palace. The highlight of the evening was a ballet performance by the legendary National Theater from nearby Weimar, accompanied by the somewhat less renowned Wismut Orchestra. Two months later on March 18, the district's newly built Agricola Hospital was officially opened at an inaugural ceremony held in the festive banquet hall of the town museum, a converted medieval Franciscan monastery. Local luminaries in attendance included the regional Soviet commandant, Lieutenant Colonel Sapolski, whose troops had helped construct this thirty-five-acre modern medical facility, built at a cost of 25 million marks. The Soviets themselves would celebrate an even more important event three weeks later when their countryman, Yuri Gagarin, became the first cosmonaut to orbit the earth – an achievement that supposedly sparked a spontaneous outpouring of "heartfelt joy and admiration" on the part of Saalfeld's residents for this "triumph of human greatness and Soviet science."

The festivities continued on April 20, when local officials organized a mass demonstration in the town marketplace to celebrate the SED's fifteenth anniversary: According to the media, no fewer than 17,000 persons attended a commemorative speech by Alexander Abusch, the former minister of culture and now deputy chairman of the East German State Council. The death in early September of Paul Dammann, one of Saalfeld's first Communists and a cofounder of the town's Spartacus League in 1918, cast only a small shadow over these events as well as over the District Council election held later that month: Only 39 (sic) dissenting votes were recorded among the more than 42,000 valid ballots, which meant that the official list of candidates had once again received a staggering 99.91 percent of the vote – a slight improvement over the 99.83 percent cast in Saalfeld at the last election held in November 1958 for the East German parliament.[1]

In Potemkin-like fashion, this spate of celebratory events masked an underlying crisis that threatened the very lifeblood of Saalfeld and the GDR, namely, the steady flow of migrants to the Federal Republic. This human hemorrhage, which had begun in the mid-1940s in the wake of Soviet occupation and creeping Stalinization, reached a crescendo following the failed upheaval of June 1953: More than 330,000 persons left the GDR that year alone, and approximately 250,000 fled annually over the next several years, i.e., roughly 1.5 percent of the East German population per annum. Two ominous developments ensured equally high numbers of emigrants during the latter part of the decade: Nikita Khrushchev's so-called Berlin Ultimatum of November 1958 and a series of high-level decisions the following year that constituted yet another concerted effort to "construct socialism" in the GDR.[2]

Growing concern about the sustained exodus of East Germans via the open border with West Berlin had partially underlain the Soviet premier's public threat to abrogate unilaterally the international modus vivendi in the divided city. This move, coupled with an official resolution in late 1959 to collectivize all agricultural holdings in the GDR, triggered a new and unprecedented wave of flight to the Federal Republic: Animated by justifiable fears that the easiest escape route to the West was about to be closed, almost 160,000 persons left during the first eight months of 1961 alone. At an emergency meeting held in March, local officials noted with alarm that more individuals had fled Saalfeld during the first two months of the year than ever before: If nothing were done, the district would "once again break the record."[3] Similar concerns at the highest levels of government prompted an extraordinary measure on the night of August 13: the construction of a twelve-foot-high, ninety-six-mile-long wall that hermetically sealed off West Berlin from the GDR.[4]

Although this infamous action effectively stanched the heavy flow of migrants to the West, several thousand East Germans still managed to make their way to the Federal Republic each year following the erection of the Wall: Saalfeld's proximity to Bavaria enabled those familiar with the local

[1] Gerhard Werner, "Chronik der Stadt Saalfeld: Teil III (1945–1978)" (unpublished manuscript, 1979), 77, 86–9.

[2] For flight statistics, see Patrick Major, "Going west: the open border and the problem of Republikflucht," in Patrick Major and Jonathan Osmond, eds., *The Workers' and Peasants' State: Communism and Society in East Germany under Ulbricht, 1945–71* (Manchester, UK, 2002), 191; Henrik Bispinck, "'Republikflucht': Flucht und Ausreise als Problem für die DDR–Führung," in Dierk Hoffmann, Michael Schwartz, and Hermann Wentker, eds., *Vor dem Mauerbau: Politik und Gesellschaft der DDR der fünfziger Jahre* (Munich, 2003), 306–9.

[3] KrA-S 12564, Prot. der Kreisratssitz., 3.8.61

[4] On the decision to construct the Wall and the history of Soviet–East German relations during this period more generally, see Hope Harrison, *Driving the Soviets up the Wall: Soviet–East German Relations, 1953–1961* (Princeton, NJ, 2003).

forests and back roads to escape across the "green border" separating the two German states, for example.[5] But for all intents and purposes, the Wall deprived all but the most determined and courageous of the so-called exit option: Famously described by Albert Hirschman, this "act of simply leaving" was supposedly one of two responses available to those who discerned a "deterioration in the quality of the goods they buy or the services and benefits they receive." The other alternative was "voice" – the "act of complaining" or protest – and, according to Hirschman, the two options usually worked at cross-purposes: "The presence of the exit alternative can ... *atrophy the development of the art of voice*." In light of the developments that led to the collapse of the GDR in 1989, Hirschman later acknowledged that the two responses can sometimes go hand-in-hand and even reinforce one another. But he nevertheless maintained that for most of the GDR's history, resistance and dissidence were "minimal" because of the way in which the availability of an exit option – even after August 1961 – effectively undermined voice.[6]

Despite the scholarly renaissance enjoyed by this conceptual framework after the fall of the Wall, its explanatory power and applicability to developments in Saalfeld and the GDR more generally remain open to question. The concepts of exit and voice identify two common reactions to unpopular developments, but other responses existed as well: Resignation and apathy were, for instance, equally widespread beyond the Elbe.[7] In addition, the model fails to explain individual choices adequately. According to Hirschman, feelings of loyalty could impede exit as well as voice. But a decision to remain in the GDR or a failure to express discontent did not necessarily reflect allegiance to the regime. Other considerations, including those of a personal nature as well as the justifiable fear of repression and other negative repercussions, often played an equally important role.

The notion that the possibility of exit often served to undercut voice is just as problematic, for this option clearly did not preclude the vocal and physical acts of defiance that shook Saalfeld in August 1951 and then much of the GDR two years later when the border was still open. In fact, it was arguably the very possibility of exit that made East Germans willing to engage in such acts: As one Western study of the East German intelligentsia concluded in 1960, "The possibility of escaping lends [them] some backbone."[8] Just as important, and as we shall see in the remainder of this study, Hirschman typically underestimates

---

[5] See the reports from the early and mid-1960s in BStU ASt-G, KD Slf 0552.

[6] Albert Hirschman, *Exit, Voice, and Loyalty: Responses to Decline in Firms, Organizations, and States* (Cambridge, MA, 1970); idem, "Exit, Voice and the Fate of the German Democratic Republic: An Essay in Conceptual History," *World Politics* 45 (1993): 173–202.

[7] On widespread apathy in the GDR, see Mark Allinson, *Politics and Popular Opinion in East Germany, 1945–68* (Manchester, UK, 2000).

[8] Infratest, *Die Intelligenzschicht in der Sowjetzone Deutschlands: Ideologische Haltungen und politische Verhaltensweisen*, vol. 3 (Munich, 1960), 196, cited in Detlef Pollack, "Die konstitutive Widersprüchlichkeit der DDR: Oder: War die DDR–Gesellschaft homogen?" *GG* 24 (1998): 120.

the surprising willingness with which many East Germans expressed their discontent during considerably less dramatic periods.

Notwithstanding its limitations with respect to developments in the GDR, Hirschman's model prompts a number of important questions about the way in which Saalfelders reacted to unpopular policies and communicated their displeasure about unwelcome developments. What were some of the main sources of dissatisfaction, what patterns of protest and resistance did they give rise to, and how did authorities typically respond? What were the possibilities for and limits on expressions of discontent, why did individuals pursue certain channels while eschewing others, and how did this change over time? Most fundamentally, what was the underlying character and significance of such behavior, and what does all of this tell us about the stability and longevity of the SED regime?

Dissenting Voices in the "Grumble *Gesellschaft*"

Even if Timothy Mason's observation about similar records produced during the Third Reich also holds true for Saalfeld and the GDR – that the "historical sources left behind by terrorist bureaucracies always document dissent better than ... consent" – it is still not difficult to reach the conclusion that East Germany was a veritable "Grumble *Gesellschaft*" in which a great deal of trenchant criticism was recited on the public or semipublic stage.[9] Regardless of age, gender, occupation, social position, or political affiliation, many of those who lived and worked in Saalfeld candidly and continuously complained about a wide variety of issues – with most grumbling tending to focus on matters of an ostensibly economic nature: low bonuses and high production quotas, harsh working conditions and long hours, poor planning and rampant bureaucracy, scant production materials and unavailable consumer goods, elevated prices and burdensome rationing, inadequate social benefits and scarce housing. In short, those who stayed spoke.[10]

Their customary reticence with regard to more sensitive (i.e., overtly political) themes nevertheless suggested that most knew the boundaries of the permissible – something many had first learned under the Third Reich: "If somebody opens their mouth nowadays, he'll be arrested, just like the comrades ... in [Ernst] Thälmann's time" – a comparison that must have been particularly galling to Communist officials.[11] Or, as one party member at the VEB Zeiss wistfully noted in the fall of 1954, the "lively discussions" that had supposedly

---

[9] Tim Mason, "The Containment of the Working Class in Nazi Germany," in Jane Caplan, ed., *Nazism, Fascism and the Working Class* (Cambridge, 1995), 252.

[10] For similar behavior elsewhere in the GDR, see Alf Lüdtke," ... Den Menschen vergessen"? – oder: Das Maß der Sicherheit: Arbeitsverhalten der 1950er Jahre im Blick von MfS, FDGB und staatlichen Leitungen," in Alf Lüdtke and Peter Becker, eds., *Akten. Eingaben. Schaufenster: Die DDR und ihre Texte: Erkundungen zu Herrschaft und Alltag* (Berlin, 1997), 189–93.

[11] Thälmann had been the head of the Weimar KPD until his arrest and subsequent execution by the National Socialists at Buchenwald in 1944.

been routine before June 17 – "even if largely negative in content" – were no longer heard on the trains carrying workers to and from their jobs. The party secretary similarly complained at the time that no one ever told him "what they really think" when it came to important political developments.[12]

The growing caution and increasingly restrained nature of public discussion did not go unnoticed, then. But this was not necessarily a reflection of indifference, as many officials apparently believed. Even though most Saalfelders were understandably more preoccupied with more mundane and immediate concerns, their silence when it came to political themes was frequently a cautious form of dissent or a way in which to avoid making unwelcome comments that might have led to serious sanctions. This was clearly related to the subsequent buildup of the state security apparatus following the brutal suppression of the June 1953 uprising. But even before that spectacular event, officials complained that most people were careful about expressing critical views: "We don't want typewritten discussions," one exasperated functionary wrote at the bottom of the minutes of a meeting held at the Maxhütte in early 1952, "but rather open ones." Many in Saalfeld nevertheless feared that captious comments would lead to imprisonment or the loss of a job.[13]

Despite the general unwillingness to express critical opinions about sensitive political issues, local authorities still had some sense of popular sentiment regarding a wide range of developments in the international arena and at home. If most criticism at public gatherings was limited to economic grievances, many were apparently less cautious when drinking in pubs or working on the assembly line – or when particularly incensed about some sanction or perceived injustice. Intercepted by attentive ears and diligently passed on to authorities, much of this grumbling found its way into official reports and analyses that began with requisite formulaic introductions: "The mood... in our district can be described as absolutely positive [and] all agree with the policies of our government.... But that doesn't mean that there aren't people here who also... hold hostile views."[14] While it is difficult to determine just how representative these hostile views were, the fact that certain criticisms continued to surface regularly over time and throughout the district suggested that they were certainly widespread.

Complaints of a more clearly political nature tended to be most concentrated during major crisis periods: During the 1956 upheavals in the eastern bloc, for example, workers at the local transportation company openly expressed their sympathy with the Hungarians and said that they had the right to demand the

---

[12] See ThStA-R IV/4/10/250, IB der SED–KL Slf, 3.11.55; ThStA-R IV/7/231/1164, Prot. der MV der SED GO–Zeiss, 29.9.54; ThStA-R IV/7/231/1165, Prot. der LS der SED GO–Zeiss, 2.9.55; ThStA-R IV/7/231/1167, IB der SED GO–Zeiss, 22.11.56.

[13] MxA-U, BGL 264, Prot. der BV in der Kranabt., 19.2.52.

[14] ThStA-R IV/4/10/248, IB der SED–KL Slf, 6.10.54. For a discussion of the special language and phraseology used by East German functionaries, see Matthias Judt, "'Nur für den Dienstgebrauch' – Arbeiten mit Texten einer deutschen Diktatur," and Ralph Jessen, "Diktatorische Herrschaft als kommunikative Praxis: Überlegungen zum Zusammenhang von 'Bürokratie' und Sprachnormierung in der DDR–Geschichte," in Lüdtke and Becker, *Akten*, 29–38, 58–75.

removal of Soviet troops if that was what they wanted. "The same question has to be posed in the GDR," they continued, before launching into a general attack on Soviet economic exploitation: "[E]verything is so scarce here... because everything is exported." A year earlier, one irate worker at the Maxhütte had similarly claimed that if East Germans did not have to work for "foreigners, the living situation here wouldn't be so bad.... You're just like the SA" (i.e., Nazi storm troopers).[15]

Outright comparisons of the SED regime with the Nazi dictatorship did surface occasionally – which casts some doubt on claims about the degree to which the regime's antifascist rhetoric had won over large segments of the population.[16] But these were far less common than complaints about the Soviet Union. Because occupation troops had arrived in Saalfeld two months after the cessation of hostilities, the district had largely been spared the mass raping and looting experienced by those Germans who lived farther east or in Berlin. Yet sporadic complaints about local soldiers molesting young women and girls indicated that sexual misconduct remained a problem, despite the tendency of some officials to dismiss these claims – such as the suggestion that a brothel be set up so that the troops would not be "forced to hit on German women so violently" – as exaggerated anti-Soviet rabble-rousing. While admitting that local soldiers had made some "errors" in the past, the party chairman at Zeiss callously lectured staff members about the offenses committed by East German citizens themselves, including that of a party member recently convicted of raping his twelve-year-old daughter.[17]

The mass arrests made by occupation officials during the immediate postwar years remained a taboo subject, much like rape, yet they occasionally prompted critical remarks by family members who wanted to know where their relatives were, or who refused to accept official pronouncements that these men had been war criminals.[18] Postwar territorial revision, which had severed off large chunks of German territory in the East, was another political taboo sometimes broken, and the most vocal critics were naturally those who had been personally affected: namely, the so-called resettlers (*Umsiedler*) from the East, many of whom continued to demand that they be allowed to return to their "homeland" (*Heimat*).[19]

[15] ThStA-R IV/4/10/249 and 252, IB der SED–KL Slf, 28.4.55, 27.9.56, 25.10.56.

[16] See the Introduction on the alleged role of antifascist rhetoric in winning support for the regime.

[17] ThStA-R IV/7/226/1137, IB der SED GO–Rotstern, 23.10.56; ThStA-R IV/7/231/1162, Rechenschaftsbericht, 14.11.53. For other reports of Soviet molestation and on the tendency of officials to dismiss this as anti-Soviet propaganda, see ThStA-R IV/4/10/246, 250, and 257, IB der SED–KL Slf, 28.10.53, 28.7.55, 22.9.58. On postwar rapes by Soviet troops, see Norman Naimark, *The Russians in Germany: A History of the Soviet Zone of Occupation, 1945–1949* (Cambridge, MA, 1995), 69–140; Anonyma, *Eine Frau in Berlin: Tagebuchaufzeichnungen vom 20. April bis 22. Juni 1945* (Frankfurt am Main, 2003).

[18] See, e.g., ThStA-R IV/7/231/1167, IB der SED GO–Zeiss, 19.10.55; ThStA-R IV/4/10/251, IB der SED–KL Slf, 16.2.56; ThStA-R IV/7/226/1137, IB der SED GO–Rotstern, 19.10.56.

[19] See, e.g., MxA-U, WL B79, Prot. der Generalversammlung der SED–BG, 1.8.47; ThStA-R, BDVP Gera 21/250, report, 27.10.54. Also see Michael Schwartz, *Vertriebene und "Umsiedlerpolitik": Integrationskonflikte in den deutschen Nachkriegs–Gesellschaften und die*

As a rule, most criticism about the Soviets tended to focus on the reparations and dismantling of the immediate postwar years, as well as on continued economic exploitation during the 1950s and 1960s. This was often cited as one main reason for the GDR's poor economic performance: "The best experts try over and over again to leave for the West. The Russians [are] to blame for this because they're always dragging people away." Or as one railroad worker quipped, "Our rails are made of Krupp steel, the Russians' of what they steal." It should be noted that the word *Russian* was usually employed in a disparaging way, and its use drew censure from local officials who insisted on more acceptable terms such as *Soviets* or *friends*. This prompted one upbraided worker whose wife had been physically attacked three times to ask "how he, as a German, could be a friend of the Soviets when they've taken everything away from him."[20]

Negative feelings toward the "Russians" were perhaps strongest on the part of those who had actually spent time in the USSR as prisoners of war – such as Walter Schilling, a skilled worker at Zeiss who performed forced labor in the Soviet Union for three years after the official cessation of hostilities. Born in Saalfeld in 1925, Schilling was the son of a former lathe operator who had also been one of the prison guards threatened with hanging during the Wismut upheaval of 1951. He himself began as an apprentice at Zeiss in the early 1940s, but had to cut his training short after being drafted into the Wehrmacht at the age of seventeen. He was wounded a year later during the battle of Normandy and, after convalescing for several months in France, was sent to fight partisans in the forests of occupied Czechoslovakia. Schilling became an American prisoner of war in mid-May 1945 but was then "delivered" (*ausgeliefert*) to Russian forces several weeks later by his erstwhile captors. He spent the next few months as a forced laborer in Czechoslovakia, Hungary, and Romania before being transported to the Soviet Union itself in the summer of 1945: That was, he recalled five decades later, when his "real internment" began.

After taking part with thousands of other German prisoners in a "funeral march" (*Trauermarsch*) through Red Square in Moscow, Schilling was transferred to a swamp region in the Ural Mountains, where he spent the next year preparing peat to help run an electric plant. Forced to march on foot for ten to twelve kilometers and then work for more than twelve hours each day (only to risk solitary confinement or a severe cut in rations if production norms were not satisfied), only 30 percent of the approximately 4,000 other prisoners survived.

Assimilationsstrategien in der SBZ/DDR, 1945 bis 1961 (Munich, 2004); Philipp Ther, *Deutsche und polnische Vertriebene: Gesellschaft und Vertriebenenpolitik in der SBZ und in Polen, 1945– 1956* (Göttingen, 1998).
20 ThStA-R IV/4/10/240, Bericht über den Einsatz der Brigade der BL der SED in Probstzella (Entwurf), 27.5.59; MxA-U, WL B79, Prot. der Versammlung der BG–Funktionäre der LEB im Kr. Slf, 26.9.47; ThStA-R IV/7/230/1158, Prot. der MV der SED GO–Wema, 14.5.52. On attempts to improve views of and relations with the USSR, see Lothar Dralle, *Von der Sowjetunion lernen . . . : Zur Geschichte der Gesellschaft für Deutsch–Sowjetische Freundschaft* (Berlin, 1993).

Schilling was one of the more fortunate ones and, thanks to his previous training as a skilled worker, was chosen in the spring of 1946 to help construct a metalworking factory in a Russian city – where he was again given "very little" to eat. He spent two winters there and was largely "left in peace," but had, by this point, given up all hope of ever returning home. In the late fall of 1948 – and after receiving a "nice meal" from the local Soviet commandant – Schilling was finally allowed to go back to Saalfeld, where he resumed work at Zeiss the following spring. By this point, the factory had been completely disassembled and stood "entirely empty," apart from a few antiquated machines: Even the water pipes had been taken away and sent to the East. As one of his colleagues later recalled with obvious bitterness, several of those who worked at Zeiss at the time were required to travel themselves to Kiev in 1946 to help rebuild what had earlier been dismantled.[21]

Many in Saalfeld were understandably critical of the East German regime's complicity in this process. In fact, they remained not only impervious to the SED's stand on these and other delicate issues regarding the Soviet Union, but also highly skeptical of official propaganda in other areas as well – especially when it came to some of its more outrageous claims. In 1955, the same year that several older residents rejected official assertions that elections had not been democratic in Weimar Germany, local functionaries described the peals of laughter prompted by a newsreel claiming that electric train lines had first been introduced in eastern Germany after 1945. They suggested that the state film studio be "a bit more diplomatic. One can also report such happy events in a way that won't make the audience chuckle." Widespread complaints about the constant barrage of propaganda in all areas of everyday life were similarly noted: "Our people want to see and hear something amusing nowadays, and we shouldn't mix culture with politics." The desire for national unity prompted many to look with an equally critical eye at official attacks against West Germany: These, they claimed, would hinder the chances of reconciliation, unity, and a lasting peace.[22]

From an official viewpoint, the often unfavorable comparisons of the GDR with the Federal Republic were just as disconcerting – such as the widespread skepticism that met the SED's boast in 1958 that the new Five-Year Plan would enable the GDR to surpass per capita consumption levels in West Germany within a few years.[23] Disdainful authorities usually attributed this "glorification" of West Germany's economic success to Bonn's "shop-window policies" (*Schaufensterpolitik*), but crude material considerations were not the only reason why so many East Germans looked so favorably across the border. In 1947, long before the so-called economic miracle, one critical party member at the Maxhütte pointed out that the vast majority of workers in the Western zones

---

[21] Walter Schilling and Horst Kämmer, in discussion with the author, August 1995.
[22] ThStA-R IV/7/231/1167, IB der SED GO–Zeiss, 25.9.57, 21.10.55, 5.12.55; ThStA-R, FDGB BV Gera 703/177, Wochenbericht, 10.9.55; ThStA-R IV/4/10/263, IB der SED–KL Slf, 23.9.60.
[23] ThStA-R IV/4/10/256, IB der SED–KL Slf, 18.7.58.

supported the leader of the SPD: "There has to be something attracting [them to Kurt] Schumacher's policies." Other reports clearly suggested that one of the main attractions was the wide-ranging political freedoms enjoyed by West Germans, such as the right to strike, vote in free elections, or "even insult [Konrad] Adenauer."[24]

Explicit calls for democracy were not limited to the June 1953 upheaval, as this suggests. But the submission of invalid ballots and refusals to participate in elections were far more common ways in which to express anger about the lack of political liberty. Protesting the undemocratic nature of factory elections, for instance, one party member at Zeiss refused to cast another vote: "[A] slip of paper is pushed into one's hand [with] all of the suggestions . . . already written on it. The party has never worked honestly. I'm no wimp (*Waschlappen*)." Such criticism obviously had little effect, given the SED's understanding of democracy: "The important thing is that the party retains leadership and control," officials at the chocolate factory explained to staff members in response to similar complaints, "so a secret ballot would be wrong because it would allow people whom the party doesn't approve of [to win]. . . . There's only one way, namely, what the party demands of us. . . . " Small wonder, then, that those who openly compared elections in East Germany to those under Hitler also concluded that the SED made all decisions and that "the worker has no say" – a popular refrain that reflected not only a widespread sense of powerlessness, but also the frustration and outrage engendered by dictatorship and imposed political infantilism.[25]

The Repertoire of Everyday Protest

However helpless many may have felt, the disgruntled nevertheless relied on a wide variety of indirect methods besides grumbling to express their economic and political discontent. In fact, the repertoire of everyday protest in Saalfeld included many acts of nonconformity and outright defiance already familiar during the Third Reich. The similarities were not surprising, given the buildup of repressive security apparatuses as well as the elimination of effective and independent forms of political and economic representation under both regimes; they suggested, moreover, that many employed surreptitious tactics learned and developed before 1945 in order to articulate discontent and assert their own personal interests.[26] The defacing of political posters (especially those with

[24] MxA-U, WL B79, Prot. der Generalversammlung der SED–BG, 1.8.47; ThStA-R IV/7/222/1060, IB der SED GO–Maxh., 7.6.56. On West German consumption in the 1950s, see Michael Wildt, *Am Beginn der Konsumgesellschaft: Mangelerfahrung, Lebenshaltung, Wohlstandshoffnung in Westdeutschland in den fünfziger Jahren* (Hamburg, 1994).

[25] ThStA-R IV/7/231/1166, Prot. der MV der SED GO–Zeiss, 14.5.57; ThStA-R IV/7/226/1136, Prot. der MV der SED GO–Rotstern, 7.8.61; ThStA-R, BDVP Gera 21/250, report, 27.10.54. For similar complaints about the absence of free elections in the GDR, see ADL, BV Gera 33127, Meinungsbildungbericht, 24.10.63; ACDP II-338–004/1, Politischer Bericht, July 1954.

[26] On similar forms of protest elsewhere in Thuringia, see Gareth Pritchard, *The Making of the GDR, 1945–53: From Antifascism to Stalinism* (Manchester, UK, 2000), 201–2. On

images of leading Communist officials), the clandestine distribution of oppositional leaflets, and the scribbling of critical graffiti in public places were among
the more popular forms of such protest. The following samples discovered by
security officials at the Maxhütte during the 1950s provide some sense of the
economic grievances as well as the wide range of political sensibilities at the
steel mill:

Heil Hitler, GDR is riffraff... 50 Stars, Hammer and Sickle, rule the German
Michel... [President Wilhelm] Pieck should be strung up... You know nothing
about our worries in bitter years, about slaving away for starvation wages... As
quickly as we work today, just as quickly will we die tomorrow, or wind up in
prison... The day will come when we'll get revenge, then we'll be the judges... Long live
June 17.

Calls for democratic elections and the overthrow of the government, as well
as an end to remilitarization and Soviet occupation ("Ivan go home"), were
other popular themes throughout the district. Local police records were also
filled with reports of swastikas scribbled on factory walls, bathroom stalls, and
other public locations.[27]

Given the dangers inherent in such activities – as Operation Scribbler made
abundantly clear – the disaffected usually resorted to more subtle forms of
protest in order to register their discontent: demonstrative coughing or mur-
muring during political speeches, for example, the silencing of loudspeakers
used to transmit propaganda, or the spreading of political jokes and rumors.[28]
The last were especially important because they revealed the grievances as well
as some of the major concerns of those who lived and worked in the district. In
so doing, these jokes and rumors offer a valuable glimpse at the so-called hidden transcript, i.e., what James Scott refers to as the critique of power spoken
behind the backs of those who dominate.[29] Much of the "gossip" pertained
to pressing material and economic issues, such as norm and wage levels or the
availability of scare consumer goods: During the 1956 disturbances in Hungary,
for instance, word spread throughout the district that factory personnel were

worker protest under the Nazis, see Klaus-Michael Mallmann and Gerhard Paul, *Herrschaft
und Alltag: Ein Industrierevier im Dritten Reich*, vol. 2 (Bonn, 1991), 353–80; Günther
Morsch, "Die kalkulierte Improvisation: Streiks und Arbeitsniederlegungen im 'Dritten Reich,'"
VfZ 36 (1988): 649–89; Michael Voges, "'Klassenkampf in der Betriebsgemeinschaft': Die
'Deutschland–Berichte' der Sopade (1934–1940) als Quelle zum Widerstand der Industriear-
beiter im Dritten Reich," *AfS* 21 (1981): 329–88; Tim Mason, "The Workers' Opposition in
Nazi Germany," *History Workshop Journal* 11 (1981): 120–37; Detlev Peukert, *Inside Nazi
Germany: Conformity, Opposition, and Racism in Everyday Life*, trans. Richard Deveson
(New Haven, CT, 1987), 101–44. For a useful overview of this literature, see, e.g., Ulrich Herbert, "Arbeiterschaft im 'Dritten Reich': Zwischenbilanz und offene Fragen," *GG* 15 (1989):
320–60.
27 See the police reports in ThStA-R, BDVP Gera 21/212 and 21/250.
28 See, e.g., ThStA-R IV/7/222/1060, IB der SED GO–Maxh., 28.3.56; ThStA-R IV/7/226/1137, IB
der SED GO–Rotstern, 11.4.56. On Operation Scribbler, see Chapter 4.
29 James Scott, *Domination and the Arts of Resistance: Hidden Transcripts* (New Haven, CT,
1990).

no longer permitted to raise production quotas.[30] On the eve of the SED's Fifth Party Congress two years later, workers at the Maxhütte speculated that the party would do away with ration cards, raise pensions, increase the lowest base wages and salaries, and cut the cost of gasoline – but that it would also raise the price of alcohol 300 percent. When officials at the steel mill subsequently prohibited the sale of beer, word soon spread that the free soft drinks offered instead caused diarrhea.[31] Rumors not only reflected the fantasies, then, but also the fears and anger of many Saalfelders.

Besides bread-and-butter issues, such "whispered propaganda" was also frequently related to and reflective of political desires and reveries – such as the rumor that Walter Ulbricht had been removed from power or that the GDR would cede Thuringia to the Federal Republic in return for West Berlin. In fact, because of the district's proximity to the Bavarian border as well as its initial occupation by U.S. forces, many local tales focused on territorial revision as well as on the so-called demarcation zone between the two postwar German states: Word spread in the 1950s and 1960s (especially following the series of forced transfers in May 1952 and then again after the construction of the Berlin Wall) that certain families and even entire villages would be removed from the restricted area located on the West German border. A rumor spread in the summer of 1962 – that the border would be redrawn straight through the middle of Probstzella – even led to fights among local children about who lived on the "right" side.[32]

While not an active form of opposition, strictly speaking, rumors could obviously have tangible consequences – like frequent hoarding in response to reports that certain staple goods would no longer be available in state-run stores. As a result, officials carefully kept track of such stories, fearing with some justification that false ones could foment serious unrest. This frequently led to lengthy discussions in which they tried to persuade local citizens that such rumors were groundless – as well as to threats that individuals caught spreading bogus tales would be subject to criminal prosecution.[33]

Rumors were also important because they demonstrated that extended communication networks existed throughout the district and beyond its borders. Through informal contacts as well as officially sanctioned meetings that allowed workers and farmers from different factories and villages to discuss their experiences at the workplace, those living in Saalfeld were able to learn about events not reported in the official media, e.g., about protests that had supposedly taken place in other parts of the GDR. Rumors of an "incident" (*Vorkommnis*) in Magdeburg and a student strike in Dresden circulated, for instance, during the

---

30 ThStA-R IV/7/226/1137, IB der SED GO–Rotstern, 29.10.56.
31 ThStA-R IV/4/10/256, IB der SED–KL Slf, 22.5.58; ThStA-R, BDVP Gera 21/250, Informationsblatt, 4.7.60.
32 ThStA-R IV/4/10/250, 263 and 268, IB der SED–KL Slf, 31.8.55, 18.11.60, 15.6.62; ThStA-R IV/7/226/1135, Prot. der MV der SED GO–Rotstern, 15.12.55; ThStA-R, Maxh. 390, report, 6.6.52.
33 See ThStA-R IV/4/10/249 and 263, IB der SED–KL Slf, 10.2.55, 18.11.60.

1956 upheaval in Hungary; two years later, word spread that fistfights had broken out at the local drilling machine factory between workers and shop-floor personnel responsible for setting norms.[34] The point is that rumors not only revealed the hopes of many East Germans, but also gave them hope.

Despite the risks involved, Saalfelders sometimes resorted to less ambiguous forms of protest to convey anger and express their discontent. These included refusals to sign the steady stream of acclamatory resolutions in endorsement of domestic or international policies (such as the introduction of compulsory military conscription in 1962), or to contribute to so-called solidarity funds in support of comrades-in-arms abroad: North Koreans and Cubans, party loyalists in Hungary, or striking workers in the Federal Republic. Such refusals were often tied to personal setbacks: As one recalcitrant woman who had not been granted permission to visit a daughter living in the Federal Republic protested, "one should first do something here about improving the most basic human interrelations. That would be real solidarity."[35]

Though it is not always easy to discern the underlying character of such resistant behavior, some refusals were clearly more political than personal in nature. In the mid-1960s, for example, many in Saalfeld categorically refused to contribute to solidarity funds earmarked for the Vietcong: While some argued that this would only serve to prolong the conflict, others suggested that authorities should first concern themselves with German unification.[36] Not all Saalfelders were convinced, incidentally, that only the party and the state had the right to make demands or draw up resolutions. Though it was rare, aggrieved individuals would occasionally collect signatures themselves in order to lend weight to some request; this included calls for higher rations, larger bonuses, or, in one instance, boneless meat.[37]

The refusal to pay party or union dues was another strategy frequently used to register discontent – and one linked, at least ostensibly, to the belief that contribution rates were too high. As one party zealot at Zeiss colorfully observed, "The colleagues say . . . 'whenever I hear the word *socialism* I reach toward my ass for my wallet.'"[38] But given the small amounts involved, widespread grumbling was obviously more than just a reflection of the financial hardship that such dues supposedly represented. Because authorities purposely made payment voluntary in order to allow the "masses" to demonstrate their attachment to the union or party, a refusal to pay was usually a clear sign of protest – and almost always by an individual who wished to make some sort of statement,

---

[34] ThStA-R IV/4/10/252, IB der SED–KL Slf, 29.10.56; ThStA-R IV/7/222/1060, IB der SED GO–Maxh., 7.6.56; ThStA-R IV/7/230/1155, Prot. der LS der SED GO–Wema, 21.5.58. The Auerbach & Scheibe drilling machine factory became a VEB after 1945.

[35] ThStA-R IV/4/10/264, IB der SED–KL Slf, 19.1.61; ThStA-R, FDGB BV Gera 1657, Analyse über die finanziell-politischen Ergebnisse vom Jahre 1964, 15.1.65.

[36] See, e.g., ThStA-R, FDGB KV Slf 6302, IB der FDGB–KV Slf, 12.8.65, 19.8.65.

[37] See, e.g., ThStA-R IV/7/231/1167, Entschließung, 2.12.49.

[38] ThStA-R IV/7/231/1162, Prot. der Berichtswahlversammlung in Zeiss, 7.4.55.

with disputes over wages, housing, vacation time, and travel to West Germany being some of the more common motives for noncompliance.[39]

Although collective actions were extremely rare, and normally limited to one department or a single brigade within a factory, there were a few prominent exceptions, such as the widespread spate of politically motivated refusals reported in Saalfeld after June 1953.[40] During the middle of the following decade, rank-and-file party members engaged in another protest, this time in response to an unpopular decision to raise dues by calculating future payments according to gross earnings. Complaining that it was unfair to include overtime and bonuses when setting the amount to be paid – especially since they were forced to put in extra hours in order to ensure plan fulfillment – many across the district consequently refused to pay any dues whatsoever. Seventy-three members at the VEB Rotstern threatened to quit the SED, in fact, and at least one retiree who had belonged to the Communist Party for forty years did eventually resign: "He doesn't want to have anything more to do with . . . social-fascists. Especially not with comrades who had earlier screamed 'Heil Hitler.' He says it's finally time to establish a Communist Party again. He doesn't care if one takes away his extra pension, he remains a Communist."[41] The District Secretariat responded to the wave of protest by putting even greater pressure on refractory members: To that end, it decided in May 1966 to repeal an earlier order stating that those who refused to pay dues would no longer be subject to punishment – as long as they otherwise participated actively in party life.[42]

Ensuring active participation by the rank-and-file had, in fact, long been an uphill battle, with mandatory attendance at party gatherings and at the so-called *Parteilehrjahr* (seminars and lectures intended to provide members with a foundation in Marxist-Leninist theory as well as the history of the Communist Party) being the one requirement in particular that usually elicited the most grumbling – when and if they took place at all, that is. Throughout the 1950s and 1960s, SED officials regularly reported participation rates of well below 50 percent: In 1952, for example, only 13 of 117 comrades at Zeiss regularly attended the *Parteilehrjahr*.[43] Such figures were not unusual, but to

---

[39] See, e.g., the KPKK reports in ThStA-R IV/A-4/10/081 and 082, 27.7.64, 5.1.65, 27.1.65. Available statistics nevertheless indicate that the vast majority of workers and party members kept up-to-date with their dues and that payment figures throughout the district usually exceeded 90 percent. See, e.g., ThStA-R, FDGB KV Slf 3549, Zusammenstellung über die Beitrags- und Soliaufkommen in der Gew. HaNaGe, 23.9.60; ThStA-R, FDGB KV Slf 6222, Stand der Erfüllung des Beitragsplanes und des Vertreibes von Solidaritätsaufkommen, 17.12.64.

[40] See, e.g., the reports from the summer of 1953 in ThStA-R, FDGB BV Gera 709/178 and 851/208. Also see Chapter 8 on the general absence of collective action in Saalfeld.

[41] ThStA-R IV/A-4/10/081, Prot. der LS der SED GO–Wema, 6.10.64; ThStA-R IV/A-4/10/082, IB der KPKK Slf, 26.2.65.

[42] This is mentioned in ThStA-R IV/A-7/220/409, Prot. der MV der SED GO–Kraftverkehr, 18.5.66. Though less common, refusals to pay dues based on gross income continued to be reported throughout the remainder of the decade. See in particular the series of KPKK reports in ThStA-R IV/A-4/10/081–2.

[43] ThStA-R IV/7/231/1166, Prot. der MV der SED GO–Zeiss, 20.5.52. For similarly low figures at other factories throughout the district, see ThStA-R IV/4/10/250, IB der SED–KL Slf, 18.8.55.

TABLE 2. *SED Membership in the Saalfeld District (all figures are percentages unless otherwise noted)*

	1954	1959	1964	1971
By social group				
Industrial workers	48.5	41.2	48.5	53.2
White-collar employees	32.8	32.6	23.2	13.7
Collective (LPG) farmers	1.6	1.8	3.0	2.9
Intelligentsia	6.6	11.5	10.9	15.6
Pensioners	3.9	5.7	6.6	11.9
Others	6.6	7.2	7.8	2.7
By gender				
Men	80.9	80.4	78.4	73.2
Women	19.1	19.6	21.6	26.8
TOTAL NUMBER	6045	6450	7670	8298

Source: ThStA Rudolstadt IV/A-4/10/086 and IV/B-4/10/106.

the even greater chagrin of local officials, attendance rates were especially low among production workers – and sometimes higher among nonmembers who were not even required to participate.[44] While this clearly suggested that party membership (Table 2) was not necessarily an indication of political sympathies or interests, high attendance by the politically unattached also might have had something to do with career considerations: Noting that half of the participants had decided to drop out of one seminar once the factory director had stopped teaching the course, the party secretary at the VEB Wema speculated that many had shown up only to impress the boss.[45]

To justify their absence, SED members would usually point to their many professional, familial, and political duties. While officials usually dismissed such excuses as "ridiculous" (e.g., that "I have to feed the goats because my wife is sick" or that "they had to chop wood at home, but actually sat in a pub and played skat," a popular card game), some admitted that party gatherings stimulated little interest because they were often boring or dry – especially because of the lengthy and usually formulaic speeches delivered by the first secretary.[46]

On irregularly scheduled meetings or no meetings at all, see ThStA-R IV/4/10/263, IB der SED–KL Slf, 28.10.60. Officials at one local school similarly reported in the late 1950s that almost all of the pupils there were in the FDJ, but that "very few actively" participated. See ThStA-R, FDJ–KL Slf 205, IB, 24.2.58.

44 According to statistics from 1953 for the entire district, regular attendance levels among party and nonparty members were 35 and 55 percent, respectively; a decade later, nonparty members still made up a quarter of all participants in Saalfeld. See ThStA-R IV/4/10/246, IB der SED–KL Slf, 28.10.53; ThStA-R IV/A-4/10/097, IB der SED–KL Slf, 17.9.65. On higher participation rates among white-collar personnel, see, e.g., ThStA-R, Maxh. 390, Teilnehmer der Kreisabendschule für das Lehrjahr 1950/51, n.d.

45 ThStA-R IV/7/230/1158, Prot. der MV der SED GO–Wema, 20.1.55.

46 See the reports from Zeiss in ThStA-R IV/7/231/1166, Prot. der MV der SED GO–Zeiss, 21.1.55; ThStA-R IV/7/231/1164, Prot. der Sitz. der SED BPL–Zeiss, 23.7.54. Also see the critical KPKK reports in ThStA-R IV/A-4/10/081.

Many members assiduously tried to avoid party gatherings for other reasons as well: because of the fear that they might somehow inadvertently incriminate themselves during discussion periods, or because of the fact that such meetings were often the place where members were called to task in front of their peers for improper behavior or otherwise unsatisfactory political performance. Yet the most common excuse by far was that too much was expected of them in general. In addition to their regular jobs, party members were required to rally their colleagues in support of party and state policy, subscribe to the official party newspaper, and participate in professional, political, and military training. Called to task for not regularly reading the official SED organ, *Neues Deutschland*, one comrade explained that he had canceled his subscription because he worked every day until 8 P.M. and was then unable to read at night because he was simply exhausted: "I'm just not able to absorb so much: First I have evening classes, then *Parteilehrjahr*, party meetings, etc. We're only human. . . . "[47]

Party functionaries were also only human, of course, and many similarly complained about being seriously overburdened with too many responsibilities. Because of a widespread reluctance to volunteer, many were forced to accept a large number of positions and then eventually quit when the pressure became too great – such as one management official at Zeiss who admitted that he would never have joined the SED if he had known that the responsibilities of party membership were so demanding. Related comments at the optical firm prompted one exasperated party member to conclude that "the lethargy is the same all over the place. Where is the spirit of someone like Lenin?"[48] Like-minded zealots frequently censured those rank-and-file members who failed to agitate sufficiently among nonmembers – which was tied, at least in part, to fears that they would alienate their colleagues by expressing unpopular views in support of official policy. As one woman at the Wema factory explained, she was the only party member in her small department and did not have the energy to cope with things alone; instead, she preferred to "look out the window" and not "say anything anymore because she's always looked at awry."[49]

That most Saalfelders lacked the fighting spirit of earlier times was a common refrain among nostalgic old-timers, who, like many officials, claimed that the widespread reluctance of party members to participate in various sociopolitical activities or assume official functions was a strong indication of political apathy and low "ideological consciousness." Yet even during the Weimar period, KPD functionaries had regularly lamented the poor participation and low turnouts

---

[47] ThStA-R IV/7/226/1135, Prot. der MV der SED GO–Rotstern, 15.12.55.

[48] ThStA-R IV/7/231/1162, Prot. der Berichtswahlversammlung in Zeiss, 10.12.55; ThStA-R IV/7/231/1166, Prot. der MV der SED GO–Zeiss, 21.1.55.

[49] The death threats received by two supposedly progressive SED members several years earlier gave some idea of what those who spoke up too forcefully in favor of official policy could sometimes expect. See ThStA-R IV/B-4/10/086, Niederschr. über Aussprachen mit Mitgliedern der SED APO–Leitung–Wema, October 1970; BStU ASt-G 0552, Lagebericht 1962 III. und IV. Quartale, 21.12.62.

at party meetings.[50] This important fact strongly suggests the need for caution when drawing conclusions about the meaning of postwar political apathy: Refusals to comply with the demands of the party and state were not *necessarily* a sign of disillusionment or a subtle form of protest, in other words, and should not automatically be construed as such. That said, and as we saw in Chapter 4, it was nevertheless true that many members failed to agitate or chastise peers who expressed politically unacceptable views because they often sympathized with them or harbored many of the same grievances themselves – thanks to shared experiences and similar everyday frustrations. As a result, party officials at Zeiss concluded, there was usually little difference between what SED members and those who were not in the party had to say at factory gatherings. Or, as officials at Rotstern complained, the former would often sit on trains or in the factory during "negative discussions" and either say nothing or just nod in agreement.[51]

All of this naturally alarmed party officials, who – because of fears that a failure to live up to certain standards would weaken respect for and diminish trust in the SED, provide the enemy with ammunition, and give nonmembers an excuse for not complying with official demands – expected the rank-and-file to set a positive example in terms of their political engagement and economic performance.[52] For similar reasons, officials were especially concerned that functionaries in responsible positions conduct themselves in a morally irreproachable manner. That was why one leading management official and party member at the VEB Wema was not given an official funeral in 1959 after suffering a fatal heart attack while away from home and in the arms of his mistress – a decision apparently influenced by comments made by several nonmembers: "If one holds sermons about socialist morals, one should also act accordingly."[53]

In most cases, improper behavior and criminal activity led to official reprimands or even expulsion from the SED. In 1968, for example, one factory

---

[50] See Eric Weitz, *Creating German Communism: From Popular Protests to Socialist State* (Princeton, NJ, 1997), 222–5, 257–63. For claims that such alleged apathy was a sign of poor ideological consciousness, see, e.g., ThStA-R IV/7/222/1060, IB der SED GO–Maxh., 24.7.56.

[51] ThStA-R IV/7/231/1166, Prot. der MV der SED GO–Zeiss, 21.1.55; ThStA-R IV/4/10/249, IB der SED–KL Slf, 17.2.55; ThStA-R IV/A-7/226/483, Prot. der MV der SED GO–TSW Rotstern, 12.11.65.

[52] See, e.g., ThStA-R IV/7/230/1153, Prot. der LS der SED GO–Wema, 19.4.52.

[53] Similar misgivings had been voiced there two years earlier about a recent decision to assign the former head of the District Party Secretariat – who had been removed from power because of an alleged extramarital affair with a younger woman – to another responsible position, this time at an MTS in the countryside. The reference to "socialist morals" was an allusion to the "Ten Commandments of Socialist Morality" proclaimed by Walter Ulbricht in 1958. See ThStA-R IV/7/230/1156, Prot. der LS der SED GO–Wema, 13.5.59; ThStA-R IV/7/230/1160, IB der SED GO–Wema, 5.7.57. These and other cases are examined in Andrew Port, "Moralizing 'from Above' and 'from Below': Social Norms, Family Values, and Adultery in the German Democratic Republic" (paper presented at the annual meeting of the German Studies Association, Salt Lake City, UT, October 1998).

party cell unanimously voted to expel a member (a former policeman, no less) who had recently been arrested for puncturing automobile tires and stabbing two deer in the town zoo while inebriated – a sensational case that attracted a good deal of local attention.[54] Damage control was obviously an important consideration in such decisions – which was why authorities also demanded that both officials and the rank-and-file maintain a united front, especially before nonmembers: Internecine disputes conducted in public, unsolicited withdrawals from the SED, and open criticism of official policy were all frowned upon because of justifiable fears that they would weaken the strength and integrity of the party and thus hamper enforcement of its more unpopular policies.[55]

Pacifism and the "Revenge of the Little Man"

Few policies were more unpopular than military recruitment and paramilitary training – and few created as much open dissension within the local party apparatus. In fact, the massive enlistment campaigns that began in the early 1950s in an effort to build up East Germany's security forces triggered widespread resistance in Saalfeld and throughout the GDR. The first major phase began in 1952 immediately following the creation of the Barracks Police, a paramilitary prototype of the National People's Army (NVA). A second phase took place after the establishment of the NVA in the fall of 1955, shortly after the GDR had been admitted to the Warsaw Pact. Local efforts to recruit young males met for the most part with resolute defiance – despite promises of higher earnings, generous vacation time, and superior provisioning reminiscent of earlier ones made to Wismut miners. Youths who refused to volunteer usually justified their decision by expressing opposition to remilitarization in general or by arguing that this would prevent them from achieving professional advancement. Many also argued that they would not shoot at other (i.e., West) Germans, or pointed to the apparent contradiction between remilitarization and official propaganda boasting of East Germany's desire for world peace. "The failure to make any progress," one party member explained, "is the fault of Walter Ulbricht, who declared in Leipzig in 1948: 'Those who take up weapons again should lose their hands'" – a statement also made, incidentally, by Franz Josef Strauß, the conservative West German politician and later minister of defense under Konrad Adenauer.[56]

---

54 ThStA-R IV/B-7/220/237, Auszug aus dem Prot. der SED GO–Kraftverkehr, 18.6.68.
55 See, e.g., the minutes of the factory party meetings in ThStA-R IV/7/230/1153 (29.1.53); ThStA-R IV/4/10/238 (1.4.58); ThStA-R IV/7/230/1157 (30.9.60); ThStA-R IV/7/226/1136 (28.9.61); ThStA-R IV/7/220/1003 (15.12.61).
56 ThStA-R IV/7/222/1060, IB der SED GO–Maxh., n.d. On widespread resistance, especially among youths, see ThStA-R IV/7/230/1160, Prot. der FDJ Konferenz, 11.7.52; ThStA-R IV/4/10/249, 253, and 266, IB der SED–KL Slf, 22.4.55, 5.5.55, 9.6.55, 26.4.57, 13.10.61. On similar resistance to remilitarization elsewhere in the GDR, see Uwe Koch, *Das Ministerium für Staatssicherheit, die Wehrdienstverweigerer der DDR und die Bausoldaten der Nationalen Volksarmee* (Schwerin, 1997); idem, *Zähne Hoch Kopf zusammenbeissen: Dokumente zur Wehrdienstverweigerung in der DDR, 1962–1990* (Kuckenshagen, 1994); Corey Ross, *Constructing Socialism at the Grass-Roots: The Transformation of East Germany, 1945–65*

The difficult task of finding enough volunteers to fill the recruitment quotas set for each firm generally fell to factory SED officials, some of whom considered this to be their main duty during the 1950s.[57] Faced with limited success as well as increasing pressure from above, they consequently resorted to a variety of coercive methods aimed at meeting the quotas. The most common form of intimidation was the prohibition of job training or enrollment at a university: As combative officials at Zeiss put it, "every youth not willing to defend his homeland is not entitled to study at the expense of the working class."[58] Distancing themselves from such aggressive tactics, many rank-and-file party members refused to assist officials in their efforts to win volunteers: "[T]he vast majority are against compulsory military service," party officials at the Maxhütte concluded in the summer of 1956. Those members whose children refused to join the Barracks Police or later the NVA were frequently subject to browbeating at party gatherings, where more acquiescent comrades often boasted of their own sons' readiness to defend the GDR.[59]

Pressure to join the army and participate in paramilitary training increased significantly during the months immediately following the erection of the Berlin Wall. In early September 1961, officials at a local secondary school announced that all male pupils would henceforth, and without exception, be required to participate in premilitary training.[60] That same week, Fritz Müller – who served as chairman of the SED District Secretariat for almost two decades beginning in 1955[61] – decreed that all youths who still refused to join the NVA would either be fired or forced to transfer to the Maxhütte blast furnace. The party secretary at Zeiss similarly announced that the "time for persuasion" was over and threatened that "difficult customers" (*Querköpfe*) who continued to oppose military participation would "soon be taken care of." This prompted several SED members at the optical firm to submit a written complaint to higher-level party officials in which they demanded to know whether the district chairman had the power to issue orders that were not "in harmony with the law" (military

(Houndsmill, UK, 2000), 72–8, 125–36. For the quotation by Strauß, see Bernt Engelmann, *Das neue Schwarzbuch: Franz Josef Strauß* (Cologne, 1980), 46.

57 See, e.g., ThStA-R IV/7/231/1163, Prot. der LS der SED GO–Zeiss, 12.8.52; ThStA-R IV/7/220/1002, Prot. der MV der SED GO–Kraftverkehr, 10.5.55.

58 ThStA-R IV/7/231/1163, Prot. der LS der SED GO–Zeiss, 12.8.52; ThStA-R IV/7/231/1165, Prot. der LS der SED GO–Zeiss, 20.5.55. Officials also tried to counter such resistance by offering stipends, greater training possibilities, and other material benefits to those who agreed to join the military. See, e.g., ThStA-R, FDGB KV Slf 3540, Prot. der erweiterten Sitz. der BGL–Brauhaus, 16.4.56; MxA-U, Kaderabt.: Abwanderung nach dem Westen (Berichte, 1949–57), Arbeitsbericht, 8.12.56.

59 ThStA-R IV/7/222/1060, IB der SED GO–Maxh., 19.7.56; ThStA-R IV/7/220/1003, Prot. der MV der SED GO–Kraftverkehr, 8.8.61. Taking a somewhat more subtle approach, local authorities also called on mothers to exert a more positive influence on their sons. See, e.g., ThStA-R IV/4/10/366, Arbeit der Frauenausschüsse, 30.6.55.

60 ThStA-R IV/4/10/266, IB der SED–KL Slf, 7.9.61.

61 For a short biography of Müller, see Heinrich Best and Heinz Mestrup, eds., *Die Ersten und Zweiten Sekretäre der SED: Machtstrukturen und Herrschaftspraxis in den thüringischen Bezirken der DDR* (Weimar, 2003), 688.

conscription was first introduced in January 1962). Müller's behavior drew a
sharp rebuke from outside officials, who warned that such methods were not
in tune with the party's leadership style.[62] The new pressure tactics employed
under the protective shadow of the Wall had the desired effect all the same: By
November 1961, more than 60 percent of all local males between ages eighteen
and twenty-three had officially declared their "readiness" to join the NVA.[63]

Local functionaries nevertheless continued to complain about the many difficulties involved in recruiting youths for the military: "When you think about
what we've been through recently," one party member at Rotstern lamented in
late 1961, "you could just go crazy hearing that nineteen-year-olds long for rest
at the end of the workday. These young people haven't yet realized what's going
on around them in the world." That was also why, officials contended, less than
10 percent of all youths in the district belonged at the time to the Society for
Sport and Technology (GST), a "mass organization" established in 1952 to provide young East Germans with premilitary training in preparation for future
armed service.[64] A series of discussions with local youths in the mid-1960s
revealed that many still remained impervious to official propaganda emphasizing the need to protect the "socialist homeland." Several asked, for example,
why authorities only spoke of western bombs when the eastern bloc had their
own as well: "[I]t doesn't make a difference if I die because of this or that atomic
bomb.... We can't do anything anyway to prevent a war. The people have
always had to bleed while their leaders just sit around and drink champagne."[65]

Given that memories of the last war were still fresh, it was not surprising that pacifist tendencies and opposition to mandatory military service were
widespread – and not just among young males. According to one report, local
women had broken down in tears at a military ceremony held at the town marketplace in 1956: "[H]ere we go again.... The uniforms are the same as the
ones worn during the fascist period. The *Volksarmee* is the same as the *Wehrmacht*."[66] For their part, many male party members were equally sympathetic
to the arguments used by their younger colleagues, in all likelihood because of
the pressure they themselves faced with regard to paramilitary participation.
In the second half of 1952, combat units (*Kampfgruppen*) were set up in factories throughout Saalfeld and the GDR. Despite increasing pressure to join these
detachments following the East German uprising of June 1953, district officials
continued to bemoan the low membership levels as well as the low turnouts

---

[62] ThStA-R IV/7/281/1349, Methoden der Armeebewerbung in Slf, 7.9.61, and correspondence,
     7.9.61, 18.9.61; ThStA-R IV/4/10/266, IB der SED–KL Slf, 7.9.61.
[63] ThStA-R, FDGB KV Slf 6178, Der politisch-ideologische Zustand der Arbeiterklasse, 15.11.61.
[64] ThStA-R IV/7/226/1136, Prot. der MV der SED GO–Rotstern, 28.11.61; ThStA-R IV/4/10/266,
     IB der SED–KL Slf, 13.10.61.
[65] ThStA-R, FDGB KV Slf 6278, Sekretariatsvorlage, 9.12.65.
[66] ThStA-R IV/7/222/1060, IB der SED GO–Maxh., 1.2.56. For similar reports of female oppo-
     sition to remilitarization, especially on the part of those who had lost family members during
     the Second World War, see ThStA-R IV/4/10/249, IB der SED–KL Slf, 24.3.55. On opposi-
     tion by members of the middle class (*Mittelstand*) to obligatory military service, see ThStA-R
     IV/4/10/250, IB der SED–KL Slf, 5.10.55.

FIGURE 5. Members of the newly created National People's Army marching along the Street of Peace in early 1960. © Bildarchiv des Stadtmuseums Saalfeld.

at training sessions, where participants would spend several hours each week learning how to use machine guns and fire rifles.[67]

Like many youths in the district, those who refused to participate frequently advanced pacifist arguments or referred to official propaganda: "I can't get used to these changes so quickly because the years 1939 to 1945 still give me pause for thought," or "I entered the party so that I would never have to pick up a weapon again. I won't go to the training sessions. I don't care if they put me up against a wall." One former soldier and standing member of the Party Secretariat at Zeiss – where opposition to remilitarization was especially strong – similarly refused to take a weapon in his hand, "and especially not if it means shooting relatives; [I'd] rather be imprisoned." Others argued that they were unable to participate because of poor health or complained that paramilitary training was too much of an added burden: "[W]e're all tensed up day and night and when our workday is over, we fall dog-tired into bed." Noncompliance was also often used in an instrumental fashion, however – and in such cases was usually linked to a personal grievance, such as the failure to receive adequate assistance with housing: "I refuse to join the combat unit," one stubborn white-collar worker told officials after not receiving a coveted apartment.

[67] On low membership rates and low turnouts throughout the district, see ThStA-R IV/4/10/247, 249, and 256, IB der SED–KL Slf, 22.4.54, 28.4.55, 2.6.55, 9.6.55, 13.6.55, 19.6.58. For a description of these training sessions, see ThStA-R IV/7/231/1165, Prot. der LS der SED GO–Zeiss, 31.3.55, 6.5.55.

"This is the revenge of the little man."[68] Other refusals were more clearly political in nature: In the early 1960s, a number of rank-and-file party members openly vented their anger about the Berlin Wall – and especially the role that combat units had played in its construction – by categorically rejecting any further paramilitary participation.[69]

Many older members of the SED – and especially former soldiers, who tended to be the most energetic paramilitary participants – showed little understanding for such refusals: "It's shameful just how little workers are prepared to defend that for which they've fought so hard. [That's] because the workforce is no longer class conscious.... Youths today don't know anything anymore about the struggles of yore." Military training was, the argument went, exactly what the younger generation needed: "[T]hat way these young smart asses [will] finally be brought up correctly ... we were also soldiers ... the draft can't hurt them: They'll just lose a bit of their smoothness."[70] Such comments shed light on a serious generational conflict at the time, one nourished by a widespread belief that most young people were spoiled because they enjoyed the fruits of the reconstruction (*Aufbau*) generation's exertions without contributing much themselves. A revealing exchange at the Maxhütte between an older colleague and a younger one who refused to join the Barracks Police – "because I want to still enjoy my life" – reflected the strong sense of resentment that such feelings engendered:

Older Colleague:	And how do you want to enjoy your life, pray tell? ...
Younger Colleague:	... we starved from 1945 to 1948 and now after four years where I and the others have finally had a chance to recuperate, it's supposed to start all over again. I repeat, I refuse to participate....
Older Colleague:	I'm forty years old now, born in 1912. My father was drafted in 1914 [and] fought until 1918. He didn't know what he fought for, and they weren't even asked if they wanted to join the military, like you, but simply had to go. They were forced. But the youths [today] have forgotten what the government has done for them. You, my friend, have it too good....[71]

Much of the resistance to recruitment was clearly motivated by self-interest; most Saalfelders simply wanted to improve their standard of living and had little desire to spend their weekends crawling around in mud while learning how to shoot automatic weapons. Yet many also objected to rearmament on

[68] See ThStA-R IV/7/231/1162, Prot. der Berichtswahlversammlung in Zeiss, 10.12.55; ThStA-R IV/7/222/1060, IB der SED GO–Maxh., n.d.; ThStA-R IV/7/231/1165, Prot. der LS der SED GO–Zeiss, 31.3.55; ThStA-R IV/7/220/1002, Prot. der MV der SED GO–Kraftverkehr, 9.12.55. Also see the series of documents related to a 1970 investigation of the APO–Technik–Wema by the KPKK in ThStA-R IV/B-4/10/086.

[69] See, e.g., ThStA-R IV/4/10/265, IB der SED–KL Slf, 16.8.61.

[70] ThStA-R IV/7/230/1158, Prot. der MV der SED GO–Wema, 7.12.56; ThStA-R IV/7/222/1060, IB der SED GO–Maxh., 18.2.56.

[71] MxA-U, BGL 264, Prot. der BV in der Gaszentrale, 29.7.52.

principle – as did many other East *and* West Germans at the time. This was important, because it suggested an important evolution in the German mentality after – and largely because of – the Second World War. Even if it is doubtful that Germans qua Germans were more inherently militaristic than other Europeans during the modern period, it is difficult to deny the strong Prussian military traditions that increasingly pervaded many aspects of German society after unification in the late nineteenth century.[72] The postwar socialist regime may have eagerly followed in that tradition, but many ordinary East Germans were obviously less than willing to do so: The experiences of the last major conflagration – along with the strong likelihood that the next military conflict would be fought against their own people – had apparently helped exorcise the militarist demons of yore.[73]

Whatever their reasons, local youths were not the only ones annoyed by continued recruitment pressures; so, too, were harried management officials angered by the way in which the loss of young men to the military exacerbated already severe labor shortages. Opposition was especially strong among top management and union officials at Zeiss, where approximately 200 youths had left the optical firm in search of employment elsewhere because of the intense pressure exerted there by party officials during the 1950s. Others responded to this sort of intimidation by fleeing to the Federal Republic, which prompted one party member to complain in response to similar developments at his factory, "Soon we won't have any skilled workers left at all."[74] That was a widespread concern throughout the district – and one that leads us back to our starting point: the flight of disgruntled Saalfelders to the West in response to unpopular policies and unfavorable developments at home.

Fleeing the Republic

Just as the Soviet cosmonaut Yuri Gagarin was preparing to escape the earth's gravity, officials in Saalfeld were struggling more than ever to prevent local residents from escaping from the GDR. At a meeting held in March 1961,

---

[72] See Ute Frevert, *Die kasernierte Nation: Militärdienst und Zivilgesellschaft in Deutschland* (Munich, 2001); Charles Maier, "German war, German peace," in Mary Fulbrook, ed., *German History since 1800* (New York, 1997), 539–45. For literature on West German resistance to rearmament at the time, see Chapter 2, footnote 78. More generally, see Manfred Messerschmidt, "Das Bild der Wehrmacht in Deutschland seit 1945," *Revue d'Allemagne* 30 (1998): 117–25.

[73] According to one report supplied to the SPD *Ostbüro*, however, there was purportedly much local support for Konrad Adenauer because of his rearmament policies – and little support for the West German SPD because of its opposition to rearmament. See AdsD, Ostbüro 00523j, report, 12.5.58. In a similar vein, one young man sent a letter to a friend in the Federal Republic stating that "he would understand why he would have to perform military service if he were in the *Bundeswehr*," i.e., in the West German army. See ThStA-R, FDJ–KL Slf 205, Beschluss, 29.9.58.

[74] See ThStA-R IV/7/230/1158, Prot. der MV der SED GO–Wema, 3.10.57; ThStA-R IV/7/230/1160, Bericht über den Einsatz einer Instrukteurbrigade in der SED BPO–Thuringia, 1.10.52. On turnover figures and flight to the West by youths at Zeiss, see the reports in ThStA-R IV/7/231/1162–3, 1166. Also see Chapter 7 on labor shortages.

members of the District Council noted with great concern the sharp rise in the number of refugees that year and especially the recent disappearance of nine medical specialists who had supposedly been lured to the West by promises of attractive positions and generous credits: If such trends continued, they warned, the district's new hospital would soon have a shortage of trained personnel.[75] In the opening statement at an emergency gathering of Saalfeld's highest-level officials that May, Fritz Müller bemoaned the apparent helplessness with which local functionaries looked on as the district's current and future labor force slowly bled away; in a lengthy harangue, the trained porcelain painter characteristically blamed those in attendance for failing to take the requisite steps to prevent further flight or discover the motivations of those who had already left.[76]

Prophylactic investigations of suspected cases as well as interviews with friends, family members, and colleagues had, in fact, regularly taken place over the past decade, giving officials some idea of the most common reasons for *Republikflucht* – or "flight from the republic." Their subsequent analyses suggested that personal reasons were usually paramount: domestic difficulties at home, for example, or a desire to join relatives or loved ones in the Federal Republic.[77] Despite frequent claims that many of the migrants had succumbed to organized recruitment by enemies in the West, the local police acknowledged in July 1961 that there was no concrete evidence of such activities: They averred at the same time, however, that few cases were motivated by negative opinions about East Germany. In a surprisingly candid address delivered several months earlier, the *Landrat* had nevertheless admitted that improper bureaucratic behavior had frequently "forced" a number of people to leave – such as one angry couple who fled to the West after an unsuccessful effort to relocate the woman's recently widowed father to Saalfeld: "We don't need any pensioners," the Town Council brusquely informed them, "we already have enough of those."[78]

Bureaucratic nastiness, familial considerations, encouragement by relatives in the West, and a "desire for adventure" (*Abenteuerlust*) undoubtedly played some part in many of the decisions to flee. But the overwhelming emphasis that officials gave to such factors clearly suggested that it was more comforting for them to accept these reasons than to admit that in most cases, a more

---

[75] KrA-S 12564, Prot. der KR–Sitz., 3.8.61. According to a discussion held with two dozen doctors at the local hospital, most of their colleagues had left because of the strict limits placed on travel to the West. See ADL, BV Gera 25070, Situation in der Wahlvorbereitung, 17.8.61. On the effects that this had on local medical treatment, see AdsD, Ostbüro 00523j, report, 25.9.58. On the flight of medical personnel more generally, see Anna-Sabine Ernst, *Die beste Prophylaxe ist der Sozialismus: Ärzte und medizinische Hochschullehrer in der SBZ/DDR 1945–1961* (Munster, 1997), 54–72.

[76] KrA-S 12636, Prot. zur Beratung über Bevölkerungsbewegung, 5.9.61.

[77] See the reports on hundreds of individual cases from the mid-1950s in KrA-S 16181.

[78] KrA-S 12636, Bericht über die Bevölkerungsbewegung im I. Halbjahr 1961, 15.7.61, Bericht über die Bevölkerungsbewegung, 3.12.61, and Niederschr. über eine geführte Aussprache mit E. J., 7.24.61.

TABLE 3. *Flight of Saalfelders to the Federal Republic (all figures are percentages unless otherwise noted)*

	1953	1954	1957	1958	1959	1960	1961 (Jan–July)
Men	NA	NA	51.4	32.9	43.6	42.4	38.7
Women	NA	NA	36.2	45.8	40.1	38.1	37.3
Children	NA	NA	12.4	21.3	16.3	19.5	24.0
TOTAL NUMBER	488	612	970	493	307	446	279
By age							
0–15	14.1	17.5	12.8	21.9	17.3	20.2	
16–18	6.1	6.9	10.8	11.2	9.4	7.2	
19–25	19.5	20.8	34.6	18.5	25.1	25.3	
26–39	25.0	25.7	19.9	16.8	20.5	18.6	
40–50	15.4	10.8	11.6	17.2	11.1	14.1	
51 and over	10.9	18.5	10.2	14.4	16.6	14.6	
By occupation							
Industrial workers	35.3	45.0	59.8	35.0	46.7	55.4	
Farmers	1.9	1.9	0.2	0.3	0.0	1.8	
Intelligentsia	1.6	2.2	1.4	1.9	3.3	2.1	
White-collar workers	21.0	22.2	17.1	19.4	22.3	17.4	
Independent/ craftsmen	8.0	5.2	3.3	5.6	7.0	3.6	
Pensioners	10.6	7.3	2.4	6.9	2.5	4.2	
Housewives	21.8	16.2	15.8	31.0	18.2	15.6	
TOTAL NUMBER	377	463	830	377	242	334	

Source: KrA Saalfeld 16181 and 12636; ThStA Rudolstadt, BDVP Gera 21/222 (statistics for 1955 and 1956 are unavailable).

general dissatisfaction with life in the GDR – coupled with the allure of better economic opportunities and greater political freedom in the Federal Republic – had ultimately led to this weighty step. Anger about military recruitment or the failure to receive a place at the university helped ensure, for example, that youths consistently made up about a third to half of all those who left Saalfeld each year (Table 3). And as this suggests, flight was often indeed an unambiguous response to, and protest against, unpopular policies and developments at home. But as in the case of sociopolitical apathy, it would be wrong to conclude from this that *Republikflucht* was necessarily an expression of fundamental political opposition to the regime as such. That was undoubtedly true in many cases. But this muted expression of protest was almost always motivated by a complex mixture of factors, among them the hope for a better standard of living elsewhere.[79]

[79] On the variety of complex reasons motivating flight, see the balanced arguments in Major, "Going west"; Bispinck, "Republikflucht"; Ross, *Socialism*, 148–53. For an analysis that

Economic improvement was relative, of course – as in the case of one comparatively well-situated young worker at the local crane factory who not only enjoyed a high income but also owned a television set and a motorcycle: Before fleeing, he boasted to his colleagues that he would now be able to buy a car.[80] It was unclear, however, that his initial experiences in the Federal Republic would have necessarily been as rosy as he had hoped. According to one elderly woman who had just returned to the GDR after having lived for a while in Munich, East Germans were involved in "constant brawls" with the Hungarians and Yugoslavians housed with them in a nearby refugee camp. Their relations with West Germans were apparently not much better: Angry about the fact that a garden colony had been torn down to make room for the migrants, local residents had supposedly told them that "if Hitler were still alive, he would have gassed all of you refugees. But Adenauer, the stupid dog, brings you over."[81]

This woman was one of almost 800 "returnees" (*Rückkehrer*) and "new arrivals" (*Zuziehende*) from the Federal Republic who had decided to swim against the current and settle down in Saalfeld by the time the Wall was built. Often fleeing economic difficulties or criminal prosecution in the West, many of these people were lured to the district by promises of an apartment or a choice job. This created even more pressure on local officials – as well as resentment among those who already lived there but were unable to secure adequate housing or a desired position themselves. Authorities nevertheless welcomed such persons in the hope that they would help offset the chronic labor shortages that plagued local industry.[82] Yet their numbers remained woefully inadequate, and they were thus unable to compensate for the steady stream westward of the skilled and the trained: Of the 970 persons who left Saalfeld in 1957 alone, approximately three-quarters were blue- and white-collar workers – consistently the two largest social groups that departed (Table 3).

Illegal escape was not without danger for those who fled or those closest to them. While unsuccessful attempts often led to hefty prison sentences – if not injury or even death at the border – the families and acquaintances of those who made it to the West normally attracted the sustained suspicion of local

emphasizes the oppositional aspect of flight, see Bernd Eisenfeld, "Die Ausreisebewegung – eine Erscheinungsform widerständigen Verhaltens," in Ulrich Poppe, Rainer Eckert, and Ilko-Sascha Kowalczuk, eds., *Zwischen Selbstbehauptung und Anpassung: Formen des Widerstands und der Opposition in der DDR* (Berlin, 1995), 192–223; idem, "Flucht und Ausreise – Erkenntnisse und Erfahrungen," in Clemens Vollnhals and Jürgen Weber, eds., *Der Schein der Normalität: Alltag und Herrschaft in der SED–Diktatur* (Munich, 2002), 341–72.

[80] KrA-S 16184, Bericht über den Stand der Bevölkerungsbewegung, 22.2.60, and Begründung der Republikflucht, 4.29.61.

[81] KrA-S 12636, Auszug aus dem Rapport Nr. 57/61, 14.5.61.

[82] KrA-S 16184, Bericht über den Stand der Bevölkerungsbewegung, 2.22.60, and Bericht über die Aufnahme und Eingliederung von Rückkehrern und Zuziehenden aus Westdeutschland und Westberlin im Kr. Slf, n.d.

authorities, with unpleasant interrogations sometimes followed by disagreeable penalties such as the loss of an apartment now deemed to be underoccupied. During postflight investigations, family, friends, and colleagues typically claimed that the departure had come as a complete surprise – followed by a letter or telegram from the Federal Republic. In a discussion with local officials in June 1961, the mother of one young woman said that she was "very disappointed" by her daughter's recent disappearance, but that she had had no prior indication of her plans: She merely "received a message not to be mad and not to waste her time doing anything because she wouldn't return." Some relatives were far more proactive: Earlier that year, another woman had warned district officials in person that her fifteen-year-old sister was planning to visit their father in the Federal Republic over Easter. Requesting that the girl not be given a travel permit (the coveted PM 12a), she feared that the man would try to persuade his daughter to remain abroad.[83]

Whatever the motivation, such warnings were not entirely uncommon – further evidence of the way in which district officials could often rely on the active participation of the local populace to report on undesired behavior. But authorities were often alerted to planned departures in other ways as well, e.g., by reports of persons selling their homes, large consumer durables, and other valuable possessions. Angry comments by some individuals that they would flee if they were not given an apartment, a promotion, or permission to visit the West frequently tipped off officials as well.[84] These were usually mere threats made in a sometimes successful attempt to achieve a concrete professional or material objective. But they were also often a last desperate act of voice – a prelude to an exit marked by the poignant image of a lone person making his or her way to the train station, a single suitcase in hand.

What was the significance of this ultimately silent form of protest for the long-term stability of the regime? The steady loss of labor and technical expertise undoubtedly helped undermine the economic viability of the GDR. But did the disappearance of those discontented individuals who decided to "vote with their feet" somehow help to shore up the regime as well? Though a relatively small percentage of the population – which was entirely understandable, given the personal hardship involved in leaving one's home, possessions, family, and loved ones behind – those who fled did help thin the ranks of the disgruntled, at least in part. And as a result, flight to the West arguably served as a safety valve of sorts that did "contribute to political stability."[85] The absence of large-scale protests following the mass exodus of many involved but not arrested during the June 1953 upheaval certainly supports this conclusion. It nevertheless remains uncertain whether those who opted for the typically individual act of exit were

---

[83] On these and similar cases, see the reports in KrA-S 12636 and 16184.
[84] Ibid.
[85] Günter de Bruyn, *Jubelschreie, Trauergesänge* (Frankfurt am Main, 1991), 36–7.

also the same persons who would have been most suitable or willing to lead more collective and offensive forms of protest.

The foregoing discussion demonstrates the many challenges local authorities faced in mobilizing the masses for the socialist project and inculcating new forms of desired behavior and attitudes. Relying on Jürgen Habermas's concept of *civil privatism*, Marc Howard has persuasively argued that those who lived under Soviet-style regimes became "organizationally passive and detached" because of their everyday experiences. That was clearly the case in Saalfeld during the early decades of the GDR, and it may have led to a distinctive type of behavior and "consciousness" – but decidedly not one in tune with the expectations of the East German leadership. In fact, large numbers of ordinary Saalfelders remained steadfastly aloof from the regime, immune to its propaganda, critical of its policies, and resistant to its onerous sociopolitical demands. If a distinct GDR identity developed east of the Elbe, then it was one that arguably came into being *after* the fall of the Wall with the rise of *Ostalgie*, i.e., a widespread nostalgia for certain aspects of the period prior to unification.[86]

Whatever their feelings since 1989 about life in the GDR, exit, voice, and apathy were three of the most common ways in which many Saalfelders chose at the time to express their discontent about unwelcome developments or resist the many unbearable demands imposed on them by the party and state. They increasingly became the most popular "weapons of the weak" after 1953, subsequently serving as a surrogate for more forceful shows of displeasure.[87] To that extent, they undoubtedly acted as a stabilizing force during the remaining years of the Ulbricht era.

Yet, the everyday strategies of resistance, refusal, and nonconformity made it abundantly clear that a great deal of ferment and potential for unrest continued to exist at the grass roots – while demonstrating at the same time that many Saalfelders were more than willing to vent their dissatisfaction, be it through incessant grumbling or the more subtle (and less than subtle) forms of protest discussed in this chapter. Why that failed to translate into a more energetic challenge to the SED regime remains to be seen. To get at this central question, the

---

[86] See Marc Howard, *The Weakness of Civil Society in Post-Communist Europe* (Cambridge, 2003) (quotation from p. 153). On official attempts at as well as the difficulty of creating a "GDR national identity," see Sigrid Meuschel, *Legitimation und Parteiherrschaft in der DDR: Zum Paradox von Stabilität und Revolution in der DDR, 1945–1989* (Frankfurt am Main, 1992), 283–91. For an insightful criticism of the way in which many scholars now use the term *identity*, see Lutz Niethammer, *Kollektive Identität: Heimliche Quellen einer unheimlichen Konjunktur* (Reinbek bei Hamburg, 2000). On the *Ostalgie* phenomenon – which arguably came in response to the open disdain of many in the West for the earlier experiences of those who had lived under Communist rule, as well as to the difficulty of adjusting to the exigencies of a liberal market economy – see the literature cited in footnote 18 of the Introduction.
[87] James Scott, *Weapons of the Weak: Everyday Forms of Peasant Resistance* (New Haven, CT, 1985).

next three chapters will focus on industrial relations on the East German shop floor and especially on the main sources of economic conflict and discontent in Saalfeld – many of which, as we saw in Part I, had sparked widespread unrest during the first postwar decade. The subsequent interaction between factory officials and those under their charge, the often successful way in which the latter endeavored to defend their everyday material interests, and the relations among workers themselves all provide, as we shall see, one important answer to the puzzle of stability.

6

Power in the People's Factories

Three years after the June 1953 uprising, the head of the VEB Rotstern's praline packaging department complained that female workers under her charge were regularly voicing their opinions about "existing problems" at the factory, which had "never been the case" under Ernst Hüther, the former owner. A member of the SED and one of the few women in Saalfeld to hold a leading managerial position at the time, she believed that this was the result of conscious "instigation" – and in a sense, she was right: Apparently animated by the disturbances in Poland and Hungary that year, local factories were abuzz with criticism about the shortcomings of the socialist economy, with many focusing in particular on wage and price levels. As the SED District Secretariat opined, "some colleagues think that this is now the time to voice their demands."[1]

But many in Saalfeld had openly expressed their discontent before, and would continue to do so well after, the 1956 upheavals abroad. In fact, East German authorities actually encouraged workers to voice their opinions and articulate their grievances, as long as they were not fundamental, overtly political attacks against the regime. At a gathering of high-level factory officials in 1958, for example, the Maxhütte's assistant director emphasized the need to stimulate greater participation at regularly scheduled production meetings. The purpose of these gatherings, he explained, was to give workers the opportunity to learn and speak out about important developments concerning the entire steel mill: This would encourage them to develop a greater sense of responsibility for "their" factory and help reduce apathy by making workers feel that their opinions were listened to and taken into consideration. Moreover, it would guard against the impression that only a few specialists ran the economy and that the working classes merely "played a subordinate role." This was, in essence,

---

[1] See ThStA-R IV/7/226/1137, IB der SED GO–Rotstern, 30.10.56; ThStA-R IV/4/10/252, IB der SED–KL Slf, 3.11.56. On similar ferment at this time throughout the GDR, see Armin Mitter and Stefan Wolle, *Untergang auf Raten: Unbekannte Kapitel der DDR–Geschichte* (Munich, 1993), 163–295.

the GDR's answer to the West German policy of factory codetermination (*Mitbestimmung*) – and an obvious attempt to forestall a repeat performance of June 1953.[2]

Similar forums for discussion and exchange between workers and factory officials had nevertheless existed in Saalfeld and the rest of the GDR since the early postwar years, e.g., at gatherings of the party rank-and-file or at more informal discussions held with entire departments or within individual production brigades.[3] At annual factory labor contract negotiations, discussion periods generally followed lengthy speeches in which management and union functionaries rendered an account of their performance, detailing the extent to which they had carried out formal resolutions or fulfilled pledges set forth in the previous contract. These exchanges gave workers the chance to air their grievances, pose questions, and make recommendations or requests about pressing issues such as wage and norm levels, poor working conditions, material shortages, and other production difficulties. Repeated complaints about the failure of officials to make requested changes or make good on their promises suggested, however, that this procedure was largely ritualistic. As a result, most workers tended to feel apathetic about these meetings: "I sense that the BKV has not really seeped into the consciousness of most colleagues," one worker commented in 1955; "if it had ... there would not be such a mass exodus like the one we have today." This had been one of the most important consequences of the first contract negotiations four years earlier, when worker protests had not led to immediate and significant modification of the original drafts.[4]

Subsequent meetings only served to strengthen the impression that these sessions were a waste of time and would not lead to any meaningful change: During the discussion period, officials usually responded to difficult demands by explaining why they could not be met, by claiming that they did not have the proper authority to deal with these issues, or by evasively promising to investigate the matter further or consult with higher-level authorities. While this would occasionally lead to partial modifications, the fact that the same grievances continued to arise over and over again strengthened the justifiable impression that little had improved as a result of these talks. The notes of one meeting in the Maxhütte's gas department suggested just how much frustration this engendered: After the minutes of the last gathering were read aloud, those in attendance "realized that not one of the adopted measures had been implemented." It was "pointless" to make further suggestions, they

[2] MxA-U, Betriebsdirektion: Prot. der WL–Besprechungen, 1957–61, Prot. der Sitz. des WL–Kollektivs, 21.5.58. More generally, see Friedrich-Ebert-Stiftung, ed., *Mitwirkung und Mitbestimmung: Die Rechte der Arbeitnehmer und ihrer Gewerkschaften in beiden deutschen Staaten* (Bonn, 1971).

[3] Based on a Soviet model, brigades were teams of workers charged with jointly carrying out given tasks within the factory. See Jörg Roesler, *Inszenierung oder Selbstgestaltungswille? Zur Geschichte der Brigadenbewegung in der DDR während der 50er Jahre* (Berlin, 1994).

[4] ThStA-R, FDGB BV Gera 855/210, Prot. über den Abschluß des BKV in der Bohrmaschinenfabrik, 22.3.55. See Chapter 1 on the first BKV.

complained, as long as officials continued to consider them "irrelevant." In 1960, the SED District Secretariat admitted itself that the BKV was still often dealt with in a "perfunctory" manner; it did claim, however, that workers now reacted with "less patience" than in the past and even criticized factory functionaries who failed to make good on their pledges.[5] But apart from incessant grumbling, extralegal forms of protest, or appeals to higher-level authorities and other mediating agencies such as the Factory Conflict Commission, workers had no effective recourse when their superiors failed to respond to complaints or comply with requests.[6]

These poorly attended gripe sessions nevertheless had several important functions; moreover, they revealed modes of behavior that were characteristic of relations between local officials and workers. In the first place, the efforts by authorities to procure support for the BKV indicated the great importance they attached to winning acclamation for their policies, even if obtained under duress. Secondly, contract negotiations demonstrated the readiness of many Saalfelders, including low-level party and union functionaries, to voice open criticism of unpopular policies. By providing them with a semipublic outlet for expressing their grievances and articulating their wishes, they served as a safety valve of sorts and allowed factory functionaries to take the pulse of popular sentiment, which was then passed on to their superiors in a steady stream of reports and analyses that occasionally led to important policy revisions. Even if the same grievances continued to surface throughout the 1950s and 1960s, one should not underestimate the symbolic significance of factory officials having to appear before assembled workers to account for their own performance and respond to questions and grievances. The point is that this practice – almost unknown before the war, as the department head at Rotstern pointed out – must have given workers some sense of empowerment. And to that extent, it represented an important shift in industrial relations in the eastern half of Germany. The following chapter looks at the way in which this helped contribute to the stability of the regime; at the same time, it examines the role of party and union representatives in the local VEB and the extent to which their own everyday behavior served to shore up the regime on whose behalf they ostensibly acted.

Shop-Floor Etiquette

According to a popular joke that made the rounds in the Soviet bloc, there was an important distinction between capitalism and socialism: The former represented the exploitation of man by man – and the latter just the opposite. To be sure, official propaganda about the replacement of capitalist with new socialist forms of ownership was, in many respects, just that: propaganda. The means of production might have belonged to the people following the mass

---

[5] MxA-U, BGL 367, Prot. der PB in der Gaszentrale, 10.12.54; ThStA-R, FDGB KV Slf 6141, Referat, n.d.

[6] On the activities of the Factory Conflict Commissions, see, e.g., ThStA-R, FDGB KV Slf 6206, Analyse über die Arbeit der Konfliktkommission innerhalb des Kr. Slf, 28.3.62. Also see the minutes of sessions that took place at the Maxhütte in ThStA-R, Maxh. 27.

FIGURE 6. A meeting of the Clara Zetkin Brigade in 1968 at the VEB Thälmann graphics factory. Zetkin and Ernst Thälmann were leading figures in the German Communist Party before 1933. © Bildarchiv des Stadtmuseums Saalfeld.

expropriation of private property in the late 1940s, but it was still clear who gave and who followed orders, who made and who carried out important policy decisions. Traditional hierarchies more or less survived the series of industrial reforms introduced during the immediate postwar years, and the East German shop floor did not experience any absolute zero hour in 1945.[7]

7 On industrial relations in the GDR, see Peter Hübner, "Um Kopf und Kragen: Zur Geschichte der innerbetrieblichen Hierarchien im Konstituierungsprozeß der DDR–Gesellschaft," *Mitteilungen aus der Kulturwissenschaftlichen Forschung* 16 (1993): 210–32; idem, "Stagnation or Change? Transformations of the Workplace in the GDR," in Konrad Jarausch, ed., *Dictatorship as Experience: Towards a Socio-Cultural History of the GDR* (New York, 1999), 285–305. Also see Claus Friedrich, *Sozialistische Betriebsdemokratie in der DDR* (Frankfurt am Main, 1975); Thomas Reichel, "Die 'durchherrschte Arbeitsgesellschaft': Zu den Herrschaftsstrukturen und Machtverhältnissen in DDR–Betrieben," in Renate Hürtgen and Thomas Reichel, eds., *Der Schein der Stabilität: DDR–Betriebsalltag in der Ära Honeckers* (Berlin, 2001), 85–110.

Yet, as the director of the local optical firm pointed out, management officials had to remain "tough" in order to maintain their authority: This made them highly unpopular, he admitted, and frequently led to serious disputes between workers and their immediate supervisors, namely, the factory foremen and brigadiers (i.e., the leaders of individual production brigades). These administrative middlemen were responsible for a wide variety of tasks: monitoring worker performance and discipline, ensuring a smooth flow of production, encouraging greater worker productivity and efficiency, procuring acceptance of modified norms and new factory labor contracts. Because of their role as taskmasters and disciplinarians, shop-floor supervisors often clashed – verbally and sometimes even physically – with those under their charge: After getting into a fistfight with his brigadier, for example, one young worker bluntly told officials, "If I'm in the right, I don't consider the director or anyone else to be my superior but rather just another person."[8]

Often chosen for their superior training and skills as well as for the authority and popularity they supposedly enjoyed among their colleagues, the brigadiers served as both worker confidantes and brigade spokesmen in dealings with shop-floor personnel or higher-level authorities.[9] But, as the foregoing suggests, this intermediary role sometimes led to strained relations within the collective itself. The brigadier might have been considered *primus inter pares*, yet he (or she) also acted as an immediate supervisor of sorts and, in this capacity, often had to deal with disciplinary infractions or make unpopular decisions concerning wages and the distribution of premiums. Though most disputes tended to focus on shop-floor performance, the higher base wages awarded to brigadiers and foremen fueled a great deal of resentment as well. And as administrative officials, they were sometimes subject to the same types of criticism often made about supposedly lazy white-collar workers: "It'll be a good thing when the time finally comes that you [idlers] have to work again."[10]

Similar tensions also existed between workers and those functionaries specifically responsible for setting production quotas. Union officials at the VEB Textima sewing machine factory reported, for example, that the latter were often greeted with "yelling and screaming" when they appeared on the shop floor. But this could cut both ways: After one official supposedly threatened to set norms that would make them "sweat blood," workers lodged a formal complaint and demanded to know if such behavior was "acceptable." One of their colleagues similarly groused about the behavior of functionaries who "grin and

---

8 ThStA-R, FDGB BV Gera 851/208, Bericht über die Vorbereitung der Volkswahlen, 18.10.54; ThStA-R, FDGB BV Gera 855/210, Prot. der Sitz. der BGL-Abus, 6.10.54.

9 See Jörg Roesler, "Die Rolle des Brigadiers bei der Konfliktregulierung zwischen Arbeitsbrigaden und der Werkleitung," in Peter Hübner and Klaus Tenfelde, eds., *Arbeiter in der SBZ–DDR* (Essen, 1999), 413–38.

10 ThStA-R IV/4/10/247, IB der SED–KL Slf, 20.6.54. On tensions between blue- and white-collar workers, see Hübner, "Um Kopf und Kragen," as well as Chapter 8.

make faces behind his back" when determining production quotas and refused to work until the "correct" norm was introduced.[11]

Many workers not only refused to shy away from confrontations, but also took their superiors to task when they failed to live up to the expectations shaped by official discourse regarding the transformed nature of industrial relations under state socialism. Besides complaints about unfulfilled pledges or discourteous and insolent treatment, their displeasure often focused on poor contact with the "laboring masses." Such grievances surfaced throughout the 1950s and 1960 but were especially common during the two years following the June 1953 uprising, suggesting that the SED's self-criticism and admission of guilt at this time had made many workers even less willing than usual to put up with what they considered to be inappropriate behavior on the part of low-level functionaries. As one worker at the VEB Abus crane factory complained in early 1954, the union chairman was seldom seen on the shop floor: "Away from the desk," he demanded, "and down to the workers." Workers at the Maxhütte similarly wanted to know how some engineers and directors, whom they had not seen "even once," could get a sense of the everyday difficulties that plagued their department.[12] Rank-and-file party members made similar complaints about SED functionaries who seldom visited the shop floor to hold personal talks with staff members about their everyday problems and concerns. Many were also deeply disappointed when members of the Factory Party Secretariat (*Betriebsparteileitung*, or BPL) neglected to visit the sick or attend important family ceremonies – a charge leveled at many low-level union officials as well.[13]

Many workers had clear ideas, then, about what constituted proper shop-floor etiquette, and official failure to live up to those expectations produced great disappointment and resentment. That was equally true of the harsh way in which some "brutal" or "bad-tempered" functionaries dealt with those who had failed to toe the official line. In October 1954, for example, workers in the Maxhütte dolomite plant criticized one functionary for the harsh way in which he had recently scolded them about poor discipline at the workplace: Appropriating the same language the SED had used in June 1953 when censuring the "dictatorial" behavior of factory officials responsible for introducing higher norms, they roundly denounced his "sledge-hammer methods.... It's correct when you (*Du*) say that working hours have to be adhered to, but one can't

---

[11] ThStA-R, FDGB BV Gera 851/208, correspondence, 31.7.57, and Prot. der Produktionsberatung in der Abt. Rund- und Flaschenlieferei, 14.10.58. The Knoch sewing-machine factory became a VEB after 1945.

[12] ThStA-R, FDGB BV Gera 855/210, Prot. der Sitz. der BGL–Abus, 22.1.54; MxA-U, BGL 367, Prot. der PV in der Thomas–Züchterei, 9.3.54. According to an informant working for the SPD *Ostbüro*, party functionaries at the Maxhütte avoided contact with workers because of their strong opposition to the regime. See AdsD, Ostbüro 00523j, report, 30.10.57.

[13] See, e.g., the KPKK reports in ThStA-R IV/4/10/238. Also see the reports and minutes in ThStA-R IV/7/231/1163, 1165, 1166; ThStA-R, FDGB KV Slf 6222, Prot. der Sondersekretariatssitz. des FDGB KV, 15.7.64.

use such words" to make the point (a product of socialist egalitarian ideology, the informal form of address widely used between workers and their superiors arguably served to weaken the authority of those in more powerful positions by subtly whittling away at social stratification).[14]

Official ideology vaunting the changed nature of industrial relations under state socialism not only emboldened many workers, then, but also contributed to the setting of new standards for appropriate behavior. As the District Party Control Commission (KPKK, a watchdog organ responsible for monitoring the performance and behavior of individual members and cells) lectured SED officials at Rotstern, one must not only "teach the masses, but also learn from them [by] listening to the voice of the people."[15] Many officials accepted – or at least paid lip service to – worker rebukes, either admitting their own mistakes or criticizing those who had failed to act in an appropriate manner.

Two incidents help illustrate these points. In January 1953, union functionaries at the VEB Wema sent an angry letter to the official FDGB newspaper, *Die Tribüne*, in which they railed against a recent decision to cut funding for a new kitchen. After describing the "intolerable sanitary and social conditions" at the factory, they emphasized in particular that most workers were forced to eat at their machines because the kitchen had only fifteen seats located directly next to a toilet: "Those in 'responsible' positions would probably object with indignation if they had to eat their meals under similar conditions.... And what you would not accept for your own person is just as intolerable for our colleagues...." The letter concluded with a request that the paper send a reporter to the factory to determine whether or not "the legs of the office chairs used by administrators [are] too long, enthroning them in the clouds and making them lose sight of the ground under their feet...." The factory received money for a new kitchen later that month.[16]

A dispute at the VEB Zeiss two years later similarly illustrated the efficacy of such public appeals. After a visit to the optical firm in December 1954, a union cadre wrote a lengthy complaint to *Die Tribüne* in which he described a recent dispute between a female worker and her male foreman: After she had borrowed his empty chair in order to make her own work somewhat easier, he demanded that she return it and then "ripped out" the chair "from under her body" when she refused. The director of the factory rejected subsequent demands by union functionaries and workers that the foreman be fired, arguing that the woman had "provoked" him because of her behavior and that a dismissal would only serve to "undermine authority." Although the workers felt "resigned," the letter continued, they would no longer "tolerate" such

---

[14] MxA-U, BGL 367, Prot. der PV, 21.10.54. Also see James Scott, *Domination and the Arts of Resistance: Hidden Transcripts* (New Haven, CT, 1990), 31–2.

[15] ThStA-R IV/4/10/238, Aussprache der KPKK Slf mit den Gen. der Partei- und Betriebsleitung, n.d., and Überprüfung vom VEB Mauxion durch die KPKK Slf, 12.2.52. On the role of the Party Control Commission, see Thomas Klein, *"Für die Einheit und Reinheit der Partei": Die innerparteilichen Kontrollorgane der SED in der Ära Ulbricht* (Cologne, 2002).

[16] ThStA-R, FDGB BV Gera 854/209, letter to *Tribüne*, 2.1.53, and Rechenschaftsbericht der BGL–Wema, n.d.; ThStA-R, FDGB BV Gera 855/210, correspondence, 28.1.53.

behavior: "We will not allow our women to be treated in this way.... Such methods were used under capitalism, under fascism, and are still being used in West Germany today." Calling for improved relations between workers and management officials more generally, the letter concluded by reminding readers that "our laws" were designed to protect workers' rights. This prompted a swift reply by union officials in Berlin, who decided that a person lacking in self-restraint could no longer remain in a position of authority. They also ordered the BGL to secure better chairs for its workers; it was not fair, they wrote, that foremen had padded chairs and normal workers more or less "bad" ones.[17]

The incidents at Wema and Zeiss were instructive for a variety of reasons. In the first place, they reflected the tensions as well as the (often material) divisions that existed between workers and their superiors. At the same time, the allusions to industrial relations under capitalism and fascism underscored the way in which official ideology was sometimes instrumentalized by officials as well as by workers themselves to defend the rights and dignity of the laboring classes. In other words, some Saalfelders apparently identified with and embraced the dogma of the regime – at least when it came to promoting their own interests. Even if the foreman at Zeiss was himself lacking in self-restraint, this could nevertheless serve more generally as an important constraining influence on official behavior – and was one way in which the East German "public transcript" affected and helped regulate relations between workers and their superiors. As James Scott has suggested, "those obliged by domination to act a mask will eventually find that their faces have grown to fit that mask...."[18] Official ideology helped transform the nature of industrial relations, in other words, by making those in power beholden to certain rules of shop-floor etiquette, in theory if not always in practice.

Finally, both disputes illustrated the way in which high- and low-level union functionaries periodically intervened on behalf of those whose interests they were supposed to represent – and not just after the "shock" of June 1953. Their endeavors, which often involved written or verbal appeals in support of workers' demands regarding wages, working conditions, production problems, and a variety of other issues, did not always meet with success. But they nevertheless indicated that at least some union officials assiduously tried to act as workers' representatives and, just as important, that workers turned to them for support. This as we shall see, occasionally led to clashes with management officials as well as with the Factory Party Secretariat, the two other main loci of power in the VEB.

The Motor versus the Transmission Belt

German Communists had successfully seized control at the highest echelons of the regime by the late 1940s but would spend the remaining years of the GDR

[17] ThStA-R, FDGB BV Gera 851/208, letter to *Tribüne*, 9.10.54, and correspondence, 1.11.54.
[18] Scott, *Hidden Transcripts*, 10–11.

endeavoring to shore up their rule at the grass roots. One of the most important instruments in this respect was the Factory Party Secretariat, whose task – as the "motor" of the firm – was to secure and extend the SED's influence on the shop floor by enforcing the official party line. Headed by an appointed chairperson known as the *first secretary*, the BPL was usually composed of up to two dozen members, each of whom was assigned a specific set of responsibilities. The secretariat normally met once a week to discuss a broad range of political, economic, and social issues related to the running of the factory, review the most recent party declarations and political developments, and adopt resolutions aimed at mobilizing rank-and-file members as well as the politically unattached.[19]

To that end, and as head of the factory party cell, the BPL was also expected to direct and control high-level management officials as well as members of the union committee in order to ensure that their work closely corresponded to the political and economic directives issued from above. Many secretariats in Saalfeld failed to live up to official expectations, however, and proved unable to establish unequivocal party hegemony within their firm – exposing themselves to high-level condemnation of their *conciliatory, liberal, opportunistic,* and *petty-bourgeois* behavior, to name only a few of the most common epithets favored by their superiors.[20] This failure supposedly reflected not only a lack of serious commitment to the party, but also the inferior ideological level, political training, and experience of those who served on the BPL. More concretely, it meant a reluctance to agitate politically or perform other essential party tasks; a widespread tendency to avoid confrontations with individuals who had either openly criticized official policies and developments in the GDR or had refused to participate in sociopolitical activities and otherwise comply with the dictates of the party and state; and a failure to establish stronger ties to the rank-and-file, carry out resolutions dictated from above or adopted at secretariat meetings, and accept criticism or practice self-criticism. In 1952, the District Secretariat sarcastically noted that there were still some party "dignitaries" who could not bear any censure whatsoever: "[M]istakes are usually not criticized because of 'friendship' or an effort 'to keep the peace.'" When asked why he had not fought against the "sectarian tendencies" exhibited by a number of older comrades, the first secretary at the Maxhütte explained that he had serious "inhibitions" about confronting those who had spent the Nazi period in prison or a concentration camp: "I sometimes have an inferiority complex because I don't have as much

[19] On the SED's role and position in the VEB, see Sandrine Kott, *Le communisme au quotidien: Les entreprises d'Etat dans la société est-allemande* (Paris, 2001), 38–64; Thomas Reichel, "'Feste Burgen der Partei': Aufbau und Rolle der SED–Betriebsgruppen in der SBZ (1946–1949)," *Internationale wissenschaftliche Korrespondenz zur Geschichte der deutschen Arbeiterbewegung* 1 (2000): 62–99. For a general overview of the BPL and its functions, see Andreas Herbst, Gerd-Rüdiger Stephan, and Jürgen Winkler, eds., *Die SED: Geschichte – Organisation – Politik: Ein Handbuch* (Berlin, 1997), 117–57.

[20] See the KPKK reports in ThStA-R IV/4/10/238; ThStA-R IV/A-4/10/081 and 086.

experience as the older comrades. I swallow a great deal out of respect for them."[21]

Those secretariats subject to the most vigorous criticism were the ones that found themselves subordinate to more powerful plant directors or union chairmen who not only failed to carry out high-level orders, but who also questioned the authority of the BPL or refused to submit to its influence, e.g., by challenging its decisions or by independently making important ones of their own without prior consultation. In fact, the BPL's official role as political and economic watchdog often led to friction, poor cooperation, and, in some cases, outright hostility between it and the two other pillars of power within the factory.[22]

Many of these disputes were rooted in personal antagonism or animosity – and nowhere more so than at the VEB Zeiss. One important reason for this was the influential role played by the union chairman, Hans Gruner, who enjoyed considerable authority among his colleagues because of his outstanding performance and lengthy tenure at the optical factory, where he had begun working as a mechanic in 1938 at the age of twenty-five. After joining the SPD and FDGB after the war, Gruner was elected head of the Workers' Council at Zeiss and later became chairman of the newly formed BGL after the official dissolution of the *Betriebsräte* in November 1948.[23] His election must have diminished somewhat the anger felt by many workers about the high-level decision to do away with their council following the adoption that year of the so-called Bitterfeld Resolution, which – by stressing the union's commitment to raising worker productivity and production norms in order to promote plan fulfillment – marked the official taming of the FDGB, as well as the initial rupture between union representatives and East German workers. The significance of this shift became immediately apparent in the late 1940s and early 1950s, when factory union officials were charged with securing shop-floor acceptance of piecework wages and the new labor contracts. The umbrella union organization not only reconfirmed its commitment to these goals at its Third Congress, held in Berlin in 1950, but also accepted its subordinate role vis-à-vis the SED by formally recognizing the party's claims to leadership.[24]

[21] See ThStA-R IV/4/10/238, Bericht des Vorsitzenden der LPKK Thür. über die Prüfung der Maxh. im Auftrag der ZPKK, 11.50; Überprüfung vom VEB Mauxion durch die KPKK Slf, 12.2.52; and Ergebnis der Untersuchung im Kulturpalast des VEB Maxh. durch die KPKK Slf, n.d. The local FDJ similarly lamented the fact that its officials tended to avoid ideological discussions about "improper" political behavior on the part of its members. See, e.g., ThStA-R, FDJ-KL Slf 209, Maßnahmeplan zur Verbesserung der Arbeit an unseren polytechnischen und erweiterten Oberschulen, 13.11.61.

[22] These are all common themes in the KPKK reports in ThStA-R IV/4/10/238.

[23] ThStA-R, FDGB BV Gera 851/208, correspondence, 27.6.55. The Workers' Councils had spontaneously formed in factories across eastern Germany after the war; until their dissolution, they oversaw production and tended to the everyday social and economic concerns of staff members. See Siegfried Suckut, *Die Betriebsrätebewegung in der sowjetisch besetzten Zone Deutschlands, 1945–1948* (Frankfurt am Main, 1982).

[24] See David Gill, *Der Freie Deutsche Gewerkschaftsbund (FDGB): Theorie – Geschichte – Organisation – Funktion – Kritik* (Opladen, 1989), 316–20. On the FDGB more generally (especially

Over the next two decades, workers in Saalfeld would regularly call on union functionaries to act more independently and stop being a mere appendage (*Anhängsel*) of the SED. Just as important, they demanded that they represent *their* interests and not merely those of the regime. As workers at the Maxhütte put it: That was, after all, what they were paid for. "The work of the BGLs is strongly criticized in all factories," the SED District Secretariat itself acknowledged in 1952, especially because of their "conciliatory behavior" toward plant directors.[25] Despite continuing complaints that union functionaries were the lackeys of management and party officials, Hans Gruner and the other members of the Zeiss BGL remained among the district's most energetic proponents of union and workers' rights. During the 1956 disturbances in Hungary, for example, they demanded that

[b]ecause staff members are either transferred from one department to another… without the union being informed, it is absolutely necessary that [we] be given greater rights in this area.… Another essential point that is very important to us is the right to codetermine the factory plan. By August 1956, no less than fifty-two modifications have taken place in our factory – changes of such magnitude that we suddenly had eighty people too many, resulting in transfers that always led to wage decreases.…

One year later, party officials reported with great concern that the BGL had tenaciously resisted a series of recent norm hikes: It "sticks to its guns" and "insists" that average earnings not be decreased.[26]

Poor cooperation and mutual hostility had marked relations between the party and the union at Zeiss from the very beginning, leading to the dismissal of several BPL chairmen during the early 1950s: According to the District

during its early years), see Stefan Paul Werum, *Gewerkschaftlicher Niedergang im sozialistischen Aufbau: Der Freie Deutsche Gewerkschaftsbund (FDGB), 1945 bis 1953* (Göttingen, 2005); Helke Stadtland, *Herrschaft nach Plan und Macht der Gewohnheit: Sozialgeschichte der Gewerkschaften in der SBZ/DDR, 1945–1953* (Essen, 2001); Sebastian Simsch, *Blinde Ohnmacht: Der Freie Deutsche Gewerkschaftsbund zwischen Diktatur und Gesellschaft in der DDR, 1945 bis 1963* (Aachen, 2002). For an overview of the literature on the FDGB, see Ulrich Mählert, "Die Massenorganisationen," in Rainer Eppelmann, Bernd Faulenbach, and Ulrich Mählert, eds., *Bilanz und Perspektiven der DDR–Forschung* (Paderborn, 2003), 100–6. Also see Chapter 1 on the role that the unions played in Saalfeld during the introduction of piecework and the BKV.

[25] See MxA-U, BGL 370, Prot. der Gewerkschaftsversammlung in der Baureparatur, 16.12.54; MxA-U, BGL 199, report, 5.4.52; ThStA-R, FDGB BV Gera 709/178, report, 22.12.52. A 1951 decision at the Maxhütte stating that the BGL's signature was no longer required on various announcements and ordinances adopted by the director clearly reflected this diminished role – and contrasted sharply with demands by the Workers' Council in the late 1940s that management recognize its right to cosign important directives as well as its "right of codetermination" (the latter had been guaranteed in a 1946 agreement). See MxA-U, WL B60, Prot. der außerordentlichen Betriebsratssitz., 11.7.47, and correspondence, 28.7.47; ThStA-R, Maxh. 616, correspondence, 7.5.48; ThStA-R, Maxh. 377, correspondence, 2.11.48; MxA-U, WL B130, Prot. der WL–Besprechung, und Aktennotiz über die Konferenz der Direktoren in Riesa, 18.12.51.

[26] ThStA-R, FDGB BV Gera 851/208, Gewerkschaftsaktivtagung, 13.9.56; ThStA-R IV/7/231/1167, IB der SED GO–Zeiss, 23.10.57.

Secretariat, the union had made each one *"kaputt."*[27] The party leadership assumed partial responsibility for these tensions, admitting that it had never invited Gruner to one of its meetings to deliver a talk or receive explicit instructions. But unlike most factory union chairmen in Saalfeld, Gruner had himself refused to become a member of the BPL, using his many other functions and responsibilities as an excuse. He was nevertheless unwilling to accept blame for the frictions at Zeiss and complained in 1955 that Helmut Dümmler, the newly appointed party secretary, had not "endeavored" to maintain strong contacts with the BGL; most of their discussions, he hastened to add, were usually held "in a hurry." Reflecting on these tensions decades later, former party members at the firm recalled that Dümmler – "a simple, primitive, ineloquent [but] good-natured dope" (*ein gutmütiger Trottel*) – and the more "cultured" Gruner could simply "not stand each another."[28]

Unlike the new party secretary, who had been transferred from the VEB Rotstern earlier that year, the BGL chairman belonged to the so-called Zeissianer, a proud elite who had joined the optical firm before 1945. The party's position was seriously undermined, in fact, by a fundamental split between these older staff members and those political functionaries who had been delegated to the factory after the war. Noting with concern the negative attitude of many old-timers toward the members of the Secretariat, SED officials claimed that the former continued to conduct themselves in the same arrogant way as the prewar "worker aristocracy" at Zeiss, who habitually wore ties and white frock coats at the workplace – "and that is unfortunately a very large number."[29]

Most of them considered the leading members of the BPL to be poorly trained outsiders, an impression strengthened by the fact that many had been required to receive additional professional training in order to learn how to run the factory properly. The firm's long-standing reputation for technical innovation, as well as its renowned commitment since the late nineteenth century to the social well-being of its workforce, made it even more difficult for the party to win over the haughty Zeissianer: Because of their tendency to "cling" to the "special rules" of the past, many disputes focused on the loss of a variety of benefits set forth in the firm's prewar Statute. Their "self-assuredness" also

[27] ThStA-R IV/4/10/150, Prot. der Sitz. der SED–KL Slf, 15.11.57.
[28] The union chairman later claimed that the trouble had begun shortly after Dümmler's arrival, and especially after he had rejected the new secretary's request to report to him each morning about the climate in the firm: Horst Kämmer, Walter Schilling, and Hans Gruner, in separate discussions with the author, August 1995. Also see ThStA-R IV/4/10/238, Bericht der KPKK Slf bzgl. der Überprüfung der SED PO im VEB Zeiss, 27.8.52; ThStA-R IV/7/231/1165, Prot. der LS der SED GO–Zeiss, 18.11.55.
[29] ThStA-R IV/7/231/1164, Prot. der LS der SED GO–Zeiss, 12.11.54; ThStA-R IV/7/231/1167, IB der SED GO–Zeiss, 19.12.56; Walter Schilling, in discussion with the author, August 1995. Also see AdsD, Ostbüro 0073f (02401), report, 16.4.59. On the history of the Zeiss branch in Saalfeld as well as developments and personnel during the immediate postwar years, see UACZ, Bestand BACZ 18940, 19998, 23453; UACZ, Bestand VA 1645.

made them skeptical about the supposed achievements of the postwar socialist system: "Zeiss was always a 'social factory'... what can the [GDR] offer us?"[30]

Frustrated party officials tried to account for such defiance by accusing the union of concentrating exclusively on social issues instead of supporting the BPL's various political activities. Calling on union functionaries to pay more attention to their political role in the firm, Dümmler declared in 1958 that the BGL "must finally be torn out of its social role...."[31] Unsatisfactory political engagement on the part of factory unions and an almost exclusive preoccupation with the social concerns of East German workers – known in official Leninist parlance as *Nurgewerkschaftlertum* – was a source of great concern to high-level officials throughout the GDR and thus was not peculiar to Zeiss. In fact, the SED Central Committee had issued a formal censure that same year calling on the unions to become "a school of socialism for the entire working class... [they] must do more to promote greater development of a socialist consciousness, new attitudes toward work, workplace discipline, and work morale...."[32] Similar rebukes earlier that decade had prompted the following response by union officials at the VEB Wema: "You people from the ministry... can't cover up your own unsatisfactory performance by accusing us of poor sociopolitical work...." Or, as the BGL chairman himself declared at the time, "[I]f I'm accused of being too generous, then I have to reply, no, some functionaries are just too narrow-minded...." Some union committees nevertheless understood the message and acknowledged – or at least paid lip service to – their official role as *transmission belts* of SED policy: "[T]he union is not an alms society," officials at the Maxhütte sanctimoniously announced in the spring of 1960, "but a social organization" with political and ideological responsibilities.[33]

Stalwart functionaries may have criticized *Nurgewerkschaftlertum*, but this was precisely what gave the Zeiss BGL and its spirited chairman such authority. As Fritz Müller, the first secretary of the district SED, admitted himself, Gruner enjoyed such "great favor" at the firm because "he solves all social

---

[30] ThStA-R IV/7/231/1167, IB der SED GO–Zeiss, 22.11.56, 13.2.57. On the progressive social policies at Zeiss since the late nineteenth century, see Felix Auerbach, *Das Zeisswerk und die Carl–Zeiss-Stiftung in Jena* (Jena, 1903); Werner Plumpe, "Menschenfreundlichkeit und Geschäftsinteresse: Die betriebliche Sozialpolitik Ernst Abbes im Lichte der modernen Theorie," in Frank Markowski, ed., *Der Letzte Schliff: 150 Jahre Arbeit und Alltag bei Carl Zeiss* (Berlin, 1997), 10–33. More generally, see Friedrich Schomerus, *Geschichte des Jenaer Zeisswerkes, 1846–1946* (Stuttgart, 1952); Wolfgang Mühlfriedel and Rolf Walter, eds., *Carl Zeiss: Die Geschichte eines Unternehmens*, 3 vols. (Weimar, 1996–2004); Armin Hermann, *Carl Zeiss: Die abenteuerliche Geschichte einer deutschen Firma* (Munich, 1992).

[31] ThStA-R IV/7/231/1165, Prot. der LS der SED GO–Zeiss, 30.5.58.

[32] Bundesministerium für gesamtdeutsche Fragen, ed., *Die Sowjetische Besatzungszone Deutschlands in den Jahren 1957–1958*, vol. 2 (Bonn, 1960), 180–1. On the concept of *Nurgewerkschaftlertum*, see Vladimir Lenin, *What Is to Be Done?* (London, 1988), esp. Chapter 3.

[33] See ThStA-R, FDGB BV Gera 854/209, letter to *Tribüne*, 2.1.53, and Rechenschaftsbericht der BGL–Wema, n.d.; ThStA-R, FDGB BV Gera 862/212, Prot. der Sitz. der BGL–Grube Schmiedefeld, 8.4.60. On official criticism of *Nurgewerkschaftlertum*, also see Gill, *FDGB*, 146–8.

problems."[34] Like their counterparts in Saalfeld's other factories, he and his colleagues responded to the grievances of those under their charge in a variety of ways: by trying to improve safety conditions, facilitate job training and professional advancement, or procure scarce consumer goods and services. Many workers also looked to the union as a repository of various forms of social assistance, as its predecessor had also been under the Third Reich. In this capacity, the BGL at Zeiss and elsewhere organized and subsidized factory parties, cultural events, excursions, and other leisure activities for staff members and their children; they also provided financial support to sick or injured workers as well as to those experiencing extraordinary financial difficulties.[35] This was, of course, why most Saalfelders were members of the FDGB – regardless of any misgivings they may have had about the efficacy of the union and its representatives more generally.

The point is that many BGLs refused to abandon entirely the classical functions of an industrial union. But just as disturbing, at least from the SED's point of view, were other forms of insubordinate activity and behavior that seriously hindered the Factory Party Secretariats from carrying out high-level political directives. That was why officials severely criticized the Zeiss BGL for scheduling its weekly meetings at the same time that the factory combat units held their practice, for example – which was supposedly typical of the poor coordination characteristic of relations there between the union and party. The three top management officials at the optical firm were similarly accused of failing to support the BPL's political activities and of not demonstrating sufficient attachment to the party. In fact, all three categorically refused to help recruit young men for the military, participate in paramilitary training themselves, or engage in other important sociopolitical activities: "If this continues," the director threatened in 1952 in response to repeated criticism, "recruitment for the People's Police will drive me to the West...." In fact, he and the technical director both withdrew from the SED that year after being openly attacked as "fascist" and "bourgeois" at a party conference.[36]

The BPL claimed that all of this insubordination made it exceedingly difficult to mobilize the masses – and was probably correct when it argued that the failure of management and union functionaries to set a proper example themselves helped account for the refusal of many ordinary workers to comply with official demands and engage in the requisite sociopolitical activities. In an attempt to

[34] ThStA-R IV/4/10/150, Prot. der Sitz. der SED–KL Slf, 29.11.57.
[35] For sample BGL expenditures, see the statistics from 1960 for the VEB Wema in ThStA-R, FDGB BV Gera 865/214. More generally, see Peter Hübner, "Der Betrieb als Ort der Sozialpolitik in der DDR," in Christoph Boyer and Peter Skyba, eds., *Repression und Wohlstandsversprechen: Zur Stabilisierung von Parteiherrschaft in der DDR und der ČSSR* (Dresden, 1999), 63–74. On similar union-related activities during the Nazi period, see Shelley Baranowski, *Strength Through Joy: Consumerism and Mass Tourism in the Third Reich* (Cambridge, 2004).
[36] See ThStA-R IV/7/231/1162, Prot. der Berichtswahlversammlung, 10.12.55; ThStA-R IV/7/231/1163, Prot. der BPO–LS, 27.11.1952; ThStA-R IV/4/10/98, Prot. und Anlage der Sitz. der SED–KL Slf, 10.9.52. Also see Chapter 5 on local resistance to military recruitment.

put his finger on the problem, one party member argued that the "fundamental mistake" had been made in 1947 "when our factory was rebuilt. Nobody, including the District Secretariat, concerned themselves with our firm. And as a result, those who had already loyally served the Kaiser and Hitler were able to carry out personnel policy in our factory as *they* wished"; as a result, the firm was now dominated by "liberal" cadres who falsely believed that politics and production were two independent spheres.[37]

Personnel policy – often considered "the most important factor in the factory"[38] – proved, in fact, to be one of the most serious bones of contention among party, union, and management functionaries at Zeiss as well as at other firms in Saalfeld. The SED realized early on that one of the surest ways to establish its dominance on the shop floor was to secure and maintain control of personnel decisions and thereby ensure the advancement of politically reliable individuals: As the Zeiss BPL observed, the question of party membership could not merely play an "abstract role" when it came to decisions about professional training, for example.[39] This strategy prompted stubborn opposition by union and management officials, who were often more interested in promoting those individuals most qualified for a given post – regardless of their political leanings. In response to such opposition, Dümmler decided to resign from the factory's Cadre Commission in 1956 so that it could not be said that "the party decides everything." But at a meeting held several months later, he and the other members of the BPL vigorously denounced a recent decision by management officials to hire a woman for a position previously designated by the SED for one of its own members: The director wanted to make this dispute a "trial of strength," they claimed, so the "prejudices...against Comrade W. have to be smashed."[40]

Because of the BGL's formal right of codetermination in this important area, personnel decisions prompted internecine quarrels at other VEBs as well. In the fall of 1958, for instance, the union committee at the washing-machine factory refused to approve a decision to fire a worker because of repeated disciplinary infractions: Arguing that proper bureaucratic procedures had not been followed, its members bluntly told the director that he could appeal to district union officials if he was not satisfied with their decision.[41] This and similar conflicts reflected a fundamental struggle over power, jurisdiction, and authority at the workplace – despite a great deal of overlap among party, union, and management personnel: Union chairmen and plant directors usually belonged to the SED and, unlike Hans Gruner, often sat on the Factory Party

---

[37] See ThStA-R IV/7/231/1165, Prot. der LS der SED GO–Zeiss, 3.2.56; ThStA-R IV/7/231/1166, Prot. der MV der SED GO–Zeiss, 7.5.57; ThStA-R IV/7/231/1167, IB der SED GO–Zeiss, 26.9.56.
[38] ThStA-R, FDGB BV Gera 854/209, Prot. der Sitz. der BGL–Waschmaschinenwerk, 30.6.54.
[39] ThStA-R IV/7/231/1165, Prot. der LS der SED GO–Zeiss, 23.1.59.
[40] ThStA-R IV/7/231/1165, Prot. der LS der SED GO–Zeiss, 26.11.56, 12.7.57.
[41] ThStA-R, FDGB BV Gera 854/209, Prot. der Sitz. der BGL–Waschmaschinenwerk, 9.10.58, 10.10.58.

Secretariat.[42] In order to strengthen their position even further, many BPLs tried to influence union elections to make sure that politically trustworthy individuals filled key positions. Such efforts were not always successful, however: In 1953, for instance, not a single member of the SED was elected to the BGL at the washing-machine factory. Two years later, only two of twenty-six candidates in an upcoming election at the local transportation company belonged to the party – prompting officials to complain that the "union is a very important mass organization, but we often let it be controlled by people over whom we have little influence. How are we going to accomplish the main tasks of the party [and] educate people in a way compatible with our goals when we are not ourselves decisively anchored in the BGL?"[43]

By the late 1950s, approximately 60 percent of all union chairmen and 85 percent of all factory directors were in the SED.[44] But as the dispute at Zeiss made abundantly clear, party membership did not necessarily guarantee compliant behavior or the forging of a united front among officials. This was true at other local factories as well, even when the relationship among officials was marked by a high degree of cliquishness: After the Party Secretariat at the VEB Rotstern decided to fire the head of the factory's radio station, for example, the director – a party cadre and a member of the BPL – told the first secretary in a "terribly excited" state that he "wouldn't dream of allowing himself to be commanded around by the District Secretariat, that it had, up to now, only sent him trash (*Schund*) for cadres, that he would not agree to anything else in the future and would henceforth decide all things by himself."[45]

Relations were not always characterized by such strong hostility, and the position of the party was not always this tenuous. In some factories, like the Maxhütte, the Party Secretariat apparently enjoyed a good working relationship with the other two pillars of power – especially after the SED succeeded in purging refractory members from the Workers' Council in the late 1940s.[46] To ensure that that situation continued, officials there and elsewhere tried to reach some sort of modus vivendi regarding the limits of their authority, particularly when it came to punitive decisions. In such cases, management and union functionaries usually deferred to the BPL when party members were involved; the reverse was true for those not in the SED, unless the matter was clearly political in nature. In January 1954, for instance, the Maxhütte union committee requested in writing that the Party Secretariat deal with a comrade who had been accused of harassing female coworkers. In an almost identical case that

[42] For evidence of this in Saalfeld, see the LPKK and KPKK reports in ThStA-R IV/4/10/238.

[43] ThStA-R IV/7/220/1002, Prot. der MV der SED GO–Kraftverkehr, 8.2.55. Also see the series of reports from 1962 on efforts to recruit union functionaries as SED candidates in ThStA-R, FDGB KV Slf 6178.

[44] ThStA-R IV/10/355, Aufstellung der VEB, Organisationen, Institutionen im Kreisgebiet, n.d.

[45] ThStA-R IV/7/226/1137, IB der SED GO–Rotstern, 4.1.56.

[46] See MxA-U, BGL 62, Fragebogen zu Schwerpunktbetrieben, 14.4.49; ThStA-R IV/4/10/238, Bericht des Vorsitzenden der LPKK Thür. über die Prüfung der Maxh. im Auftrag der ZPKK, 11.50; ThStA-R, FDGB BV Gera 862/212, Prot. der Sitz. der BGL–Grube Schmiedefeld, 8.4.60.

same month, a worker employed at the VEB Abus appealed to the Party Secretariat to overturn a recent decision to fire him: Because he did not belong to the
SED, the BPL decided to turn the matter over to union officials.[47] Comparable
examples of such deference were few and far between at Zeiss.

Showdown at Zeiss

Tensions at the optical firm finally came to a head in the winter of 1956–7
because of a major dispute over two recent decisions announced by officials
in Berlin: Following the upheavals in Poland and especially Hungary, the SED
Central Committee decided in November to introduce a shorter, forty-five-hour
workweek and set up so-called Worker Committees in all East German factories.
These new administrative bodies – intended, in all likelihood, as a prophylactic
measure taken in response to the creation of similar bodies in Hungary – were,
according to authorities, supposed to strengthen the power and influence of
ordinary workers. Despite the fact that it never precisely formulated their exact
rights, the decree met throughout the GDR with widespread opposition by high-
and low-level union officials, many of whom apparently feared that this was
a new strategy aimed at "pulling the rug out from under the FDGB's feet."[48]
At a union conference held in December, Gruner openly attacked the recent
decisions in no uncertain terms:

I'm an old hand in the union. What's being created today is the old Workers' Council of yore. I've already expressed my opinion to the comrades on the District Secretariat.... The Worker Committees belong in the ministries, I've already said that three
times (applause). If there are production problems, then we can assign people ourselves
[to take care of them]; there's no need to establish a new committee. One is scared to say
anything negative about the recent discussion in the newspapers. Many BGL chairmen
were at a [recent] meeting of the SED District Secretariat [and sat silent] until I finally
saw red.... It's just not necessary to create another type of BGL....[49]

Because of plans that would have allowed members of this new organ to be
present at all factory meetings, Gruner worried that it would eventually come
to control the BGL – a concern apparently shared by members of other local
union committees as well. Underlying such fears was the suspicion that the SED
would try to pack the body with obedient party members, which was clearly

---

[47] ThStA-R, Maxh. 379, correspondence, 27.1.54; ThStA-R, FDGB BV Gera 855/210, Prot. der
Sitz. der BGL–Abus, 4.1.54.
[48] Wolfgang Eckelmann, Hans-Hermann Hertle, and Rainer Weinert, *FDGB Intern: Innenan-
sichten einer Massenorganisation der SED* (Berlin, 1990), 48. On the Worker Commit-
tees episode and the FDGB's oppositon, also see Gill, *FDGB*, 216–20; Thomas Reichel,
"Konfliktprävention: Die Episode der 'Arbeiterkomitees' 1956/58," in Hübner and Tenfelde,
Arbeiter, 439–52; Dietrich Staritz, "Die 'Arbeiterkomitees' der Jahre 1956/58: Fallstudie zur
Partizipations–Problematik in der DDR," in *Der X. Parteitag der SED: 35 Jahre SED–Politik –
Versuch einer Bilanz* (Cologne, 1980), 63–74.
[49] ThStA-R IV/4/10/140, Anlage der Sitz. der SED–KL Slf, 4.1.1957.

the intention at Zeiss and at the VEB Wema.[50] To justify their opposition, some union officials argued that another factory commission was simply unnecessary, not only because a union already existed but also because the new measure would only lead to more bureaucracy: "[I]n a few more years... we'll have more functionaries than workers.... If one adds together the amount of time already lost because of meetings, there'd be no housing shortages anymore." Many workers were equally skeptical: "Why create another new institution? If the unions couldn't get things done, then the new committees surely won't either."[51]

The concurrent decision to introduce a shorter workweek kindled a great deal of discussion as well, and Gruner, like many of his colleagues, demanded that officials grant three Saturdays off each month instead; this was, after all, "what the vast majority desired."[52] The length of the workweek had long been an important source of tension in Saalfeld, especially during the early postwar years, when some workers had even been required to work on Sundays. The resulting loss of leisure time understandably became a major source of discontent throughout the district.[53] To make weekend work more attractive, factory officials had initially agreed to pay a 50 percent bonus on Sunday, but the practice was abolished in early 1951: Because workers were guaranteed one day off each week, they reasoned, there was no "Sunday work" anymore in the "conventional sense... it doesn't make a difference whether the day off is, by chance, a Monday or a Friday." Such arguments fell on deaf ears, and the issue became a serious point of contention during the first BKV negotiations held later that year.[54]

Tensions about weekend work flared up once again in response to the 1956 decision to reduce the workweek to forty-five hours. But instead of accepting this olive branch, many in the district characteristically called instead for a five-day week so that they could have their weekends off. While some argued that the reform would not make life any easier for them (the "half hour earlier that we stop working each day won't... get us home any earlier" because of the poor transportation system), others feared that the reform would simply lead to lower earnings and a drive to increase productivity. As one worker at Rotstern

---

[50] See ThStA-R IV/7/230/1154, Prot. der LS der SED GO–Wema, 4.1.57; ThStA-R IV/7/231/1165, Prot. der LS der SED GO–Zeiss, 22.1.57.

[51] ThStA-R, FDGB BV Gera 705/177, Prot. der Sitz. der KV IG Metall Slf, 6.12.56; ThStA-R IV/7/226/1137, IB der SED GO–Rotstern, 1.12.56.

[52] See ThStA-R IV/7/231/1165, Prot. der LS der SED GO–Zeiss, 22.1.57; ThStA-R IV/7/231/1167, IB der SED GO–Zeiss, 19.12.56.

[53] On disputes related to the length of the workweek, see Peter Hübner, *Konsens, Konflikt und Kompromiß: Soziale Arbeiterinteressen und Sozialpolitik in der SBZ/DDR, 1945–1970* (Berlin, 1995), 89–129.

[54] In a conciliatory measure, factory officials agreed the following year to award bonuses for supposedly irregular work performed on Sundays, a stipulation that could obviously be broadly interpreted. See MxA-U, WL B130, Prot. der WL–Besprechung, 5.1.51, 19.4.51; MxA-U, BGL 170, Bericht über die BV in der Kranabt., 14.6.51. Also see the discussion of the first BKV in Chapter 1.

griped, the reduced workweek only meant that she would have to achieve even
more than she had before, and "even now she doesn't have enough time to take
a single breath."[55]

The decision to shorten the workweek remained one of the most heated
topics of discussion in Saalfeld through the summer of 1957, and the complaints
voiced at the time – as well as Gruner's public attack at the conference – were
clearly connected to the political thaw initiated by Khrushchev's attack on
Stalin in February 1956. As in other countries within the eastern bloc, the
destalinization campaign prompted a more open and critical discussion focusing
on the need for urgent economic and political reform. While it is true that most
participants were either intellectuals or high-level functionaries, it would be
wrong to conclude that East German workers failed to take much notice of this
"superstructural phenomenon."[56] Few might have been aware of the details of
the reform debate, yet the reaction to the Worker Committees as well as to the
shorter workweek strongly suggested that many had nevertheless been infected
by the more critical atmosphere – and also, of course, by the recent events in
Poland and Hungary.

Gruner's criticism of the new committees and his plea for weekends off nevertheless gave the Party Secretariat at Zeiss an opportunity to finally dispose
of their old adversary. This was not the first time that the BGL chairman had
expressed misgivings about or opposition to official policies, but that he had
now done so in a public setting was an entirely different matter. Despite reservations by some members that someone who had been elected by the masses also
had to be dismissed by them,[57] the BPL sent a tape of Gruner's speech to the
District Secretariat, which held a formal discussion with the renitent chairman
in January 1957:

Comrade [Fritz] Müller	read a few excerpts from [Gruner's] concluding remarks and asked whether... this was his own opinion.
Comrade Gruner:	That's not only my opinion but the opinion of many party members and many workers.
Müller:	[addressing Party Secretary Helmut Dümmler] Do you agree that that is the opinion of many party members?

[55] Such suspicions were not entirely unwarranted, for management and union officials realized
themselves that productivity would have to be increased in order to make up for the loss
of production time. But with the East German upheaval of June 1953 and the 1956 disturbances in Hungary and Poland still fresh in mind, factory officials were careful not to force
higher productivity levels on workers. As discussed in Chapter 7, skyrocketing overtime during
the latter part of the decade was one important way in which they dealt with this challenge.
See ThStA-R, FDGB BV Gera 855/210, Prot. der Delegiertenkonferenz zur Wahl der BGL–
Bohrmaschinenwerk, 14.12.56; ThStA-R IV/7/230/1158, Prot. der MV der SED GO–Wema,
7.12.56; ThStA-R IV/7/226/1137, IB der SED GO–Rotstern, 28.3.56. Also see the information
reports in ThStA-R IV/4/10/252–4.

[56] Dietrich Staritz, *Geschichte der DDR, 1949–1985* (Frankfurt am Main, 1985), 101–18. For
another study whose finding implicitly call Staritz's claims into question, see Mitter and Wolle,
Untergang, 163–295.

[57] ThStA-R IV/4/10/150, Prot. der Sitz. der SED–KL Slf, 29.11.57.

Dümmler:	It was primarily party members who spoke up....
Müller:	Then we really do need to talk about this. What led [Gruner] to such conclusions.... I've never read such things anywhere in our newspapers.
Gruner:	Forty-five hour workweek: I believe that mistakes were made on high.... The opinion of the workers was that Saturdays should be given off... Worker Committees[:] We had many difficulties in 1956. We had fifty-two plan modifications. One of these made a hundred people in the factory unnecessary. That's the focal point of much discussion in the factory. A Worker Committee could not have done anything to avoid these plan changes and [other] deficiencies. That was decided by the ministry. It is irresponsible to adopt such plans. The workers receive assignments involving more complicated work, so they earn less. That naturally leads to discussions....
Müller:	What has been the main concern in Zeiss since 1945?
Gruner:	If you mean by that the Zeiss Statute: One can't treat one factory differently [from others]. But there are also other factories with special rights, for example...coal allotments for coal miners.
Müller:	Do you believe that ideology... still plays a role?
Gruner:	Sure, but not in Saalfeld.... We don't have different types of people than in other factories. The opinion of those working for us is the same as in the Maxhütte, the drilling machine factory, Rotstern, etc. They want Saturdays off.... I'd advise you to come once to our factory and speak with twenty colleagues at random. When I talk to BGL chairmen from other factories, they say the same things we do.... If we continue to work like this, it makes you lose all desire. I don't have one party member in the BGL who goes along 100 percent with the [official line]....[58]

The shorter workweek was introduced that month, but authorities ultimately decided not to establish a Worker Committee at Zeiss (in fact, fewer than two dozen were set up in the entire GDR, suggesting that high-level officials had more or less decided to quietly drop this unpopular measure).[59] The dispute nevertheless led to an important administrative shakeup at the optical firm. Following recommendations by the Party Control Commission, the SED ordered Hugo Schrade, the head of the Zeiss combine in nearby Jena, to break up the concentration of former SED members that occupied the top echelons of management at the Saalfeld branch. The technical director was sent to the main headquarters, where he assumed another high-level managerial position, but

---

58 ThStA-R IV/4/10/140, Prot. und Anlage der Sitz. der SED–KL Slf, 4.1.57. For further discussions by the District Secretariat about the tensions at Zeiss, see the minutes in ThStA-R IV/4/10/92 (26.10.51); /98 (10.9.52); /131 (6.10.55); /150 (15.11.57, 26.11.57, 29.11.57); /151 (13.12.57).

59 See Gill, *FDGB*, 219–22. The five-day workweek was first introduced a decade later in 1967; see Chapter 7.

Hans Kohler, the director of the factory, remained at his post until his retirement in the 1970s. According to a former employee, connections might have played an important role here: Kohler was a "passionate fisherman" who regularly supplied Schrade with trout. More to the point, and reminiscent of some of the personnel decisions made during the immediate postwar period, party officials apparently considered it impossible to do without these two highly trained specialists despite their defiant behavior.[60]

They nevertheless dealt more stringently with the union chairman, who was unceremoniously removed from his position despite protestations of loyalty to the party and despite subsequent efforts to distance himself from his earlier criticisms.[61] This took several months, however, because of the SED's inability to find a suitable individual willing to take over Gruner's job. In accordance with the Control Commission's insistence that his successor come from the BPL's own ranks, the Party Secretariat finally chose, or rather persuaded, one of its members to accept the position in January 1958 (the same man, incidentally, who had earlier referred to high-level party officials as "rascals" during the June 17 upheaval).[62] Gruner himself was subsequently placed in charge of procuring production materials and remained at Zeiss until his retirement in 1978. Looking back on the dispute, he wistfully described himself as a "dead man" who "completely withdrew" from all activities at the firm after 1957; he nevertheless remained in the party until 1988.[63]

Why did the SED hesitate so long before finally taking action against its main adversaries at Zeiss? The valuable expertise of the technical intelligentsia as well as the union chairman's personal stature had certainly played an important role, of course. But why did high-level SED officials first decide in October 1957 to sack Gruner and disperse the concentration of former party members in key managerial positions, i.e., ten months _after_ the acrimonious meeting held in the District Secretariat's office? Gruner himself believed that he would have been kicked out much earlier if he had not always received the most votes during union elections.[64] But there was an equally plausible explanation involving high-level political developments, namely, the end of the political thaw initiated by Khruschchev, which began in the GDR in March 1957 with the trial of philosopher Wolfgang Harich. In the fall of that year, East German officials launched a sweeping campaign against all those who had spoken out in favor of revisionist policies since 1956. The effects of this political _revirement_ at the grass roots have largely been overlooked: While the available sources do not permit any definite conclusions, it was probably no coincidence that the union chairman was removed precisely at this time.

---

[60] Horst Kämmer, in discussion with the author, August 1995; ThStA-R IV/2/3/265, Bericht der BPKK Gera, 29.10.57.
[61] ThStA-R IV/7/231/1165, Prot. der LS der SED GO–Zeiss, 22.1.57, 15.11.57; ThStA-R IV/7/231/1166, Prot. der MV der SED GO–Zeiss, 14.5.57.
[62] ThStA-R IV/7/231/1165, Prot. der LS der SED GO–Zeiss, 24.1.58.
[63] Hans Gruner, in discussion with the author, August 1995.
[64] Ibid.

Interference by high-level SED officials did not necessarily secure the party's hegemony and leading role in the optical firm, however. The Secretariat continued to have disputes with management officials over personnel decisions, and the BPL was still not in a position to secure automatic compliance with its demands; for that reason, it now tended to seek compromise instead.[65] Yet with the appointment of a more acquiescent party member as union chairman, it did succeed in making the factory union committee somewhat more obedient. The minutes of two BPL meetings held a little more than a year after the 1957 showdown illustrated this evolution – as well as the heightened politicization of decision making at Zeiss. In early January 1959, the new union chairman announced that holiday checks were – "for the first time" – not to be paid automatically to all those who received a vacation spot, but would instead be allocated according to the level of sociopolitical participation. And at a meeting he attended three weeks later, the Party Secretariat confidently recommended candidates for the upcoming union election: "These suggestions," the minutes ominously read, "will be taken into account by the BGL."[66]

The Schizophrenic Role of the Unions

There were other noticeable changes at Zeiss as well following Gruner's departure: In the mid-1960s, for example, FDGB officials severely criticized the union committee for not reacting to a continuous stream of complaints about unsatisfactory working conditions at the optical firm.[67] Such criticism and neglect would have been unthinkable there a decade earlier. But, as noted previously, those employed at other factories had long expressed dissatisfaction with the overall performance of the unions – despite the efforts of many BGL functionaries to fulfill their role as advocates and benefactors of the industrial working classes. Most criticism focused on their failure to exercise their official duties properly, represent workers' interests in a satisfactory manner, or make good on their promises – prompting complaints that the FDGB "doesn't do anything anyway" or that the BGL "merely talks" but doesn't "change a thing."[68] This widespread perception served to undermine the authority of many union officials, and helped account for the numerous reports that emphasized just how little trust and respect they enjoyed: When workers "sit together and are suddenly approached" by union functionaries, the Maxhütte reported, "the discussion stops immediately and they act very embarrassed."[69] Should this suggest that the East German unions had no useful function and were thus

---

[65] See, e.g., ThStA-R IV/7/231/1165, Prot. der LS der SED GO–Zeiss, 23.1.59.
[66] ThStA-R IV/7/231/1165, Prot. der LS der SED GO–Zeiss, 2.1.59, 23.1.59.
[67] ThStA-R, FDGB KV Slf 6222, Prot. der Sondersitz. des FDGB KV, 15.7.64.
[68] ThStA-R, BDVP Gera 21/250, reports, 26.7.54, 26.2.55; ThStA-R IV/A-7/230/498, IB der SED GO–Wema, 13.5.63.
[69] MxA-U, BGL 264, report, 26.9.51.

rejected by most of those under their charge as entirely powerless, as unable or unwilling to represent their own everyday interests?[70]

The history of Zeiss in the 1940s and 1950s clearly calls into question such generalizations. In fact, many workers there and elsewhere continued to approach the BGL with their grievances and demands, suggesting that they still entertained the hope that this body would or could fulfill the classic role of a union. It was nevertheless true that such expectations were often frustrated, primarily because of the precarious position in which union members found themselves. On the one hand, they were supposed to represent workers' interests and provide for their economic, social, and cultural well-being. But at the same time, they were obliged to enforce official policies aimed at ensuring high productivity levels and satisfactory fulfillment of the Plan. As the episode at Zeiss made clear, it was extremely difficult for union functionaries – serving simultaneously as representatives of both the workforce and the regime – to balance their discordant responsibilities and allegiances.

Like many foremen and brigadiers, those who dutifully exercised their role as taskmasters or ideologues often earned the enmity and resentment of those whom they reprimanded, lectured, or penalized. When BGL officials at the local washing-machine factory gave one worker a public warning because of his supposedly wasteful production practices, the chastised individual responded with a series of "unbridled comments" and threatened to appeal their decision to the factory director. This incident, in which a worker sought support from management against the union, suggested the often incongruous constellations that sometimes arose in the VEB. So, too, did a comment made by one union chairman with regard to a recent surge in sickness rates at the Maxhütte: "Many colleagues have simply not yet understood for whom they work...."[71]

Regular complaints by management and party officials that many low-level union functionaries went out of their way to avoid confrontations with workers nevertheless suggest the difficulty of generalizing about union behavior in the factories of Saalfeld – or, for that matter, in any single factory. It usually depended on the individuals involved: Some functionaries were clearly more solicitous of workers' demands and more willing or able to defend their economic and social interests. This was clearly the case at Zeiss, at least during the tenure of one particularly mettlesome chairman. But even the BGL under Hans Gruner had, for example, consistently and rigorously penalized those who were

---

[70] For such arguments, see, e.g., Simsch, *Ohnmacht*; idem, "Ausgeschlossenheit und Indifferenz: Deutsche Arbeiterinnen und Arbeiter, Deutsche Arbeitsfront und Freier Deutscher Gewerkschaftsbund, 1929–1962," in Hübner and Tenfelde, *Arbeiter*, 751–87; Gareth Pritchard, *The Making of the GDR, 1945–53: From Antifascism to Stalinism* (Manchester, UK, 2000), 6, 138–48, 205–6. For a more positive assessment of the role played by the unions, see Stadtland, *Herrschaft*; Günter Simon, *Ohne sie geht nichts: Gewerkschaften im Alltag der DDR* (Frankfurt am Main, 1979).

[71] ThStA-R, FDGB BV Gera 854/209, Prot. der Sitz. der BGL–Waschmaschine, 18.8.55; MxA-U, BGL 264, Prot. der PV im Hochofen (Kollektiv Eisen), 21.2.52.

allegedly ill when spotted on the streets after the official curfew imposed on sick workers.[72] Representing the interests of the East German workforce and carrying out the dictates of the party and state were, in short, contradictory tasks that were almost impossible to harmonize – leading many to play a schizophrenic role, to say the very least.

By revealing the possibilities and limits of dissenting behavior at the factory level, the conflicts at Zeiss as well as at other VEBs in Saalfeld vividly illustrated just how difficult it was for the SED to establish its authority at the grass roots and enforce the party line. This was especially true when it confronted established mentalities and milieus that felt threatened by official policies and developments, as was clearly the case at the local branch of the world-famous optical firm. Such conflicts cast doubt, in short, on misleading claims that the "SED's authority in the factories was never seriously called into question after June 17, 1953" – or that that uprising marked the "final death spasm of the East German labour movement."[73] As we have seen, the assignment of party members to leading positions in the People's Factories did not necessarily guarantee that high-level orders would be followed with blind obedience, and many union functionaries adamantly refused to act as spineless instruments of the SED. Their intermediary role between the regime and the workforce nevertheless placed them in a difficult position: As a result, they were often subject to a great deal of criticism from below – despite the various ways in which they often tried to represent the interests of their workers and provide them with important social benefits.

Although the SED apparently did not see it this way, those efforts arguably contributed to the stability of the regime. But at the same time, the fact that union and management officials were able to disobey or criticize party injunctions for years without suffering any real consequences must have served as an inspiration for – or at least emboldened – the workers under their charge. The evolving nature of industrial relations in the GDR clearly played an important role in this respect as well. As we shall see in the next chapter, all of this translated into widespread attempts by many Saalfelders to defend their everyday material interests on the shop floor and resist official schemes aimed at boosting output and productivity. We will look in particular at the success of such defensive strategies and try to determine above all their relationship to the longevity of the regime.

---

[72] According to a factory ordinance, sick workers were not allowed outside their homes after 6 P.M. See ThStA-R, FDGB Gera 851/208, Prot. der Sitz. der BGL–Zeiss, 30.11.56.

[73] See Reichel, "Arbeitsgesellschaft," 91; Pritchard, *Making*, 4. Compare these claims with the assertion that the uprising had "effectively crippled the regime on the shop floor," in Jeffrey Kopstein, *The Politics of Economic Decline in East Germany, 1945–1989* (Chapel Hill, NC, 1997), 37. Also see Kott, *Communisme*, 62–4.

7

Economic Struggles on the Shop Floor

With the possible exception of Soviet directives, one historian has argued, the SED leadership "respected, even feared, nothing" as much as industrial workers: "The greatest freedom in the GDR prevailed at the workbench...." If that were indeed the case, it appeared to be especially true in Saalfeld itself after the statewide uprising – or "learning shock" – of June 1953.[1] With memories of that dramatic event and especially its economic component in mind, most local factory officials now assiduously tried more than ever to avoid serious disputes with workers – above all those that threatened to escalate, disrupt production, and thus endanger fulfillment of the almighty Plan. Informal ad hoc meetings on the shop floor were the most common venue for dealing with specific conflicts, which were generally related to income levels and which often involved attempts by individuals or small groups of workers to boost their earnings by requesting – or demanding – lower production quotas or higher base wages and bonuses. Their efforts met with varying success, but usually resulted in a prolonged discussion or series of discussions leading to some sort of settlement amenable to both sides.[2]

The customary search for compromise as well as the general disinclination to antagonize workers clearly reflected a widespread desire to maintain harmony. That did not mean, of course, that officials automatically gave in to all demands.

---

[1] Quotation from Lutz Niethammer, cited in Ulrich Plenzdorf and Rüdiger Dammann, eds., *Ein Land, genannt die DDR* (Frankfurt am Main, 2005), 137. On the idea of *Lernschock*, see Martin Jänicke, *Der dritte Weg: Die antistalinistische Opposition gegen Ulbricht seit 1953* (Cologne, 1964).

[2] See, e.g., the minutes of the production meetings (*Produktionsversammlungen*) in MxA-U, BGL 199, 262, 264, 304, 366, 367, 412, 541. Also see the correspondence and minutes in ThStA-R, FDGB BV Gera 711/179, 854/209, 855/210, 862/212; ThStA-R, FDGB KV Slf 3245, 3540. On the tendency of officials elsewhere in the GDR to give in to wage-related demands, see in particular Peter Hübner, *Konsens, Konflikt und Kompromiß: Soziale Arbeiterinteressen und Sozialpolitik in der SBZ/DDR, 1945–1970* (Berlin, 1995), 187–204; Sandrine Kott, *Le communisme au quotidien: Les entreprises d'Etat dans la société est-allemande* (Paris, 2001), 182–97.

In fact, they often responded to customary calls for higher pay or lower norms by reminding workers of the performance principle or by summarily dismissing unwarranted requests that contravened official wage regulations. In response to demands for additional bonuses normally given to workers who performed especially arduous tasks, for example, a member of the Maxhütte's Wage Committee told one production brigade that its request could not be granted because it would lead to an illegal wage hike. Besides, he reminded them, they already received other bonuses that exceeded officially sanctioned levels – a rebuff that in itself clearly underscored the lenient practices of many factory officials.[3]

To avoid unwelcome disputes, shop-floor functionaries resorted to a number of other strategies that usually involved "passing the mark," so to speak. These included claims that they did not have the proper authority to comply with workers' demands, as well as evasive pledges to investigate the matter further or speak with their own superiors in order to find an equitable solution.[4] The latter was not always just an empty promise, however, and often led to negotiations with higher-level authorities in an attempt to pacify those under their charge. To that end, district and factory officials regularly appealed to central agencies for higher wages and extra bonuses for their workers or for assistance in maintaining a smooth – or at least a less bumpy – flow of production that would ensure satisfactory income levels. The Maxhütte even sent a permanent representative to Berlin to champion its concerns. Crisis situations often prompted urgent appeals to outside authorities as well: When workers at the washing-machine factory threatened to quit the union in protest against a decision excluding them from a special bonus awarded at larger firms in the district, officials quickly dispatched a delegation to the capital to speak directly with high-level party, union, and ministerial officials about the matter.[5]

If demands were not met by their immediate supervisors, particularly intransigent workers sometimes appealed to higher-level authorities themselves – which almost always prompted some form of external intervention, usually in the form of a written exchange between the VEB and outside agencies. During subsequent investigations that led to modifications in favor of the workers, those factory officials who had proven less than flexible when dealing with disgruntled subordinates were frequently subject to censure. In 1955, for instance, a wage dispute at one factory prompted a strong rebuke by the head of the district metal union: While admitting that there was no legal basis for workers' demands that they receive remuneration when summoned to appear before state or party authorities (i.e., to make up for lost time on the job), he reminded factory officials that the "laws and decrees in our workers-and-farmers' state

---

[3] MxA-U, BGL 367, Prot. der PV im Thomas–Stahlwerk, 26.2.54. For similar conflicts as well as comparable rebuffs, see the primary sources in the previous footnote.

[4] "Passing the mark" was an especially common tactic at Zeiss, where functionaries often claimed that their hands were tied by higher-level decisions made at the main headquarters in Jena. See, e.g., the reports in ThStA-R IV/7/231/1165, 1166; ThStA-R, FDGB BV Gera 709/178, 711/179.

[5] MxA-U, BGL 58, correspondence, 24.1.48; ThStA-R, FDGB BV Gera 709/178, correspondence, 13.12.52.

are created in the interest of our working masses, and should not merely be interpreted literally," but rather to the advantage of those who labor.[6]

Such admonitions placed lower-level officials in a difficult position. They were often discouraged from dealing too harshly with those under their charge and were usually reluctant to do so in any event. But they were nevertheless taken to task when labor costs exceeded – and production levels fell short of – official plan figures because of their often indulgent shop-floor practices. This chapter examines the dilemma more fully. It also looks at how workers responded to a variety of schemes aimed at boosting productivity while keeping wage levels in check, the effect that this had on the economy, and what all of this meant for the long-term stability of the regime.

Spiraling Wages and Stagnating Productivity

Leaving aside the endemic scarcity of basic goods and services in the GDR, the economic position of industrial workers improved considerably during the two decades following the Second World War: Real wages rose steadily over this period, especially after June 1953, and would even surpass prewar levels by the end of the decade. This favorable development was linked to a succession of official price decreases as well as to a piecemeal series of wage hikes that affected specific categories of workers and industrial sectors at different times and in varying degrees. As a result, the average income of production workers almost doubled between 1949 and 1960 and continued to climb during the following decade, though at a slower pace.[7] Workers in Saalfeld nevertheless continued to grumble about low earnings and the supposedly high cost of living: In response to typical complaints about "poor pay" in late 1957, one district union official admitted to a group of workers at the local brewery that despite a recent increase in the lowest base wages as well as the elimination of the lowest territorial tariffs, "one knows 'on high' that a thing or two still have to be changed."[8]

In fact, high-level authorities constantly worried that income levels were rising far too rapidly, with wage increases consistently outstripping those in

---

[6] ThStA-R, FDGB BV Gera 855/210, correspondence, 27.6.55, 5.7.55. For similar cases of appeals to as well as intervention and censure by outside officials, see the other documents in this file as well as those in ThStA-R, FDGB BV Gera 851/208, 854/209.

[7] For example, the average monthly wages of production workers at the Maxhütte rose from 176 marks in 1946 to 579 marks in 1960 and then to 658 marks in 1967. See the statistics in MxA-U, BGL 2, 165; ThStA-R, Maxh. 80. On wage and price developments in the GDR more generally, see Hübner, Konsens, 16–88; Johannes Frerich and Martin Frey, Handbuch der Geschichte der Sozialpolitik in Deutschland: Sozialpolitik in der DDR, vol. 2 (Munich, 1993), 51–3, 98–105, 132–5; Jörg Roesler, "Privater Konsum in Ostdeutschland," in Axel Schildt and Arnold Sywottek, eds., Modernisierung im Wiederaufbau: Die westdeutsche Gesellschaft der 50er Jahre (Bonn, 1993), 294–6.

[8] ThStA-R, FDGB KV Slf 3540, Prot. der BV am 25.11.57. On the various factors that influenced the configuration of wages in the GDR, see Chapter 1, footnote 82.

worker productivity as a result.[9] Most local functionaries candidly acknowledged this problem themselves, especially during the latter 1950s, when wage costs regularly exceeded – and worker productivity consistently failed to meet – the levels set forth in the annual plans determined for each factory. "In many cases," local FDGB functionaries concluded, "the current wage formulas provide no incentive to raise productivity."[10]

Workers and officials both remained preoccupied with income levels, then, but for entirely different reasons: While the former habitually complained that their wages were far too low, the latter were primarily concerned about reining in rising labor costs in an attempt to reverse the distorted wage/productivity trend and jumpstart the economy. To that end, they adopted a variety of strategies specifically aimed at stimulating worker performance. The most important ones were organized industrial competition (*Wettbewerb*) and the introduction of supposedly new production methods (*Neue Methoden*) devised in the GDR or elsewhere in the Soviet bloc. The latter would not only help reduce manufacturing costs, officials believed, but also increase worker productivity by speeding up production, eliminating mistakes, and increasing efficiency.[11]

Both campaigns met with widespread suspicion and resistance in Saalfeld: While some workers suspected that the new methods constituted a covert attempt to raise production quotas, others characteristically feared that they would lead to lower earnings. Pride in German technological prowess apparently played an important role as well – especially at Zeiss, where skilled workers vigorously rejected such methods by arguing that there was not much to improve there anyway. The proud Zeissianer were not the only skeptics, however: As one foreman at the Maxhütte put it, German workers had already become "hard-working" and "efficient" without having to rely on Soviet pedagogy; "besides, the Russians are more backward, what could they offer us anyhow...." He explained that his contentious views were based on wartime experiences with slave laborers from the East; this, along with years of National Socialist propaganda, had apparently made him immune to the

---

[9] For such trends at the Maxhütte, see the statistics in MxA-U, Betriebsdirektion: Personalfragen, 1950–4; MxA-U, Betriebsdirektion: Prot. der WL-Besprechungen, 1954–61.

[10] ThStA-R, FDGB BV Gera 862/212, Bericht über den Einsatz im VEB Saalfelder Hebezeugbau, n.d. On the tendency of wage increases to outstrip those in productivity throughout the GDR, see, e.g., Hübner, *Konsens*, 16–88; Jeffrey Kopstein, *The Politics of Economic Decline in East Germany, 1945–1989* (Chapel Hill, NC, 1997), 38; Jörg Roesler, "Wende in der Wirtschaftsstrategie: Krisensituation und Krisenmanagement, 1960–1962," in Jochen Cerny, ed., *Brüche, Krisen, Wendepunkte: Neubefragung der DDR–Geschichte* (Leipzig, 1990), 171–84. For evidence of this in Saalfeld itself, see the reports and correspondence in ThStA-R, FDGB BV Gera 851/208, 853/209, 855/210, 865/214; ThStA-R IV/7/230/1154, 1155, 1158.

[11] See ThStA-R, FDGB KV Slf 6190, Bericht über die Mitranow und Seifert Methoden, 20.12.61; Axel Bust-Bartels, *Herrschaft und Widerstand in den DDR–Betrieben: Leistungsentlohnung, Arbeitsbedingungen, innerbetriebliche Konflikte und technologische Entwicklung* (Frankfurt am Main, 1980), 73–5.

catchy East German slogan "To learn from the Soviet Union means to learn victory."[12]

Local officials acknowledged similar resistance to organized forms of industrial competition. Based on a Soviet model and evaluated according to a point system, these contests pitted worker against worker, brigade against brigade, department against department, and factory against factory in an effort to stimulate productivity and assure plan fulfillment. Decorations and titles as well as monetary premiums and other material rewards were given to collectives or individuals who had either produced the most or had done the best job of fulfilling written pledges to increase productivity, lower production costs, and improve the quality of manufactured goods.[13]

Despite the many incentives offered to participants, there was little initial interest in industrial competition following its introduction in the late 1940s; this was true of blue- and white-collar workers as well as members of the intelligentsia. Their reluctance largely reflected a widespread unwillingness to go along with yet another official scheme aimed at boosting output. At the same time, the early failure of many factory officials to encourage greater involvement suggested their general disinclination to upset shop-floor harmony by pressing staff members to act against their own wishes. Participation nevertheless grew steadily over the course of the 1950s, which supposedly reflected a growing realization that success in industrial competition often brought with it attractive material rewards: According to officials at the Maxhütte, attitudes had changed significantly after distribution of the first premiums. Whatever the reason, almost 65 percent of all workers in the district were involved in some form of factory-level competition by 1958, with participation rates continuing to climb during the following decade. In 1967, for example, more than 86 percent of all blue- and white-collar workers in the light industrial sector were involved in some form of competition; similar figures were reported at the steel mill as well, where almost 6,300 staff members participated in 1969 alone.[14]

Despite the growing number of participants, resistance and apathy remained widespread, leading to complaints by local officials that many contests were carried out in a merely perfunctory manner.[15] Severe material shortages accounted in part for this continuing aloofness: Throughout the 1950s and 1960s, many factories were periodically forced to suspend competition because of production

[12] ThStA-R IV/4/10/98, Prot. und Anlage der Sitz. der SED–KL, 10.9.1952; ThStA-R, Maxh. 390, Berichterstattung der SED BPO–Maxh., 9.10.51.

[13] See the useful overview in Kurt Erdmann, "Sozialistischer Wettbewerb," in Hartmut Zimmermann, ed., *DDR Handbuch*, vol. 2, 3rd ed. (Cologne, 1985), 1192–1208.

[14] See the statistics in ThStA-R, FDGB KV Slf 3555; ThStA-R, FDGB BV Gera – KV Gew. HaNaGe Slf 3576; ThStA-R, FDGB KV Slf 8007. On early resistance, see, e.g., ThStA-R, FDGB BV Gera 855/210, Bericht über den Instrukteureinsatz in dem Abus, 16.12.52.

[15] See, e.g., the various reports in ThStA-R IV/4/10/270, and ThStA-R IV/A-4/10/081, 090, 091, 095; ThStA-R, FDGB KV Slf 6141, 6278, 6302; ThStA-R, FDGB KV Slf 3540, 3555, 3567. Also see BStU ASt-G 0552, Lagebericht 1962 III. und IV. Quartale, 21.12.62.

bottlenecks or the irregular delivery of essential supplies. Such disturbances adversely affected both performance and income and consequently dampened the enthusiasm of many workers, who characteristically complained that they were unfairly penalized by production factors beyond their control: "The steel workers show little understanding for inter- and inner-factory competition because they simply don't receive enough iron...."[16] The continuing lack of interest also reflected anger or dismay on the part of less successful contenders, who were often upset about their failure to receive awards or about supposedly unfair practices by competitors.

But to what extent did industrial competition nevertheless achieve its main economic goals, i.e., did it effectively stimulate worker productivity and thus help ensure satisfaction of the plan? Local officials pointed to some positive results as participation levels increased toward the latter part of the 1950s: According to union functionaries at Zeiss, for example, industrial competition had saved the optical firm 389,000 marks in 1957 by spurring productivity and helping to reduce production backlogs.[17] Such claims must be treated with caution, of course, especially given the often mendacious nature of official economic analyses: Many functionaries simply exaggerated the success of their factories in order to avoid censure from above.[18] Just as important, the continuing regularity of pessimistic reports about participants who failed to make good on their promises, or about competitions that were no more than "purely formal affairs," similarly suggests the need for skepticism. Finally, the ways in which some workers tried to disadvantage their competitors in order to improve their own chances of success must have had an adverse effect on overall economic performance as well.[19]

Even if industrial competition and the new methods did spur at least some Saalfelders to improve their own performance, the overall sluggish performance of the East German economy clearly suggested that these strategies alone could not help overcome the many congenital shortcomings of centralized planning and the socialist production system.[20] Moreover, and whatever the impact of competition and the new methods, wage increases continued to outstrip those in

---

[16] ThStA-R IV/7/222/1060, IB der SED GO–Maxh., 18.2.56. For similar supply difficulties there and elsewhere, see the reports in ThStA-R, FDGB KV Slf 6141, 6278, 6302, 8007, 9541; ThStA-R, FDGB BV Gera 850/208, 851/208, 865/214.

[17] ThStA-R, FDGB BV Gera 850/208, Bericht über den Wettbewerb im Jahre 1957 im VEB Carl Zeiss Fertigungsstätte, 17.2.58.

[18] See Burghard Ciesla, "Hinter den Zahlen: Zur Wirtschaftsstatistik und Wirtschaftsberichterstattung in der DDR," in Alf Lüdtke and Peter Becker, eds., *Akten. Eingaben. Schaufenster: Die DDR und ihre Texte: Erkundungen zu Herrschaft und Alltag* (Berlin, 1997), 39–55.

[19] See Chapter 8.

[20] Besides Kopstein, *Politics*, a good place to start on the congenital problems of the East German economy is André Steiner, *Von Plan zu Plan: Eine Wirtschaftsgeschichte der DDR* (Munich, 2004). Also see Christoph Buchheim, "Die Wirtschaftsordnung als Barriere des gesamtwirtschaftlichen Wachstums in der DDR," *Vierteljahrschrift für Sozial- und Wirtschaftsgeschichte* 82 (1995): 194–210.

worker productivity – thanks in large part to the liberal distribution of bonuses as well as the widespread assignment of soft norms, a major problem since the immediate postwar period.

Leaving aside the occasional protests that norm levels "border on death,"[21] workers in almost all of Saalfeld's factories could easily satisfy and even exceed their assigned quotas and thereby substantially boost their earnings – much as they had before June 1953. Average fulfillment levels steadily climbed over that decade, in fact, rising at the Maxhütte from approximately 120 percent in 1950 to 145 percent by the end of the decade.[22] This was no isolated phenomenon, despite desultory efforts to introduce more stringent technically determined quotas: By the spring of 1958, average norm fulfillment at the local VEBs exceeded 140 percent – with three firms reporting average figures above 160 percent.[23] The minutes of a meeting convened by the metal union that year clearly illustrated the extent to which district functionaries had capitulated to workers on the norm issue: No objections were raised, for example, when a representative from the steel mill characterized fulfillment of 125 to 150 percent as "healthy." While noting that some quotas had to be modified in order to prevent much higher figures, the chairman of the union nevertheless hastened to add, "But it can't look as if the colleagues are taking home less money. . . ."[24]

High fulfillment rates were not a postwar novelty.[25] Yet this exchange hinted at several reasons why norms became even softer after June 1953 and why officials were either unable or unwilling to introduce more realistic quotas, despite high-level pressure to lower labor costs and increase productivity. In the first place, many appear to have tacitly accepted weak norms in order to forestall worker protest and maintain harmony on the shop floor. This was one of the most important legacies of both the 1948 progressive piecework fiasco and the more serious upheaval that took place five years later. Given the nature of piecework, workers were clearly interested in securing norms that could be easily satisfied, and there were several reasons why officials tended to indulge them on this issue: Because those functionaries specifically responsible for introducing and enforcing stricter norms were sometimes subject to verbal and even physical attack, many would vacillate when assigning new production quotas or meekly defer to union officials to secure acquiescence instead.[26] Apart

[21] ThStA-R IV/4/10/251 and 252, IB der SED–KL Slf, 16.2.56, 9.11.56.

[22] See footnote 9.

[23] See the figures in KrA-S 15673; ThStA-R IV/4/10/263; ThStA-R IV/7/230/1155; ThStA-R, FDGB BV Gera 862/212. For similar figures and reports about the difficulty of introducing TANs at these and other factories, see ThStA-R, FDGB KV Slf 3245, 6191; ThStA-R, FDGB BV Gera 705/177, 851/208, 855/210, 865/214.

[24] ThStA-R, FDGB BV Gera 853/209, Prot. der Sitz. der KV IG Metall Slf, 12.9.58.

[25] See, e.g., Alf Lüdtke, "What Happened to the 'Fiery Red Glow'? Workers' Experiences and German Capitalism," in Alf Lüdtke, ed., *The History of Everyday Life: Reconstructing Historical Experiences and Ways of Life*, trans. William Templer (Princeton, NJ, 1995), 226.

[26] See, e.g., the reports in MxA-U, BGL 26, 262; ThStA-R, FDGB BV Gera 711/179, 851/208.

from intimidation, many workers also succeeded in maintaining low norms by resorting to the same types of deceptive tricks common before June 1953, such as holding back labor reserves. Such practices suggest that official wage policy had the paradoxical and unintended effect of promoting behavior that served as a brake on worker productivity – thus undermining one of its most important goals. Although productivity levels rose in Saalfeld over the course of the 1950s, they did not necessarily do so because of piecework, but rather in spite of it.[27]

The same was true of official guidelines regarding the distribution of bonuses and premiums – or, more precisely, of the generous way in which such policies were carried out in everyday practice. In theory, these monetary incentives, intended to stimulate worker productivity, were to be awarded for outstanding performance, satisfactory plan fulfillment, and success in industrial competition. But in practice, most workers received premiums regardless of actual achievement – which contributed to spiraling labor costs without bringing about the expected increases in productivity. As one Soviet officer told management officials at the Maxhütte in 1947, "It would be better to distribute 500,000 marks in premiums . . . than to book a loss of one million marks." These words eventually came back to haunt local officials, however, as the various types of bonuses proliferated and as premium amounts skyrocketed over the next two decades.[28]

This development reflected, at least in part, the growing tendency of many factory officials to divide bonuses equally among workers – a widespread practice in Saalfeld despite high-level condemnation of this strategic attempt to maintain harmony on the shop floor as egalitarianism (*Gleichmacherei*). As officials at the VEB Rotstern readily acknowledged, premiums were not distributed according to the performance principle but rather according to the number of persons in a given brigade.[29] Union functionaries elsewhere similarly admitted that quarterly premiums were handed out without workers having to "demonstrate a certain degree of achievement." As a result of such liberal practices, many Saalfelders came to expect bonuses as a matter of course and felt that they were entitled to them regardless of actual performance.[30]

---

[27] See Alf Lüdtke, "'Helden der Arbeit' – Mühen beim Arbeiten: Zur mißmutigen Loyalität von Industriearbeitern in der DDR," in Hartmut Kaelble, Jürgen Kocka, and Hartmut Zwahr, eds., *Sozialgeschichte der DDR* (Stuttgart, 1994), 193–6.

[28] MxA-U, WL B60, Prot. der WL–Besprechung, 29.3.47. On premium policies more generally, see Hübner, *Konsens*, 62–70; Frerich and Frey, *Handbuch*, 97–8, 101–2, 134–5.

[29] ThStA-R IV/4/10/257, IB der SED–KL Slf, 13.11.58. For similar reports of *Gleichmacherei* at the Maxhütte, see MxA-U, BGL 58, 367, 611.

[30] In fact, bonuses eventually became the single most important source of supplementary income in the GDR, especially after authorities introduced a new ordinance in 1957 that led to a further increase in the amount of available bonuses by creating factory premium funds subsidized by the state. Average premiums at the VEB Wema almost doubled as a result, and the total amount of bonuses increased fourfold between 1954 and 1957 alone. See ThStA-R, FDGB KV Slf 3540, Prot. der erweiterten BGL–Sitz., 29.8.57; Hübner, *Konsens*, 64.

The Limits of Economic Reform in the 1960s

The first concerted effort to combat such attitudes and halt the worrisome wage/productivity trend of the 1950s came one month after the construction of the Berlin Wall, when emboldened high-level officials launched a statewide Production Challenge (*Produktionsaufgebot*) that sought to increase industrial output and thus forestall the adverse economic effects expected after the closing of the border. To that end, and in a move reminiscent of the fateful policies that had ostensibly led to the disturbances of June 1953, the new campaign once again called on workers to raise their production quotas and improve workplace discipline.[31] Taking its lead from the official motto – "Produce more in the same amount of time for the same amount of money" – a youth brigade at the Maxhütte initiated the local drive to change current norms, and duly issued a public pledge in which its members proclaimed that they "won't tolerate wages rising faster than productivity." Thousands of other workers in Saalfeld eventually yielded to increasing pressure and joined the movement as well, with a fourfold increase in pledges between October and December 1961.[32]

Local authorities nevertheless complained that most of these declarations were merely perfunctory and that few had come about as a result of worker self-initiative. In fact, the new productivity campaign met with widespread criticism throughout the district. While some workers claimed that current norms could not be increased further because they were already realistic enough, others suggested that material shortages and other production factors prevented any further hikes in productivity: "Why do you always begin with us, we're supposed to give time back to the state and work better, [but] what do the *Intelligentsia* do?" Despite similar protests that the Production Challenge was a "modern form of exploitation," most workers did not merely oppose the campaign on principle: Many feared that the drive to increase production quotas would only lead to lower earnings.[33]

Much of this opposition went beyond mere grumbling or a stubborn refusal to accept higher norms. This was especially true at the supposed site of greatest resistance, the VEB Wema, where some workers engaged in acts of industrial sabotage or called for a go-slow movement in protest. Hostile workers vented

---

[31] On this campaign as well as similar developments elsewhere in the GDR, see Hübner, *Konsens*, 79–82; Steiner, *Plan zu Plan*, 124–9; Corey Ross, *Constructing Socialism at the Grass-Roots: The Transformation of East Germany, 1945–65* (Houndsmill, UK, 2000), 165–72; Rüdiger Beetz, "Zur Geschichte des Produktionsaufgebotes 1961/1962 in der Industrie des Bezirks Potsdam," *Wissenschaftliche Zeitschrift der Pädagogischen Hochschule Potsdam* 29 (1985): 283–93.

[32] ThStA-R, FDGB KV Slf 6190, report, 16.2.62. For participation rates, see ThStA-R IV/4/10/266 and 268, IB der SED–KL Slf, 10.10.61, 1.12.61, 8.6.62.

[33] As workers elsewhere demanded at the time, "Communists, give us more to eat, or have you already forgotten June 17?" See ThStA-R IV/4/10/266, IB der SED–KL Slf, 10.10.61, 8.12.61; Steiner, *Von Plan zu Plan*, 128. On similar resistance and criticism, especially at Wema, also see the reports in ThStA-R, FDGB KV Slf 6190, 6191; ThStA-R, FDGB KV Slf 6178, Der politisch-ideologische Zustand der Arbeiterklasse, 15.11.61.

their anger as well by attacking colleagues who had broken ranks by agreeing to join the movement: Branded as "traitors" and "scabs" (*Lohndrücker*, an epithet that had inspired an earlier play by the East German author Heiner Müller), the latter were subject to frequent harassment as well as personal acts of sabotage – such as one worker who "had an inner tube tied to her machine [and] its oil pipe loosened so that when she turned [it] on she was sprayed with hot oil." Local authorities attributed such egregious behavior to a "lack of clarity" among many workers – or blamed it on the lack of interest and even outright opposition exhibited by many factory officials themselves.[34]

Along similar lines, district authorities suggested that the primary shortcoming of the new campaign lay in the failure of union and management officials to recognize its vital economic importance: To maintain harmony on the shop floor, they characteristically "[shied] away from disputes" and were "afraid to deal with such touchy issues." Like many workers, however, the latter defended their opposition by arguing that existing norms were already fair or that severe material shortages made further increases in productivity impossible.[35] That might have been true, but their justifiable concerns about the difficulty and danger of securing worker acquiescence must have played an important role as well.

To make matters worse, at least from an official standpoint, many rank-and-file party members also criticized the campaign openly or refused to set a positive example by taking part themselves. According to several at Rotstern, it was impossible to raise productivity because there were "hardly any [labor] reserves left." By the summer of 1962, in fact, only 16 percent of all participants belonged to the SED – which meant that only two-thirds of all party members in the district were somehow involved. Despite such widespread resistance, local authorities were nevertheless able to report by this time that three-quarters of all workers had already joined the campaign.[36] Noting how "incredibly difficult" it had previously been to introduce higher quotas, management officials at the Maxhütte even boasted that "after August 13" (i.e., the day the Berlin Wall went up) and "thanks to the Production Challenge . . . it's first become possible again to carry out norm modifications on a large scale."[37]

Notwithstanding such figures and despite such optimism, the *Produktionsaufgebot* only achieved mixed economic results overall: Most production

34 Several management officials at Wema were even accused of trying to discriminate against the head of one department who had publicly come out in support of the *Produktionsaufgebot*. See ThStA-R, FDGB KV Slf 6178, Der politisch-ideologische Zustand der Arbeiterklasse, 15.11.61; ThStA-R, FDGB KV Slf 6186, Anhang zum IB vom 12.12.61. Also see Heiner Müller and Inge Müller, *Der Lohndrücker* (Berlin, 1958).

35 ThStA-R, FDGB KV Slf 6186, Einschätzung zur gegenwärtigen Stand des Produktionsaufgebotes, 27.9.61, and Ergänzung zum IB, 25.10.61. For other examples of lackluster participation by officials, see the reports in ThStA-R, FDGB KV Slf 6178, 6191.

36 See ThStA-R IV/4/10/266 and 268, IB der SED–KL Slf, 10.10.61, 13.10.61, 8.6.62.

37 See MxA-U, Betriebsdirektion: Prot. der WL–Besprechungen (1962–3), Bericht über die nicht erfüllten Verpflichtungen des BKV 1961, n.d.

quotas remained unchanged at Wema, for example, where average norm fulfillment exceeded 200 percent in some departments by early 1962. In response to criticism from their superiors, officials there explained that those responsible for introducing more realistic norms still tended to be lenient with workers; as a result, only 61 percent were technically determined – and many of these were not really TANs at all but had instead been pulled from the proverbial desk drawer.[38] In essence, then, little had changed in Saalfeld over the past decade.

In reaction to similar reports throughout the GDR, the East German Council of Ministers issued a directive in March 1962 entitled "New Technology – New Norms," which insisted on the introduction of production quotas that supposedly reflected current technological and organizational conditions more accurately. The directive also tried to combat phony norms by calling for the enforcement of industrywide quotas based on so-called best times, i.e., the minimum time required by workers in a given sector to perform a given task rationally. Despite widespread objections – e.g., that the specific technical conditions and production procedures used in a certain factory prevented the application of the normative times prescribed by the sector to which it belonged – the new measure apparently succeeded, at least in part, in reining in runaway labor costs.[39] Although the average income of production workers at the Maxhütte increased slightly in 1963, for example, ten departments suffered significant pay cuts that year, with wages falling below plan figures in nine other firms as well during the first half of 1962. As a result, local officials could finally report a partial reversal of the distorted relationship between wage and productivity levels: In the first quarter of 1962, the increase in worker productivity at Zeiss outstripped a concomitant rise in wages by more than 5 percent. Increases in productivity exceeded plan figures in eight other firms as well during the first six months of that year.[40]

East German officials obviously welcomed these and similar reports – yet they had not necessarily intended to reduce net wages, but merely block further increases in an attempt to reverse the disturbing wage/productivity trend. Complaining that official policy only meant more work and less pay, several angry workers at Wema threatened in late 1963 that authorities were "in for a surprise": A series of strikes earlier that year that had come in response to wage decreases elsewhere suggested that they had already had one.[41]

[38] ThStA-R, FDGB KV Slf 6190, Bericht über die Mitranow und Seifert Methoden, 20.12.61; FDGB KV Slf 6191, Analyse über die Tätigkeit der Gewerkschaftlichen Leitungen und der ökonomischen Situation im VEB Wema, 8.2.62. On habitually soft norms at Wema, also see AdsD, Ostbüro 0523j, report, 24.11.60.

[39] See, e.g., ThStA-R, FDGB KV Slf 6232, Bericht zur Arbeit mit neuen Lohnformen, 4.6.63; ThStA-R, Maxh. 381, Bericht über die Verwirklichung der Direktive "Neue Technik – Neue Normen," 17.12.64. Also see Bust-Bartels, *Herrschaft*, 79–80, 100.

[40] See BStU ASt-G 0552, Lagebericht 1962 III. und IV. Quartale, 21.12.62; ThStA-R, FDGB KV Slf 6191, IB Nr. 22, 21.9.62; ThStA-R IV IV/4/10/213, Anhang zur Bürovorlage, 7.9.62.

[41] See BStU ASt-G 0552, Quartalsanalyse für die III. und IV. Quartale 1962, 20.12.62, and Halbjahresanalyse I. Halbjahr 1963, n.d; ThStA-R IV/A-4/10/091, IB der SED–KL Slf, 25.5.63.

To pacify workers and maintain shop-floor tranquility, some factories tried to offset these decreases by offering new supplementary bonuses (*Lohnausgleiche*), which, as one foreman at Wema explained, soon became standard in his department: "The amount to be paid rose continually and was on average 1,500 marks" – leading once again to inflated labor costs well above plan figures:

[W]asted time (*Bummelzeit*) was also rewarded at the end of the month because of the supplementary payments.... [T]he colleagues no longer had the same incentive they had had with [normal] piecework because they now earned even more. So they said to themselves: No one notices if I complete ten pieces more or less, I still receive my compensatory payment anyway at the end of the month.[42]

Partly in response to such uneven achievements throughout the GDR, high-level officials unveiled a major economic reform program in January 1963 that aimed once again at increasing productivity and efficiency while keeping wage levels in check. Brimming with buzzwords that would become increasingly familiar to East Germans over the next several years, the so-called New Economic System (NÖS) proclaimed by Walter Ulbricht at the SED's Sixth Party Congress promised to correct the "mistakes" of the past by introducing a variety of measures aimed at modernizing the economy and rationalizing the production process. To that end, it called for a "scientific-technical revolution" based on the introduction of cutting-edge technology and automation; it also emphasized the need to train a new, technically proficient elite capable of applying more scientific management methods, such as the use of cybernetics.[43]

The New Economic System heralded, in effect, the age of the East German technocrat: If functionaries were slow at first to master the new vocabulary and style of the period, their reports would become increasingly laden with – and leadened by – social-scientific jargon by the end of the decade. In more concrete economic terms, the NÖS was a concerted attempt to reduce rigid centralized control of the economy by delegating greater powers and responsibility to state-run enterprises, whose performance was now to be measured primarily in terms of profitability.

The creation of a new system of structural incentives – known in NÖS parlance as *economic levers* – constituted an equally important component of the reform program, and one that would supposedly stimulate performance and productivity by appealing to the "material interests" of both factories and workers themselves. What that meant in practice was that the VEBs would now have a greater interest in making a profit because they could now use it for reinvestment and finance. Along similar lines, and in an attempt to strengthen workers' interest in the overall performance of their factory, authorities decided

---

[42] ThStA-R, FDGB KV Slf 6232, Bericht des Meisters M., 4.6.63.

[43] Important studies of the NÖS include André Steiner, *Die DDR–Wirtschaftsreform der sechziger Jahre: Konflikt zwischen Effizienz- und Machtkalkül* (Berlin, 1997); Jörg Roesler, *Zwischen Plan und Markt: Die Wirtschaftsreform 1963–1970 in der DDR* (Berlin, 1990); idem, *Das Neue Ökonomische System (NÖS): Dekorations- oder Paradigmawechsel* (Berlin, 1994); Kopstein, *Politics*, 41–73.

to introduce year-end premiums that were to be distributed only if the entire firm had satisfied the financial and production goals set forth in the annual plan.[44] Because the size of the premium fund in each enterprise was now to be determined largely by profits, the amount paid to each worker depended on individual accomplishment as well as the performance of the entire firm, i.e., low factory earnings would mean low year-end premiums – at least in theory. In practice, these bonuses, which ranged from one-third to double average monthly wages, quickly became a lucrative source of supplementary income and one of the most important premiums available to local workers – regardless of their factory's actual accomplishment.

As an additional incentive, and in an effort to militate against the widespread practice of blanket distribution, the NÖS increasingly tied other bonuses (as well as extra vacation time) to the satisfactory performance of a given task or special assignment. Other economic levers directed specifically at workers included new types of wages and norms intended to counter other unwelcome developments – besides soaring income levels and lagging productivity – that officials had routinely criticized since the late 1940s: poor-quality goods, high production costs, and wasteful production practices.[45] Premium piecework, for example, partially reduced the traditional emphasis on quantity – now roundly denounced as "tonnage ideology" – by making individual earnings more dependent on other factors besides mere output: the quality of goods produced, for example, the full use of all labor reserves, cleanliness and order in the workplace, more careful treatment of machinery and tools, and (with an eye to the effect that the complete closure of the border with West Germany in 1961 had had on already chronic material shortages) less wasteful production practices. The reforms made a good deal of sense, given the way in which many workers had habitually manipulated piecework to their own advantage without regard to quality or cost. In essence, authorities had finally come to recognize that the satisfaction of plan figures alone was neither a reliable gauge nor an effective measure of performance.[46]

Broadly speaking, the new reforms achieved some initial success in reversing the wage/productivity trend of the 1950s. This provoked widespread grumbling and a spate of work stoppages on the part of those who suffered wage cuts, but

---

[44] By paying these substantial bonuses at the end of the year, officials also hoped to discourage labor turnover – the perennial bugbear of local authorities, as we shall see in the next section.

[45] ThStA-R, Maxh. 132, Bericht über die Verwendung der Prämienmittel 1966, 21.3.67. For the ways in which local officials interpreted and tried to implement the NÖS more generally, see the information reports (*Informationsberichte*) in ThStA-R IV/A-4/10/091 and 092, 19.6.63, 17.7.63; ThStA-R IV/B-4/10/99 and 100, 17.2.66, 9.4.68. Also see the reports and minutes in ThStA-R, FDGB KV Slf 3564, 6256, 8007, 9541; ThStA-R, Maxh. 100, Einführung von leistungsabhängigen Gehältern im Kombinat, n.d.; MxA-U, Bandnummer 851 (Betriebsdirektion: Prot. der Direktorensitz., I. Halbjahr 1968), Methodik zur komplexen Durchsetzung des Systems der fehlerfreien Arbeit, 22.1.68.

[46] On the efforts to encourage more efficient production practices, see, e.g., MxA-U, Bandnummer 633 (Betriebsdirektion: Prot. der Direktorensitz., I. Halbjahr 1964), Prot. der Dienstbesprechung, 24.6.64; ThStA-R, FDGB KV Slf 6302, IB der FDGB KV Slf, 30.9.65, 14.12.65; ThStA-R, FDGB KV Slf 3564, Prot. der Sekretariatssitz., 6.6.66. Also see Bust-Bartels, *Herrschaft*, 92–4.

local security officials noticed a decrease in such behavior by the summer of 1964: They attributed this, at least in part, to a recent rise once again in earnings.[47] Average wages had, according to one investigation, risen in sixteen of eighteen factories that year but average productivity in only thirteen; moreover, growth in productivity had outpaced wage increases in only eleven. Developments during the latter part of the decade were equally uneven and, from an official viewpoint, equally disconcerting: The VEB Wema continued to report an "unfavorable relationship" between wages and productivity, for example, and at the Maxhütte, income levels regularly surpassed – and productivity levels consistently fell short of – plan figures throughout the period. In mid-1971, the steel mill reported that it had already exceeded the amount available in its wage fund for the entire year by 310,000 marks.[48]

Local authorities accounted for these mixed results by arguing that many of the NÖS reforms had not been properly implemented. They characteristically censured factory officials for not taking the measures seriously enough and criticized in particular their alleged failure to introduce the various economic levers of incentive. In short, they claimed, the new way of thinking had not yet become second nature to those in charge of the People's Factories. As a result, many functionaries continued to award bonuses despite inadequate performance, and the old practice of blanket distribution continued apace: "One constantly encounters egalitarian tendencies," the SED District Party Secretariat complained in early 1965, and the "equal distribution of premiums . . . means that bonuses no longer act as a material incentive."[49] Whether they ever had was, of course, entirely debatable.

The failure of many functionaries to enforce stricter criteria when deciding on the distribution of bonuses may have had unfavorable consequences for the East German economy. This was nevertheless part of a well-established strategy aimed at maintaining tranquility on the shop floor. As one foreman at the Thälmann graphics factory admitted in 1965, "We are sometimes still too soft and tend to shy away from honest disputes. . . . We even pay bonuses to workers who don't participate in industrial competition."[50] That old habits died hard was also underscored by continued reports of "tonnage ideology," i.e., the use of quantity and not quality as the primary measure of performance. While factory functionaries typically blamed poor quality on carelessness, indifference, thoughtlessness, and the failure of workers to take proper care of their equipment or maintain a clean, orderly workplace, the latter responded to such censure by attributing deficient production quality to poor working conditions as well as the substandard material and old machinery they were still forced to

---

[47] BStU ASt-G 0552, Quartalsanalyse I. und II. Quartale 1962, 3.7.62; Halbjahranalyse I. Halbjahr 1964, 3.6.64; and Lagebericht I. Halbjahr 1965, 29.6.65.

[48] ThStA-R IV/A-7/230/498, IB der SED GO–Wema, 22.9.67; ThStA-R, Maxh. 80, Arbeitskräfte und Lohnsummenvergleich, 22.1.68; ThStA-R, Maxh. 373, report, 18.8.71.

[49] MxA-U, Bandnummer 633 (Betriebsdirektion: Prot. der Direktorensitz., I. Halbjahr 1964), Vorlage über Arbeit mit den Neueren, 23.3.64; ThStA-R IV/A-4/10/095, IB der SED–KL Slf, 26.1.65, 8.3.65.

[50] ThStA-R IV/A-4/10/096, IB der SED–KL Slf, 21.4.65.

use. As one retired worker from the city of Leipzig colorfully recalled following the collapse of the regime, he and his colleagues often had to make "candy out of shit."[51]

Official strategies aimed at boosting worker productivity and keeping labor costs under control were largely imperfect, then, following the uprising of June 1953. As one student of the 1960s reform experiment has concluded, "[T]he implementation of new instruments created new contradictions and consequently new inefficiencies. . . . [H]alf-hearted corrections failed to help, and for that reason, the behavior of the economic subjects [i.e., the workers themselves] hardly changed during the entire period." This failure reflected, at least in part, the fears of dogmatic Communist officials about the possible loss of central control – and not just over the economy.[52] But it also attested to the successful ways in which many workers continued to defend their own *immediate* material interests by successfully resisting many of the economic demands placed upon them by the party and state.[53] At the same time, it underscored the inability or unwillingness of local functionaries to rigorously enforce high-level economic directives, despite the pressure brought to bear upon them by their superiors. This leniency reflected not only their eagerness to maintain shop-floor harmony, but also the considerable power that industrial workers enjoyed – in large part because of chronic labor shortages.

"A Real Traveling Circus"

Insufficient labor had plagued local industry since the early postwar years, despite the influx of thousands of refugees from the East as well as the large-scale entry of women into the labor force after 1945.[54] This challenge became especially worrisome during the latter part of the 1950s, however, following

[51] Lüdkte, "Helden," 202. On the failure to implement many of the NÖS reforms properly, especially the use of economic levers, see the information reports in ThStA-R IV/A-4/10/082 (31.1.64), 091 (19.6.63), 093 (24.1.64), 095 (26.1.65, 8.3.65), 100 (14.7.66). Also see the minutes of the union meetings in ThStA-R, FDGB KV Slf 3589, 8007, 9541.

[52] André Steiner, "Wirtschaftsgeschichte der DDR," in Rainer Eppelmann, Bernd Faulenbach, and Ulrich Mählert, eds., *Bilanz und Perspektiven der DDR–Forschung* (Paderborn, 2003), 232.

[53] The long-term economic effect of such behavior (especially in terms of continuing scarcity and poor-quality goods) was an entirely different matter, of course, i.e., it could be argued that workers were, in effect, cutting off their noses to spite their faces.

[54] Apart from important ideological considerations, the recruitment of women into the local workforce was initially intended to make up for the significant loss of men killed or imprisoned during the war. In the late 1940s, approximately 55 percent of the district's population was female, as was a similar percentage of all those considered fit for employment. Efforts to attract women into the local labor force met with considerable success: By the mid-1950s, approximately one-third of all those employed in Saalfeld were female. Thanks to continuing recruitment as well as a steady increase in the number of women employed part-time, more than 40 percent of all workers in Saalfeld were female by the close of the following decade. See the statistics in KrA-S 23268, 23739, 23740; ThHStA-W, KR Slf 559, 872; ThStA-R, FDGB KV Slf 7609, 7610. More generally, see Gunilla-Friederike Budde, ed., *Frauen arbeiten: Weibliche Erwerbstätigkeit in Ost- und Westdeutschland nach 1945* (Göttingen, 1997).

the second Berlin crisis: In 1958 alone, the district's twenty largest firms were short some 600 workers – a situation that did not improve significantly in the following decade despite the subsequent closure of the border.[55] East German authorities were themselves largely responsible for this dire state of affairs. Military recruitment as well as the other unpopular policies that had earlier prompted mass flight had all taken their toll, of course. But to make matters worse, the new emphasis placed on high-tech sectors in the mid-1960s only served to exacerbate the acute labor shortages already present in other branches of the economy.

In Saalfeld itself, Ulbricht's "scientific-technical revolution" led to the massive expansion of the VEB Zeiss, which produced important technological devices as well as military hardware. As a result, local factories were forced to yield large numbers of blue- and white-collar workers to the optical firm despite having already insufficient labor. This understandably met with widespread resistance among factory officials as well as among many workers themselves, who balked at the requisite retraining that this involved. The loudest objections were heard at the washing- and sewing-machine factories, which – after a century-old tradition – halted the manufacture of their old wares after a forced merger with Zeiss in 1968. Compulsory labor transfers had serious consequences for other major firms in the district as well: This was especially true at the Maxhütte, which was obliged to part with approximately 200 workers each year. The loss of many young skilled workers and apprentices to the optical firm contributed to the superannuation of what was already an aged workforce, forcing the steel mill – once the pride of East German industry – to close down several departments and mines because of resulting labor deficits.[56]

To counter this worrisome development, officials at the Maxhütte not only relied on the use of forced labor – a practice that had first begun during the Third Reich under Flick – but also became increasingly preoccupied with recruiting teenagers about to complete their studies. Despite the allure of relatively high earnings, such efforts met with limited success because most youths were making job choices according to their own personal interests – opting for "fashionable careers" (*Modeberufe*), as disparaging officials put it, instead of ones that were supposedly essential for the economic well-being of Saalfeld and the GDR as a whole. Their general reluctance to become apprenticed in the metallurgy sector reflected a widespread aversion to strenuous manual labor and shift work, and many were supported in their decision by parents employed

---

55 See ThStA-R, FDGB KV Slf 6151, Prot. der Sekretariatssitz., 3.12.58; ThStA-R, Maxh. 128, Arbeitskräftebedarf, 25.7.65; ThStA-R, FDGB KV Slf 9541, Prot. der Sekretariatssitz. der KV IG Metall Slf, 27.6.68.

56 See ThStA-R IV/B-4/10/087, ABI Bericht über die durchgeführte Kontrolle zur Durchsetzung des Beschlusses des Präsidiums des Ministerrates zur Entwicklung des wissenschaftlichen Gerätebaus im VEB Carl Zeiss Jena, 18.4.68; ThStA-R, Maxh. 28, Fluktuationsanalyse I. Quartal 1968, 21.5.68, and Analytische Einschätzung der Arbeitskräfte-Situation und -Fluktuation, 30.5.68.

at the Maxhütte themselves; according to investigators, the latter tended to put up the greatest resistance because of their own everyday experiences there.[57]

Regardless of the reasons, what was the ultimate significance of continuing labor shortages more generally? In the first place, and as factory officials knew themselves, the maintenance of an adequate and permanent staff (or *Stammbelegschaft*) was essential for high-quality production and the timely satisfaction of plan goals. As one union chairman warned, "[S]omething must be done at all costs to prevent job turnover [because] one works better with those who know the ropes...."[58] Aware of such considerations, high-level authorities actively tried to dissuade factories from luring workers away from each another. In the summer of 1959, for example, the District Council decided to prohibit all factories in Saalfeld from hiring construction workers, whose numbers had decreased by almost a quarter the previous year alone because of low wages and an inadequate supply of production materials. With the help of the People's Police, it subsequently tracked down many of those who had left and tried to persuade them to return to their old jobs. Several months later, the local Planning Commission went a step further by placing a general ban on all labor recruitment through newspapers and the radio and by decreeing that it alone would mediate all job placement in the future.[59] Recruitment nevertheless remained a serious problem during the following decade, eventually prompting the District Council to announce a complete freeze on the recruitment of workers already employed at the largest and economically most important factories in Saalfeld: "[W]e realize that we don't have a right to force a worker into a certain factory, but we can certainly decide along with the director whether or not he can leave." That was clearly wishful thinking, as continued reports of high turnover rates made clear: "[W]ork was much different years ago when we had a more permanent staff," one nostalgic union official remarked in 1967; "today it's just a coming and going . . . a real traveling circus."[60]

From the standpoint of East German authorities, the absence of a *Stammbelegschaft* could nevertheless have at least one positive effect: The constant

---

[57] See MxA-U, Betriebsdirektion: Prot. der WL–Besprechungen (1962–3), Prot. der erweiterten Dienstbesprechung der Direktoren, 12.11.63, and Bericht zum Stand des polytechnischen Unterrichts, 5.1.61; MxA-U, Bandnummer 633 (Betriebsdirektion: Prot. der Direktorensitz., I. Halbjahr 1964), Einschätzung der Arbeit der Betriebsberufsschule, 18.1.64. For similar recruitment difficulties throughout the district, especially at Zeiss, see the reports and minutes in ThStA-R, FDGB KV Slf 6256, 6302, 9541. On the use of forced labor at the steel mill, see MxA-U, Kaderabt.: Abwanderung nach dem Westen (Berichte, 1949–57); BStU ASt-G 0552, Lagebericht II. Halbjahr 1964, 4.1.65.

[58] ThStA-R, FDGB KV Slf 3540, Prot. der BV–Brauhaus, 25.11.57.

[59] ThStA-R, FDGB KV Slf 6148, Prot. der Sitz. der FDGB KV Slf, 9.11.59. More generally, see Dierk Hoffmann, *Aufbau und Krise der Planwirtschaft: Die Arbeitskräftelenkung in der SBZ/DDR, 1945 bis 1963* (Munich, 2002). Also see Ross, *Constructing Socialism*, 97–8.

[60] See ThStA-R, FDGB KV Slf 9541, Prot. der Sekretariatssitz. der KV IG Metall Slf, 14.3.68; ThStA-R, FDGB KV Slf 3567, Prot. der Sitz. der BGL–Kohlenhandel, 22.11.67.

shuffling and reshuffling of the workforce within any single factory, as well as between different ones, must have helped impede the creation of shop-floor solidarity that might have posed a potential threat to stability. But there was another important consequence as well, and one that also helped ensure domestic peace, at least indirectly: The opportunity made possible by labor shortages of transferring to another department or factory not only served to empower but also strengthen the economic position of many workers in Saalfeld. Even if most avoided the *Parteilehrjahr*, as we saw in Chapter 5, they apparently had an implicit understanding of basic Communist economic theory – and especially Karl Marx's ideas concerning the so-called industrial reserve army. What that meant in practice was that they knowingly took advantage of labor deficits in order to advance their demands for higher wages, larger bonuses, and lower production quotas, usually by threatening to seek employment elsewhere or transfer to another department.[61] And because many actually made good on this threat, factory functionaries came under added pressure to give in to workers' demands. This was, in short, yet another important reason why norms remained so weak after June 1953, why factory officials regularly lobbied their superiors in order to secure higher wages and bonuses for those under their charge – i.e., to *keep* them under their charge – and why, as a result, increases in income continued to outstrip those in productivity.

But there was another important connection as well between labor shortages and soaring wage costs during the post-1953 period, namely, the increasingly high levels of overtime in Saalfeld. To make up for chronic labor deficits – as well as production bottlenecks or disturbances caused by sudden modifications of the plan – workers were frequently required to put in extra hours, with overtime always rising sharply at the end of a quarter in order to meet production goals (a practice known as *Stoßarbeit*). As a result, factory personnel were usually willing to turn a blind eye to a December 1953 ordinance that restricted annual overtime to 120 hours per worker; in turn, obliging state and union authorities frequently granted factory requests to surpass the legal limit.[62]

The number of additional hours put in by workers consequently skyrocketed during the 1950s and 1960s. In 1958, for instance, overtime at the local transportation company far exceeded the legal limits, jumping from 36,000 hours in the third quarter of 1957 to more than 53,000 hours one year later – a result, in all likelihood, of the SED's recent decision to reduce the workweek to forty-five hours. Noting that this would have normally been enough to keep a small factory going for a quarter of a year, and arguing that such excesses not only inflated labor costs but were also an important cause of industrial accidents,

---

[61] See, e.g., MxA-U, BGL 264, Prot. der BV im MB–Hochofen, 12.12.52; ThStA-R, FDGB KV Slf 3795, Prot. der BGL–Sitz. Rotstern, 16.7.58. Also see Karl Marx, *Capital*, vol. 1, trans. Ben Fowkes (New York, 1977), 781–94.

[62] See, e.g., the correspondence and minutes in ThStA-R, FDGB BV Gera 705/177, 851/208, 855/210. Also see Frerich and Frey, *Handbuch*, 110–12, 135–6.

the District Council responded by calling for a significant reduction in overtime there and elsewhere. Several years earlier, one union official at the transportation company had already declared that he was no longer willing – "as a member of the BGL and as the one responsible for worker safety protection" – to approve so much overtime.[63]

These warnings and protests had little effect. In fact, and despite their legitimate concerns, factory officials would grant even higher levels of overtime the following decade: In 1964, some truck drivers at the transportation company worked 120 hours of overtime *each month*.[64] Comparable increases were also reported elsewhere: Overtime at the Maxhütte rose from approximately 64,000 hours in 1962, for example, to almost 138,000 hours during the first half of 1971 alone.[65] Actual figures were often much higher because management officials at the steel mill often assigned workers to a second job in order to conceal the amount of overtime they actually worked. Such illicit practices as well as continued reports of wildly excessive overtime figures prompted East German authorities to censure or even take legal action against derelict factory functionaries in the 1960s.[66] Yet, the latter were in a difficult position: They were supposed to abide by official guidelines and keep overtime at a healthy minimum, but they were also under constant pressure to meet plan targets set by central authorities. Staying within the legal limits became even more of a challenge once the five-day workweek was formally introduced in 1967.[67]

High-level efforts to keep wage costs in check by reducing inordinate amounts of overtime remained more or less ineffectual, then. But economic necessity was not the only explanation for this failure. Despite complaints about the number of extra hours they were asked to put in, many Saalfelders explicitly demanded the right to perform overtime by arguing that their regular wages were insufficient: "[T]he party has to guarantee me high amounts of overtime," one driver at the transportation company argued in 1966, "so that my living standard remains secure." For similar reasons, many workers opposed obligatory breaks that were not remunerated or that hindered them from satisfying their norms.[68] In short, official efforts to reduce overtime met with widespread resistance on the shop floor, not only by functionaries constrained by the dictates

---

[63] KrA-S 12560, Kreisratssitz., 7.1.59; ThStA-R IV/7/220/1002, Prot. der MV der SED GO–Kraftverkehr, 28.2.55. On excessive overtime elsewhere in the GDR, see Hübner, *Konsens*, 104–20.

[64] ThStA-R IV/A-4/10/082, IB der KPKK Slf, 21.12.64.

[65] See the statistics in ThStA-R, Maxh. 80, 128, 373; MxA-U, Bandnummer 633 (Betriebsdirektion: Prot. der Direktorensitz., I. Halbjahr 1964).

[66] See, e.g., ThStA-R IV/A-7/230/496, Prot. der LS der SED GO–Wema, 30.9.65; ThStA-R IV/B-7/220/237, Monatsbericht der SED GO–Kraftverkehr, Oct. 1969.

[67] See Hübner, *Konsens*, 120–9.

[68] See ThStA-R IV/A-4/10/081, Zwischenbericht der KPKK Slf über den gegenwärtigen Stand der geführten Untersuchung in der APO KOM des VEB Kraftverkehr Slf-Rudolstadt, 2.3.66; ThStA-R IV/7/231/1167, IB der SED GO–Zeiss, 24.6.58, 2.7.58.

of the plan but also by workers who viewed additional shifts as a way in which to boost their income.

Not all of them were merely concerned with high pay, of course, especially when health and leisure time were at risk. In fact, one investigation of turnover rates at the Maxhütte found that unpopular hours at the steel mill had prompted "not a few" to search for employment elsewhere. The most common complaint there concerned double shifts, a major source of discontent since the late 1940s, when a three-shift system had first been introduced at the factory. In response to understandable objections that sixteen-hour workdays were simply not permissible, one functionary explained that they had been working on this problem for twenty years (i.e., since the Nazi period) but could still not make any headway because of continuing labor shortages.[69] Night work was equally unpopular in Saalfeld, not only because of general health concerns but also because of poor public transportation and inadequate supplies of food and drink after hours. "Party members tell us that one can no longer even speak with night-shift workers," alarmed officials at Zeiss reported in 1956. "For nine years these people have had to perform a night shift every three weeks; this has had an adverse effect on their physical condition. Over time, most of them suffer from stomach ailments. The elimination of the night shift is their greatest demand [but we] don't exactly know when or even if this wish can be fulfilled."[70]

As this once again suggests, some local officials were quite sympathetic to workers' demands, at the very least because of their interest in maintaining industrial harmony and a healthy labor force. Their apparent inability to introduce necessary changes nevertheless created a serious dilemma. Many workers were forced to put in overtime, as well as work double shifts and at night, in order to make up for labor shortages and production disturbances. But the excesses just described had a negative effect on the labor supply by leading to elevated sickness and accident rates, which, in turn, undermined worker productivity even further and thus wreaked havoc on production. This was, in short, a vicious circle.[71] But, as we shall see in the next section, the high incidence of illness and injury reflected more than just the demographic and economic constraints engendered by the regime's own failed policies.

---

[69] Complaints about shift work would continue there and at other local factories throughout the remainder of the Ulbricht era. The Maxhütte even decided in 1969 to introduce a four-shift system in some departments in response to a Politbüro decree calling for maximal use of the workday. See the reports in MxA-U, Betriebsdirektion: Personalfragen (1950–4); also see MxA-U, BGL 367, Prot. der BV im Hochofen, 7.1.54; ThStA-R, Maxh. 28, Fluktuations-analyse I. Quartal 1968, 21.5.68, and Analytische Einschätzung der Arbeitskräfte-Situation und -Fluktuation, 30.5.68; ThStA-R IV/B-4/10/100, Bericht über Maßnahmen zur vollen Ausnutzung der Arbeitszeit, 25.7.69.

[70] ThStA-R IV/7/231/1167, IB der SED GO–Zeiss, 27.3.56.

[71] On lost production time at the Maxhütte because of industrial accidents (almost 150,000 hours in 1958 alone), see the statistics in MxA-U, Betriebsdirektion: Personalfragen (1950–4); MxA-U, Bandnummer 633 (Betriebsdirektion: Prot. der Direktorensitz., I. Halbjahr 1964).

The Sick, the Slacker, and the Slovenly

According to an April 1949 investigation, sickness levels at one of the Maxhütte's mines had increased enormously in January and February of that year. This appeared, on the one hand, to have been a protest against the recent Soviet decision to abolish progressive piecework wages, a source of indignation throughout the eastern zone. But that was not the only reason for high sickness levels, as the author of the report hastened to point out: Many workers had put in long hours during the last three months of 1948 in order to take advantage of the new wage system and earn more money. As a result, and especially in light of widespread malnutrition at the time, many were now physically "overspent." Yet, that was not all: The fact that the previous month's earnings were used to determine the amount of sick pay explained as well why so many workers suddenly stayed at home during the first two months of 1949.[72] This is a particularly instructive example because it identifies several of the most important factors contributing to high sickness rates in Saalfeld then and throughout the following two decades: physical exhaustion or actual illness, manipulation of East Germany's social welfare policies, and, last but not least, absenteeism as protest.

Management officials and medical personnel attributed most illness to natural causes, such as flu epidemics or colds during the winter months, when sickness rates generally peaked. Other important factors included arduous or unsanitary work conditions, poor nourishment, shortages of protective clothing and medical personnel, long waits for frequently unheated buses and trains – and, above all, the steady and widespread increase in overtime. As the head of the local railway station explained in September 1958, because "we are understaffed by 10 percent... approximately 6,000 hours of overtime were performed last month. And that is the main cause of sickness."[73]

As suggested, other factors came into play as well, such as the tendency of many workers to feign illness in order to take advantage of the monetary benefits accruing to the indisposed. Sickness rates were, in other words, not just a medical problem: "Some colleagues think very rationally about material things. They figure out, for example, that sickness benefits... amount to almost as much as" they would receive if they "continued to work in the factory, especially when production problems arise...." Because sick workers received 90 percent of their base wages as well as additional compensation, many could earn more in such cases by simply staying at home. This "false understanding... of our social achievements," members of the District Council angrily concluded, was widespread among blue- and white-collar workers, who "try at all costs to take 'their' six sick weeks each year...." In fact, absenteeism as a result of

---

[72] MxA-U, BGL 62, Bericht über meinen Einsatz [von Rudolf F.], 11.4.49. See Chapter 1 on the progressive piecework episode.

[73] KrA-S 12559, Prot. der Kreisratssitz., 17.9.58.

illness – feigned or otherwise – was higher in the GDR than anywhere else in the Soviet bloc.[74]

Abuse of the regime's generous social welfare system remained endemic throughout the 1950s and 1960s, made possible in part by local doctors who knowingly connived with workers wishing to stay at home – or at least away from the workplace. Those employed in the Maxhütte blast furnace admitted as much themselves at one gathering, where they acknowledged that doctors tended to hand out sick notes for even minor ailments – and that they would go to another physician if the first one did not comply with their request for a certificate excusing them from work. Monetary benefits were not the only motivation for calling in sick, however: Increases in the incidence of "illness" were especially common during the harvest season, for instance, particularly among those who owned small parcels of land.[75]

Officials tried to keep tabs on and expose the "half-sick" (*Halbkranken*) and other "slackers" (*Bummelanten*) by carrying out periodic checks, i.e., by going to the homes and speaking with the neighbors of those who had suspicious histories – a common practice under capitalism as well. In the summer of 1958, for example, officials at the Maxhütte investigated eighteen colleagues who had repeatedly reported in sick; according to cooperative neighbors, one of these men did not appear to be ill since he was always working in his garden or performing household repairs.[76] Officials also relied on voluntary reports exposing allegedly sick workers who had been seen drinking at pubs or out on the streets after their curfew: This could lead to some form of sanction or even dismissal in cases involving chronic absenteeism. In addition, the names of those who habitually abused the system were often displayed on the shop floor or printed in local and factory newspapers – "for educational purposes."[77]

High sickness rates and chronic absenteeism were not the only manifestations of deficient "working morale" (*Arbeitsmoral*) and poor discipline at the workplace. Others included arriving late to work or departing early, drinking during the workday or not showing up because of a binge, refusing to carry out certain tasks, acting carelessly on the job, leaving assigned work areas without permission, or taking unscheduled pauses during shifts – often to play skat, a popular card game. "Once the clock strikes four no one really works anymore," party officials at the drilling machine factory complained in 1956.

74 See MxA-U, Sozialversicherung (Sammelordner, 1960–1), Besprechung über den Krankenstand im Hochofen, 19.9.60; KrA-S 12560, Prot. der Kreisratssitz., 7.1.59. On comparisons to the rest of the Soviet bloc, see Kopstein, *Politics*, 39.

75 See ThStA-R, Maxh. 377, BV im Hochofen, 13.2.52; MxA-U, Sozialversicherung (Sammelordner, 1964–71), Prot. der Beratung des Kranken/Unfallstandes, 15.2.65, 22.9.65; MxA-U, WL B130, Prot. der WL–Besprechung, 28.5.52.

76 MxA-U, Sozialversicherung (Sammelordner, 1954–9), Bericht über die Krankenkontrolle, 12.8.58.

77 See ThStA-R, FDGB BV Gera 851/208, Prot. der Sitz. der BGL–Zeiss; also see the reports in MxA-U, Sozialversicherung (Sammelordner, 1954–9), Sozialversicherung (Sammelordner, 1960–1), and Sozialversicherung (Sammelordner, 1962–3).

"The colleagues disappear one after the other. Or they just stand around and chitchat."[78]

Such *eigensinnig* behavior – not peculiar to the GDR, of course – has often been interpreted as a form of protest against increasing industrial regimentation, and this undoubtedly held true for many Saalfelders.[79] Yet, certain conditions in the GDR, and in the socialist states of Eastern Europe more generally, also helped account for much of this behavior. Because of the chronic shortage of production materials, for example, some workers would leave their machines and wander about their factories in search of scarce supplies. Those who left early or for short periods during the workday often did so in order to procure consumer goods that were either rationed or in short supply – an especially common practice when word spread that certain coveted items had just appeared in a local store, and one that sometimes led resentful workers to squeal on their less conscientious colleagues. The poor transportation system also helped explain why so many arrived late to work or left early: "[I]f those on high don't do a better job taking care of us," angry staff members at the Maxhütte threatened when complaining about buses that were either overfilled or failed to arrive on time (if at all), "then we don't have to worry about starting work punctually."[80]

Such threats and arguments notwithstanding, local factory officials introduced a number of measures aimed at combating this type of behavior and improving shop-floor discipline. Some required that staff members hand in their work passes each morning to keep track of those who arrived late; others occasionally reported the names of habitual slackers to local police officials.[81] In response to widespread alcohol consumption, which not only affected performance but also heightened the risk of industrial accidents, officials decided in the mid-1950s to forbid the sale of beer at the workplace – to the chagrin of workers throughout the district. Complaining that this was unfair (especially since local miners continued to receive schnapps: Because of their arduous working conditions, German miners had traditionally received a periodic allotment of spirits gratis), workers subsequently devised a number of clever strategies to smuggle beer into the workplace. As a result, the official prohibition remained

[78] ThStA-R IV/7/230/1154, Prot. der LS der SED GO–Wema, 11.10.56. Also see the minutes in MxA-U, BGL 262, 367, 430; ThStA-R, FDGB BV Gera 854/209, 855/210; ThStA-R IV/7/230/1156, 1157; ThStA-R, FDGB KV Slf 3540.

[79] See, e.g., Alf Lüdtke, *Eigen–Sinn: Fabrikalltag, Arbeitererfahrungen und Politik vom Kaiserreich bis in den Faschismus* (Hamburg, 1993); E. P. Thompson, "Time, Work-Discipline, and Capitalism," in *Customs in Common: Studies in Traditional Popular Culture* (New York, 1991), 352–403.

[80] See MxA-U, Sozialversicherung (Sammelordner, 1962–3), Besprechung über den Krankenstand in der Abt. Hochofen, 15.3.62. On issues related to local commuting, see Josef Wustelt, "Untersuchungen zum Berufspendelverkehr des Kreises Saalfeld," *Wissenschaftliche Zeitschrift der Friedrich-Schiller-Universität Jena* 14 (1965): 165–71. On the type of behavior described here, see, e.g., MxA-U, BGL 367, Prot. der BV im Hochofen, 29.4.54; ThStA-R, FDGB BV Gera 855/210, Prot. der Sitz. der BGL–Hebezeugbau, 2.3.53; ThStA-R, FDGB KV Slf 3245, Prot. der Sitz. der BGL–Rotstern, 24.7.57.

[81] See the minutes in ThStA-R, FDGB BV Gera 851/208 and 854/209.

more or less a dead letter – as one colorful incident at a construction site in Unterwellenborn made clear: When officials there decided to reduce the wages of workers who had recently held a long drinking bout during the workday, they "staged a protest... by holding a new drinking bout and refusing to work" at all.[82]

Similar to the way in which they dealt with the chronically "ill," management and union functionaries also responded to poor discipline by issuing warnings and threats, by displaying the names of idlers in public, by withholding bonuses, or by placing pressure on foremen, brigadiers, and even entire brigades to hold talks with chronic slackers in order to "educate" them.[83] Most of these efforts were in vain, however, because many shop-floor supervisors tended to treat problem workers leniently and overlook poor discipline – as in the case of one habitual shirker who spent most of his time at the crane factory drinking beer. When he noticed at the end of one shift that his wages were not what he had expected, he attributed his "lost time" to "waiting for a crane". The foreman "accepted this without any commentary" and simply readjusted his pay. Similarly indulgent foremen at the Maxhütte were inclined to excuse poor discipline by pointing to unsatisfactory working conditions or to the fact that many workers lived so far away and had to commute. In defense of such tolerant practices, low-level functionaries typically argued that shirkers only hurt themselves because they were unable to satisfy their own norms.[84] The East German economy suffered as well, of course. But such leniency nevertheless helped maintain shop-floor tranquility – which was the obvious intent.

They may have frowned upon this, but higher-level management and union officials tended to be as forthcoming as most foremen in everyday practice. Dismissals were rare, in fact, and usually occurred after several warnings had been issued or a particularly grievous offense had taken place: "In order to put an end to shirking," one factory union committee warned at the height of the 1953 norm campaign, "those colleagues who stay away unexcused for three days will be fired without notice" – an indulgent policy by any standard. Three years later, the chairman of the district FDGB informed the local brewery that sackings were now possible only in cases involving economic or criminal activity.[85]

---

[82] ThStA-R IV/4/10/243, report, 14.10.60. On alcohol consumption at the workplace as well as the various measures taken to prevent it, also see the series of reports and minutes in ThStA-R, Maxh. 367, 370, 390; ThStA-R, FDGB KV Slf 3245, 3540, 3550, 3567, 6302; ThStA-R, FDGB BV Gera 851/208, 855/210, 862/212; ThStA-R, BDVP Gera 21/250; ThStA-R, VPKA Slf 101.

[83] See, e.g., ThStA-R IV/7/230/1154 and 1156, Prot. der LS der SED GO–Wema, 11.10.56, 1.10.59.

[84] See ThStA-R, FDGB KV Slf 6178, report, 30.11.60, and Der politisch-ideologische Zustand der Arbeiterklasse, 15.11.61; ThStA-R IV/4/10/253, Die Lage unter den Meistern in der Maxh., 29.5.57.

[85] ThStA-R, FDGB BV Gera 855/210, Prot. der Sitz. der BGL–Hebezeugbau, 11.4.53; ThStA-R, FDGB KV Slf 3540, Prot. der erweiterten Sitz. der BGL–Brauhaus, 16.4.56. For examples of dismissals after repeated warnings or especially egregious behavior at the workplace, see the correspondence, reports, and minutes in ThStA-R, FDGB BV Gera 851/208, 854/209, 855/210, 862/212.

Chronic labor shortages and a desire for harmony certainly played a role here, but the many bureaucratic obstacles faced by factory officials who wished to let go of disobedient workers helped account for such restraint as well. The East German Labor Code included a series of stipulations intended to protect the rights of those to be sacked, which meant that workers could sometimes successfully block a dismissal by appealing to their legal rights. After being fired for striking an apprentice, for example, one plucky instructor at the Maxhütte lectured members of the Factory Conflict Commission about the Labor Code's special protection of the handicapped: "You are surely aware that nowadays one can no longer deal in such a manner with a severely disabled person."[86] Workers could also impede dismissal by securing the support of factory union officials, who were required by law to review and approve all dismissals ordered by management. One BGL reversed the sacking of a worker at the VEB MEW electric motor plant, for instance, because it had not taken place within the given period prescribed by law. Several years later, union officials at the washing-machine factory similarly blocked a dismissal there because management had failed to hang up a public reprimand or warning, also required by law.[87]

These cases demonstrated once again that East German workers could sometimes count on union functionaries to represent their interests against management and that the rule of law was not entirely moribund in the GDR. Not all decisions were necessarily made by the book, however. In fact, more subjective factors such as an individual's political actions and attitude could play an equally significant role. A 1951 addendum to the Labor Code even placed "behavior against the principles of the antifascist-democratic order" at the top of a list of proper causes for dismissal. But the reverse was also taken into consideration: The head of the district metal union had personally intervened in the case at the electric motor plant, for example, arguing against dismissal because the worker was a "progressive colleague" – coded language suggesting that he was politically reliable. Union officials at the crane factory apparently felt less remorse about firing a woman because of poor shop-floor discipline: Among the reasons cited for her dismissal was her flawed political "outlook."[88] Politics may have played some part in such decisions, but the tendency in Saalfeld was a general reluctance to dismiss workers solely because of poor discipline on the job. This undoubtedly reflected the insurmountable challenges posed by chronic labor shortages. After all, it was

---

[86] ThStA-R, BDVP Gera 21/212, Prot. der Sitz. der Konfliktkommission, 15.4.55.

[87] See ThStA-R, FDGB BV Gera 854/209, Prot. der Sitz. der BGL–MEW, 17.6.53; Prot. der Sitz. der BGL–Waschmaschinenwerk, 10.10.58.

[88] Such politically motivated decisions prompted one worker at the washing-machine factory to complain, "It's always said that we don't have enough competent people; we do have them but they're taken out of action (*kaltgestellt*) because they supposedly don't act in a progressive manner, even though they are very conscientious." See ThStA-R, FDGB BV Gera 855/210, Prot. der Sitz. der BGL–Hebezeugbau, 28.3.53; ThStA-R, FDGB BV Gera 854/209, Prot. der BV in dem Waschmaschinenwerk, 2.6.53.

better to have workers who came to work occasionally than to have none at all.

That Saalfelders enjoyed a certain degree of leverage because of this and that many took advantage of full employment was not surprising. But was there more to poor workplace discipline than a desire to relax, pursue leisure activities, or take care of personal needs? In other words, was such behavior also an indication of dissatisfaction with official policies or a hidden form of protest and opposition?

Apart from resentment against shop-floor regimentation, there was little evidence suggesting that large-scale sickness or absenteeism was linked to specific policy decisions or political developments. In fact, statistics for the Maxhütte indicate that sickness levels remained seasonally constant. That they peaked during the winter months was not in itself remarkable, as officials themselves admitted. But if feigned illness were tied to widespread discontent, one might have expected an increase in the winter of 1956–7, for example, when unrest was reported throughout the GDR in connection with the disturbances in Poland and Hungary. Yet, there was no conspicuous surge at this time – or at any other point (apart from an outbreak of influenza in October 1957).[89] The point is not that phony illnesses or poor discipline were not ways in which to express discontent, but rather that they rarely took place in epidemic proportions suggestive of large-scale collective action, as Tim Mason has argued for the Third Reich.[90]

There were exceptions, of course, e.g., the hike in sickness rates that followed the abolition of progressive piecework wages in late 1948. That the number of workers at the Maxhütte who called in sick or who suffered work-related injuries tended to increase on Saturdays was another case in point – behavior clearly tied to the unpopularity of weekend work and the desire for a five-day workweek.[91] There were also certain periods when sickness levels would predictably rise (during the harvest season, for instance) or fall: The latter usually occurred during occupational competitions, when workers had the opportunity to increase their earnings substantially. As union officials at the steel mill remarked in 1959, it was noticeable that sickness and accident rates suddenly fell during every steel competition (*Stahlschlacht*).[92]

When protests involving absenteeism or other forms of poor workplace discipline did take place, they were almost always limited to individuals or small

---

[89] See the figures in MxA-U, Sozialversicherung (Sammelordner, 1954–71); MxA-U, Bandnummer 406 (Betriebsdirektion: Sekr., 1957), Prot. der Auswertung des Brigadeeinsatzes des Ministeriums Berg- und Hüttenwesen, 26.10.57.

[90] See Tim Mason, *Social Policy in the Third Reich: The Working Class and the "National Community,"* ed. Jane Caplan, trans. John Broadwin (Providence, RI, 1993); idem, "The Workers' Opposition in Nazi Germany," *History Workshop Journal* 11 (1981): 120–37.

[91] MxA-U, WL B130, Prot. der WL–Besprechung, 15.6.51.

[92] ThStA-R, FDGB BV Gera 853/209, Prot. der Aktivtagung über die Übernahme der vollen Verantwortlichkeit über die Sozialversicherung durch die IG Metall, 1.8.57; MxA-U, Sozialversicherung (Sammelordner, 1954–9), Prot. der Sitz. der BGL, 24.9.59.

groups within a single brigade or department – as was most nonconformist or oppositional behavior in Saalfeld, an important point that we shall return to in Chapter 8. Such protests were frequently prompted by disputes over wages, poor performance, or norm levels: When one foreman instructed a subordinate at the VEB Wema to write down for once the actual time he needed to perform his job, the worker "immediately claimed to be sick" and went home.[93]

Production slowdowns were another way in which industrial workers sometimes expressed their discontent – another traditional practice not peculiar to the GDR. But drops in productivity are notoriously difficult to interpret: Were they caused by willful behavior on the part of angry workers, or were they instead the result of the everyday production bottlenecks and material shortages that plagued the East German economy because of poor planning? While there was little evidence of coordinated large-scale behavior resulting in lower productivity, it was nonetheless true, as we have seen, that individual workers purposely held back labor reserves in protest or in order to maintain low production quotas. According to officials at the VEB Wema, work was often left lying about in order to conceal actual norm fulfillment.[94] This might have been a form of protest against piecework, but it was also an effective way in which to exploit that unpopular wage system to the workers' monetary advantage.

Gender and generational variations in behavior also underscore the difficulty of attributing shoddy performance and poor discipline to economic or political discontent. Statistics for Zeiss indicate that sickness rates tended to be somewhat higher among women, a trend noted in other factories as well. Even if we discount the sexist explanation offered by one physician at the optical firm – "that the work in this factory . . . places certain demands on the nervous system. People who are somewhat labile drop out sooner or later" – it was still not surprising that women tended to call in sick more often than men: After all, they were the ones who bore the "triple burden" of having to work outside the home, perform sociopolitical duties, and do housework. As a result, they were often forced to give priority to their domestic responsibilities, such as caring for sick children: This accounted for 20 percent of all lost production time at seventeen major factories and state organizations during the first five months of 1965, in fact.[95]

Another important factor contributing to high sickness rates in Saalfeld was the growing superannuation of the workforce – above all at the Maxhütte, which reported especially high illness levels among administrative employees,

93 ThStA-R IV/7/230/1160, IB der SED GO–Wema, 9.10.58.
94 ThStA-R IV/7/230/1158, Prot. der MV der SED GO–Wema, 27.4.55.
95 See KrA-S 9137, Prot. der KR–Sitz., 31.5.55; ThStA-R IV/A-4/10/147, Analytisches Material über Ausfallstunden der Frauen durch die Pflege erkrankter Kinder, 30.5.65. Also see the statistics on sickness rates broken down by gender in ThStA-R, FDGB BV Gera 851/208; KrA-S 12559. On the situation of female workers more generally, see Chapters 8 and 10.

many of whom were over age seventy. Despite repeated encouragement to retire, most were unwilling to do so, an entirely understandable decision given the low pensions awarded to most of East Germany's elderly.[96] Natural causes did not necessarily account for the absenteeism or poor work habits supposedly prevalent among many of Saalfeld's younger workers, however. In early 1968, for instance, more than 37 percent of all workers under age eighteen were supposedly ill at the steel mill, placing this age cohort ahead of all of those unable to work at the time: "We don't know what to do anymore to keep our youths in check.... [T]hey hang around in dance clubs on Sunday and then sleep all day on Monday."[97] The widespread impression that poor work habits were especially prevalent among the young prompted one foreman at the Maxhütte to request that he no longer be assigned any youths: They tended to shirk and call in sick more frequently than married men, who, he claimed, were forced to work more seriously because of their weightier familial responsibilities.[98] Besides criticizing their supposedly poor discipline, shoddy performance, and general apathy (except when it came to dancing), many older workers also lamented the poor camaraderie of younger colleagues who refused to help them out in a pinch; more commonly, they complained that younger colleagues showed little respect for their shop-floor elders.[99]

The tendency of older people to criticize the behavior of the young was certainly not an East German novelty. But was there any substance to such charges – and if so, what might have accounted for poor shop-floor discipline on the part of many youths? One worker at Zeiss offered a possible clue when he pointed out that his young apprentices had only known war and the immediate postwar years of dearth and disease – recalling the comments made by one young man at the Maxhütte who had refused to join the army because he finally wanted to enjoy his life after so many years of hunger and deprivation.[100] Just as important, the younger generation had not been exposed to the discipline of factory life or to the solidarity and values of the pre-1933 working-class movement. But such arguments should not be taken too far; after all, poor work morale was frequently reported among older, experienced, and well-paid

[96] See the reports in MxA-U, Sozialversicherung (Sammelordner, 1960–1), Sozialversicherung (Sammelordner, 1962–3), Sozialversicherung (Sammelordner, 1964–71).

[97] See MxA-U, Sozialversicherung (Sammelordner, 1964–71), Prot. der SV–Haushaltsplankontrollberatungen in der BGL, 12.2.68, 15.5.68; ThStA-R IV/7/231/1163, Prot. der MV der SED GO–Zeiss, 28.9.53.

[98] ThStA-R IV/4/10/253, Bericht über die Lage der Meister in der Maxh., 29.5.57; ThStA-R IV/7/222/1060, IB der SED GO–Maxh., 27.2.56. Also see the KPKK reports related to a 1952 investigation of a serious dispute over workplace discipline between the FDJ and high-level management officials at the VEB Rostern in ThStA-R IV/4/10/238.

[99] Such claims were clearly impressionistic but undoubtedly reflected the generational conflict alluded to in Chapter 5. For tensions between the young and old, also see Chapter 8 as well as Kott, *Communisme*, 228–36.

[100] ThStA-R IV/7/231/1162, Prot. der Berichtswahlversammlung in Zeiss, 7.4.59. For the exchange at the Maxhütte, see Chapter 5.

workers in Saalfeld as well. As one party zealot pointed out, her colleagues at Zeiss "often instruct young people...not to work so much since they'll be paid anyway." Or, as several SED members at the VEB Rotstern purportedly told apprentices, "don't work so conscientiously for the two or two and a half marks you earn each day...."[101] It would seem that poor discipline in the GDR was not so much generational as pandemic.

In the end, it may be difficult to pinpoint the exact motivation for such habits at the workplace. And there may have been few signs of large-scale and coordinated forms of shop-floor protest in Saalfeld – especially ones animated specifically by political discontent. It would nevertheless be a mistake to ignore the high *collective* economic impact of such behavior, regardless of actual motivation. The strategic tendency of workers to hold back labor reserves in order to secure lower norms clearly served, for one, as a significant brake on productivity. The cumulative effect of rampant absenteeism and poor workplace discipline had enormous economic costs as well, not only in terms of productivity but also because of the serious strain that this placed on factory budgets. In the second half of the 1950s, sickness benefits at the Maxhütte hovered between 1.0 and 1.3 million marks annually and thus regularly exceeded planned expenditures – a major problem reported at other local factories as well:

The average sickness rate...in the Saalfeld district was 6.15% in 1958. That corresponds to a loss of approximately 435,000 workdays and means, for example, that the Wema factory would have to work an additional four years uninterrupted in order to make up for this loss of time. A one percent decrease in the sickness rates at these firms would mean an additional 70,500 workdays – a savings of 487,000 marks in sickness benefits alone.... Additional goods worth millions could be produced instead....[102]

This failure to produce the goods was, of course, one of the most important factors fueling discontent in Saalfeld and in the GDR more generally. But can one really blame the workforce itself for the regime's economic deficiencies? The reasons for the relatively poor performance of the East German economy have been fiercely debated: While some scholars have focused on the unpropitious starting point of the late 1940s, others have emphasized poor decision making by East German authorities later on, as well as the structural shortcomings of state socialism more generally. Was the economy, in other words, doomed from the outset because of wartime destruction, Soviet dismantling, and the adverse effects of national division? Or did it ultimately fail instead because of bureaucratic ineptitude, the inefficiency of rigid centralized planning, and the

---

[101] See MxA-U, BGL 367, Prot. der BV im Hochofen, 7.1.54; ThStA-R IV/7/231/1162, Prot. der Berichtswahlversammlung in Zeiss, 7.4.55; ThStA-R IV/A-7/226/483, Niederschr. über die durchgeführte Wahlberichtsversammlung in Rotstern, 27.2.65.

[102] KrA-S 12560, Prot. der Kreisratssitz., 7.1.59. Also see the figures in MxA-U, Sozialversicherung (Sammelordner, 1954–71).

absence of self-correcting market mechanisms?[103] An answer to this question lies beyond the scope of this study. Yet, as the foregoing clearly suggests, the everyday behavior of ordinary East Germans at the grass roots only served to reinforce whatever structural deficits already plagued the economy – thus undermining its performance even further.

Most workers in Saalfeld were remarkably adept at defending their own material interests and resisting the economic demands placed on them by the party and state. This reflected, in large part, the power that they enjoyed because of chronic labor shortages. It was also made possible by the indulgent practices of their immediate supervisors on the shop floor. The solicitousness of factory officials – above all their tendency to tolerate undesired behavior, as well as their conciliatory attempts to resolve disputes and reach consensus through negotiation and compromise – undoubtedly defused much potential for unrest. But by hindering the introduction of necessary reforms and by failing to enforce more stringent production habits, all of this had a devastating economic impact. More to the point, it helped create a material situation that proved intolerable to most East Germans and that was thus potentially destabilizing – as Jeffrey Kopstein has argued and as the events leading to the eventual collapse of the GDR made abundantly clear.[104] That said, appeasement by officials and far-ranging "freedom at the workbench" helped ensure industrial peace and shop-floor tranquility for many decades: They forestalled a repeat performance of June 1953 and thus significantly contributed to the long-term stability of the SED regime. One can, in other words, look at the glass as half empty or half full.

But that in itself cannot fully explain so many years of worker quiescence. After all, rising real wages – a result of successive wage hikes, official price cuts, soft norms, soaring overtime, and generous premiums – failed to satisfy most workers in Saalfeld, who continued to complain regularly and ritualistically about low earnings and the supposedly high cost of living. Moreover, the failure or inability of local officials to rectify many of their other grievances, especially with regard to poor working conditions, unpopular working hours, and endemic shortages of basic goods and services, proved to be a continuous source of dissatisfaction and frustration as well. Disgruntled workers nevertheless tended to act in a defensively refractory, passive, or resigned manner.

---

[103] Compare, e.g., Wilma Merkel and Stefanie Wahl, *Das geplünderte Deutschland: Die wirtschaftliche Entwicklung im östlichen Teil Deutschlands von 1949 bis 1989* (Bonn, 1991), with Christoph Buchheim, ed., *Wirtschaftliche Folgelasten des Krieges in der SBZ/DDR* (Baden-Baden, 1995), and Oskar Schwarzer, *Sozialistische Zentralplanwirtschaft in der SBZ/DDR: Ergebnisse eines ordnungspolitischen Experiments, 1945–1989* (Stuttgart, 1999). For an overview of this debate, see Corey Ross, *The East German Dictatorship: Problems and Perspectives in the Interpretation of the GDR* (London, 2002), 69–96; Steiner, "Wirtschaftsgeschichte," 229–38.

[104] See Jeffrey Kopstein, "Chipping Away at the State: Workers' Resistance and the Demise of East Germany," *World Politics* 48 (1996): 391–423; idem, *Politics*.

They were seldom actively rebellious and no longer expressed their discontent through open and offensive actions akin to those of August 1951 and June 1953 – in part, but only in part, because of the justifiable fear that such behavior would have highly undesirable consequences. Why they failed to join together and launch more energetic and more collective challenges to the regime is the subject of the next chapter.

8

Divide and Rule?

On October 3, 1959 – exactly three years after the head of the praline packaging department at Rotstern had raised concerns about the many complaints voiced by her staff – approximately thirty female workers from two brigades left their workplace at 8 A.M. and went to the chocolate factory's Labor Division to complain about the bonuses they had received in a recent industrial competition. Alarmed management officials summoned the department's male head foremen, who instructed them to return to work immediately. Although the order was obeyed without further incident and the disruption lasted less than a quarter of an hour, the directors at Rotstern nevertheless convened an emergency meeting with department heads as well as with the factory union committee.

According to a subsequent investigation by the Party Control Commission, the women were angered that members of other brigades in the same department had received bonuses two to three times higher than their own: "[T]hey hadn't known that the modified rules of competition meant an end to equal premium distribution and that only the best brigades would now be awarded higher bonuses. . . ." Two days later, the alleged ringleader, a woman employed at the factory since 1936, went to the party secretary at the start of the workday and "tearfully assured him that this had not constituted a work stoppage. . . ." Despite her obvious fears about possible sanctions, the party leadership responded to the incident by recommending that a wage investigation be carried out at the factory and that those SED members who had taken part be reprimanded at the next party gathering. The only serious disciplinary measure was taken against a brigadier who had acted as spokeswoman for the other striking workers: She was transferred to another department, and it was decided that she would never again lead an industrial brigade.[1]

This incident was typical of most shop-floor protests in Saalfeld that involved the laying down of tools: They were almost always limited to a small group of workers in one brigade or one department within a single factory and were

---

[1] ThStA-R IV/4/10/238, Bericht über das besondere Vorkommnis im Pralinen–Packsaal, 3.10.59.

normally linked, at least ostensibly, to economic issues such as wage and norm levels, the distribution of bonuses, or poor working conditions. Such protests were usually more or less spontaneous, lacked organization and firm leadership, and lasted no longer than a few hours at most. The fact that the incident at the chocolate factory prompted an investigation by the Party Control Commission not only indicated the seriousness with which authorities viewed even such minor disturbances but also suggested their rarity – even though the 1949 constitution had formally guaranteed East German workers the right to strike.

In general, officials tended to forego taking punitive measures against all participants, opting instead to single out a few of the alleged ringleaders for disciplinary action or censure the workers' immediate supervisors. This was intended, in all likelihood, to avoid escalation and prevent further disruption of production. Officials also responded to open protest by holding talks with the participants about the reasons for their strike – almost always referred to euphemistically as an "episode" (*Vorkommnis*) – and by promising to look into the alleged deficiencies that had prompted the incident. These meetings were customarily followed by a formal investigation that often led to the introduction of measures aimed at rectifying the causes for unrest – if officials believed that the grievances were justified. In essence, then, local functionaries usually did all they could to avoid alienating angered workers even further.

Despite isolated instances of collective action like the one at Rotstern, most acts of protest or defiance in Saalfeld involved single individuals. Some scholars have nevertheless emphasized various manifestations of industrial solidarity in the GDR and, in particular, the important mediating role that factory brigades supposedly played in shop-floor disputes. Peter Hübner has led the way, arguing that the creation of a new type of worker collective in the late 1950s (the so-called *Brigade der sozialistischen Arbeit* discussed later) allowed many brigades to obtain greater rights and expand their functions within East German factories, especially with regard to the representation of workers' interests – an alarming development branded as "syndicalism" by high-level party and union officials.[2]

It is probably no coincidence that most of Hübner's "conflict scenarios" involving strikes by brigades took place around 1960, for such disputes were

---

[2] See Peter Hübner, *Konsens, Konflikt und Kompromiß: Soziale Arbeiterinteressen und Sozialpolitik in der SBZ/DDR, 1945–1970* (Berlin, 1995); idem, "Arbeitskonflikte in Industriebetrieben der DDR nach 1953: Annäherungen an eine historische Struktur- und Prozeßanalyse," in Ulrike Poppe, Rainer Eckert, and Ilko-Sascha Kowalczuk, eds., *Zwischen Selbstbehauptung und Anpassung: Formen des Widerstandes und der Opposition in der DDR* (Berlin, 1995), 182–91; idem, "Syndikalistische Versündigungen? Versuche unabhängiger Interessenvertretung für die Industriearbeiter der DDR um 1960," in *JHK* (Berlin, 1995): 100–17. Also see Thomas Reichel, "'Jugoslawische Verhältnisse'? Die 'Brigaden der sozialistischen Arbeit' und die 'Syndicalismus'–Affäre' (1959–1962)," in Thomas Lindenberger, ed., *Herrschaft und Eigen–Sinn in der Diktatur: Studien zur Gesellschaftsgeschichte der DDR* (Cologne, 1999), 45–73.

rare in the 1940s and 1950s. This was not altogether surprising, given the fact that collectives were still a recent creation and that new forms of worker representation do not develop overnight. More to the point, the emphasis placed by Hübner and others on their informal role in collectively articulating the interests of their members misleadingly suggests a degree of solidarity not generally characteristic of relations among Saalfeld's workers – even in the 1960s after the formation of the new "socialist brigades." Most disputes continued to involve individuals or small groups that did not usually comprise an entire collective, and the focus on brigades draws attention away from this individualistic negotiation process. Collective behavior was the exception in East Germany, not the rule.[3]

The 1959 strike at Rotstern was nevertheless instructive for a number of reasons. The joint action by the two brigades certainly demonstrated that workers were able, however fleetingly, to join together in an attempt to advance their own interests. But this instance of solidarity paradoxically highlighted at the same time the serious divisions that existed within the East German labor force. To put it somewhat differently, these small pockets of solidarity underscored the absence of greater cohesion among larger groups of workers: After all, the two collectives laid down their tools in order to protest the fact that other brigades in their department – and not they – had received premiums in a recent competition.

Like Hübner, Jörg Roesler has emphasized the stabilizing effect that brigades supposedly had through "their contribution to the elimination, or at least reduction, of the daily potential for economic and social conflict in the factories and also, as a result, in society as a whole."[4] Yet, the tensions that existed *among* workers in general and within or between brigades in particular were

---

3 Studies that also emphasize worker solidarity include Rüdiger Soldt, "Zum Beispiel Schwarze Pumpe: Arbeiterbrigaden in der DDR," *GG* 24 (1998): 88–109; Francesca Weil, "Betriebliches Sozialverhalten in der DDR der 70er und 80er Jahre am Beispiel zweier sächsischer Betriebe," in Peter Hübner and Klaus Tenfelde, eds., *Arbeiter in der SBZ–DDR* (Essen, 1999), 321–54; Dorothee Wierling, "Work, Workers, and Politics in the German Democratic Republic," *ILWCH* 50 (1996): 44–63. For a less sanguine view of worker solidarity in the GDR, see Ulrich Voskamp and Volker Wittke, "Industrial Restructuring in the Former German Democratic Republic (GDR): Barriers to Adaptive Reform Become Downward Development Spirals," *Politics & Society* 19 (1991): 362. Thomas Reichel, "Die 'durchherrschte Arbeitsgesellschaft': Zu den Herrschaftsstrukturen und Machtverhältnissen in DDR–Betrieben," in Renate Hürtgen and Thomas Reichel, eds., *Der Schein der Stabilität: DDR–Betriebsalltag in der Ära Honeckers* (Berlin, 2001), 107, claims that brigades no longer acted as worker representatives after the 1960s; the present study doubts that they ever had, at least to the extent suggested by Hübner and others.
4 Jörg Roesler, "Die Produktionsbrigaden in der Industrie der DDR: Zentrum der Arbeitswelt?" in Hartmut Kaelble, Jürgen Kocka, and Hartmut Zwahr, eds., *Sozialgeschichte der DDR* (Stuttgart, 1994), 164. Roesler has written about brigades in a number of other publications as well; see, e.g., *Inszenierung oder Selbstgestaltungswille? Zur Geschichte der Brigadenbewegung in der DDR während der 50er Jahre* (Berlin, 1994); "Die Rolle des Brigadiers bei der Konfliktregulierung zwischen Arbeitsbrigaden und der Werkleitung," in Hübner and Tenfelde, *Arbeiter*, 413–38; "Jugendbrigaden im Fabrikalltag der DDR, 1948–1989," *APuZ* B28 (1999): 21–31; "Probleme

just as important in accounting for East German stability: Such frictions hardly contributed to the building of extended solidarity networks that would have allowed workers – like their counterparts in Poland at a later date – to present a broader united front against authorities.[5]

What might have accounted for the absence of greater solidarity? The placatory way in which low-level officials usually responded to shop-floor disputes by trying to reach individual arrangements that often involved concessions certainly played a significant role. The absence of independent and effective institutional forms of worker representation was obviously important as well – as was repression or the fear engendered by the threat of repression. But the many divisions created unwittingly or not by official policies, as well as by a variety of social and economic frictions at the grass roots (including ones along the gender divide), constituted another important structural factor hindering collective action – and one that arguably provides a more persuasive explanation for East German stability than a monocausal emphasis on state terror and the confines of dictatorship.[6] Those divisions are the subject of this chapter.

Schichtegoismus, or "Shift Selfishness"

As the incident at Rotstern made clear, industrial competition was often an important source of anger and jealousy on the shop floor – especially on the part of less successful contenders, who frequently maintained that the rules of competition had somehow handicapped them or that their competitors had enjoyed an unfair advantage.[7] Besides causing mutual resentment, industrial competition divided the labor force in other ways as well, above all by encouraging certain types of behavior that heightened tensions among workers even further. Participants often accused rival brigades or departments of adopting illicit or unfair practices that increased their own chances of winning – usually by hurting the performance of their adversaries. The term *shift selfishness* (*Schichtegoismus*) surfaced regularly at the Maxhütte to describe such behavior, as workers there charged those on earlier shifts with purposely leaving

---

des Brigadealltags: Arbeitsverhältnisse und Arbeitsklima in volkseigenen Betrieben, 1950–1989," *APuZ* B38 (1997): 3–17.

[5] For an attempt to explain the difference in behavior between East German and Polish workers, especially with an eye to the events of 1989–90, see Linda Fuller, *Where Was the Working Class? Revolution in Eastern Germany* (Urbana, IL, 1999), 154–74. On the Solidarity movement more generally, see Timothy Garton Ash, *The Polish Revolution: Solidarity*, 3rd ed. (New Haven, CT, 2002); Roman Laba, *The Roots of Solidarity: A Political Sociology of Poland's Working-Class Democratization* (Princeton, NJ, 1991).

[6] On the limits of terror in accounting for regime stability, see Chapter 4.

[7] See, e.g., the minutes in MxA-U, BGL 125 (12.3.51); ThStA-R, FDGB KV Slf 3540 (17.1.56, 25.7.57); ThStA-R IV/7/220/1003 (17.2.61). Also see ThStA-R IV/7/222/1060, IB der SED GO–Maxh., 18.2.56.

their workplace in poor condition or acting in other ways disadvantageous to those who followed them on the shop floor. Such accusations were not merely self-serving: In the early 1950s, functionaries at the steel mill admitted themselves that worker interest in industrial competition had significantly increased following the announcement of the first competition results – "and with that shift selfishness."[8]

Such behavior remained a source of perennial concern to local officials, above all because of its deleterious economic consequences. To avoid further discord, promote greater cooperation, and ensure that competition did not degenerate into a "nasty contest" (*Wettstreit*), factory supervisors actively encouraged brigades to make pledges explicitly stating that they would not behave in a manner detrimental to colleagues in other collectives. Workers at the Maxhütte were asked, for example, to promise in writing that they would turn over their machines without delay to those who followed. The inclusion of this provision in a 1959 contract indicated that shift selfishness and poor cooperation continued to remain problems there. That was the case at other factories as well: As union officials at Zeiss lamented at the time, "there was still no sign of mutual assistance among colleagues or foremen during industrial competition." More than a decade later, in 1971, party officials at Rotstern similarly noted that there was still little cooperation among collectives, largely because of competition over work space.[9]

Besides adversely affecting the economy by hindering cooperative efforts on the shop floor, industrial competition failed to achieve one of its most important ideological goals: the development of a socialist consciousness that would, at least in theory, have made workers more willing to work collectively for the common good instead of for their own immediate and personal benefit. In response to disputes among several brigades during a competition at a factory in Leutenberg, the district's second largest town, union officials reminded workers that winning was not what counted but rather the positive experience they would gain by merely participating: That would enhance performance "so that in the end, all of them and all of society [would] win."[10] Such exhortations apparently fell on deaf ears. Even though industrial competition was supposed to be an "honorable affair" and not merely a "supplementary source of money," officials at Zeiss continued to bemoan the fact that higher earnings and larger bonuses were of considerably greater interest than anything else to those employed at the optical firm. Material concerns even led some workers

---

[8] Or as one brigadier concluded at the time, industrial competition will be more successful once "shift selfishness is overcome." See MxA-U, BGL 367, Prot. der PB im Kollektiv Feuer, 9.7.54; MxA-U, BGL 264, report, 23.7.52.

[9] See ThStA-R, FDGB BV Gera 850/208, Bericht über den Wettbewerb im Jahre 1957 im VEB Carl Zeiss Fertigungsstätte, 17.2.58; ThStA-R, Maxh. 373, Stellungnahme der BGL zur Arbeitsstudie im Thomas–Stahlwerk, 17.10.68; ThStA-R IV/A-7/226/280, Prot. der SED GO–TSW Rotstern, 29.9.71.

[10] ThStA-R, FDGB KV Slf 6302, IB der FDGB KV Slf, 26.8.65.

to demand revision of the criteria used to judge contests in order to improve their own chances of winning. This might have reflected sustained interest in industrial competition but, from the perspective of East German authorities, for all the wrong reasons.[11]

At the root of such tensions were disparities in income levels resulting from officially sanctioned variations in wages, norms, and premiums – something first attacked on a large scale during the factory labor contract negotiations of 1951 and then again in June 1953. Besides making many workers openly critical of the regime for adopting incentive policies considered to be flagrantly unjust, anger about supposedly unfair discrepancies also created serious tensions and engendered strong feelings of resentment *among* workers themselves: As one man employed at the Maxhütte explained, the assignment to different base wage groups only led to divisions among his colleagues. Local officials themselves recognized the way in which differential treatment undermined solidarity: "[P]remium distribution always creates bad blood," they admitted, and "the differences in payment always lead to discord." The same was true of unequal production quotas: According to the SED District Secretariat, local miners were often jealous when "the earnings of one colleague greatly surpasses that of another. They have the good work, they claim... while we work ourselves to death and earn nothing" because of supposedly more rigorous norms.[12] As this suggests, workers did not shy away from denouncing their colleagues or naming names in an attempt to eradicate perceived inequities. To keep tabs on what their colleagues earned, especially suspicious workers even insisted that premium lists be posted in public.[13]

Other incentive policies aimed at stimulating performance engendered jealousy and anger as well – and thus hindered collective action by promoting feelings of mutual hostility that served to pit worker against worker. Beginning in the late 1940s, authorities actively recruited volunteers who agreed to increase their productivity substantially in order to set a positive example for their less industrious colleagues; in recompense, they were honored with monetary rewards and other material benefits such as superior provisioning and housing. Based on the Soviet Stakhanovite model, this so-called activist movement produced a great deal of rancor and resentment on the part of non-activists. As one angry steel worker complained, "There are colleagues who aren't activists but who certainly achieve a great deal even though their work

---

[11] See ThStA-R, FDGB BV Gera 850/208, Bericht über den Wettbewerb im Jahre 1957 im VEB Carl Zeiss Fertigungsstätte, 17.2.58; MxA-U, BGL 367, report, 13.1.54; ThStA-R, FDGB BV Gera 865/214, Prot. der Delegiertenkonferenz im Waschmaschinenwerk, 12.1.61.

[12] See MxA-U, BGL 125, Prot. der AGL–Versamml., 26.1.51; MxA-U, BGL 170, Prot. der BV im Elektrostahlwerk, 25.6.51; ThStA-R IV/4/10/247, IB der SED–KL Slf, 18.6.54; ThStA-R, FDGB KV Slf 6178, Einschätzung der Situation im Hochofenbetrieb in Durchführung des Stahl–Wettbewerbs, 3.11.69.

[13] On calls for public displays of premiums, see, e.g., the minutes from meetings at the local brewery in ThStA-R, FDGB KV Slf 3540.

isn't valued like that of an activist. There are also activists who never achieve as much as non-activists."[14]

Such resentment reflected more than jealousy about the monetary and material benefits enjoyed by activists: By demonstrating what was theoretically possible, their outstanding production performance gave officials an excuse to demand more of their colleagues. This led to aggressive expressions of anger about these so-called traitors to the working class – as Adolf Hennecke, the first East German Stakhanovite, learned firsthand: "You shabby scoundrel," read one anonymous card he received from the city of Erfurt, "you pimp of Soviet exploitation of German labor ... you will not escape your well-deserved punishment."[15] In Saalfeld itself, a well-known railroad activist was physically attacked outside a village pub in 1952. Later that decade, the head of a local construction site similarly reported that the vehicles driven by his two best drivers had been willfully damaged by nails found in their brakes. Besides committing acts of sabotage against individuals known for their outstanding production performance, local workers tried to intimidate compliant colleagues by resorting to anonymous letters or phone calls – as in the case of one worker at Zeiss who was told that he would "get a punch in the face" if he continued to raise his own norms.[16]

Collective Divisions

In a similar attempt to promote production and enhance performance, authorities actively encouraged the formation of model brigades whose members were expected to spur on less ambitious or less obedient colleagues, e.g., by issuing public proclamations in which they themselves not only promised to boost output, increase norms, and adopt new production methods, but also called on fellow workers to follow suit. As we saw in the previous chapter, this divisive strategy was used in Saalfeld to launch the Production Campaign of 1961, when a youth brigade at the Maxhütte "set an honest example" by adopting more stringent production quotas: "After that the others were more amenable" – and

---

[14] MxA-U, BGL 170, Prot. der BV in der Forschungsstelle, 19.6.51.

[15] On Hennecke, see Norman Naimark, *The Russians in Germany: A History of the Soviet Zone of Occupation, 1945–1949* (Cambridge, MA, 1995), 198–204; Klaus Ewers, "Aktivisten in Aktion: Adolf Hennecke und der Beginn der Aktivistenbewegung, 1948/49," *DA* 14 (1981): 947–70. On the Stakhanovite movement as well as the tensions it created in the Soviet Union and China, see Lewis Siegelbaum, *Stakhanovism and the Politics of Productivity in the USSR, 1935–1941* (Cambridge, 1988); Andrew Walder, *Communist Neo-Traditionalism: Work and Authority in Chinese Industry* (Berkeley, 1986), 162–89.

[16] The publicity campaigns that popularized their impressive feats made sure that especially prodigious activists were known to all. See ThStA-R IV/4/10/261, IB der SED–KL Slf, 3.2.60; ThStA-R IV/4/10/256, IB der SED–KL Slf, 19.6.58; ThStA-R IV/7/231/1166, Prot. der MV der SED GO–Zeiss, 21.1.55. On similar resentment elsewhere, see Gareth Pritchard, *The Making of the GDR, 1945–53: From Antifascism to Stalinism* (Manchester, UK, 2000), 202.

obviously more than a bit resentful, for such "positive forces" were frequently mocked and harassed by their estranged colleagues on the shop floor.[17]

That had obviously not been the official intent. In fact, authorities promoted brigades as a way in which to improve shop-floor relations in the belief that greater cooperation among workers would heighten performance and encourage the development of a socialist consciousness. Based on a Soviet model, the so-called collective – the most fundamental unit of the socialist production process – was composed, on average, of a dozen workers charged with jointly carrying out given tasks within the factory.[18] At least in theory, it was a voluntary merger whose members were allowed to choose a leader, or brigadier, from their own ranks. In practice, and ever since the FDGB's first major campaign in 1950 to create brigades on a large scale, local officials had been forced to exert considerable pressure on workers to join up: As a result, the percentage of production workers organized in brigades increased in Saalfeld from approximately one-third to one-half by the middle of the decade.[19]

In an attempt to spur even greater interest (and combat sociopolitical apathy), officials decided in the late 1950s to introduce a new type of worker collective whose members agreed not only to work but also to "learn and live" in a socialist manner. Competing for the title *Brigade der sozialistischen Arbeit*, those who joined these new collectives formally committed themselves to active participation in cultural and sociopolitical activities as well as to the social life of the brigade after hours. Factory officials agreed to support such endeavors by providing space for social get-togethers as well as funding for outdoor excursions and visits to concerts and the theater. The movement took off rapidly: By the second half of 1960, almost 43 percent of all workers in the district were competing for the title. That number would surpass 80 percent by 1968.[20]

Despite this impressive increase, local officials typically complained that many of these brigades merely existed on paper, and that they had only been created through pressure from above and not as a result of worker initiative. Moreover, most brigades simply did not understand what it meant to work, learn, and live in a socialist manner – which meant, more concretely, a widespread failure to participate more actively in cultural, convivial, and sociopolitical activities.[21] Brigades throughout the district refused to join mass organizations such as the Society for German–Soviet Friendship (DSF), for example, participate in

---

[17] ThStA-R, FDGB KV Slf 6178, Der politisch-ideologische Zustand der Arbeiterklasse, 15.11.61.

[18] For literature on the brigade movement, see footnote 4.

[19] Reports complaining that some brigades were "just informal" suggested that these figures were somewhat inflated. See, e.g., MxA-U, BGL 199, report, 5.4.52; also see the statistics in ThStA-R, FDGB KV Slf 6151 and 6255.

[20] See ThStA-R IV/4/10/261 and 263, IB der SED–KL Slf, 6.1.60, 21.10.60; ThStA-R, Maxh. 400, Führung des sozialen Wettbewerbs für 1960, 24.6.60. On the supposed centrality of these brigades in the lives of East German workers, see the works by Roesler in footnote 4 as well as Martin Kohli, "Die DDR als Arbeitsgesellschaft? Arbeit, Lebenslauf und soziale Differenzierung," in Kaelble, Kocka, and Zwahr, *Sozialgeschichte*, 48–51.

[21] See, e.g., ThStA-R, FDGB KV Slf 8007, Prot. der Sekretariatssitz. der KV IG Metall Slf, 6.9.66.

combat unit training, attend cultural events, contribute to so-called solidarity funds, or serve as school sponsors charged with persuading young Saalfelders to pursue certain occupations. In 1968, functionaries from the district metal union even admitted that most brigade get-togethers had just been "drinking bouts" up to that point.[22]

High-level FDGB officials nevertheless claimed that the movement had led to "much closer ties" among colleagues, who now "tackled their tasks with a new élan." Members of individual brigades supposedly assumed greater responsibility for their own performance as well as for that of the collective as a whole. As a result, they would help each other adopt new production methods because they did not want to "remain behind" other brigades.[23] The extent to which this optimistic evaluation corresponded to shop-floor reality was questionable – and not only because of the way in which it conveniently overlooked endemic disciplinary problems as well as the general reluctance of many workers to accept new methods. In the first place, it greatly overstated the degree of camaraderie among individuals within each collective: While it was true that the leisurely activities organized by brigades outside the workplace often comprised an important part of each member's social life – promoting, in effect, a certain degree of clubbiness – there were nevertheless significant sources of friction among those working together in a single collective. This was largely tied to the fact that success in industrial competition, as well as the ability to satisfy production quotas and meet plan figures, often depended on the performance of one's immediate coworkers. As a result, many Saalfelders complained when their own performance and income were adversely affected by carelessness, poor work, or laziness on the part of undisciplined or less talented cohorts within their brigade – or, for that matter, in other departments or collectives upon which they were dependent. A 1957 report by union officials at Rotstern captured many of these tensions:

> . . . we need to stop placing newly hired workers into experienced brigades. That leads to anger on the part of older and more experienced colleagues because they have to carry along the new ones and then sometimes don't meet their own norms as a result. . . . We think that colleagues should not suffer wage decreases if it's not their own fault. For example, there was great discontent in the packaging department because the candy department covered the candy containers with cardboard that stuck to the candy. This made their packaging work more difficult and, as a result, they were unable to satisfy their norms.[24]

---

[22] See ThStA-R IV/B-4/10/100, IB der SED–KL Slf über den Kampf um die kontinuierliche Planerfüllung, 9.4.68; ThStA-R, FDGB KV Slf 9541, Prot. der Sekretariatssitz. der KV IG Metall Slf, 31.10.68. Compare the optimistic account of relations between factory sponsors and school-age children in Roesler, "Produktionsbrigaden," 158–9, with the reports and minutes in ThStA-R, FDGB KV Slf 3555, 3567, 6302.

[23] Roesler, *Inszenierung*, 18–19.

[24] ThStA-R, FDGB KV Slf 3245, Beschluß der BGL–Rotstern über das Ergebnis der Rechenschaftslegung des BKV, 24.7.57. Frictions between members of the SED and those not in the party exacerbated such conflicts: This was linked, at least in part, to the resentment created by the

Mutual dependence, which prompted some workers to denounce shirkers and other poor performers to shop-floor supervisors, led to serious frictions among workers in other ways as well. Because they were obviously eager to obtain conditions that would allow them to satisfy their norms and outproduce industrial rivals, workers were greatly concerned about assuring an adequate supply of tools and other essential production materials – no easy task given the chronic supply shortages that plagued the local economy. The struggle to procure scarce items consequently led to fights among workers, departments, and brigades over access to the so-called means of production, as well as to accusations about the hoarding of materials, tools, and machinery: "[W]hen there are no tools available one has to go begging to one's colleagues. . . . [W]ill he give it to you or not?"[25] By effectively cutting off access to scarce materials previously available through clandestine channels in the West, the Berlin Wall made the struggle over scarce supplies even more pronounced in the 1960s.[26] A series of new wage and norm schemes introduced in that decade as part of the New Economic System (e.g., brigade piecework wages, collective norms, and collective forms of premium-based hourly wages) exacerbated existing tensions within many collectives by making workers even more dependent on the performance of their immediate colleagues.[27]

All of this led to widespread efforts by many workers to discipline the undisciplined themselves: As a member of one brigade at the Maxhütte argued, "whoever doesn't do his work should just go to the devil" – or simply receive less pay and lower premiums.[28] The punishment of such individuals was, in fact, actively encouraged by local officials, who held brigades responsible for taking "educational measures" against their own members. This was ordinarily done during a "friendly discussion" within the brigade, in which offenders

---

burdensome sociopolitical duties of the rank-and-file, especially when the flood of mandatory gatherings they were required to attend affected the performance of their colleagues. Such ill feelings were further intensified when the party rank-and-file tried to set a positive example on the shop floor and agitate in favor of official policy. The suspicion and hostility that this bred prompted frequent accusations of opportunism on the part of many SED members, who had supposedly joined not out of political conviction but rather in order to advance their careers and get ahead. For evidence of such frictions – which contributed little, of course, to solidarity on the shop floor – see, e.g., MxA-U, BGL 367, Prot. der PB in der Verw., 19.2.54; ThStA-R IV/7/226/1135, Prot. der MV der SED GO–Rotstern, 15.12.55; ThStA-R IV/4/10/252, IB der SED–KL Slf, 27.9.56; ThStA-R, FDGB KV Slf 3567, Prot. der Sitz. der BGL–Mitropa, 13.2.67.

[25] ThStA-R, FDGB BV Gera 855/210, Prot. der Sitz. der BGL–Hebezeugfabrik, 22.1.54, and Prot. der Vollversammlung der Vertrauensleute, 7.8.58. On fights among Wismut miners for access to scarce materials, see Rainer Karlsch, "Der Aufbau der Uranindustrien in der SBZ/DDR und CSR als Folge der sowjetischen 'Uranlücke,'" *ZfG* 44 (1996): 11.

[26] Gerhard Friedrich (a former engineer at the VEB Wema), in discussion with the author, September 1995.

[27] See, e.g., the reports in ThStA-R, FDGB KV Slf 6232.

[28] MxA-U, BGL 170, Prot. der BV im Hochofen, 7.6.51.

were called to account by their peers, usually for disciplinary infractions.[29] Such discussions were not limited to cases involving poor economic performance, however: Many brigades also engaged in political disputes (*Auseinandersetzungen*) with those who had demanded the right to travel to the Federal Republic, for example, or who had refused to vote in elections and otherwise participate in sociopolitical activities. Collectives were especially concerned about such apathy because it could count against them in certain types of industrial competition. For similar reasons, brigades often served as moral watchdogs who took their own members to task for a variety of failings such as alcoholism, adultery, or criminal activity – especially when this had had an adverse effect on the brigade's overall performance.[30]

The willingness of workers to take action against their colleagues spoke volumes about the nature of industrial relations in the GDR. So, too, did the way in which many jumped on the proverbial bandwagon once they smelled blood during a supposedly collegial get-together. Collective education was not particularly friendly or always performed in a spirit of camaraderie, in fact, and many workers frequently assailed their problem colleagues with apparent gusto. That was particularly true when it came to the habitually sick, especially when they placed their coworkers at a distinct disadvantage during industrial competition. Workers at the steel mill were outraged, for instance, when the chief physician at the Maxhütte decided to grant one intoxicated colleague sick leave as well as a short stay in the factory sanatorium: "[T]hey believe that their money should not be used for such people."[31] Poor workplace discipline and the abuse of sickness benefits apparently raised the ire of many workers as much as that of most officials.

The distribution of bonuses constituted an additional source of friction and resentment that did little to promote solidarity on the shop floor. Despite regulations to the contrary, some brigades assumed responsibility themselves for deciding on the internal allocation of these monetary incentives, a practice that often led to rancor on the part of those who received lower amounts or none at

---

[29] In 1962, for instance, one Factory Conflict Commission decided to dock a driver an entire month's wages after he caused an accident – but "first after his colleagues had expressed their opinion...and explained that he had already often violated workplace discipline...." See ThStA-R, FDGB KV Slf 6206, Analyse über die Arbeit der Konfliktkommission innerhalb des Kr. Slf, 28.3.62.

[30] Local police officials reported that discussions almost always took place within the collective when one or more members were involved in some sort of criminal investigation. See ThStA-R, VPKA Slf 114, Halbjahresbericht I/64, 7.7.64. For actual examples of such gatherings, see the reports and correspondence in MxA-U, Kaderabt.: Abwanderung nach dem Westen (Berichte, 1949–57). Also see Roesler, "Produktionsbrigaden," 153; Andrew Port, "Moralizing 'from Above' and 'from Below': Social Norms, Family Values, and Adultery in the German Democratic Republic" (paper presented at the annual meeting of the German Studies Association, Salt Lake City, UT, October 1998).

[31] See the reports and minutes in MxA-U, Sozialversicherung (Sammelordner, 1954–9, 1960–1, 1962–3); MxA-U, BGL 367, 370; KrA-S 9137, 12559, 12560.

all. After failing to receive his "fair share," for example, one angry steelworker called his brigadier a liar and denounced his colleagues as lazy and reactionary. The latter responded in kind and demanded unanimously that he be removed from the collective: It was impossible to work with him, they argued, because of his hostile attitude, poor workplace discipline, and reactionary political sensibilities.[32] To avoid similar disputes, some brigades suggested that premiums be distributed equally among all members – except, of course, for shirkers and the chronically sick.[33]

Based on developments in Saalfeld, the FDGB's assertion that the brigade movement had led to closer ties among workers was misleading, to say the least. There may have been more truth to claims that many felt a greater sense of responsibility for the entire brigade's performance or that they were loath to perform more poorly than their counterparts in other collectives. But what officials neglected to point out was the way in which this pressure to perform helped undermine worker solidarity – not only by creating tensions within individual collectives and among competing brigades, but also by making many workers prone to police their colleagues in order to expose perceived inequities as well as behavior that endangered their own income. It is unclear whether officials consciously pursued policies aimed at weakening worker solidarity, as Victor Zaslavsky has posited for the Soviet Union. Functionaries at the Maxhütte nevertheless admitted to themselves that a certain "material incentive" was often necessary to make sure that "the mates keep close tabs on each other."[34]

Gender Discrimination and the Battle of the Sexes

Besides denouncing and attempting to punish allegedly irresponsible or delinquent colleagues, some collectives in Saalfeld actively tried to exclude these and other workers whose poor performance purportedly hurt their own. Youths and women were among the most common targets and, as a result, many brigades were exclusively composed of older and experienced workers – or just men. Union officials reported in the late 1960s, for example, that only one of seventy-five female workers employed at the Abus crane factory was in

---

[32] MxA-U, BGL 264, Prot. der BV im MB–Hochofen, 12.12.52.
[33] This was arguably motivated by material self-interest (i.e., by a desire not to be left out) and did not necessarily reflect real solidarity with one's colleagues. For such demands in Saalfeld, see, e.g., MxA-U, BGL 370, Prot. der BV im Hochofen, 30.11.54. On supposedly egalitarian impulses elsewhere in the GDR, see Jeffrey Kopstein, *The Politics of Economic Decline in East Germany, 1945–1989* (Chapel Hill, NC, 1997), 27; Axel Bust-Bartels, *Herrschaft und Widerstand in den DDR–Betrieben: Leistungsentlohnung, Arbeitsbedingungen, innerbetriebliche Konflikte und technologische Entwicklung* (Frankfurt am Main, 1980), 29.
[34] ThStA-R Maxh., Sozialversicherung (Sammelordner, 1954–9), Prot. der BGL–Sitz., 24.9.59. See Victor Zaslavsky, *The Neo-Stalinist State: Class, Ethnicity, and Consensus in Soviet Society* (Armonk, NY, 1994), 44–65.

a collective.[35] Those women who did belong to sexually integrated brigades frequently complained about the disparaging behavior of male colleagues who openly expressed displeasure about their presence. In response to objections by male workers at one factory that they were forced to earn money for their supposedly less talented female cohorts, the latter decided to establish their own brigade – and then gave the lie to such claims by filling their production quotas by 120 percent.[36]

Despite such positive examples by local women, many factory officials tended to think along similar lines. Young female colleagues "view their work as a game," functionaries at Rotstern characteristically complained, "and as a result, the entire department suffers financially." There may have been some truth to this, but poor workplace discipline was by no means gender specific in Saalfeld. More to the point, the superior performance of many local women suggested that the negative and largely impressionistic claims about them were simply unwarranted: After all, six female brigades won the title *Brigade der sozialistischen Arbeit* in 1961. And in response to similar views at the Maxhütte, the personnel director was able to provide the SED Central Committee with a number of positive examples to demonstrate that such complaints were groundless – the "best evidence," he noted, for official claims that women were just as able as men to carry out tasks corresponding to their "capabilities and physical condition."[37] Sexist bias nevertheless remained widespread in Saalfeld, leading to various forms of discrimination, above all in the form of lower pay, harassment on the shop floor, and a failure to train women or promote them to leading positions.

All of this flew in the face of Article 7 of the 1949 constitution, which officially proclaimed the principle of equal rights for men and women. Official efforts to ensure greater equality of the sexes had begun even earlier with a series of decrees that embraced equal pay for equal performance, a prescript first set forth in late 1945 at a meeting of high-level union officials and then again in SMAD Order 253 of August 1946.[38] Progressive attitudes toward women had long been a mainstay of Communist ideology, of course, yet economic considerations were arguably as important as ideological ones at the time: Faced with severe labor shortages as well as the daunting task of reconstruction, Soviet and East German authorities supported equal pay in order to encourage female entry into the labor force. To their dismay, many local functionaries assiduously

---

[35] See ThStA-R, FDGB BV Gera 855/210, Brigadenaufstellung in Abus, n.d.; ThStA-R IV/4/10/252, IB der SED–KL Slf, 6.12.56. On efforts to exclude certain workers, also see Roesler, "Produktionsbrigaden," 148, 151–4.

[36] ThStA-R IV/4/10/366, report, 3.12.52.

[37] See ThStA-R, FDGB KV Slf 3245, Beschluß der BGL–Rotstern über das Ergebnis der Rechenschaftslegung des BKV, 24.7.57; ThStA-R IV/4/10/276, correspondence, 10.5.61; ThStA-R, Maxh. 400, Führung des sozialen Wettbewerbes für das Jahr 1960, 24.6.60; MxA-U, Betriebsdirektion: Personalfragen (1950–4), correspondence, January 1951.

[38] See Gunnar Winkler, ed., *Geschichte der Sozialpolitik der DDR, 1945–1985* (Berlin, 1989), 63–7.

tried to thwart these and other high-level efforts aimed at prohibiting discrimination based on gender. While acknowledging that equal pay should serve as an important incentive to attract female workers, one leading management official at the Maxhütte typically argued that this should not apply to tasks that were "exclusively female" in nature – whatever that meant – or in cases where women were unable to achieve as much as men.[39]

The reluctance to pay equal wages reflected not only traditional male prejudices, but also fears that this would contribute even further to spiraling labor costs. Criticizing an earlier appeal by the Maxhütte Workers' Council to pay the same wages to women who had taken over positions previously occupied by men, the chairman of the BGL later called for an end to such "egalitarianism" by arguing that this had made wage costs inordinately high: "It's not right that a cleaning lady receives the same pay as a skilled worker or a director" – a claim that was patently false.[40] According to members of the Factory Women's Committee, officials at the steel mill tried "to circumvent official orders and purposely prevent women from receiving better pay" by arbitrarily labeling certain jobs as "women's work.... [M]en are taken out of these positions and the women continue to receive the old wages...." In a letter sent to the Soviets thanking them for their enlightened policies, which had "paved the way to liberation from a servitude that has lasted for centuries," the Committee skillfully attempted to politicize these dilatory efforts: "Yes, one can even suspect certain intentions by persons who are not amenable to the progressive measures of our democratic order, and who are attempting to anger part of the workforce in order to upset our reconstruction efforts."[41]

Available evidence suggests that active wage discrimination based on gender gradually diminished there and elsewhere in the district. Yet, most local women continued to earn considerably less than men because the vast majority remained in low-paying, unskilled, or semiskilled positions – despite official calls to promote female training in order to satisfy the urgent need for skilled workers. As late as 1971, almost three-quarters of all women employed at the local VEBs received less than 550 marks each month, and less than 5 percent received more than 700 marks; the corresponding figures for men were one-quarter and one-half.[42] So-called female promotion plans (*Frauenförderungspläne*) did spur some factories to intensify their efforts to train women, but as these numbers suggest, the results were modest at best. In response to the 1951 Law to Promote Women (*Gesetz zur Förderung der Frau*), for example, the Maxhütte set up a special commission charged with investigating ways in which more of its female staff members could be qualified for skilled

---

[39] MxA-U, WL B64, Meldung, 6.12.45.

[40] MxA-U, BGL 142, Prot. der BV, 22.3.49.

[41] MxA-U, WL B64, correspondence, 15.10.46.

[42] BStU ASt-G, KD Slf 2MA 2317, Jahresbericht 1971 über die Entwicklung des Kr. Slf, 30.3.72. Also see Annemette Sorensen and Heike Trappe, "The Persistence of Gender Inequality in Earnings in the German Democratic Republic," *American Sociological Review* 60 (1995): 398–406.

positions. Yet by the close of the decade, less than 8 percent of all women at the steel mill had undergone training: This corresponded to only slightly more than 6 percent of *all* workers and employees trained there in 1959. The situation would improve somewhat by the close of the following decade, thanks in large part to the Women's Communiqué (*Frauenkommunique*) issued by the Politburo in 1961, which called on officials to make greater strides in this area. As a result, one-quarter of all trainees in the district were women by 1966 – even though they now made up more than 40 percent of the district's workforce. The number of women who performed unskilled or semiskilled tasks consequently decreased over the course of the decade, yet more than 83 percent of all skilled workers were still men by the end of the 1960s.[43]

The appointment of women to high-level shop-floor or management positions progressed at an equally sluggish pace, which meant that there were relatively few female cadres in Saalfeld despite official ideology professing equality of the sexes. Women were equally underrepresented on factory union committees and Party Secretariats – even in firms or sectors where they comprised a significant portion of the workforce. In 1952, for instance, only one of thirty-four foremen was a woman at Rotstern – a "purely female factory" (*reiner Frauenbetrieb*) where only one woman sat on the BGL. The situation was not much better at the Maxhütte, where women made up a significant percentage of the labor force as well: The union and party chairmen in all twenty-eight divisions at the steel mill were all men, and only one woman headed a department in 1958.[44]

As with female training, the situation improved somewhat in the 1960s following the release of the *Frauenkommunique*, largely because of the increasing pressure it brought to bear on local officials. The greatest progress was made in the light industry and service sectors, where the proportion of women was especially high. By the mid-1960s, the overwhelming majority of those who sat on the district secretariat of the foodstuffs union were women, for example (there had only been one a decade earlier). And by 1970, approximately sixty women held mid- and high-level managerial positions at Rotstern. These were the proverbial exceptions to the rule, however. Only a handful occupied similar positions elsewhere in Saalfeld – despite the increasing number of women

43 See MxA-U, WL B130, Prot. der WL–Besprechung, 24.10.52; ThStA-R, FDGB KV Slf 7609, Auftragsinformation, 9.10.69; ThStA-R IV/A-7/230/495, Bericht der Parteileitung zur Delegiertenkonferenz 1965, n.d.; ThStA-R IV/A-4/10/147, Bericht über die Verwirklichung des Kommuniques "Die Frau," n.d. Also see the statistics in ThStA-R, Maxh. 397, 584. More generally, see Susanne Kreutzer, "'Sozialismus braucht gebildete Frauen': Die Kampagne um das Kommunique 'Die Frauen – der Frieden und der Sozialismus' in der DDR, 1961/62," *ZfG* 47 (1999): 23–37.
44 See ThStA-R IV/4/10/238, Überprüfung vom VEB Mauxion durch die KPKK Slf, 12.2.52; MxA-U, WL B130, Prot. der WL–Besprechung, 24.10.52; ThStA-R, Maxh. 401, list, 8.1.58; ThStA-R IV/4/10/366, Auswertung der Beratung mit den Frauen–Instrukteuren in SED BL–Gera, 31.5.61. Also see Dagmar Langenhan and Sabine Roß, "The Socialist Glass Ceiling: Limits to Female Careers," in Konrad Jarausch, ed., *Dictatorship as Experience: Towards a Socio-Cultural History of the GDR* (New York, 1999), 177–91.

with advanced professional training: Of the 364 women employed at the VEB Wema, only one held a high-level post in 1971, the year that Ulbricht fell from power.[45]

What accounted for the general failure to make greater strides in the training and promotion of women? One important explanation lay in the reluctance of many working women themselves to pursue job-related training because of the added burden that this represented. As female party officials noted after a visit to the Rotstern factory in the early 1950s, "The women could not be recruited for anything.... [T]hey had a hard enough time filling their norms, getting home quickly evenings to do domestic work around the house, power shortages, etc...." Like their male colleagues, many also feared that training would adversely affect their income, at least in the short term, because of the time they would lose on the job. Yet, many were also unwilling to attend courses scheduled after the close of the workday because of their duties at home.[46] This was also why many working women refused to participate in sociopolitical activities or even attend meetings set up by committees specifically designed to represent their own particular interests.[47]

Such apathy was by no means gender specific, of course. Yet the "triple burden" borne by most laboring women – i.e., work outside the home, domestic chores, *and* sociopolitical activities – made it even more difficult for them to comply with the rigorous demands of the party and state. The fact that some were "laughed at and shouted down" during shop-floor discussions or told by dismissive male colleagues that they were "just here for popular amusement" must have made many even more reluctant to participate at factory gatherings or assume leading social, economic, and political roles. "Our women want to work," female officials explained, "but they often don't have the necessary self-confidence" – which was not surprising, given the reactions of their male colleagues and superiors. As party functionaries at Zeiss admitted, many female workers justifiably "fear that they'll just be passed over." Management officials at the Maxhütte similarly acknowledged that "some of us still tend to shunt women off to the side." All of this confirmed what female workers and their representatives on the Women's Committees had long maintained: that despite repeated promises, most male officials were neither committed to nor interested

---

[45] See ThStA-R, FDGB KV Slf 3569, Prot. der Sekretariatssitz. der Gew. HaNaGe, 1.2.65; ThStA-R IV/B-4/10/112, Information über die Beratung der Frauenkommission, 28.5.70; ThStA-R, FDGB BV Gera 2461, Prot. der Beratung, 11.2.71; ThStA-R, FDGB KV Slf 6191, Analyse über die Tätigkeit der Gewerkschaftlichen Leitungen und die ökonomische Situation im VEB Wema, 8.2.62. Also see the statistics on female training and women in leading sociopolitical positions in ThStA-R IV/4/10/366 and IV/B-4/10/087.

[46] See ThStA-R IV/4/10/366, report, 5.1.53; ThStA-R IV/B-4/10/112, Analyse über das Thema: Probleme der jungen Mädchen in der BBS, LWH, und anderen Ausbildungsstätten, 25.7.69, and Information über die Beratung der Frauenkommission, 28.5.70; ThStA-R, FDGB KV Slf 6191, Bericht über die Überprüfung der Frauenarbeit in Wema, 31.1.62.

[47] See, e.g., ThStA-R, Maxh. 584, report, 8.12.54; MxA-U, WL B130, Prot. der WL–Besprechung, 24.10.52.

in training and promoting women, who "often have to fight against the arrogance of . . . male colleagues who don't want to recognize them as equal."[48]

Discrimination and neglect reflected a widespread belief on the part of many men that women were simply not up to the challenges of industrial production. In response to plans to train a woman in his brigade as foreman, for example, one worker at the VEB Wema characteristically scoffed that "she just won't make it. Besides, she's married and will certainly have children and then leave the factory. So what's the use?"[49] Others took a somewhat different tack when defending their opposition to female employment: Arguing that "we can't afford to raise children only in kindergartens," a district official of the CDU demanded that mothers remain at home and not "jeopardize" the education of their children. Many were forced to do just that, in fact, because of insufficient space at most local child-care institutions.[50]

Such "false attitudes" not only reflected prevailing prejudices but also the fears and resentment of many men in Saalfeld. Because of official calls to fill traditionally male positions with women, many were concerned that they might lose their jobs to female colleagues: "You're not any different from the Nazis," one worker at the steel mill bitterly complained after being transferred to make room for a woman. "You want to place women in this position so that you can later put us in a soldier's uniform."[51] The reverse situation was actually much more common: Several months earlier, a supervisor at the blast furnace had decided to replace a female crane operator with a male colleague who could no longer perform his old job because of health reasons. Echoing widespread complaints about the employment of so-called *Doppelverdiener* (i.e., married women with working husbands), the official justified his decision by pointing out that the woman's husband also worked: "It's said . . . that there are no unemployed in the district, but there are unemployed fathers. One should think about letting go of dual-earners in order to give these people some work." To their credit, high-level officials not only criticized such views but also endeavored to

[48] See ThStA-R IV/4/10/366, report, 29.11.52; MxA-U, BGL 367, Prot. der BV im Hochofen, 7.1.54; MxA-U, BGL 397, Prot. der Sitz. des Frauenausschusses, 27.8.52; ThStA-R IV/4/10/366, Überprüfung der Frauenarbeit in der Industrie im Kreisgebiet Slf, n.d.; ThStA-R, FDGB KV Slf 8007, Prot. der Sekretariatssitz. der KV IG Metall Slf, 1.3.66. Also see Birgit Bütow, "Politische Nichtpartizipation von Frauen?" in Birgit Bütow and Heidi Stecker, eds., *EigenArtige Ostfrauen: Frauenemanzipation in der DDR und in den neuen Bundesländern* (Bielefeld, 1994), 261–8.

[49] ThStA-R, FDGB KV Slf 6191, Bericht über die Überprüfung der Frauenarbeit in Wema, 31.1.62. Notwithstanding the sexist nature of such comments, available evidence did suggest that a large number of women sent for training did not return to their factories after marrying. See, e.g., ThStA-R IV/B-4/10/087, Prot. der Massenkontrolle der Durchsetzung der Anordnung über die Aus- und Weiterbildung der Frauen für technische Berufe, 7.7.68.

[50] ThStA-R, FDGB KV Slf 9541, Prot. der Sekretariatssitz. der KV IG Metall Slf, 15.10.68; BStU ASt-G 0552, Halbjahranalyse II. Halbjahr 1965, 17.12.65. On similar views in the West, see Robert Moeller, *Protecting Motherhood: Women and the Family in the Politics of Postwar West Germany* (Berkeley, 1993). Also see Chapter 10 on the lack of adequate child-care facilities.

[51] MxA-U, Betriebsdirektion: Personalfragen (1950–4), report, November 1951.

reverse unjust decisions in which women had been made redundant in order to make room for men.[52] It was nevertheless understandable why many women continued to fear that they would simply be pushed to the side and their jobs given to men.

Besides being subject to various forms of discrimination, laboring women faced verbal and sometimes even physical harassment – which also did little, of course, to promote shop-floor solidarity in Saalfeld. Though not exclusively, this treatment was often directed against women known for their outstanding performance – as in the case of one woman at Zeiss who had made herself highly unpopular because of her thorough work habits: "Her life is made unbearable, anonymous threats are placed on her desk." Despite fears that this would lead to new struggles at the workplace, she eventually overcame serious reservations and decided to accept an offer to train as a shift supervisor. One of her coworkers proved less willing to endure the everyday taunts of her male colleagues, however: "[T]hey played around with her machine while she was away from her workplace. . . . She can't bear the hostile atmosphere and has asked to be transferred."[53]

Hostility toward those who performed especially well was not limited to women, of course. But unlike their female counterparts, few men complained about aggressive, sometimes violent colleagues who made sexual advances or lewd remarks. As one female worker at the sewing-machine factory noted with considerable understatement in 1960, "the tone of the male colleagues often leaves a lot to be desired." Earlier that month, one of them had slapped a woman in the face after obscenely threatening her with a water hose and asking if he should "shove it inside" her. Noting that similar incidents had previously occurred without leading to any serious sanctions, her colleagues warmly applauded the decision to fire the man; they hoped that this would set an example for others and preserve the "honor of a woman."[54]

Not all authorities reacted this firmly, however. Several years earlier, a male worker at the Maxhütte had seriously injured a pregnant women by thrusting an iron rod into her vagina. According to the high-level factory officials who met to discuss this disturbing incident, the man not only acted "irresponsibly" toward female colleagues but also had an "especially bad influence" on young male workers (earlier that year, an apprentice there had struck a woman so hard that she suffered a concussion). But because of fears that a dismissal would cause him to flee to the West, they decided to fire the man *only* if the personnel department was unable to find him another position where he could

[52] See ThStA-R IV/4/10/238, Bericht von der Überprüfung der Maxh. durch die KPKK Slf, 3.4.51; ThStA-R, FDGB BV Gera 854/209, Prot. der BV im Waschmaschinenwerk, 2.6.53, and Prot. der Sitz. der BGL–Waschmaschinenwerk, 1.12.54.

[53] ThStA-R IV/4/10/366, report, 5.1.53; ThStA-R IV/7/231/1166, Prot. der MV der SED GO–Zeiss, 21.1.55. For similar tensions in the USSR, see Diane Koenker, "Men Against Women on the Shop Floor in Early Soviet Russia: Gender and Class in the Socialist Workplace," *AHR* (1995): 1438–64.

[54] ThStA-R, FDGB BV Gera 862/212, Prot. der Sitz. der BGL–Nähmaschinenwerk, 15.2.60.

put his "excessive strength" (*überschiessende Kraft*) to better use – a scandalous decision that underscored once again the power enjoyed by many workers because of chronic labor shortages.[55]

This should not suggest that aggression – sexual or otherwise – characterized relations between all men and women on the shop floor; romantic ties between male and female colleagues were not uncommon, in fact. Yet, the reaction to such liaisons further underscored prevailing attitudes toward women. In April 1953, for example, members of the VEB Abus's all-male factory union committee gathered to discuss an extramarital affair between a female employee and an official responsible for setting norms there: "[T]he entire staff was furious about the relationship" because it had supposedly affected workplace discipline. According to the minutes of the meeting, a delegation of four male brigadiers and two male foremen called on the BGL to dismiss the woman:

Foreman H.:   This pigsty has to be cleaned up. Colleague S. has it too good, he should work on the production floor. Colleague J. should be fired immediately. This is an intolerable situation for the factory. As foremen we can't tolerate such filth. . . .

Brigadier G.:   I'm of the same opinion: Kick the wench out, and Colleague S. should finally get to work. . . .

Their comments obviously reflected the customary resentment toward norm officials as well as shirkers. But what was more interesting in this case was the demand that harsher sanctions be taken against the young woman. After deciding to allow the man to remain in his position if he agreed to end the relationship – and after noting that he had been "a hard-working, decent person before Colleague J. joined the factory" – officials ultimately decided to fire the female employee.[56] Poor Adam had, in short, once again succumbed to the baleful influence of wily, scheming Eve.

Neither the outcome nor the sexist language was unusual. In similar cases there and at other local factories, allegedly "man-crazy" (*männertolle*) women were also fired or severely penalized for conducting supposedly immoral relationships – while their male accomplices got off with a mild slap on the wrist.[57] The reaction to one such affair at the Thälmann graphics factory revealed the attitudes often underlying such decisions: "[B]ecause it's a female factory, things couldn't be different from a moral standpoint." Or, as one union official commented during the investigation of a case involving the rape of a young virgin who had drunk to excess during a factory excursion, "She can't be completely innocent." Sexual promiscuity was apparently not the only flaw in the female character that led innocent men astray – as the chairman of the District Party Control Commission suggested himself when alluding to petty criminal offences

[55] MxA-U, BGL 370, Prot. über den Betriebsunfall Erz und Brennstoffbunker Rennlage, 16–17.10.54.
[56] ThStA-R, FDGB BV Gera 855/210, Prot. der Sitz. der BGL–Abus, 11.4.53.
[57] See, e.g., ThStA-R, Maxh. 27, Prot. der Sitz. der Konfliktkommission, 7.5.54, 24.5.55, 6.12.56.

committed by a male SED member under interrogation at the Maxhütte: "He steals pipes, he steals light bulbs. Are there wenches behind this, is it the aunt in Zwickau?"[58]

Such comments epitomized prevailing male attitudes toward women, even on the part of supposedly more enlightened Communist officials.[59] They – along with the various sexist practices common on the shop floors of Saalfeld during the early decades of the regime – clearly call into question facile claims about the supposed progress made in the GDR with respect to the emancipation and advancement of East German women. It *is* true that approximately 90 percent were active members of the labor force by the year the Berlin Wall fell. And to that extent, they may have enjoyed a "lead in equality" (*Gleichstellungsvorsprung*) compared to those living in the Federal Republic. Such progress was only relative, of course, for as the foregoing suggests, traditional forms of discrimination and bias remained alive and well in the GDR – further undermining the potential for solidarity among those who lived and labored there.[60]

---

[58] See ThStA-R IV/4/10/238, Prot. der Verhandlung im Maxhüttewerksverkehr, 7.2.53; Bericht der KPKK Slf über die Untersuchung des VEB Ernst Thälmann, 1.4.58; and Prot. der Sitz. der BPL–Thälmann, 6.1.58; ThStA-R IV/4/10/239, report, 20.6.60, and Prot. der MV der Deutschen Versicherungs Anstalt, 28.6.60.

[59] This was not altogether surprising, given the traditionally masculine self-image cultivated by the German Communist movement. See, for example, Catherine Epstein, *The Last Revolutionaries: German Communists and Their Century* (Cambridge, MA, 2003), 32; Eric Weitz, *Creating German Communism, 1890–1990: From Popular Protests to Socialist State* (Princeton, NJ, 1997), esp. 188–232.

[60] On the alleged *Gleichstellungsvorsprung*, see Rainer Geißler, *Die Sozialstruktur Deutschlands: Ein Studienbuch zur Entwicklung im geteilten und vereinten Deutschland* (Opladen, 1992), 259–61. In addition to the ones already cited, important studies that call into question such claims and that support many of the trends identified in this chapter include Sandrine Kott, *Le communisme au quotidien: Les entreprises d'Etat dans la société est-allemande* (Paris, 2001), 237–69; Annegret Schüle, *"Die Spinne": Die Erfahrungsgeschichte weiblicher Industriearbeit im VEB Leipziger Baumwollspinnerei* (Leipzig, 2001); Grit Bühler, *Mythos Gleichberechtigung in der DDR: Politische Partizipation von Frauen am Beispiel des Demokratischen Frauenbunds Deutschlands* (Frankfurt am Main, 1997); Leonore Ansorg and Renate Hürtgen, "The Myth of Female Emancipation: Contradictions in Women's Lives," in Jarausch, *Dictatorship*, 163–76; Heike Trappe, *Emanzipation oder Zwang? Frauen in der DDR zwischen Beruf, Famile und Sozialpolitik* (Berlin, 1995); Susanne Diemer, *Patriarchalismus in der DDR: Strukturelle, kulturelle und subjektive Dimensionen der Geschlechterpolarisierung* (Opladen, 1994); Gunilla-Friederike Budde, ed., *Frauen arbeiten: Weibliche Erwerbstätigkeit in Ost- und Westdeutschland nach 1945* (Göttingen, 1997); Gisela Helwig and Hildegard Maria Nickel, eds., *Frauen in Deutschland, 1945–1992* (Bonn, 1993); Ina Merkel, *"... Und Du, Frau an der Werkbank": Die DDR in den 1950er Jahre* (Berlin, 1990); Gunnar Winkler, ed., *Frauenreport '90* (Berlin, 1990); Donna Harsch, "Squaring the Circle: The Dilemmas and Evolution of Women's Policy," in Patrick Major and Jonathan Osmond, eds., *The Workers' and Peasants' State: Communism and Society in East Germany under Ulbricht, 1945–71* (Manchester, UK, 2002), 151–70; Ute Gerhard, "Die staatliche institutionalisierte 'Lösung' der Frauenfrage: Zur Geschichte der Geschlechterverhältnisse in der DDR," in Kaelble, Kocka, and Zwahr, *Sozialgeschichte*, 383–403. For a useful collection of essays that helps to place gender relations in the GDR in a historical perspective, see Lynn Abrams and Elizabeth Harvey, eds., *Gender Relations in German History:*

The Unmaking of the East German Working Class?

By the early decades of the twentieth century, the German working class had long been regarded as the strongest and best organized in Europe, and its behavior in Saalfeld at the time would not have cast doubt on that assessment. During the years leading up to the outbreak of the First World War, periodic waves of large-scale industrial unrest took place there involving workers from a number of different factories and economic sectors. This earlier unrest, which continued well into the 1920s, demonstrated that the local labor force had a strong tradition of industrial militancy and that working-class solidarity was not unknown in Saalfeld.[61] The main issues at stake – higher wages, better working conditions, and shorter hours – would generate a great deal of shop-floor discontent after 1945 as well, but without leading to much collective action. Why did the behavior of local workers after 1945 stand in such stark contrast to their behavior in this earlier period?

In an attempt to explain why acts of worker protest and resistance were largely individual and scattered during the Nazi era, a number of studies have focused in particular on the important divisions in the German working class that first developed during the late Weimar Republic and then under the Third Reich. They have stressed the effects of the Great Depression and mass unemployment, the destruction of the labor movement and the weakening of the working-class milieu following the Nazi seizure of power, the tensions that existed between the old and the young, the skilled and semiskilled, Social Democrats and Communists, and – last but not least – men and women.[62] The point is that the absence of working-class solidarity after 1945 has to be considered in a larger historical context: The earlier divisions did not disappear in East Germany, and the "shift away from traditional collective solidarity" did not abate. Rather, both phenomena became even more pronounced for many of the reasons discussed in this chapter. With some qualifications, what Detlev

---

Power, Agency and Experience from the Sixteenth to the Twentieth Century (Durham, NC, 1996).

[61] See Gerhard Werner, *Geschichte der Stadt Saalfeld*, vol. 3 (Bamberg, 1997), 82–5, 96, 99.

[62] On the history of the prewar German working class, a good place to start is Jürgen Kocka, *Lohnarbeit und Klassenbildung: Arbeiter und Arbeiterbewegung in Deutschland, 1800–1875* (Berlin, 1983); Josef Mooser, *Arbeiterleben in Deutschland, 1900–1970: Klassenlagen, Kultur und Politik* (Frankfurt am Main, 1984); Heinrich August Winkler, *Der Weg in die Katastrophe: Arbeiter und Arbeiterbewegung in der Weimarer Republik, 1930 bis 1933* (Berlin, 1983). On the Nazi period in particular, see Michael Schneider, *"Unterm Hakenkreuz": Arbeiter und Arbeiterbewegung, 1933 bis 1939* (Bonn, 1999); Tim Mason, *Social Policy in the Third Reich: The Working Class and the "National Community,"* ed. Jane Caplan, trans. John Broadwin (Providence, RI, 1993); idem, *Nazism, Fascism and the Working Class,* ed. Jane Caplan (Cambridge, 1995); Ulrich Herbert, "Arbeiterschaft im 'Dritten Reich': Zwischenbilanz und offene Fragen," *GG* 15 (1989): 320–60. Also see Horst Groschopp, "Überlegungen zur Kontinuität der deutschen Arbeiterbewegungskultur in der DDR," in Wolfgang Kaschuba, Gottfried Korff, and Bernd Jürgen Warneken, eds., *Arbeiterkultur seit 1945: Ende oder Veränderung?* (Tübingen, 1991), 123–40.

Peukert has written with regard to industrial relations in the Federal Republic holds true for the GDR as well:

The longer-term impact became evident only after the war, when, although workers parties and trade unions emerged once again, the old traditional proletarian social environment did not.... [T]he Nazis' destruction of the old structures of solidarity in the labour movement paved the way for a new, more individualistic, more achievement-oriented 'sceptical' type of worker, of the sort described by sociologists in the 1950s....[63]

But an important question still remains: Did East German authorities purposely pursue strategies aimed at dividing the workforce? That was certainly not the case for those designed to integrate women. And the various incentive policies introduced by the regime were clearly intended first and foremost to spur productivity. Yet, this could cut both ways: They gave rise to divisive shop-floor practices that certainly proved beneficial to the performance of some workers but seriously impaired that of their colleagues. As a result, the overall economic benefits of these official incentive schemes remain unclear. Such policies nevertheless had other, less tangible benefits for the regime and its leaders, above all the frictions that they created – frictions that promoted domestic stability by seriously undercutting worker solidarity. In the absence of conclusive documentary evidence, it is difficult to say whether or not such policies were consciously pursued with that aim in mind. But regardless of their actual intent, this was clearly an unintended consequence that wary officials in Saalfeld must have warmly welcomed, especially after the double shocks of August 1951 and June 1953.

[63] Detlev Peukert, *Inside Nazi Germany: Conformity, Opposition, and Racism in Everyday Life*, trans. Richard Deveson (New Haven, CT, 1987), 114, 117.

9

"I Comes before We" in the Countryside

The preceding chapters have focused primarily on industrial workers, the social group that received the most attention in the reports and analyses of local officials. This preoccupation undoubtedly reflected their economic and ideological importance as well as their overwhelming numerical superiority in Saalfeld. Yet approximately half of the district's population lived in small villages located outside the core industrial region between the administrative capital and Unterwellenborn. Not all were farmers, of course, but the vast majority were somehow engaged in the primary sector and therefore were greatly affected by the major developments that took place in the countryside during the remaining years of the Ulbricht era – above all the forced transition to collectivization that began again in the late 1950s.

Much as they had since the immediate postwar period, Communist officials remained committed to gaining the support of, or at least taming, this traditionally hostile constituency, whose performance was considered to be of the utmost importance for the well-being of the East German economy – and in whose name the SED *also* claimed to rule. The active involvement of many landholders in the statewide uprising of 1953 clearly made this an imperative, and the extent to which such endeavors met with success was intimately related to the subsequent political and economic stability of the regime. With that overarching theme in mind, this chapter looks at the fundamental changes that took place in the countryside after the June disturbances, focusing in particular on the response of local farmers to official policies, their relationship to the regime and its direct representatives, and their own everyday interaction.[1]

[1] On comparable developments elsewhere in the GDR during this period, see in particular Arnd Bauerkämper, *Ländliche Gesellschaft in der kommunistischen Diktatur: Zwangsmodernisierung und Tradition in Brandenburg, 1945–1963* (Cologne, 2002); Barbara Schier, *Alltagsleben im "sozialistischen Dorf": Merxleben und seine LPG im Spannungsfeld der SED–Agrarpolitik, 1945–1990* (Munster, 2001); Antonia Maria Humm, *Auf dem Weg zum sozialistischen Dorf? Zum Wandel der dörflichen Lebenswelt in der DDR und der Bundesrepublik Deutschland, 1952–1969* (Göttingen, 1999); Corey Ross, *Constructing Socialism at the Grass-Roots: The*

Struggling (Not) to Deliver

Whatever their differences, most farmers in Saalfeld had at least one thing in common with industrial workers: an often steely determination to limit the weighty demands imposed on them by the party and state. They, too, chafed at their many sociopolitical obligations, and they similarly resisted the regime's unrelenting pressure to increase productivity. The refractory behavior of many farmers during the period leading up to and during the dramatic events of June 1953 had made this abundantly clear, and the mass exodus from the first LPGs established on the eve of the upheaval revealed in no uncertain terms their strong aversion to collective forms of production. After the disturbances – and despite a subsequent series of placatory reforms – opposition to mandatory requisitioning and a frequent failure to satisfy official obligations remained among the most important sources of tension between authorities and local landowners.

The regime responded to the protest by quickly adopting a number of corrective measures aimed at promoting agricultural production and assuring future deliveries: It distributed more than 200 tons of feed in 1954 alone, awarded hundreds of thousands of marks in credit to the remaining LPGs in Saalfeld, and reduced production quotas by up to 15 percent that year because of poor weather – and, in all likelihood, because of widespread anger about previous norm levels. District officials also dispatched hundreds of paid volunteers to help farmers harvest their crops, and delegated a phalanx of agricultural specialists and industrial workers to the countryside to provide the LPGs with additional assistance and guidance.[2] But despite this and other valuable forms of aid, farmers in Saalfeld still continued to complain – much like their industrial counterparts – about inordinately high production quotas that could not be met given their available resources. In turn, district officials regularly lamented the failure of both independent landowners and agricultural collectives to satisfy plan targets and honor their production pledges.[3]

Transformation of East Germany, 1945–65 (Houndsmill, UK, 2000), 105–24, 172–4, 188–93. For a brief overview of the literature on East German farmers, also see Jens Schöne, "Landwirtschaft und ländliche Gesellschaft in der DDR," in Rainer Eppelmann, Bernd Faulenbach, and Ulrich Mählert, eds., *Bilanz und Perspektiven der DDR-Forschung* (Paderborn, 2003), 254–9.

[2] See KrA-S 12553, Informatorischer Ratsbericht: Unterstützung und weitere Festigung unserer LPG'en, 16.5.55.

[3] In 1955, the LPGs managed to fill plan figures by only 73 percent overall. Despite improvements in some areas or the occasional report praising satisfactory performance, production figures and deliveries continued to fall well below official expectations – and tended to depend on the product itself (milk and livestock were generally poor) as well as on the individual collective. It was reported in 1967, for example, that twenty-nine LPGs had not met their milk quotas and that more than half of all the collectives in Saalfeld had similarly fallen behind in meat production. See ThStA-R IV/4/10/135, Bericht über die Entwicklung der LPG, 6.3.56; ThStA-R IV/B-4/10/100, IB der SED–KL Slf: Stimmung unter den Genossenschaftsbauern über die X. Deutsche Bauernkonferenz, 10.6.68. On unsatisfactory plan fulfillment more generally, also see the reports and analyses in ThStA-R IV/4/10/124, 174, 177, 269, 306; ThStA-R IV/A-4/10/26, 40, 60, 67, 100, 119, 120, 154. More generally, see Dieter Schulz, *"Kapitalistische Länder überflügeln": Die DDR-Bauern in der SED-Politik des ökonomischen Wettbewerbs mit der Bundesrepublik von 1956 bis 1961* (Berlin, 1994).

Local authorities typically attributed this failure to the machinations of real or imagined enemies: A drop in milk deliveries during the 1955 Geneva Summit was supposedly linked, for example, to the hostile influence of Western radio broadcasts.[4] Derelict producers, for their part, blamed their often unsatisfactory performance on factors beyond their control: inclement weather, labor shortages, damage caused by wild boars, and, above all, insufficient state aid. Chronic shortages of feed, they contended, was the main reason why livestock holdings continued to decrease in Saalfeld throughout the 1950s and 1960s. To make matters worse, construction backlogs meant that some LPGs did not have proper facilities to store the feed they *had* managed to procure from state agencies.[5]

No matter how vehemently farmers criticized the regime because of its policies, they were clearly dependent on its services. And as a result, its failure to supply them with enough feed, seed, and manure, with necessary tools and machinery, or with adequate buildings, credit, and other forms of assistance led to repeated calls for lower and supposedly more realistic production quotas. Others went a step further by rejecting production figures altogether, by declining to make further pledges, or by categorically refusing to surrender their products to official agencies: "The state gradually takes everything from us and one day we'll just stand there and own nothing anymore." Or as one former LPG chairman quipped after learning that increased milk production was now the primary task in Saalfeld, "If it were up to me, the dairy wouldn't get another drop of milk. . . ."[6]

High-level authorities usually responded to such resistance by issuing calls for even higher production levels and by further increasing pressure on local officials to ensure plan fulfillment. Caught between two hostile fronts, the latter often joined farmers in criticizing plan figures themselves or in arguing that it was not possible to raise rural productivity any further. In fact, the administrative heads of many LPGs seldom fought to assure fulfillment of the plan, which most collectives regarded as a "burdensome scourge" – or, in the words of one SED member, "political nonsense." Just like those engaged in the industrial sector, party organizations in several villages similarly complained in response to the statewide Production Challenge of 1961, which was also launched in the countryside, "Always something new, more and more should be produced even though there's not enough feed. They should just be content for once and not always apply pressure to get even more."[7]

---

4 The Geneva Summit was the first meeting of the former wartime Allies since the Potsdam Conference of 1945. See KrA-S 9137, Prot. der Sitz. des KR, 15.6.55, 6.8.55; ThStA-R IV/4/10/130, Bericht über die Erfüllung des Ministerratsbeschlusses, 9.9.55.

5 See, e.g., the minutes and analyses in KrA-S 9137, 12554, 12556.

6 ThStA-R IV/A-4/10/119 and 120, Einschätzung der Lage der Landwirtschaft, 17.12.65; Politische Arbeit in den LPG Typ I, n.d.; and IB, 18.7.64. On similar resistance elsewhere to the regime's economic demands, see Bauerkämper, *Ländliche Gesellschaft*, 436–90.

7 See ThStA-R IV/4/10/127, Prot. der Sekretariatssitz. der SED–KL Slf, 18.3.55; ThStA-R IV/4/10/177, Prot. der Sekretariatssitz. der SED–KL Slf (Vorlage), 26.10.59, 30.10.59; ThStA-R IV/4/10/266, IB der SED–KL Slf, 8.12.61. See Chapter 7 on the Production Campaign of 1961.

In essence, then, many of those who ostensibly supported the regime readily acknowledged the adverse effect that objective difficulties had on plan fulfillment. But their frequent appeals for additional support usually fell on deaf ears because of the severe economic constraints of state socialism and the many shortcomings of centralized planning. In 1959, for example, one local mayor desperately appealed to district officials for help because his village did not have enough buildings to house their livestock. Their hands were tied, however, because the construction program planned for that year could not be completed due to severe labor and material shortages; to cap it off, regional authorities had refused to give them the full amount requested for investment in this important sector. Financial assistance did increase in the following decade, yet complaints about serious construction backlogs persisted throughout the 1960s.[8]

Besides pointing to inadequate aid and other obstacles beyond their control, many farmers also justified their defiance by arguing that the official prices offered for their goods were too low – which prompted them to sell their wares on the black market or disregard the dictates of state planners by specializing in more remunerative products at the expense of less profitable ones. When authorities decided in 1958 to offer higher prices for beef than for pork, many collectives began to concentrate on the former and consequently failed to fill plan quotas for the latter.[9] As this suggests, vestiges of a market economy not only survived under but were also unwittingly encouraged by socialist forms of planning. But officials steadfastly refused to abandon such policies; instead, they decided at the time to try and spur agricultural production by accelerating once again the GDR's relentless march toward socialism.

Forced Collectivization (Round Two)

To reduce tensions in the countryside following the "shock" of June 1953, East German authorities prudently decided to relax the pressure on landowners to join and remain in collective farming units. Many of Saalfeld's rural residents eagerly took advantage of this reprieve, and from November 1955 to July 1957, the number of LPG members decreased by 40 percent; another half dozen collectives dissolved themselves entirely during this period. As a result, the remaining LPGs worked less than 10 percent of all arable land in the district.[10] Confronted with similar developments throughout the GDR, and for a variety of political, economic, and ideological reasons, the SED launched a new offensive in 1958 at its Fifth Party Congress, where it called on local officials to accelerate the

---

[8] See, e.g., the analyses and minutes in ThStA-R IV/4/10/167, 174, 177, 307; ThStA-R IV/A-4/10/119–20.

[9] See the information reports from this period in ThStA-R IV/4/10/251, 264, 266, 270.

[10] ThStA-R IV/4/10/135, Bericht über die Entwicklung der LPG, 6.3.56; ThStA-R IV/4/10/254, IB der SED–KL Slf, 25.7.57.

collectivization process and effect a complete "social transformation" of the countryside.[11]

Once again, party members and industrial workers dutifully descended on Saalfeld's villages en masse to recruit independent farmers and persuade local communities to set up new LPGs. Because of low attendance at the public gatherings convened to discuss the new measures, the agitators were often forced to go from farm to farm to conduct individual discussions with resistant landowners. Besides emphasizing the ideological necessity of collectivization, they promoted its purported economic benefits, such as higher income, greater state assistance, and more leisure time. Notwithstanding official complaints about sluggish progress, and as a result of these efforts, the number of collectives doubled during the second half of 1958, and by December, fifty LPGs cultivated slightly more than 30 percent of the land. These figures remained more or less constant until early 1960, when the SED abandoned all pretense of voluntarism and decided to embrace more forceful measures in an all-out effort to surmount the recent standstill: "[F]ull collectivity"– a euphemism for forced collectivization – now became the order of the day.[12]

To accomplish this new task, the District Secretariat adopted a series of emergency decrees in late February and March that delegated half of all local functionaries to the countryside and – to the chagrin of factory officials already faced with severe labor shortages – required worker brigades to live in the villages in order to assure a steady barrage of exhortation. Local "sheriffs" (*Abschnittsbevollmächtigte*, or ABVs) were charged with reporting any signs of activity by the class enemy so that repressive measures could be immediately taken; in the belief that this would bring others in line, they were instructed to pay special attention to wealthy farmers, who usually had the greatest influence in their community.[13]

The earlier policy of excluding *kulaks* from the LPGs now came back to haunt officials: "The main focus in Breternitz is the largest farmer... who argued that he had wanted to join the LPG when it was first established but wasn't accepted, so he won't join now. Whether or not the others join depends primarily on his decision." Despite similar refusals elsewhere, the agitators' determined efforts at persuasion ultimately paid off. After "working on" the "strongest" farmer in Lositz-Jemichen until 3 A.M. one night, representatives from the sewing-machine factory successfully reported that the entire village had finally agreed to join the collective. Several days later, on March 31, the District Secretariat proudly announced that all farmers

---

[11] On the second collectivization campaign, see Jens Schöne, *Frühling auf dem Lande? Die Kollektivierung der DDR–Landwirtschaft* (Berlin, 2005). Also see Bauerkämper, *Ländliche Gesellschaft*, 159–94; Ross, *Constructing Socialism*, 110–20; Schier, *Alltagsleben*, 61–74.

[12] See the reports and minutes in KrA-S 12557, 12561; ThStA-R IV/4/10/147, 163, 177, 185, 255, 257, 261, 306, 307.

[13] See, e.g., ThStA-R IV/4/10/182, Prot. der Sekretariatssitz. der SED–KL Slf, 1.3.60, 22.3.60; ThStA-R, FDGB BV Gera 860/211, IB Nr. 3 zur sozialistischen Umgestaltung der Landwirtschaft, 25.3.60.

FIGURE 7. Members of an agricultural collective in the village of Remschütz planting turnips during the GDR's second major collectivization campaign of the late 1950s. © Bildarchiv des Stadtmuseums Saalfeld.

in Saalfeld were now joined together in seventy-seven LPGs: Their number had increased almost eightfold to more than 3,000 since the SED's 1958 Congress.[14]

Despite this apparent success, the new campaign had obviously met with as little enthusiasm as the first one earlier that decade. Resistance was once again most tenacious among middle-sized farmers, who voiced concerns about relinquishing their freedom or who claimed that collectivization would only lead to more work or to a decline in social status: "One is branded a day laborer in an LPG."[15] Others argued that they were too old to join or that they were generally satisfied with their present situation, especially since their own performance usually surpassed that of most LPGs. Unwilling to accept the fact that most independent landowners were simply opposed to collectivization of their own volition, officials attributed their obduracy to the usual scapegoats: devious class enemies, Western media, the clergy, and even female farmers. "We always noticed that the women wore the pants" and that they "browbeat" their husbands not to join (in fact, many Saalfelders did claim that their wives'

---

[14] See ThStA-R, FDGB BV Gera 860/211, IB Nr. 4 zur sozialistischen Umgestaltung der Land-wirtschaft, 28.3.60; ThStA-R IV/4/10/185, Stand der Bildung der SED GO auf dem Lande, 2.6.60.

[15] ThStA-R IV/4/10/177, report, 26.10.59.

stubborn opposition to collectivization was the main reason they could not comply with official demands).[16]

Supposedly incompetent functionaries and industrial workers were similarly taken to task for failing to agitate sufficiently or for even opposing the campaign themselves. Such accusations were characteristically exaggerated, yet many did admit that they tended to avoid disputes with hostile landowners, often because of their own reservations about collectivization. As the VdgB chairman in one village rhetorically asked, how could he persuade the farmers to join "when I am not even convinced myself?"[17] Not all functionaries were this sympathetic or forbearing, of course. One disgruntled agitator reported with contempt the "complete underestimation of the importance and necessity of socialist management" and accused farmers of neglecting their responsibility toward their children: "[T]hey'll do it better someday and then call you to account." Urging greater patience and warning delegated workers not to bring to a head the traditional antagonism between themselves and those living in the countryside, a visiting Soviet professor nevertheless reminded local officials that "the farmer is contradictory by nature. He's won over to the LPG today, but then says 'no' tomorrow."[18]

These were prophetic words, in fact, for a number of farmers who had caved in to pressure and joined an LPG during the campaign subsequently withdrew during the period leading up to the construction of the Berlin Wall. The reasons they offered for their decision were all familiar: They were better off financially on their own, they did not get along with the other members of their collective, or they found it difficult to administer such large holdings: "If it were my farm, I'd manage just fine because then you don't have forty-five to fifty opinions, just a single one."[19] Conveniently forgetting earlier promises guaranteeing them the right to quit if dissatisfied, local authorities frequently strong-armed these farmers into taking back their resignations, usually by engaging them in lengthy discussions or by reporting them to state security officials. Such pressure tactics were largely effective: By September 1961, just as the cement in Berlin had hardened and the possibility of fleeing the GDR had all but vanished, only twenty-two farms in the entire district were not in an LPG. Few withdrawals were reported later that decade, and most of these were ostensibly linked to old age or retirement.[20]

---

[16] ThStA-R IV/4/10/177, Prot. der Sekretariatssitz. der SED KL–Slf, 30.10.59. On resistance to collectivization, also see the reports and minutes in ThStA-R IV/4/10/159, 175, 177, 182, 253–5, 260, 298, 306, 307. See in particular ThStA-R IV/4/10/243, Bericht der KPKK Slf an die ZPKK über feindliche Einflüsse und hemmende Faktoren bei der Entwicklung der sozialistischen Umgestaltung der Landwirtschaft, 16.2.60.

[17] See KrA-S 12557, Prot. der Sitz. des KR, 9.4.58; ThStA-R IV/4/10/298, Bericht über den Instrukteureinsatz in Arnsgereuth, n.d.

[18] See ThStA-R IV/4/10/260, IB der SED–KL Slf, 28.10.59; ThStA-R IV/4/10/307, Bericht über den Agit-Einsatz in Arnsgereuth zur Bildung einer LPG, 24.10.59.

[19] ThStA-R IV/4/10/264, IB der SED–KL Slf, 1.2.61.

[20] See, e.g., the information reports in ThStA-R IV/4/10/265–6. On efforts to socialize the artisanal sector at this time, as well as similar resistance on the part of local craftsmen and other

Old Wine in New Bottles

Authorities may have blamed class enemies and other alleged foes for the widespread resistance to collectivization, yet most realized that LPG profitability was one of the most important keys to winning the hearts and minds of the agrarian populace and effecting a social transformation of the countryside. In other words, they had to convince independent farmers that they would produce more and be better off financially once they had joined a collective. Yet, many LPGs had failed to turn a profit in the 1950s, and some even suffered serious financial losses. The value of the work units (*Arbeitseinheiten*) that collective farmers earned for performing a specific task fluctuated accordingly – decreasing in ten LPGs from 1957 to 1958, for example. Forced to borrow short-term credit to stay afloat, many complained that the LPGs did not provide a real living and that they had nothing to show for their efforts but increasing debt.[21]

Even the SED itself admitted that the collectives were not economically superior to most independent holdings, which was why officials had decided to dissolve several local LPGs in the mid-1950s. This would, they hoped, counteract the negative impression they had made on those farmers who justified their refusal to join by pointing to "poor work by this or that LPG" – or who, during the height of the campaign in late 1959, had argued that the LPGs could not compete with middle-sized independent holdings, which had finished harvesting much earlier that year. The dissolutions also allowed local functionaries to concentrate their efforts on model LPGs or on those that showed most promise, yet more than half of all of Saalfeld's collectives remained unprofitable in the latter 1950s. In fact, official agencies were sometimes forced to pay independent farmers for additional products in order to make up for the failure of many collectives to meet their production targets.[22]

District officials and LPG members accounted for such disturbing developments by arguing that individual proprietors had had an unfair advantage because they supposedly received more assistance than the collectives themselves: "Housewife brigades and others don't work in the LPGs but rather for the private farmers. We sometimes thought that a field belonged to an LPG because so many people were on it, but it actually belonged to a private farmer. It's no surprise when many of them still say they're doing well."[23] There were other reasons as well for the superior performance of most independent farmers. For one, state agencies usually furnished them with more manure and

private tradesmen, see the reports in ADL, BV Gera 33107; AdsD, Ostbüro 00523j. More generally, see Frank Ebbinghaus, *Ausnutzung und Verdrängung: Steuerungsprobleme der SED–Mittelstandspolitik, 1955–1972* (Berlin, 2003), 66–128.

[21] See the reports and minutes in ThStA-R IV/4/10/118, 135, 147, 156, 167, 243, 306, 307, 309; KrA-S 9137, 12554, 15582.

[22] See the reports and minutes in ThStA-R IV/4/10/177, 306, 307; see in particular ThStA-R IV/4/10/243, Bericht der KPKK Slf an die ZPKK, 16.2.60. Also see Horst Brezinski, "Private Agriculture in the GDR: Limitations of Orthodox Socialist Agricultural Policy," *Soviet Studies* 42 (1990): 535–53.

[23] ThStA-R IV/4/10/177, Prot. der Sekretariatssitz. der SED–KL Slf, 30.10.59.

feed because they were required to pay more for these essential supplies. For similar reasons, they also tended to receive greater attention from the MTSs because of official policies requiring them to pay higher fees for their services (another incentive to join a collective) and because their holdings tended to be in better condition and were thus easier to work.[24] Official policies designed to penalize those who insisted on remaining independent had, in other words, backfired.

Whatever the objective reasons, district authorities attributed the relatively weak performance of the LPGs first and foremost to the poor morale of the farmers themselves, who – like those in the industrial sector – supposedly worked in a slothful, undisciplined manner, avoided work altogether, or drank to excess while on the job. Because their "sense of responsibility" for the collective was "not yet fully developed," crops often lay unharvested in the fields, which not only hurt production but also reduced the fertility of the soil. It was purportedly even difficult to mobilize all the members of the LPG Marktgölitz – the first and one of the most successful collectives in Saalfeld – during the height of the season: "One female farmer went to the beauty parlor, the other went shopping in Saalfeld, a third washed clothes, etc., etc."[25] In response to official rebukes, some farmers began to argue in the early 1960s – at a time when the average yearly income of local LPG members exceeded 3,000 marks – that they simply did not need to work so hard because they were already satisfied with their standard of living: "Why should we always produce more, we already have everything we need (television, car, motorcycle)."[26] Though obviously self-serving, such claims represented a major shift from the previous decade, when most collective farmers had complained that their income was far too low.

Faced with incessant criticism and under constant pressure to produce even more, many local farmers attributed their own poor performance to that of low-level bureaucrats and especially the machine-and-tractor stations. In fact, the same grievances voiced about the MTSs following the June 1953 upheaval continued to surface regularly over the next two decades: They repeatedly reneged on their contracts, they worked carelessly and inefficiently, and they wasted the farmers' time by using old or defective machinery. All in all, many concluded, the MTSs did more harm than good. As one representative from the LPG in Aue am Berg complained, it was intolerable that "one can already recognize MTS fields from afar because of poor work.... [T]he MTS once arrived at 8 A.M. with their machines but couldn't use them because a cogwheel was missing."[27] In

---

[24] See the various reports in KrA-S 9137.

[25] ThStA-R IV/4/10/298, Abschlußbericht über den Einsatz der Kreisparteischullehrer in LPG/Gemeinde Marktgölitz, 26.6.58. On reports of high alcohol consumption as well as the supposedly poor working habits of local farmers more generally, also see the reports, minutes, and correspondence in KrA-S 9137, 12554; ThStA-R IV/4/10/182, 187, 298, 307, 309; ThStA-R IV/A-4/10/27 and 120. Also see ThStA-R, VPKA Slf 8, correspondence, 13.1.71.

[26] See ThStA-R IV/4/10/270, IB der SED–KL Slf, 28.11.62; ThStA-R IV/A-4/10/090, IB der SED–KL Slf, 27.2.63.

[27] KrA-S 9137, Prot. der Sitz. des KR, 15.6.55.

response to such complaints as well as to frequent reprimands by local officials, MTS workers characteristically pointed to factors beyond their control, such as shortages of spare parts and essential tools. In 1962, for instance, tractor drivers blamed state agencies for not supplying them with enough tires, even though a large supply supposedly lay unpacked in a regional warehouse: They were not responsible, they concluded, for the backlogs caused by bureaucratic ineptitude.[28] Their unsatisfactory performance also reflected, in all likelihood, widespread anger about low earnings, poor working conditions, and frequent pressure to work additional shifts because of perennial labor shortages. The response of most MTS officials to such grievances was typical: They tended to avoid disputes and give in to the demands of their subordinates in order to discourage job turnover and maintain harmony – another important parallel to the situation in many local factories.[29]

Echoing the complaints of many farmers, leading district authorities frequently censured these and other low-level functionaries for incompetence, flagrant neglect, and a lack of resolve – especially when production levels fell short or when high-level policies failed to win support at the grass roots. Under pressure from their own superiors, it was obviously easier to blame these whipping boys than to admit that official policies were flawed or that the regime enjoyed little backing among large segments of the agrarian population. It was not, in other words, the endemic shortages and shortcomings of a planned economy that accounted for poor plan fulfillment, but rather the supposed ineptitude of low-level district and village officials – local mayors and community councils, agronomists and other members of the agricultural intelligentsia – who failed to provide sufficient guidance and support, who neglected to carry out the flood of orders handed down from on high, or who made too many concessions in an effort to maintain peace and tranquility.[30]

Despite the tendency to blame unsatisfactory performance on supposedly lazy producers and other scapegoats, some district officials nevertheless admitted that rigid planning had indeed often served as a brake on agricultural production and initiative. To counter the many difficulties caused by such bureaucratic deficiencies, they recommended greater use of modern technology in the countryside. This would not only help boost production but also make up for the worsening shortage of rural labor, a problem that could "only be solved" by greater mechanization.[31] From 1959 to 1966, in fact, the number of agricultural workers decreased from 32.2 to 24.8 per 100 hectares, and authorities feared that this figure would drop even further to 17.9 by 1970 – largely because the children of those reaching retirement age were not taking over their

[28] ThStA-R IV/4/10/267 and 269, IB der SED–KL Slf,16.3.62, 2.8.62.
[29] See, e.g., KrA-S 24075, Niederschr. über die Sitz. der Kommission "Industriearbeiter aufs Land," 24.2.55; ThStA-R IV/4/10/177, Prot. der Sekretariatssitz. der SED–KL Slf (Vorlage), 30.10.59; ThStA-R IV/4/10/276, correspondence, 17.2.60.
[30] See, e.g., the minutes in KrA-S 9137.
[31] ThStA-R IV/4/10/306, Plan des Kr. zur Entwicklung der Landwirtschaft, 12.11.57.

parents' holdings but instead were migrating to cities and towns in search of better-paying jobs in the industrial sector.[32] A serious challenge since the early 1950s, the steady loss of rural youths to urban centers was, of course, a global phenomenon and not peculiar to East Germany. Yet, local officials characteristically placed the blame on hostile forces intent on undermining the economy: "A very popular method of the enemy is to draw youths away from the countryside" by convincing them "that they had no perspectives in this area."[33] Opponents of the GDR had, in other words, unwittingly served as the agents of modernity.

To counter this troublesome trend, local authorities intensified their efforts to win over school-age children for the primary sector. Yet, their endeavors – much like those aimed at recruiting urban adolescents for key industries and factories – met with limited success. That was not altogether surprising, especially given the attitude of many older farmers in Saalfeld, who claimed that "their sons and daughters would have earlier taken over their farmstead [but the] love of agriculture (meaning private farming) was taken away from them. This explains the exodus to industry, which offers them much more."[34] Some even counseled village youths to acquire occupational training in the city before joining an LPG. Such advice apparently found a receptive audience among local youths, who typically complained that they were not given much responsibility in the LPGs, that agricultural apprentices were much worse off than their industrial counterparts, or that there was simply no future in farming. By 1962, those under age twenty-five made up less than 0.5 percent of the LPG membership in Saalfeld. The average age of farm workers in the district steadily increased as a result, and there were very few young people in some villages by mid-decade, when 40 percent of those still active in the primary sector had already reached retirement age.[35]

As officials recognized themselves, the introduction of modern technology and greater mechanization was one viable way in which to counter the adverse effects that a dwindling, aging labor force had on agricultural performance and productivity. Yet, despite some advances – one-third of all field work was mechanized by 1959 and approximately 13 million marks were invested at the time in new machinery for the MTSs – local farmers and officials continued to complain about shortages of advanced technology and the negative consequences

[32] See the statistics in KrA-S 15590; ThStA-R IV/4/10/177 and IV/A-4/10/67.

[33] ThStA-R IV/4/10/243, Bericht der KPKK Slf an die ZPKK, 16.2.60. On labor shortages and the flight of youths from the countryside, also see the reports and minutes in ThStA-R IV/4/10/136, 177, 267, 298, 306; KrA-S 12556, 15590. See in particular ThStA-R IV/A-4/10/67, Perspektivplankonzeption der sozialistischen Landwirtschaft, 25.8.67; ADL, BV Gera 33024, Erfahrungsaustausch, 20.3.64.

[34] ThStA-R IV/4/10/243, Bericht der KPKK Slf an die ZPKK, 16.2.60. Also see ThStA-R, FDGB KV Slf 6256, Bericht über EOS Erziehung/Nachwuchs, 6.12.65.

[35] See ThStA-R IV/A-4/10/22, Bericht über die politisch-ideologische Arbeit der Partei in LPG Typ I, 27.9.63; ThStA-R IV/A-4/10/27, Einschätzung der Entwicklung der LPG, 23.3.64; ThStA-R IV/A-4/10/67, Perspektivplankonzeption der sozialistischen Landwirtschaft, 25.8.67.

this had for production.[36] In response to a state ordinance calling for even higher yields, landowners in the Drognitz region griped in the mid-1960s that they still did not have even the most basic implements – while pointing out that special technology readily available in West Germany had enabled two farmers in a neighboring Bavarian village to harvest forty hectares of hay all by themselves: "We have to perform the same work here using considerably more manual labor and the same tools used by our grandfathers...."[37] To make matters worse, many machines and tools could not be used at all because they were defective and because spare parts were still in short supply.

Despite such complaints, a number of farmers showed little interest in utilizing whatever new equipment was placed at their disposal. There were many reasons for this: Prior to collectivization, for example, several of the larger landowners had opposed the use of tractors so that they could earn additional income by making their neighbors dependent on their own draft animals for heavy tasks – a practice roundly denounced by local officials as "horse ideology." For their part, many smaller proprietors believed that they could only amass enough work units by performing strenuous physical labor; others remained highly suspicious of newfangled time-saving devices or doubted that modern technology would really lessen their workload. Many were equally impervious to official arguments calling for the adoption of modern, scientific techniques designed to improve productivity and enhance fertility. District authorities may have been correct in attributing such resistance to traditional rural "backwardness." But it was equally plausible that many farmers – like their industrial counterparts – simply feared that these supposedly more rational methods only represented yet another devious strategy aimed at squeezing out even more labor from them.[38]

That was why many farmers similarly resisted official efforts aimed at stepping up socialist competitions like those conducted in the VEBs. Pitting village against village, collective against collective, and farmer against farmer, the contests rewarded winners with monetary premiums and other material incentives in an effort to improve discipline, boost output, and draw on supposedly untapped labor reserves.[39] Like industrial workers, many farmers argued that organized competition was a disguised form of exploitation that only led to higher norms and increasing demands by the state. Reminding visiting officials that no one was supposed to be exploited anymore in the GDR, disgruntled party members from the village of Unterloquitz even compared competition to capitalism. Those who did compete typically complained that their bonuses

---

[36] ThStA-R IV/4/10/307, Stand der sozialistischen Umgestaltung der Landwirtschaft, Patenschaften; Zwischenbilanz der bisherigen Erfahrungen der Brigade der Maxh., n.d.

[37] See ThStA-R IV/A-4/10/120, Eingabe laut Staatseinlaß, 28.7.65; ThStA-R IV/A-4/10/101, IB der SED–KL Slf, 4.8.66.

[38] See, e.g., the reports and minutes in ThStA-R IV/4/10/124, 127, 263, 266, 307, 309; KrA-S 9137, 12553, 12561.

[39] For an overview of organized competition in the countryside, see KrA-S 12553, Informatorischer Bericht über die Durchführung des Wettbewerbs in der Landwirtschaft, 1955.

were too low, that they had been unfairly excluded or penalized because of factors beyond their control, and that competition only led to "quarrels and fights" over premiums – not just between organizers and competitors, but also *among* the participants themselves.[40]

For all of these reasons, participation levels remained consistently spotty: In the spring of 1956, for example, less than 40 percent of all farmsteads in Saalfeld were nominally involved in some form of rural competition. Organized programs did exist in more than 70 percent of all LPGs by the latter 1960s, but local officials still complained about a lack of real interest or admitted that the degree of actual participation tended to vary widely.[41] As usual, they placed the blame on low-level apparatchiks. Accused of poor agitation and shoddy organization, the latter usually defended themselves by explaining that they did not have enough funds to award premiums or enough time to popularize and discuss the importance of rural competition. More to the point, their efforts to promote competition were usually a waste of time because their arguments were ignored or met with pronounced hostility: "What are you thinking? When we're supposed to speak with farmers who are falling behind and give them instructions about how to work better and produce more, they just laugh at us. . . ."[42]

The achievement of full collectivization had done little, then, to promote agricultural production, ensure satisfactory deliveries, and solve many of the challenges that had plagued the local countryside since the immediate postwar period. High-level authorities responded to this failure in Saalfeld and elsewhere in the GDR by introducing important aspects of the New Economic System to the primary sector in the mid-1960s. In an effort to raise productivity, improve performance, and heighten discipline, they called for the adoption of more rational and scientific industrial farming and management methods and encouraged the use of economic levers that would appeal to the "material interests" of producers and officials alike. Special bonuses (so-called *Zielprämien*) were introduced, for example, that rewarded farmers for successfully carrying out specific tasks, and local cadres were either rewarded or penalized financially, depending on their own achievement as well as that of their immediate subordinates.[43]

---

[40] See, e.g., the reports and minutes in ThStA-R IV/4/10/127, 236, 270; ThStA-R IV/A-4/10/22, 27, 092–3.

[41] See the statistics in ThStA-R IV/4/10/251, IB der SED–KL Slf, 26.4.56; ThStA-R IV/B-4/10/100, Stimmung unter den Genossenschaftsbauern, 10.6.68.

[42] See KrA-S 9137, Prot. der Sitz. des KR, 6.8.55; KrA-S 12553, Informatorischer Bericht über die Durchführung des Wettbewerbs in der Landwirtschaft, 1955; ThStA-R IV/4/10/270, IB der SED–KL Slf, 28.11.62; ThStA-R IV/A-4/10/22, Bericht über die politisch-ideologische Arbeit der Partei in LPG Typ I, 27.9.63; ThStA-R IV/A-4/10/119, Referat zur Aktivtagung in der KG Könitz in Unterwellenborn, 11.4.67.

[43] See, e.g., ThStA-R IV/A-4/10/20, Bericht über den Einsatz in die LPG Aue über materielle Interessiertheit, 12.7.63; KrA-S 16382, Konzeption über die politisch-ideologischen, organisatorischen, und technischen Vorbereitungen und Durchführung der Frühjahrsbestellung 1966, 17.2.66; ThStA-R IV/A-4/10/69, Entwicklung einer wissenschaftlichen Führungs/Leitungstätigkeit durch die Produktionsleitung der KLR, 20.10.67; ThStA-R

The buzzwords and strategies were similar to those used in the industrial sector at the time and represented, in many respects, little more than old wine in new bottles. Yet, many farmers and low-level functionaries reacted with predictable hostility, arguing that it was not possible to raise productivity any further or reminding district officials that improved technology had its limits. As one exasperated party member from the village of Fischersdorf angrily asked, "What use are economic laws to us? We're dependent on the weather, no matter what we do...." Functionaries in Dorfilm even threatened to relinquish their posts in protest following the German Farmers Congress of March 1964, where many of the reforms were announced.[44] Resistance continued throughout the remainder of the decade, and even though most LPGs had supposedly introduced some type of economic lever by the latter part of the 1960s, local authorities admitted that there was still no systematic use of NÖS planning and leadership methods. This intransigence, they concluded, had largely accounted for the district's uneven economic growth during that decade, as well as the continuing failure of many collectives to satisfy their plan targets.[45] This truly was old wine in new bottles.

Rural Divisions and Traditional Mentalities

Even if rural performance failed to meet official expectations in the 1960s, production figures had nevertheless risen substantially since the end of the war: Average yields per hectare increased more than threefold between 1946 and 1966, and despite a substantial decline in overall numbers, livestock holdings increased as well over this period. Saalfeld was even the first district in the region to fill its plan targets in 1964, despite sustained resistance to state requisitioning – and despite the serious social and economic tensions that continued to rent many collectives and hinder performance.[46]

Such frictions had already existed prior to the June 1953 upheaval, as we saw in Chapter 3, but ill feelings were not limited to the collectives themselves: Prior to the achievement of full collectivization in 1960, competition over scarce goods and access to various forms of state aid had soured relations between many independent farmers and those already in the LPGs. The two groups

IV/B-4/10/101, IB der SED–KL Slf, Gestaltung des ökonomischen Systems des Sozialismus in der Landwirtschaft, 7.8.70. On rural aspects of the NÖS more generally, see Bauerkämper, *Ländliche Gesellschaft*, 194–205.

[44] See ThStA-R IV/A-4/10/082, 093, and 094, IB der KPKK Slf, 31.3.64, 25.11.64, and Quartalsanalyse über die Arbeit der SED GO im Aufgabenbereich Landwirtschaft, n.d.; BStU ASt-G 0552, Lagebericht II. Halbjahr 1964, 4.1.65.

[45] ThStA-R IV/A-4/10/154, Zuarbeitung der Abt. Landwirtschaft zur Jahresanalyse 1967, 21.12.67; ThStA-R IV/A-4/10/60, Analyse des Kreislandwirtschaftsrates zur Kritik auf der 8. Kreisdelegiertenkonferenz der SED, 19.1.67.

[46] On these positive economic achievements, see ThStA-R IV/A-4/10/120, correspondence, 17.8.64. For social divisions elsewhere in the GDR similar to the ones discussed in this section, see Bauerkämper, *Ländliche Gesellschaft*, 347–97.

were "generally opposed to each other," officials concluded, and most collectives still "cut themselves off" from their neighbors. In a rare moment of candor, the *Kreisrat* admitted in 1957 that "even we on the District Council have supported that ourselves." This was another important reason, of course, why it had been so difficult to persuade many independent landowners to join an LPG in the first place – especially since functionaries could not even manage to get the two groups to sit down together at one table. Relations may have improved somewhat by 1960, as one official contended, but many collectives still adamantly refused to recruit their independent neighbors and "instead hold the view that they don't need them."[47]

Such feelings of animosity did not disappear overnight, and they arguably contributed to the tensions that continued to divide many LPGs in the 1960s after the second collectivization campaign had come to an end: *Vollgenossenschaftlichung* did not, in short, mean "full collectivity." In fact, local officials regularly criticized the LPGs – much as they had in the 1950s – for failing to uphold their founding statutes and work in a collective manner. What that meant, in practice, was a widespread resistance to land mergers, the sine qua non of collective farming for ideological as well as practical economic reasons: Because the district had originally been divided into many small farms with an average size of seven hectares, only land consolidation would have allowed for the deployment of large machinery needed to spur production. But by the end of the 1950s, approximately half of the LPGs in Saalfeld had not yet merged their individual holdings. In response to official demands that they finally consolidate their property, a number of farmers and functionaries threatened to quit or dissolve their LPGs in protest.[48]

Land consolidation may have been essentially completed by the fall of 1963, according to officials, but rural individualism remained both widespread and a continuing source of concern to them throughout the decade.[49] The opposition to mergers was, in fact, symptomatic of a much larger problem: the reluctance of many LPG farmers to work together. Instead, they tended to focus first and foremost on their own holdings, which legally remained in their possession even after joining a collective. Besides sowing, cultivating, and harvesting their own fields first – and sometimes last as well – many farmers also continued to raise their livestock individually, a common practice throughout the 1960s and another important reason why, apart from construction shortages, many LPGs had no common enclosures for their animals. As farmers from one village poetically put it, "LPG Type I: Everyone looks out for Number One"

[47] See ThStA-R IV/4/10/144 and 146, Bericht über die politisch/ökonomischen Ergebnisse der 5. LPG Konferenz und des 5. deutschen Bauerntages, 15.5.57, and Die Aufgaben der Landwirtschaft in unserem Kr., n.d.; KrA-S 12561, Prot. der Sitz. des KR, 9.9.59; ThStA-R IV/4/10/182, Bericht über die sozialistische Umgestaltung, 11.3.60.

[48] See the reports in ThStA-R IV/4/10/118, 127, 146, 147, 250, 306, 307; KrA-S 9137, 12553, 12554.

[49] ThStA-R IV/A-4/10/22, Bericht über die politisch-ideologische Arbeit der Partei in LPG Typ I, 27.9.63.

(*LPG I – jeder macht seins*).[50] The "desire for private property," authorities similarly concluded, continued to outweigh a "collective spirit" – "I comes before We."[51]

There were a number of reasons why so many farmers adamantly refused to cooperate. While some claimed that they had earned and produced more while on their own, others simply resented having to follow orders. Expressing this widespread desire to be "free" once again, one villager from Kamsdorf protested that it was "not right that everyone has to dance to the same tune.... As a private farmer I was my own boss, now I'm just a farmhand (*Knecht*) and have to let myself be pushed around by every fop" and "do things I often don't agree with." That was not the only reason for such resistance, however: In anticipation of future political changes in the Soviet bloc that might some day bring back individual holdings, the members of the LPG in Oberwellenborn characteristically refused to erect a communal building on one member's land because of fears that he would eventually own it himself.[52]

All of this reflected the persistence of traditional mentalities in the countryside, above all a stubborn attachment to one's own property and independence.[53] That, along with the serious dissension that existed within many LPGs, only served to undermine the communal spirit desired by East German authorities, who habitually scolded farmers for accepting the benefits of collective farming but not the requisite duties. Internal frictions, often the product of personal animosity or petty differences (*Zwistigkeiten*), were further fueled by disputes over the distribution of premiums or the allocation of agricultural goods produced by the entire collective. This frequently prompted accusations that a certain clique – usually members of the LPG's governing board – had made important decisions without consulting the entire collective, or that it unfairly favored certain individuals by giving them privileged access to scarce resources and valuable commodities. Complaints that some members failed to do their share of the work were common as well, especially among smaller proprietors: "[W]e're exploited by the larger ones, we have to do the work for them but receive much less." Such personal and professional quarrels prompted some

---

[50] There were three categories of LPG (Type I, II, and III), which were classified according to their degree of collectivity: In Type III, the most advanced socialist form, the only remaining private property – at least in theory – consisted of an individual farmer's household possessions. See Andreas Kurjo, "Landwirtschaftliche Betriebsformen," in Hartmut Zimmermann, ed., *DDR Handbuch*, vol. 1, 3rd ed. (Cologne, 1985), 803–4.

[51] ThStA-R IV/4/10/298, Tätigkeit in der Gemeinde Neidenberg, n.d. On the absence of and resistance to collective work, also see the reports and minutes in KrA-S 9137, 12554, 15581, 15582; ThStA-R IV/4/10/133, 136, 146, 154, 253, 298; ThStA-R IV/A-4/10/60, 120; ADL, BV Gera 33118.

[52] See ThStA-R IV/A-4/10/154, Information, 12.5.66; BStU ASt-G 0552, Lagebericht 1962 III. und IV. Quartale, 21.12.62.

[53] For a useful overview of the literature on German farmers and the agrarian sector, see Ulrich Kluge, *Agrarwirtschaft und ländliche Gesellschaft im 20. Jahrhundert* (Munich, 2004).

farmers to quit their collectives in anger or attempt to dissolve dysfunctional ones altogether.[54]

Many of these issues came to a head in the mid-1950s in Aue am Berg, an LPG located on the outskirts of the town of Saalfeld. The dispute, which pitted two families against the other members of the collective, eventually became so severe that it prompted an investigation by the SED District Secretariat. According to reports based on lengthy discussions with the antagonists, the two families accused the others of secretly distributing products among themselves and of forming a clique within the LPG that determined everything: Because the governing board rarely met, all decisions were supposedly made in a "dictatorial" manner or "just discussed in passing on the field." In an attempt to incriminate their neighbors politically, the two families alleged as well that the others had referred to the SED as a "party of rascals," that their children wore Western-style clothing sent by siblings who had fled to the Federal Republic, and that at least one of them had previously worn a "brown uniform," i.e., that he had been a National Socialist.

The other members of the LPG responded in kind to these and similar accusations and explained to authorities that the quarrel had begun several years earlier when the head of one of the two families had been reported to authorities for possessing weapons, a criminal offense in the GDR. They claimed that the two families did little work and that they vehemently resisted all efforts to improve the collective – including a recent decision to become an LPG Type III, which would have required each family to share all of its products and goods with all of the others (the two families justified their opposition to this move by characteristically arguing that one should concentrate on developing one's own farm first). Their neighbors subsequently submitted a request to expel the two families and warned that the collective would fall apart if the dispute were not resolved. But in 1968 – more than ten years after the initial contretemps and despite the collective's promising name (*Frohe Zukunft*, or Happy Future) – farmers there were *still* fighting and still complaining that the governing board ignored their suggestions and only did what it wished: "We don't always have time," functionaries in another LPG explained in response to similar charges, "to postpone decisions until every individual approves of them."[55]

---

54 ThStA-R IV/4/10/144, Bericht über die politisch/ökonomischen Ergebnisse, 15.5.57; ThStA-R IV/4/10/136, Bericht über Parteiarbeit auf dem Land, 20.6.56. Also see the reports in KrA-S 12553–4, 15582.

55 See ThStA-R IV/4/10/309, Situationsbericht über Aue, 18.2.55, and Überprüfung der LPG Aue auf Grund des Situationsberichts der Politischen-Abt. der MTS, 22.2.55; ThStA-R IV/B-4/10/134, Einschätzung der Arbeitsgruppe in der LPG "Frohe Zukunft" Aue/Berg, 1.8.68, and Einschätzung der Arbeitsgruppe "Roter Berg," 31.3.69. In another long-standing dispute, LPG members from Kaulsdorf hung up a sign ("Prussians go home") that expressed in no uncertain terms their contempt for neighboring farmers whose hamlet, located on Prussian territory before the war, had later been incorporated into their own village. See ThStA-R IV/A-4/10/092, IB der SED–KL Slf, 20.9.63. For similar tensions elsewhere, see the reports in ThStA-R IV/4/10/263, 266, 307; ThStA-R IV/A-4/10/119 and 120.

In a classic display of Orwellian doublethink, the SED concluded at the time that "farmer unity had been established in our district, but [not yet] the internal unity of the collective farmer class...."[56] As we shall see in the following section, official attempts to forge closer ties between industrial and agricultural workers and overcome their traditional antagonism remained largely ineffective as well – though not for lack of trying.

The Limits of Interclass Unity

Beginning in the mid-1950s, East German authorities launched a large-scale program to recruit factory workers and party members for agricultural service. This campaign, known as Workers to the Countryside (*Arbeiter aufs Land*), was primarily motivated by the need to make up for severe labor shortages in the primary sector. At the same time, party ideologues believed that greater contact between workers and farmers would not only improve relations between the two classes but also raise the political level of those who lived outside the cities. Most workers and party members vehemently rejected the appeal for volunteers, however, usually by arguing that they were too old or unhealthy, that they had no agricultural experience ("I understand as much about agriculture as a Neanderthal does about the Ninth Symphony"), that they did not want to be separated from their families, or that earnings were too low in the countryside. Others wittily suggested that they might be more willing to go if high-level party and management officials would set a positive example themselves: "If one would at least delegate some of the comrades on the SED District Secretariat, with their wealth of experience, there'd be a revolutionary change."[57]

Though frustrated by this widespread lack of interest, some officials were surprisingly sympathetic to the excuses offered by those who refused to comply: "None of our colleagues volunteer because they have it much better working for me," the director of Saalfeld's electric motor plant explained in 1956 at the height of the recruitment campaign. "They earn 500 marks in my factory; they'd never get that much there." Or, as one union official admitted later that year, those delegated to the countryside had absolutely no idea about agriculture and usually did more harm than good. As a result, many asked that they be allowed to return to their factories, a request frequently accompanied by complaints about unsatisfactory lodging and provisioning.[58]

The difficulties involved in recruiting and retaining volunteers also helped explain why many factory sponsors (*Patenbetriebe*) failed to honor their contractual obligations and provide farmers with adequate assistance. The LPG in Arnsgereuth reported in 1964, for example, that its sponsor – the members of the FDGB District Council, no less – offered almost no aid whatsoever and

[56] ThStA-R IV/A-4/10/119, Einschätzung der Lage der Landwirtschaft, 17.12.65.

[57] ThStA-R IV/7/231/1165, Prot. der LS der SED GO–Zeiss, 6.7.56.

[58] See ThStA-R IV/7/231/1165, Prot. der LS der SED GO–Zeiss, 6.7.56; ThStA-R IV/4/10/252, IB der SED–KL Slf, 13.9.56; ThStA-R, FDGB BV Gera 853/209, Prot. der konstituierenden Sitz. des KV IG Metall Slf, 9.5.58.

had not visited the village in more than two years. Even if a few factories did perform useful services for the collectives they were supposed to support (such as helping out during the harvest season or keeping the books), local officials admitted that the situation in Arnsgereuth was no "isolated case" and that "the compulsory working-class alliance with collective farmers" continued to play a "subordinate role" in most factories: "[I]t would do these colleagues some good if they'd put on work clothes, go to the collective farmers, and show them how to organize and improve [their] work."[59]

Those who did supply adequate assistance were often called to task for not providing the requisite political and ideological education (*Aufklärung*) deemed so essential to winning farmers over to socialism. In their own defense, many sponsors claimed that those engaged in the primary sector either refused to listen to their political arguments or remained impervious to their ideological agitation. In fact, they argued, the latter only served to alienate them even further from the regime and from the industrial working class as a whole: If one said too much, one volunteer cautioned, one ran the risk of getting kicked out. That was exactly what happened to one visiting worker during a political speech he held in the village of Herrschdorf: Shouted down by disgruntled residents angered by the SED's failure to make good on past promises, he was told to "get rid of the wild boars first and then we'll talk some more."[60]

Much of the tension between local workers and farmers was not really political in nature, but fueled instead by traditional class stereotypes. "History has taught us," the *Kreisrat* informed party members at the VEB Zeiss in 1955, "that the countryside was consciously held back behind the city...." Paternalistic efforts aimed at reversing this situation tended to elicit a great deal of skepticism: "[W]hat do dumb farmers understand about men like Goethe?" SED members at the Maxhütte asked in response to endeavors aimed at raising the "cultural level" of those working in the primary sector. In fact, greater contact between the two groups often only served to fortify the hoary stereotype that farmers were either lazy or indolent. As one party member quipped in 1962, "I don't understand why we have to go off to the fields... and encourage their laziness: They sit for hours in the pub and play skat while we do all the work."[61]

Disputes over provisioning were another major source of friction – and had been since the immediate postwar period, when many of Saalfeld's industrial workers openly advocated the use of harsh measures to ensure that essential foodstuffs be made available at affordable prices. Farmers had not yet experienced the "true plight of the people," resentful workers at the Maxhütte declared in 1947, and did not know what it meant to survive on ration

[59] ThStA-R IV/A-4/10/26, Bericht über den Bewußtseinsstand der verschiedenen Schichten der Landbevölkerung, 26.4.65; KrA-S 9137, Prot. der Sitz. des KR, 15.6.55.

[60] ThStA-R IV/7/231/1167, IB der SED GO–Zeiss, 6.6.56.

[61] See ThStA-R IV/7/231/1166, Prot. der MV der SED GO–Zeiss, 14.1.55; ThStA-R IV/7/222/1060, IB der SED GO–Maxh., 27.2.56; ThStA-R IV/4/10/263 and 270, IB der SED–KL Slf, 30.9.60, 10.10.62.

cards: "It would only be just to take their entire harvest away from them." Taking a somewhat different tack, some of their colleagues later claimed that East German farmers owed their entire well-being to the exertions of the industrial working class. For their part, those who lived in the countryside complained that factory workers lived too well and earned too much, and even suggested that their supposedly higher standard of living came at the cost of those who toiled on the land. Widespread anger about the role that many workers had played during the two major collectivization campaigns only reinforced existing rancor. As villagers from one small hamlet told a visiting worker in the fall of 1960, "You rascals are responsible for the confusion here in Crösten. ... It won't hurt you that you now have no butter, you should eat garbage" instead.[62]

The timing of this angry outburst was not purely coincidental: The second campaign had just come to an end, and conditions in the countryside were indeed chaotic – and tensions high – because of the recent transformation. Yet, the barrier between Saalfeld's urban and rural populations was not as rigid as the foregoing account might suggest. A number of farmers supplemented their income by taking secondary jobs in the industrial sector, for example, and many factory workers cultivated small parcels of land themselves in order to improve their supply situation.[63] All of this served to broaden contact and make the town–country divide somewhat more porous. Yet, feelings of mutual hostility and vestiges of the traditional enmity between German workers and farmers had clearly survived the war and continued to surface throughout the early decades of the GDR – giving the lie to official slogans claiming that a strong alliance had been forged between the two groups in whose name the SED claimed to rule.[64]

Given their common antipathy toward a wide array of official policies, one is almost tempted to ask why workers and farmers did not form a different type of alliance, one directed against the regime itself. After all, both groups were similarly averse to – and often equally adept at resisting – the many unwelcome

[62] See MxA-U, WL B79, Prot. der Generalversammlung der SED BG, 1.8.47; ThStA-R IV/4/10/317, Prot. der Arbeitsgebietskonferenz, 13.6.48; Prot. der Sitz. der landwirtschaftlichen Sachbearbeiter, 14.8.48; and Bericht über Arbeitsgebiet Tagung in Kleinkamsdorf, 29.8.48; ThStA-R IV/4/10/177, Prot. der Sekretariatssitz. der SED KL–Slf, 30.10.59; ThStA-R IV/4/10/263, IB der SED–KL Slf, 30.9.60.

[63] In 1960, for example, approximately fifty workers at the steel mill and sewing-machine factory worked more than 100 hectares of land located in nearby villages. See ThStA-R, FDGB BV Gera 860/211, IB Nr. 3 zur sozialistischen Umgestaltung der Landwirtschaft, 25.3.60. Also see Christel Nehrig, "Industriearbeiter im dörflichen Milieu: Eine Studie zur Sozialgeschichte der Niederlausitzer Nebenerwerbsbauern von 1945 bis 1965," in Peter Hübner, ed., *Niederlausitzer Industriearbeiter, 1935 bis 1970: Studien zur Sozialgeschichte* (Berlin, 1995), 167–92.

[64] On the alleged achievement of class unity, see ThStA-R IV/4/10/307, Bericht/Referat, 23.4.58. In the 1980s, leading East German sociologists admitted that a social and material gap continued to exist between workers and farmers and that it had, in fact, grown larger over the past decades. See Manfred Lötsch, "Sozialstruktur der DDR – Kontinuität und Wandel," *APuZ* B36 (1988): 3–16. Such conclusions were based on high-level confidential studies that reflected the regime's

demands placed on them by the party and state. Yet in the end, each group went its own way, so to speak, and largely succumbed to a wide range of highly unpopular policies: collectivization and forced requisitioning in the countryside, piecework and other official schemes aimed at boosting productivity in the industrial sector. The repressive nature of the regime provides one obvious clue to why that was the case: Any concerted attempt to join forces and make common cause for change would have undoubtedly led to an immediate crackdown by vigilant security forces. The mutual recriminations, longstanding prejudices, and otherwise disparate interests that strained relations between these two major social groups nevertheless played an important role as well – and were reinforced, paradoxically, by the very policies of a regime ostensibly committed to eliminating social antagonism among the ideologically acceptable.

In fact, for a party that talked incessantly about ending class conflict, its leadership certainly pursued strategies – unwittingly or not – that helped keep such tensions alive. That was equally true of the effect they had on relations *within* each of these social groups, i.e., *among* their own members. In the case of farmers, the introduction of socialist production methods only served to fragment the rural population by creating new frictions or reinforcing existing ones – effectively making sure that it would remain that "vast mass" of "potatoes in a sack" with "no unity . . . and no political organization" famously described by Karl Marx in a different historical context.[65] That characterization, which applied to East German workers as well, reflected an ongoing process of social disintegration that tore apart the very fabric of East German society – and, in so doing, helped forestall mass unrest from below. As we shall see in the next chapter, such divisions were further compounded by everyday struggles over access to housing, scarce goods, and a variety of coveted privileges.

---

apparent interest in monitoring the traditional disparity between life in the cities and in the countryside, as well as continuing divisions between workers and farmers. See, e.g., Klaus Fischer and others, "Entwicklungsprozesse der Genossenschaftsbauern und der Arbeiter in der Landwirtschaft, der Annäherung der Lebensbedingungen des Landes an die der Stadt" (Berlin, 1979). Copies of this and similar investigations are available in the archive of the Institut für Sozialdatenanalyse e.V. in Berlin. For an overview of this research, see *Sozialforschung in der DDR: Dokumentation unveröffentlichter Forschungsarbeiten*, 6 vols. (Berlin, 1992–4). Also see Lothar Mertens, "'Was die Partei wusste, aber nicht sagte . . .' Empirische Befunde sozialer Ungleichheit in der DDR–Gesellschaft," in Lothar Mertens, ed., *Soziale Ungleichheit in der DDR: Zu einem tabuisierten Strukturmerkmal der SED–Diktatur* (Berlin, 2002), 119–57.

[65] Karl Marx, "The Eighteenth Brumaire of Louis Bonaparte," in Robert Tucker, ed., *The Marx–Engels Reader*, 2nd ed. (New York, 1978), 608.

"Whatever Happened to the Classless Society?"

During union elections held in the fall of 1958, a speech about classes and social strata in the GDR sparked a heated discussion at the Moritz Hädrich KG, a manufacturer of writing utensils and one of the few remaining private firms in the district.[1] The ensuing debate, which focused primarily on various forms of privilege in East Germany, began with a series of pointed questions by the head of the factory union committee: "How many categories of people are there in a socialist society," he wanted to know, "what position do clerks have in our social order; do white-collar workers (*Angestellte*) belong to the laboring masses (*Werktätige*), the workers, or the capitalists?" The union chairman then went on to allege that his son had recently been denied admission to secondary school – the only path to higher education – because he himself was a white-collar worker.

Apparently emboldened by the functionary's remarks, the other participants followed up with a series of equally critical questions about the many privileges enjoyed by members of the so-called intelligentsia, i.e., highly trained specialists who performed nonmanual tasks in the workplace – or, according to the minutes of the meeting, "a social stratum regarded and subsequently treated as a necessary evil." While accepting the fact that this group received higher earnings "related to their achievement and ability," those in attendance could not understand why they also enjoyed "special privileges" allowing them to travel more easily to West Germany. Criticizing in particular a new law that regulated travel between the two states, they suggested that "many disagreeable disputes" could be avoided if the limitations on travel "were applied equally to all citizens." After this heated exchange, and after asking whether unmarried mothers could also have a paid "domestic day" off (*Haushaltstag*) each month, one colleague complained in particular about women who belonged to "financially more privileged strata, who don't work as a rule but have servants, while

---

[1] ThStA-R, FDGB BV Gera 854/209, Bericht über die Wahlversammlung in der Fa. Füllhalterfabrik Moritz Hädrich, 16.10.58. A *Kommanditgesellschaft* (KG) is a limited commercial partnership.

the laboring woman, who has no provider, serves society year in and year out, and only finds time to take care of her own personal concerns under the most difficult of conditions."² The visiting functionary who had come to the firm to address the group proved unable to respond adequately to their questions and complaints. But as one management official at another local factory would warn his staff several years later, "if we speak today about class differences between *Intelligentsia* and workers, we have to realize that this gives the class enemy a powerful impetus. This is a systematically controlled discussion aimed at splitting the former from the latter."³

According to the official party line, there were only two classes in East Germany – collective farmers and workers (of both the blue- and white-collar variety) – and one social stratum, the intelligentsia. Since the collapse of the GDR, a number of empirical studies have painted a much more nuanced portrait of East Germany's social makeup, especially during its last two decades. In so doing, they have called into question scholarly claims that the GDR was a classless society without significant social inequalities. Moreover, they have argued that such differences produced widespread discontent that eventually helped bring down the regime by fomenting serious unrest in the late 1980s.⁴ A confidential series of sociological analyses commissioned at the highest levels of the regime suggested that the East German leadership itself had long been aware of considerable social differentiation – and that it was very much interested in reducing, or at least keeping an eye on, the material disparities that distinguished various social groups from one another.⁵

Such efforts were, as we shall see, largely in vain. Picking up on themes that run like a red thread throughout this study, this chapter examines the various sources of anger and frustration that such "fine distinctions" and privileges had already engendered since the late 1940s – largely as a result of unequal access to scarce goods and attractive privileges doled out selectively by the regime and its local representatives. Much of this resentment was heightened by the expectations created by a constant barrage of official rhetoric about the way in which state socialism had successfully helped reduce material disparities and eradicate social inequality more generally. Not surprisingly, and as the exchange at the Hädrich factory made clear, this produced vehement criticism of the regime itself. But at the same time, it engendered deep-seated feelings of mutual antipathy and jealousy that tore at the social fabric of Saalfeld by

---

² In 1960, the East German satire magazine *Der Eulenspiegel* published a fictitious letter that contained many of the same resentments voiced at this meeting; it was supposedly written to a doctor by a woman who ran a newpaper stand in his neighborhood. The letter is reprinted in Christoph Kleßmann and Georg Wagner, eds., *Das gespaltene Land: Leben in Deutschland, 1945 bis 1990: Texte und Dokumente* (Munich, 1993), 399–400.
³ ThStA-R IV/7/220/1003, Prot. der MV der SED GO–Kraftverkehr, 29.8.61.
⁴ Compare Sigrid Meuschel, *Legitimation und Parteiherrschaft in der DDR: Zum Paradox von Stabilität und Revolution in der DDR, 1945–1989* (Frankfurt am Main, 1992), with the studies listed in footnote 29 of the Introduction.
⁵ See Chapter 9, footnote 64.

creating cleavages and fomenting tensions among those who lived and labored there. The significance of this atomization for the long-term stability of the regime lies at the heart of the following discussion.

The Traditional "Collar Divide"

Outbursts about privilege and social difference in the GDR rarely dominated entire discussions as they did at the gathering that took place at the Hädrich factory. Yet, the exchange clearly suggested that many blue- and white-collar workers deeply resented the privileged position of the intelligentsia – an impression supported by similar objections voiced sporadically in Saalfeld throughout the early decades of the regime. "The word *Intelligentsia* has the same effect on me that a red cape has on a bull," one party member at the Maxhütte had typically complained several years earlier. "Some belong to the *Intelligentsia* even though they aren't very intelligent." Much of the grumbling about these "stuffed pigs" tended to surface during crisis situations: On the eve of the June 1953 uprising, for example, workers at the washing-machine factory demanded to know "whose earnings have risen in the past? The salaries of the *Intelligentsia*, that's whose, and the worker doesn't know how he's supposed to survive on his 200 marks." Three years later, during the upheavals in Poland and Hungary, staff members at the steel mill similarly groused that "everything's invested in the *Intelligentsia*; they should receive less so that pension levels can be increased.... By paying them salaries of 10 to 15,000 marks, we're breeding capitalists ourselves once again. They'll become exploiters, even if they just hire maids, chauffeurs, etc...." That same year, moviegoers at a local theater were similarly overheard comparing the high salaries awarded to local factory directors with the "inadequate pensions" given to most East Germans: Another June 17 was necessary, they suggested, in order to bring about some necessary changes.[6]

Besides complaining about the "crass differences" between normal earnings and top monthly salaries of more than 1,000 marks, many Saalfelders also criticized the preferential treatment enjoyed by the intelligentsia when it came to

---

[6] Shortly after the tenth anniversary of the 1953 uprising, one angry retiree complained to the chair of the local LDPD that he had had a completely different image of socialism after the war: "I thought that it would eliminate all crass distinctions. But in reality it's now worse than before. Look at the difference between my pension and the salary of Walter Ulbricht, who receives 34,000 marks [sic] each month. That's more than the large industrialists and bankers earn in the West." See ThStA-R, BDVP Gera 21/250, report, 26.7.54; ThStA-R, FDGB BV Gera 854/209, Prot. der Funktionärssitz. im Waschmaschinenwerk, 2.6.53; ThStA-R IV/7/222/1060, IB der SED GO–Maxh., n.d.; ThStA-R IV/4/10/249, IB der SED–KL Slf, 17.3.55; ADL, BV Gera 33127, Meinungsbildungsbericht, 24.10.63. On the anger and jealousy created by low pension levels, especially among pensioners themselves, see Lutz Niethammer, Alexander von Plato, and Dorothee Wierling, *Die Volkseigene Erfahrung: Eine Archäologie des Lebens in der Industrieprovinz der DDR* (Berlin, 1991), 533–6.

rationing and the distribution of scarce goods.[7] Beginning in the late 1940s, authorities offered these highly trained specialists a wide variety of monetary and material benefits in a concerted effort to keep them in the GDR because of the need for their valuable expertise. To that end, they were awarded generous retirement benefits, as well as individual labor contracts that guaranteed relatively high salaries, bonuses, and far-reaching job security. Besides enjoying less stringent travel restrictions both within the GDR and beyond its borders, many also received preferential treatment with respect to housing, scarce goods, and choice vacation spots. Officials at the Maxhütte went to especially great pains to assure their intelligentsia an elevated standard of living as well as adequate professional resources: They were provided with first-rate apartments, specialized technical literature from the West, personal access to company cars, subsidized gasoline and oil, extra fuel in the winter, and other coveted commodities that were in limited supply.[8] The beneficiaries undoubtedly welcomed such privileged treatment, and this may have been at least one reason for their reserved behavior during the June 1953 upheaval – largely a working-class affair in Saalfeld, where "almost nothing was heard from members of the *Intelligentsia* during the entire time."[9]

Their superior incomes and other material advantages nevertheless fostered a great deal of anger and resentment on the part of less-privileged social groups. As Fritz Müller, the head of the SED District Secretariat, admitted in 1970, some "workers could say to us right now [that] this is no longer a worker-and-farmers' state, it's just a state of *Intelligentsia* and craftsmen. They live well, not the worker. If we continue to tolerate this, then we're lost...."[10] Resentment about their superior material position was not the only issue that fueled animosity toward the intelligentsia, however: The widespread perception that these highly educated specialists were haughty apparently played an important role as well. Pointing out that conduct and "style" were "decisive" because many workers "set great store in this," management officials at the district's pumped-water storage plant in Hohenwarte cautioned their engineers not to display any signs of "arrogance." The director of the Maxhütte similarly demanded that

---

[7] See ThStA-R IV/4/10/252, IB der SED–KL Slf, 25.10.56. On similar complaints elsewhere in Thuringia, see Gareth Pritchard, *The Making of the GDR, 1945–53: From Antifascism to Stalinism* (Manchester, UK, 2000), 196.

[8] On the special benefits provided to members of the Maxhütte intelligentsia, see the series of reports and analyses in MxA-U, Finanzbuchhaltung: Förderung der Intelligenz (1949–62). On the privileged position of the East German intelligentsia more generally, see Peter Hübner, ed., *Eliten im Sozialismus: Beiträge zur Sozialgeschichte des SED Regimes* (Stuttgart, 1999); Thomas Baylis, *The Technical Intelligentsia and the East German Elite: Legitimacy and Social Change in Mature Communism* (Berkeley, 1974); Dolores Augustine, "Frustrierte Technokraten: Zur Sozialgeschichte des Ingenieursberufs in der Ulbricht–Ära," in Richard Bessel and Ralph Jessen, eds., *Die Grenzen der Diktatur: Staat und Gesellschaft in der DDR* (Göttingen, 1996), 58–61.

[9] ThStA-R IV/4/10/246, IB der SED–KL Slf, 3.8.53. On another possible reason for the limited participation of the intelligentsia, see Chapter 3, footnote 19.

[10] ThStA-R IV/B-4/10/086, Prot. der MV der SED APO–Technik des VEB Wema, 19.10.70.

the relationship between workers and the intelligentsia be characterized by a
greater degree of "camaraderie," which strongly intimated that this had not
been the case previously.[11]

Despite such exhortations, officials were, of course, largely responsible themselves for having created tensions and fomented divisions. In fact, the preferential treatment they bestowed upon the intelligentsia only served to harden
the dividing line between them and other groups – literally as well as figura-
tively. The steel mill decided in the mid-1950s, for example, to set up a dining
hall reserved for the former, where they could have "thoughtful exchanges"
and take their meals "in peace." The factory similarly organized special out-
ings and private social gatherings (*Intelligenzabende*) limited to factory intelligentsia.[12] Besides grumbling about the separate dining hall, those who found
themselves in a less privileged position complained that members of the intelligentsia could offer their children "much more" than a "simple worker" could,
especially when it came to vacations for their children (they were referring to
so-called *Kinderferienaktionen*, summer camps set up for the children of staff
members).[13] Coupled with economic disparities, the organization of these and
other exclusive activities not only strengthened divisions between workers and
the intelligentsia, but also between their families. It was still difficult, the SED
District Secretariat admitted in 1960, to persuade the wives of male members
of the intelligentsia to work more closely with other women in groups like the
DFD. This was not surprising, given the views of at least one wife: "I would
have never married a proletarian.... [M]y husband is educated and only deals
with professors in the West."[14]

---

[11] See ThStA-R IV/7/224/1116, Prot. der MV der SED GO–Pumpspeicherwerk Hohenwarte,
25.6.58; MxA-U, Betriebsdirektion: Prot. der WL–Besprechungen (1957–61), Prot. der Sitz.
des WL–Kollektivs, 14.8.58.

[12] See the reports in MxA-U, Finanzbuchhaltung: Förderung der Intelligenz (1949–62). For
a list of those allowed to eat in the special dining room, see MxA-U, Bandnummer 406
(Betriebsdirektion: Sekr., 1957), Mitteilung, 18.2.57.

[13] ThStA-R, BDVP Gera 21/250, report, 26.7.54.

[14] See ThStA-R IV/4/10/261 and 247, IB der SED–KL Slf, 6.4.60, 5.3.54. In an attempt to improve
relations between workers and members of the intelligentsia – and in an attempt to tackle increasingly complex production challenges by promoting greater coordination between the technical
know-how of highly trained specialists and the everyday experiences of workers on the shop
floor – authorities set up a new type of factory collective in the late 1950s composed of individuals from both social groups. Complaints by officials at the Maxhütte that participating workers
had not been included sufficiently and that their practical experiences had not been seriously
taken advantage of suggest that these new Socialist Research and Work Associations enjoyed
only moderate economic success. That said, the fact that most members reportedly limited
their cooperation to "after-hours activities" indicates that the associations must have helped
improve somewhat social relations between the two groups. See MxA-U, Betriebsdirektion:
Prot. der WL–Besprechungen (1954–6), Entwicklung der sozialistischen Gemeinschaftsarbeit im
Kombinat, 15.5.61; MxA-U, Betriebsdirektion: Prot. der WL–Besprechungen (1957–61), Prot.
der Sitz. des WL–Kollektivs, 28.4.59; MxA-U Betriebsdirektion: Prot. der WL–Besprechungen
(1954–61), Entwicklung der sozialistischen Gemeinschaftsarbeit im Kombinat, 15.5.61; ThStA-
R IV/A-7/230/497, Bericht über die sozialistische Gemeinschaftsarbeit, 16.7.65.

Many of the same types of mutual recrimination and traditional prejudice common before 1945 continued to characterize and sour relations between blue- and white-collar workers as well. Pointing to their supposedly poor organizational abilities, bureaucratic behavior, and reputed laziness, industrial workers regularly blamed factory clerks and other administrative personnel for production problems that negatively affected their own earnings.[15] That was why, one mechanic at the Maxhütte explained, he could not accept the fact that white-collar employees (*Angestellte*) also received pay for overtime – especially "since eight hours of intensive work are more fruitful than ten hours of just sitting around" and doing nothing or "spending the workday in the HO or at the beauty parlor." In response to these and similar allegations, many white-collar workers in Saalfeld vigorously emphasized their own important contribution to the economy. As one employee at the Maxhütte put it, "Do we still have such an inferiority complex today" to think that "our mental work is not at least as valuable as that of a simple unskilled production worker[?] . . . The belief that *Angestellte* are just a bunch of potato sacks (*Bürohocker*) must end." Arguing along similar lines, his colleagues in the accounting department called for higher salaries and the allotment of more generous rations, especially since they – unlike "simple" workers – had to continue thinking about social and economic problems after the whistle blew at the end of the day.[16] These and similar arguments failed to impress most production workers, who repeatedly called for a reduction in the number of office personnel by arguing that factory staffs were inordinately top-heavy and that this posed a threat to their own earnings: As workers at the VEB Wema characteristically complained after the hiring of yet another white-collar employee, "there's one more who draws away from our money."[17]

The shop-floor tensions described in Chapter 8 may have effectively undermined working-class solidarity in the GDR, yet class consciousness had obviously not vanished entirely under Communist rule.[18] In fact, and as the foregoing suggests, many industrial workers continued to view themselves as a distinct social group, largely in contrast to white-collar employees and the

---

[15] For similar developments elsewhere, see Peter Hübner, "Um Kopf und Kragen: Zur Geschichte der innerbetrieblichen Hierarchien im Konstituierungsprozeß der DDR–Gesellschaft," *Mitteilungen aus der Kulturwissenschaftlichen Forschung* 16 (1993): 210–32.

[16] See MxA-U, WL B129, Prot. der WL–Besprechung, 24.5.50; MxA-U, BGL 262, Monatsbericht der Kommission für Arbeit und Löhne, 28.1.52; MxA-U, BGL 170, Prot. der BV im Rechnungswesen und im Technischen Büro, 21.6.51, 22.6.51. On income differentials between blue- and white-collar workers at the Maxhütte, see the statistics from the first half of the 1950s in MxA-U, WL B146.

[17] ThStA-R IV/7/230/1160, Rechenschaftslegung der SED BPO–Wema, 19.3.58.

[18] A useful introduction to the question of class consciousness and working-class solidarity is Ira Katznelson and Aristide Zolberg, eds., *Working-Class Formation: Nineteenth-Century Patterns in Western Europe and the United States* (Princeton, NJ, 1986).

intelligentsia.[19] That was important, because although the members of all three social groups shared many of the same political and economic grievances, mutual recriminations and reciprocal feelings of resentment effectively hindered them from working together in a way that might have allowed them to present their common demands for change more successfully. By hampering social unity and collective shows of solidarity, these tensions and frictions further contributed to the stability and longevity of a largely unpopular regime.

Endemic Scarcity: The Great Equalizer?

Reflecting on their experiences in Saalfeld under socialism, local residents vividly conveyed the strong sense of social resentment just described. The reminiscences of Friedrich Jung are particularly instructive in this respect. Born in a village near the Thuringian city of Erfurt in 1926, this former teacher attended a local high school (*Gymnasium*) until 1943 and spent the last two years of the war working in an antiaircraft unit until being wounded in Italy. Captured by British troops in May 1945, Jung remained a prisoner of war for two years and then returned to the Soviet zone of occupation to be with his family. After working for his father, a shopkeeper who sold incidentals in the countryside, Jung returned to school and received his *Abitur* in 1949, only to have his application to study at the University of Jena be rejected three times – because, he claimed, of his father's occupation, i.e., because of his low social standing in a state where the children of workers and farmers were normally given preference in admission decisions. Jung was nevertheless allowed to enroll at the University of Halle in 1952 and spent the remaining years of the GDR teaching at a vocational school in Saalfeld (he had moved there two years earlier to be with his fiancée).[20]

Despite earning a modest monthly salary of about 300 marks in the 1950s, Jung was relatively well situated: He and his wife lived together in a spacious villa that they had inherited from her parents and – at a time when less than 10 percent of East Germans enjoyed modern forms of private transportation – owned their own cars: first a P70 (the forerunner of the famed Trabant) and then a used Wartburg (the East German automobile of choice) in the 1950s, two used Trabis the following decade, and finally, after a sixteen-year wait and at a cost of 24,000 marks, a new Wartburg in 1972.[21] Explaining the key to all material acquisitions in the GDR, Jung emphasized that "he who had neither money nor connections was in poor shape" (*der sah alt aus*). Jung himself was in relatively good shape, thanks not only to his in-laws but also to the ties that

---

[19] See Günter Erbe, *Arbeiterklasse und Intelligenz in der DDR: Soziale Annäherung von Produktionsarbeiterschaft und wissenschaftlich-technischer Intelligenz im Industriebetrieb?* (Opladen, 1982).

[20] Friedrich Jung, in discussion with the author, May 1995.

[21] See Jonathan Zatlin, "The Vehicle of Desire: The Trabant, the Wartburg, and the End of the GDR," *German History* 15 (1997): 358–80. For statistics on car ownership in the GDR, see Annette Kaminsky, *Wohlstand, Schönheit, Glück: Kleine Konsumgeschichte der DDR* (Munich, 2001), 163.

he was able to forge with the parents of his pupils, who often provided him with valuable goods and services.

This was part of the GDR's vaunted *Notgemeinschaft*, an informal social network of mutual assistance that allowed East Germans to obtain desired commodities that were usually in short supply: "If you had something," Jung pithily recalled, "you got something." And those who got the most, he claimed with more than a bit of resentment, were the production workers – in his words, the "kings" of East German society. They earned more than teachers, lived in inexpensive apartments subsidized by the state, and enjoyed cheap meals at their factories. In Saalfeld itself, those supposedly best off were the workers employed at major factories like the Maxhütte, Zeiss, and Wema. Shop-floor activists and members of the intelligentsia who performed well and were politically active (unlike Jung himself, who never joined the SED) purportedly benefited from a number of other enviable privileges as well – such as quicker access to automobiles, a subject apparently dear to his heart.

The accuracy of Jung's observations was arguably less important than his impression that others were consistently better off than he – a claim that members of almost every social group in Saalfeld made about those belonging to other societal categories. As his recollections suggested, perceptions of privileged treatment and the struggle for limited goods and resources were often at the root of such allegations. Endemic scarcity was, in fact, one of the most important sources of discontent and social resentment in the district, and remained a serious problem despite official promises to improve the supply situation following the June 1953 upheaval. As a result, many local residents continued to complain regularly about fluctuating availability, uneven distribution, limited choice, and poor quality – not only of industrial wares and so-called luxury goods, but also of more essential items such as coal and fuel, clothing and shoes, spare parts, and daily foodstuffs: "Well, great plans are being made," one party member bitterly remarked in early 1963 in an obvious allusion to the New Economic System, but "we don't even have enough tropical fruit for our children."[22]

The overall situation *had* improved by that time, of course – especially when compared to the so-called hunger years of the late 1940s and early 1950s.[23] More to the point, complaints about shortages of coal and butter gradually gave way in the 1960s to grievances about insufficient quantities of televisions, washing machines, and refrigerators, and many of the same individuals who had grumbled a decade earlier about the scarcity of spare parts for their bicycles and motorcycles would later complain about long waits for cars and shortages of tires for their Trabis.[24]

---

[22] ThStA-R IV/A-7/230/498, IB der SED GO–Wema, 18.1.63.

[23] See the statistics in BStU ASt-G, KD Slf 2311; KrA-S 17416. On general trends in the GDR, see Kaminsky, *Konsumgeschichte*; Peter Hübner, *Konsens, Konflikt und Kompromiß: Soziale Arbeiterinteressen und Sozialpolitik in der SBZ/DDR, 1945–1970* (Berlin, 1995), 130–49.

[24] See, e.g., the information reports in ThStA-R IV/4/10/247, 251, 253, 260–3, 269; also see the Stasi reports from the early 1960s in BStU ASt-G 0552. On everyday supply shortages more generally, see Mark Landsman, *Dictatorship and Demand: The Politics of Consumerism in East*

Expectations may have increased over time and the variety of available goods may have significantly improved, yet the recurrent supply crises and bottlenecks characteristic of all postwar socialist economies nevertheless continued to plague Saalfeld, leading to long lines and periodic scarcity of even the most basic consumer goods. Following a major crop failure in the fall of 1961, for example, local officials reported serious shortages of meat, butter, eggs, and vegetables – a disconcerting development that dominated discussion throughout the district for a year. One worker at the Rotstern chocolate factory claimed that she had lost fourteen pounds as a result, and several women at a small private firm even threatened to go on strike if the supply of meat was not increased immediately. Security officials noted a marked decrease in such critical discussion and other "negative phenomena" over the next two years, which they attributed to improved deliveries. Yet local authorities continued to report widespread grumbling and long lines in front of state-run stores throughout the second half of the decade – especially in the summer of 1965, when meat and produce were once again in particularly short supply.[25] Another major crisis in the winter of 1969–70, this time statewide, prompted a new flood of written complaints about coal, gas, and potato shortages, as well as somewhat exaggerated claims that the supply situation had "gone downhill" since the late 1950s: "We can understand that we have to wait a long time for a car, but can't understand why goods needed on a daily basis are [still] inadequately distributed."[26]

Many Saalfelders naturally blamed the regime and its policies for the chronic scarcity of basic goods, claiming, for instance, that the supply crisis of the early 1960s had been a result of the recent collectivization campaign or that there were saboteurs at the highest levels of government. A rumor that 100 tons of spoiled butter had to be thrown away did little to allay such suspicions or

Germany (Cambridge, MA, 2005); Kaminsky, *Konsumgeschichte*; Philipp Heldmann, "Negotiating Consumption in a Dictatorship: Consumption Politics in the GDR in the 1950s and 1960s," in Martin Daunton and Matthew Hilton, eds., *The Politics of Consumption: Material Culture and Citizenship in Europe and America* (Oxford, 2001), 185–202; Burghard Ciesla and Patrice Poutros, "Food Supply in a Planned Economy: SED Nutrition Policy between Crisis Response and Popular Needs," in Konrad Jarausch, ed., *Dictatorship as Experience: Towards a Socio-Cultural History of the GDR* (New York, 1999), 143–62; Ina Merkel, *Utopie und Bedürfnis: Die Geschichte der Konsumkultur in den 60er Jahren* (Cologne, 1999); idem, "Working People and Consumption under Really-Existing Socialism: Perspectives from the German Democratic Republic," *ILWCH* 55 (1999): 92–111; Jeffrey Kopstein, *The Politics of Economic Decline in East Germany, 1945–1989* (Chapel Hill, NC, 1997), 173–94; Hübner, *Konsens*, 130–77. More generally, see David Crew, ed., *Consuming Germany in the Cold War* (Oxford, 2003).

[25] See the reports from this period in ThStA-R IV/4/10/266, 269, 270; ThStA-R IV/A-4/10/097; ThStA-R, FDGB KV Slf 6185, 6188, 6191, 6278, 6302, 9541; BStU ASt-G 0552; ThStA-R, VPKA Slf 94, 113.

[26] See ThStA-R IV/B-7/230/284, Monatbericht der SED GO–Wema, October 1971; ThStA-R IV/A-7/226/280, Monatsbericht der SED GO–TSW Rotstern, May 1971. Also see ThStA-R IV/B-4/10/088, Übersicht über die Eingaben und deren Probleme im II. Halbjahr 1969, 8.1.70. Also see Gerhard Naumann and Eckhard Trümpler, *Von Ulbricht zu Honecker: 1970, ein Krisenjahr der DDR* (Berlin, 1990).

increase confidence in the authorities.[27] Others argued that "everything here was so scarce, like butter and eggs," because so many goods – especially high-quality products – were sold abroad: "[W]hy do we export so many valuable things when we could use many of these items ourselves in our own country?" Responding to a similar question several years later, a low-level party official offered workers the customary justification, i.e., that the GDR had few raw materials besides lignite and potash, which meant that "we're not in a position to provide for ourselves agriculturally. That's why the best machines are exported: so that necessary raw materials and food can be imported."[28]

That might have been true, yet such explanations did little to improve the supply situation or assuage frustrated consumers. Local officials nevertheless realized – with memories of the 1951 and 1953 upheavals still fresh – that shortages were a highly explosive issue and that adequate provisioning was an "extremely important political task" that significantly affected public attitudes and behavior: "Even little bread pores are a determining factor in public opinion. They make the bread feel older. It's not as elastic as bread with large pores...."[29] Because of such concerns, district authorities – like the SED Politburo itself – regularly discussed and kept tabs on the availability and quality of key goods. In fact, some even shared the same grievances voiced by local residents: "Our exports will only be accepted by other states if they are of impeccable quality," perturbed party officials at Zeiss noted in response to complaints there about the high cost of low-quality shoes imported from Czechoslovakia. "Why doesn't that also hold true for states that deliver to us?"[30]

Like many frustrated consumers, authorities frequently attributed supply shortages to the maddening distribution practices of those who managed or worked at state-run stores. Several years after being censured by the SED District Secretariat for not offering enough "proper" goods in the countryside, the *Konsum* cooperative came under fire once again for neglecting Saalfeld's rural areas, where it was the main supplier: After learning in late 1961 that village stores had recently received a large contingent of pickles, functionaries noted that "not one of the nine jars in each store was sold" and concluded that "such distribution practices shouldn't lead us to expect anything else." This was especially disconcerting at a time when many farmers were complaining about the failure of *Konsum* to offer its customers more indispensable items like blankets.[31]

[27] See ThStA-R IV/4/10/249, IB der SED–KL Slf, 11.3.55; ThStA-R IV/7/231/1167, IB der SED GO–Zeiss, 10.4.57; BStU ASt-G 0552, Gesamteinschätzung der politisch-operativen Lage im I. Halbjahr 1962, 4.7.62.

[28] See ThStA-R IV/7/226/1137, IB der SED GO–Rotstern, 29.10.56; ThStA-R IV/4/10/257, IB der SED–KL Slf, 7.11.58; ThStA-R IV/A-7/226/483, Prot. der MV der SED GO–TSW Rotstern, 4.10.65.

[29] See KrA-S 9137, Prot. der Kreisratssitz., 7.9.55; ThStA-R, FDGB KV Slf 3569, Prot. der Sekretariatssitz. der Gew. HaNaGe, 14.10.65.

[30] ThStA-R IV/7/231/1167, IB der SED GO–Zeiss, 5.12.55.

[31] See ThStA-R IV/4/10/130, Prot. der Sekretariatssitz. der SED–KL Slf, 9.9.55; ThStA-R IV/4/10/177, Vorlage, n.d.; ThStA-R, FDGB KV Slf 3550, Prot. der Besprechung der

Besides criticizing merchants for failing to satisfy local demands, officials often took more proactive measures aimed at defusing widespread discontent.[32] They were especially concerned about assuring a continuous flow of foodstuffs and industrial wares during election periods or on the eve of important holidays such as Christmas – something of an irony in an atheistic state where most elections were rigged: "It's important that provisioning function well in the fourth quarter. The residents will not tolerate a single mishap."[33] Local officials were also quick to react to emergency situations that threatened to escalate: After learning that shortages of fruit and vegetables had intensified an already heated wage dispute at a major construction site in Hohenwarte, the District Secretariat reported several days later that "bananas, tomatoes, cherries, etc." were all now available there.[34] Volunteers who sat on so-called Worker-and-Farmer-Inspection committees (ABIs) were particularly sensitive to complaints about shortages and generally did their best to introduce corrective measures as well: They successfully negotiated with ministerial officials and coal distributors during the energy crisis of early 1970, for instance, to ensure that fuel was promptly delivered to all households that had submitted written complaints.[35]

Since open protest and grumbling occasionally led to at least a temporary improvement in supply, it apparently paid to make noise and complain. But even if local officials were often able to find expedient solutions in crisis situations or during the holiday season, their efforts were usually frustrated by circumstances beyond their control, e.g., by snags in planning, by arbitrary decisions from on high to decrease assigned quotas of foodstuffs and other merchandise, or by poor deliveries from other regions and districts. All of these difficulties were exacerbated by the failure or unwillingness of local farmers to satisfy production quotas or of factories and distributors to honor their contracts and assure a steady supply of goods.[36] Because of bureaucratic mismanagement on the part of ministerial officials, to cite one particularly illuminating example, the district

---

Versorgungsaktiv, 15.12.61; ThStA-R IV/A-4/10/26, Prot. der Sekretariatssitz. der SED–KL Slf, 30.4.64.

[32] At the height of the unrest in Poland and Hungary in 1956, for example, the union committee at the VEB Wema instructed the head of their factory store to procure immediately "all of the desired items" demanded by staff members. And when a high-level FDGB functionary learned during the supply crisis of 1961 that one rural region had not received any citrus fruit for three weeks, he ordered that a delivery be made the next day "at all costs." See ThStA-R, FDGB BV Gera 855/210, Prot. der Sitz. der BGL–Wema, 3.10.56; ThStA-R, FDGB KV Slf 3551, Niederschr. über die Beratung der Versorgungsaktiv im Rat des Kr., 22.12.61.

[33] KrA-S 12555, Prot. der Kreisratssitz., 28.11.56. Also see, e.g., KrA-S 12553, Wie wurden die Weihnachtsfeiertage in Fragen der Versorgung unserer Bevölkerung seitens der Handelsorgane vorbereitet, 2.12.55.

[34] ThStA-R IV/4/10/262, IB der SED–KL Slf, 15.7.60. On the active role that SED district officials played elsewhere in helping to surmount supply difficulties, see Landolf Scherzer, *Der Erste: Protokoll einer Begegnung* (Rudolstadt, 1989).

[35] ThStA-R IV/B-4/10/088, Übersicht über die Eingaben und deren Probleme im II. Halbjahr 1969, 8.1.70.

[36] See, e.g., the reports in ThStA-R IV/4/10/247, 262; ThStA-R, VPKA Slf 94; ThStA-R, FDGB KV Slf 6278, 6302.

received more potatoes in late July 1955 than its residents could consume – and this at the time when a neighboring district had gone without any potatoes for two weeks. The surplus, which could not be stored because of its poor quality, was given to local farmers to fatten their pigs. One month later, officials reported "serious difficulties" after suppliers from the northern provinces had fallen behind in their deliveries and local farmers had failed to meet their quotas. As a result, factory kitchens, state-run restaurants, and Soviet troops were unable to procure any potatoes whatsoever in late August and early September. There was nevertheless some consolation at the time for those who enjoyed seafood: The district suddenly received more fish than it could readily dispose of that fall, and local pigs once again benefited from the surplus.[37]

In response to habitual dearth, Saalfelders resorted to a variety of resourceful strategies aimed at procuring items that were in short supply. Because scarce articles were often sold out by the late afternoon (a major source of discontent, particularly among laboring women), many would leave work early or for short periods in order to obtain goods that were hard to come by – an especially common practice when word spread that a coveted item had just appeared in a local store. The sudden availability of scarce goods also led to hoarding, which usually occurred in waves and which was frequently prompted by rumors of future shortages or by worrisome domestic and international developments: As one woman explained to a party functionary in the mid-1950s, she was stocking up on food because of rumors that the GDR was planning to create a new Wehrmacht and that this would lead to reduced rations.[38] Besides running from shop to shop in search of daily provisions, many would also line up in front of state-run stores to get first – or at least last – pick: When the Maxhütte radio station announced that the factory HO would take orders for televisions sets beginning at 5:30 A.M. on February 15, 1961, more than 100 hopeful workers assembled in front of the store the evening before, equipped with sleeping bags, blankets, and felt-lined shoes.[39]

Because state-run stores were often unable to satisfy demand, many consumers were forced to rely instead on private merchants for their daily needs: The widespread impression that their prices were lower and that their selection was often superior helped explain why the 535 private shops in Saalfeld accounted for almost one-third of all sales in the district in 1957. Even party personnel at the *Konsum* in Leutenberg admitted that private vegetable dealers were able to offer a wider variety of higher-quality goods at lower prices – while they themselves had nothing to offer local residents.[40] For similar reasons, and despite the threat of official sanctions, many Saalfelders – including, no less,

---

37 See KrA-S 12553, Die Versorgung im Kr. Slf, n.d.; KrA-S 9137, Bericht über die Versorgungslage im Kr. Slf, 7.9.55.
38 See ThStA-R IV/4/10/249, IB der SED–KL Slf, 17.3.55; ThStA-R IV/7/220/1003, Prot. der MV der SED GO–Kraftverkehr, 29.8.61.
39 ThStA-R IV/4/10/264, IB der SED–KL Slf, 15.2.61.
40 ThStA-R IV/4/10/247 and 253, IB der SED–KL Slf, 27.5.54, 26.4.57.

those who themselves worked at state-run stores – traveled to West Berlin to do their shopping. In the winter of 1954, for example, the People's Police apprehended more than a dozen HO personnel who had gone on an illicit shopping spree in the western half of the former capital. During the ensuing investigation, one woman explained that she had purchased luxury food items (coffee, cocoa, and chocolate) as well as medication for her chronically sick daughter because they were cheaper, better, and more readily available in the West. The authorities showed little understanding, however, and subsequently fired her as well as several of her colleagues for this transgression; the others only received a warning because they were supposedly "just hangers-on ... and didn't realize that this helped finance class enemies."

After the erection of the Wall, those with contacts in the West increasingly came to rely on care packages sent by mail or personally delivered by relatives and friends during short trips to Saalfeld. The number of visits increased considerably following a 1963 agreement between East and West Berlin, which – to the dismay of local authorities – led to even more unfavorable comparisons with the Federal Republic.[41] As one former clerk at the local police precinct recalled, visitors from the West always stood out because of their finer clothing and "relaxed" faces – supposedly unlike the "cramped" ones of the Saalfelders themselves. Responsible for registering Western visitors to the city, she also noted how their perfume never failed to impress her and her colleagues: They could always "smell the difference." Such contacts were a cherished "privilege," she hastened to add. The less fortunate had to rely instead on the informal consumption networks described by Friedrich Jung.[42]

Local factories remained an important source of everyday provisioning as well. Obliged by the East German Labor Code to provide for the social welfare of their staff members, the larger and wealthier VEBs offered a number of important services. These included privileged access to state-run stores located directly on factory premises as well as warm meals and snacks provided at subsidized prices; some firms also distributed fuel and valuable scrap material to their personnel or helped them gain access to scarce consumer durables.[43] Many Saalfelders came to expect such assistance as a matter of course, and either surreptitiously helped themselves by pilfering or openly complained when factory personnel failed to satisfy their needs – as well as their growing sense of entitlement. In 1965, for example, one party member at the Maxhütte submitted a written grievance to the District Council after management officials had failed to

[41] See, e.g., the analyses in BStU ASt-G 0552. Also see Christian Härtel and Petra Kabus, eds., *Das Westpaket: Geschenksendung, keine Handelsware* (Berlin, 2000). On increased contact between East and West Germans, see, e.g., Peter Bender, *Die "Neue Ostpolitik" und ihre Folgen: Vom Mauerbau bis zur Vereinigung* (Munich, 1995), 244–62, 359–65. On the illegal visit of HO personnel to West Berlin, see ThStA–R, FDGB Gew. HaNaGe 3171, IB, 9.11.54.

[42] Friedel Appelt, in discussion with the author, February 1995.

[43] See, e.g., the minutes in ThStA-R, FDGB BV Gera 854/209. Also see Peter Hübner, "Betriebe als Träger der Sozialpolitik, betriebliche Sozialpolitik," in Dierk Hoffmann and Michael Schwartz, eds., *Geschichte der Sozialpolitik in Deutschland seit 1945: DDR, 1949–1961: Im Zeichen des Aufbaus des Sozialismus*, vol. 8 (Baden-Baden, 2004), 729–73.

provide him with a bathtub. Responding to a subsequent censure by his superiors, the director of the steel mill angrily wrote that "the supply of staff members with desired goods was not among the responsibilities of an industrial factory" but admitted that the Maxhütte had "helped a large number of workers secure such items" in the past. Despite his obvious indignation, the man subsequently received the bathtub. The director himself had personally appealed to high-level authorities one year earlier, in fact, in response to repeated complaints about provisioning at the steel mill; this led to a new contract that assured that the Maxhütte HO as well as those located in the immediate vicinity would receive better deliveries in the future.[44]

Such interventions were largely motivated by concerns about maintaining shop-floor harmony – and were not limited to the Maxhütte, of course. But certain factories were more successful at this than others because high-level authorities continued to favor certain groups of East Germans when deciding on the disposition of scarce commodities – despite the anger and resentment that such policies had engendered during the formative years of the GDR and despite official promises after June 1953 to assure a more equitable distribution of food and industrial wares. Most decisions were guided by social, political, and economic considerations: As part of the ongoing effort to direct the flow of labor, those industries, factories, and regions deemed most essential to the economy continued to enjoy preferential access to items that were in short supply. That was equally true of privileged individuals such as activists, members of the intelligentsia, security personnel, those who lived within the five-kilometer demarcation zone that bordered West Germany, and – because of an increasing emphasis on pronatalist policies in the late 1960s families with large numbers of children.[45]

Distribution decisions often fell to the District Council, which helped supervise the periodic allocation of popular consumer durables. The following excerpt from the minutes of a council meeting gives some sense of how such decisions were made in practice: "According to the principle that those working in leading factories are to be given priority with respect to supplies, special allotments of highly valuable industrial products will be given to the Maxhütte and the pumped-water storage plant in Hohenwarte in 1963. This includes cars, televisions, washing machines, and refrigerators."[46] Angered by the preference

---

44 The fact that the director had to lodge such a complaint suggested the declining status of the steel mill in the 1960s, especially when compared to the first postwar decade. See ThStA-R, Maxh. Bandnummer 722 (Betriebsdirektion: Sprechstunden, 1961–6), Bevölkerungsbeschwerde des Gen. M., 22.5.65; MxA-U, Bandnummer 635 (Betriebsdirektion: Prot. der Direktorensitz., September bis Dezember 1964), Vorlage über Probleme der Arbeiterversorgung, 31.8.64.

45 See, e.g., ThStA-R, Maxh. 390, Aufstellung über die Verteilung von Briketts, 5.4.49; ThStA-R IV/B-4/10/087, Bericht über die durchgeführte ABI–Kontrolle "Verbesserung der Lebenslage von Familien mit 4 und mehr Kindern," 24.9.68.

46 KrA-S 20812, Analyse zur Planerfüllung 1963, 22.1.64. For the factories and regions that were given preferential treatment at the time, also see ThStA-R, FDGB KV Slf 6225, Komplexer Versorgungsplan 1963 des Kr. Slf; ThStA-R IV/A-4/10/093, IB der SED–KL Slf, 7.2.64.

given to those employed by priority firms – and echoing repeated calls for a "fair distribution" of basic foodstuffs and better provisioning for the "entire population" – workers at the sewing-machine factory protested during the supply crisis of 1965 that they "perform their work just like their colleagues at the Maxhütte, Wema, and Zeiss." Or, as one frustrated sales clerk complained at the time, "All the top nobs (*Leute mit Rang und Namen*) get eyeglasses in three or four days while mere mortals have to wait no less than a year. Whatever happened to the classless society?"[47]

The supposedly inequitable distribution practices of those who worked in state-run stores themselves were an equally important source of discontent. Besides complaining about rude behavior on the part of beleaguered sales personnel, many Saalfelders claimed that customers with connections – humorously referred to as Vitamin B (for *Beziehungen*, or connections) – enjoyed privileged treatment and unfair access to scarce goods, an allegation often grounded in fact. As security officials admitted in 1965, "mutual corruption and dependence as well as under-the-counter selling" were widespread; this was seen as a "great injustice" that understandably led to "negative" discussions among local consumers.[48] Many similarly resented the fact that only those with sufficient earnings could afford to shop at special stores that offered rare goods at exorbitant prices; this included the HO (which had provided expensive but virtually unlimited access to rationed goods prior to the elimination of official rationing in 1958) as well as the so-called *Exquisitläden*, which, beginning in 1962, allowed wealthier East Germans to purchase cars, luxury food items, textiles, televisions, and other valuable household appliances for tidy sums of money.[49]

Differential treatment and unequal access to limited goods generated a pervasive sense of injustice, as well as heartfelt anger about the obvious discrepancy between the regime's egalitarian rhetoric and its actual practices. The impression that provisioning in other towns, districts, and regions was far superior to that in Saalfeld only fueled such feelings – leading to complaints that the HO in nearby Rudolstadt provided its customers with more butter, for example, that coffee was always available in Eisfeld, or that the northern regions had a better selection of textiles and other industrial wares. The priority given to those who lived in the East German capital and other major cities drew especially heavy

---

[47] See ThStA-R IV/4/10/269, IB der SED–KL Slf, 6.9.62; ThStA-R, FDGB KV Slf 6302, IB der FDGB KV Slf, 16.3.65, 12.8.65, 2.9.65, 9.9.65.

[48] BStU ASt-G 0552, Lagebericht II. Halbjahr 1964, 4.1.65.

[49] See, e.g., ThStA-R, BDVP Gera 21/250, report, 26.2.55; ThStA-R, FDGB KV Slf 6185, Nachtrag zum IB Nr. 7, n.d. Also see Katherine Pence, "Building Socialist Worker-Consumers: The Paradoxical Construction of the Handelsorganisation – HO, 1948," and Jonathan Zatlin, "Consuming Ideology: Socialist Consumerism and the Intershops, 1970–1989," in Peter Hübner and Klaus Tenfelde, eds., *Arbeiter in der SBZ/DDR* (Essen, 1999), 497–526, 555–72; Annette Kaminsky, "Ungleichheit in der SBZ/DDR am Beispiel des Konsums: Versandhandel, Intershop und Delikat," in Lothar Mertens, ed., *Soziale Ungleichheit in der DDR: Zu einem tabuisierten Strukturmerkmal der SED–Diktatur* (Berlin, 2002), 57–79.

criticism: "They sit in Berlin and stuff their faces and we receive less and less money." Others tried to account for the continuing scarcity by suggesting that "everything was probably sent off to Leipzig." Even privileged workers at the Maxhütte joined in the chorus of protest: "Everything goes to Jena. But we're not any worse than they."[50]

A number of cities and regions did, in fact, enjoy a distinct advantage because of their greater economic and political importance, especially when compared to the border region of Saalfeld.[51] It was also true that because of limited supplies, central planners were obliged to favor certain areas over others during certain periods – lending further credence to complaints that scarce items were sometimes available only in other districts and towns, a grievance many district officials tended to share themselves. But their regular efforts to bring about a change in the proportion of goods allocated to Saalfeld usually met with "tenacious resistance" from above – which was quite understandable, given the fact that officials elsewhere were making comparable demands.[52] In the end, the accuracy of such self-serving claims was again less important than the tenacity with which many Saalfelders clung to the belief that individuals in other factories, regions, and social groups were, in some way or other, almost always better off than they. This conviction fostered a profound sense of injustice that only served to undermine social solidarity – and accounted just as much as actual material circumstances for the high levels of discontent regularly voiced and registered across the district.

The "Triple Burden" of Working Women

As the heated exchange that took place at the Hädrich factory made clear, local women had their own particular grievances on this score. That was especially true of those who not only worked but also had families – and were thus strad-dled with the triple burden of performing their jobs, running their households, and participating in sociopolitical activities. To ensure and encourage the entry of women into the labor force, authorities acknowledged and responded to these challenges by adopting a number of measures specifically aimed at easing their burden. Those with young children, for instance, were granted extended leaves of absence during and after pregnancy as well as a paid day off each month (*Haushaltstag*) to shop and perform other household chores. Local offi-cials also constructed a variety of public and workplace facilities in the VEBs

[50] See the information reports in ThStA-R IV/4/10/249–51; ThStA-R IV/A-4/10/090, 100; ThStA-R IV/B-4/10/104; BStU ASt-G 0552. Local craftsmen similarly complained that they were "discrim-inated against" (*stiefmütterlich behandelt*) when it came to the distribution of raw materials. See ADL, BV Gera 25111, Kreisparteitag, 6.3.55. More generally, see Rainer Gries, *Die Rationen–Gesellschaft: Versorgungskampf und Vergleichsmentalität: Leipzig, München und Köln nach dem Kriege* (Munster, 1991).

[51] See Siegfried Grundmann, "Räumliche Disparitäten in der DDR," in Mertens, *Ungleichheit*, 159–201.

[52] See ThStA-R, FDGB KV Slf 6302, IB der FDGB KV Slf, 2.9.65, 9.9.65.

and LPGs specifically designed to lighten the load of laboring women: These included laundry, shoe-repair, and sewing services.[53]

Most women in Saalfeld nevertheless continued to grumble about inadequate care or claim that officials showed little consideration for their special social concerns – with many pointing in particular to poor and insufficient laundry facilities that were usually filled to capacity.[54] A source of even greater concern for most, however, was the chronic lack of space in public nurseries, kindergartens, and day-care centers, a keystone of the GDR's vaunted social welfare system. By the late 1960s, there were more than a dozen kindergartens in the town of Saalfeld, as opposed to only one in 1945; in addition to those located in factories with large numbers of women, similar institutions were set up in many LPGs in response to demands for child care, especially during the harvest season. As a result, the number of places available at local nurseries and kindergartens more than tripled for children under age three, and almost doubled for those between three and six, between 1958 and 1970 – clearly an encouraging development. Yet, overcrowding and insufficient capacity remained serious challenges: The town of Saalfeld alone was still unable to accommodate more than 1,100 children in 1970.[55]

Because the number of requests for child care far outstripped the number of available spaces, women who had no place to leave their children during the workday were often prevented from accepting employment.[56] For similar

---

[53] See, e.g., ThStA-R IV/7/230/1157, Vorlage über die Arbeit des Frauenausschusses–Wema, 17.11.60; ThStA-R, FDGB KV Slf 6205, Verwirklichung des Frauenkommuniques in Rotstern, n.d.; ThStA-R IV/4/10/366, Bericht über den Stand des Kommuniques des Politbüros "Die Frau – der Frieden und der Sozialismus," 18.12.62; ThStA-R IV/B-4/10/112, Information über die Beratung der Frauenkommission, 28.5.70. Also see Johannes Frerich and Martin Frey, *Handbuch der Geschichte der Sozialpolitik in Deutschland: Sozialpolitik in der DDR*, vol. 2 (Munich, 1993), 396–406; Gunnar Winkler, ed., *Geschichte der Sozialpolitik der DDR, 1945–1985* (Berlin, 1989), 65.

[54] See the reports and minutes in ThStA-R, FDGB BV Gera 851/208, 854/209; ThStA-R, FDGB KV Slf 6222, 6278, 6302; ThStA-R IV/4/10/275, 365. Also see ThStA-R IV/A-4/10/148, Prot. der Auswertung des Lehrganges für die Frauenkommission, 18.1.58; ThStA-R IV/B-4/10/100, Erleichterung der Lebensbedingungen der Werktätigen besonders Frauen, 20.8.68.

[55] See ThStA-R IV/4/10/365 and 366, Tätigkeitsbericht, n.d.; Bericht über die Kreisfrauenkonferenz, 31.7.48; and Bericht über den Stand des Kommuniques des Politbüros "Die Frau – der Frieden und der Sozialismus," 18.12.62; ThStA-R IV/A-4/10/147, Bericht über den derzeitigen Stand der Kapazitäten der Kinderkrippen im Stadtgebiet Slf, 14.9.63; ThStA-R IV/B-4/10/100 and 112, Erleichterung der Lebensbedingungen der Werktätigen besonders Frauen, 20.8.68; Zuarbeit der Frauenkommission für die Sekretariatssitz. der SED–KL Slf, 1.8.69; and Information über die Beratung der Frauenkommission, 28.5.70; BStU ASt-G 0552, Analyse über die Entwicklung der Arbeits- und Lebensbedingungen der Werktätigen, 1970, Tabelle 6. On childcare establishments in the town of Saalfeld, see the statistics in KrA-S 22632; BStU ASt-G, KD Slf 2311. Also see Gerhard Werner, "Chronik der Stadt Saalfeld: Teil III (1945–1978)" (unpublished manuscript, 1979), passim. More generally, see Winkler, *Sozialpolitik*, 145–9.

[56] Available evidence suggests that few couples chose to have the father remain at home instead of the mother to take care of their children. This was not entirely surprising, given prevailing social mores as well as the fact that men generally earned more than women. It nevertheless underscored the dogged preservation of traditional gender roles in the GDR. See Jutta Gysi and

reasons, those who did work were frequently forced to forego job-related training, settle for part-time positions, stay home when their children became ill, or send them away for the entire workweek to underoccupied nurseries located in other towns and villages – a practice actively encouraged by local officials.[57] All of this gave rise to a great deal of grumbling, especially when the children of women not employed by a given factory occupied a space in its kindergarten or nursery. Many were equally upset about the preference given to certain groups of women on official "urgency lists" similar to those used to decide on the distribution of housing; these included single mothers, the wives of men serving in the army, women who had college degrees or advanced technical training, and those with large numbers of children or jobs in important branches of industry and the service sector. Their anger not only reflected the extent to which working mothers were dependent on such facilities but also underscored the sense of entitlement many felt with respect to state social care – as well as the typical resentment engendered by what many considered to be unequal access to limited goods and services.[58]

The same held true for disputes over the so-called *Haushaltstag*, which was intended to ease the burden of working mothers by providing them with more time for shopping and other household chores.[59] Even if the "domestic day" obviously reinforced the division of domestic labor along traditional gender lines, the measure was evidently applauded by overtaxed working women – so much so that an early decision to curtail the number of women entitled to this benefit prompted vigorous protest during the first factory labor contract negotiations of 1951 and then again following the June 1953 uprising. A source of widespread indignation over the next two decades, the decision prompted many single women, widows, and mothers with older children to demand a day off each month as well, arguing that they had to perform many of the same domestic duties as those legally entitled to the benefit.

In turn, local officials relied on a mixture of economic and moral arguments to explain why the GDR could ill afford to extend the day to more women. In an article that appeared in the Maxhütte newspaper in March 1955, the head of the Factory Conflict Commission publicly responded to frequent complaints by those who lived in a "concubinary" relationship. While admitting that exceptions had been made during the immediate postwar years, when the term *life*

Dagmar Meyer, "Leitbild: berufstätige Mutter – DDR–Frauen in Familie, Partnerschaft und Ehe," in Gisela Helwig and Hildegard Maria Nickel, eds., *Frauen in Deutschland, 1945–1992* (Bonn, 1993), 157–61.

[57] See, e.g., the reports in ThStA-R, FDGB KV Slf 6151, 6191, 6205, 7609, 7610; ThStA-R IV/4/10/365, 366; ThStA-R IV/A-4/10/147.

[58] See, e.g., ThStA-R IV/7/226/1137, IB der SED GO–Rotstern, 5.11.56; ThStA-R IV/A-4/10/148, Prot. der Auswertung des Lehrganges der Frauenkommission, 18.1.58; ThStA-R IV/B-4/10/100, IB der SED–KL Slf, Erleichterung der Lebensbedingungen der Werktätigen besonders Frauen, 20.8.68; ThStA-R, FDGB KV Slf 7610, Information, 4.11.70.

[59] See Carola Sachse, *Der Hausarbeitstag: Gerechtigkeit und Gleichberechtigung in Ost und West, 1939–1994* (Göttingen, 2002).

companion (*Lebenskamerad*) had been included in labor contracts, he argued that one only needed to look at recent developments in order to understand why the new stipulations only applied to married women and "why concubinage is no longer considered today the same as marriage":

> Our constitution says that marriage and family are the basis of collective living.... [T]he foundation of every state is a healthy marriage conducted with a high level of consciousness toward the state and profound morality...toward society.... There is no obstacle to making a real concubinary relationship into a legal marriage. But when concubinage is regarded from the start only as a temporary living arrangement between two people, then both persons don't have enough responsibility toward one another or toward society.... [60]

The working woman was not only expected, then, to perform domestic chores and be prepared to sacrifice her own career when not enough kindergarten spaces were available: The more upstanding ones were also expected to enter into lawful matrimony. The excluded nevertheless continued to clamor for an extra day off each month for a variety of understandable reasons: Besides resenting the fact that only certain categories of women were granted this privilege, many desperately needed the additional time to perform household chores and provide for their family's sustenance.

Even if the triple burden was obviously difficult for many women to bear, employment outside the home certainly brought with it undeniable advantages: higher income, some degree of financial independence, and greater access to scarce goods and superior rations. That said, entry into the labor force had a number of major drawbacks: It often prevented women from procuring items usually sold out during the workday, for instance – which prompted repeated demands for extended store hours as well as for factory shops catering exclusively to the VEB's own staff. In response to such requests and in an effort to stop women from leaving the workplace in order to run errands and go shopping, district authorities gradually lengthened opening hours, set up more factory shops accessible only to staff members, and allowed women to hand in order forms before the beginning of the workday (few took advantage of this last measure, however, because of fears that they would not receive the items they desired most). [61]

While obviously well intended, these accommodating efforts failed to eradicate many of the most pressing difficulties faced by working women – especially those employed in less privileged factories, which usually had neither their own stores nor greater access to coveted goods and supplies. In fact, most laboring women in Saalfeld were at a distinct *structural* disadvantage because they tended to work in industries deemed least essential to the economy – an

---

[60] See the copy of the article that appeared in the March 30, 1955, edition of *Hütte* in ThStA-R, Maxh. 27. Also see the reports and correspondence from the late 1940s in MxA-U, BGL 10, 170, 384.

[61] See, e.g., ThStA-R, FDGB BV Gera 851/208, Prot. der Sitz. der BGL–Zeiss, 7.9.56; ThStA-R, FDGB KV Slf 6205, Niederschr. des Betriebseinsatzes der Frauenkommission im VEB Waschmaschine, 3.12.59; ThStA-R IV/B-4/10/100, IB der SED–KL Slf, 20.8.68.

important source of resentment alluded to at a meeting held at the VEB Wema one week after the June 1953 upheaval: "[I]f a distribution of scarce goods should take place in the factories at all, then firms in light industry should be included as well [because] so many women work in this sector [and] have to worry about providing [for] their families."[62] Official ration guidelines, which remained in place until 1958 and which favored those who performed especially dangerous or arduous tasks, placed most working women at a similar disadvantage: Because men occupied most of these positions, they were usually the primary beneficiaries.

Complaints about low rations and severe shortages were certainly not limited to women. In fact, supply difficulties remained a major preoccupation of all Saalfelders regardless of gender, which meant that the difficult task of procuring scarce food items often fell to both husbands and wives. This may have contributed to a partial breakdown of traditional gender roles, yet most women remained the ones primarily responsible for cooking, shopping, and cleaning – which was why complaints about long lines, high prices, and recurrent shortages of everyday goods and even electricity tended to dominate their customary litany of grievances in particular.[63] And it was also why, as the woman at the Hädrich factory made clear, they were highly sensitive to and extremely critical of policies and practices that gave preference to certain groups of women over others.

The Local Housing Crisis

Chronic housing shortages were a similar source of friction and social resentment – and, as a result, remained one of the most explosive issues in the district throughout the 1950s and 1960s.[64] Local authorities responded to this serious challenge by resorting to many of the same strategies adopted during the immediate postwar years. But with an eye to the role that housing had played during the twin upheavals of the early 1950s, they now tried to defuse discontent by avoiding some of the more drastic measures common earlier, such as the excessive use of force. Compulsory transfers nevertheless continued apace,

---

[62] ThStA-R, FDGB BV Gera 854/209, IB der BGL–Wema in der Mittagspause, 23.6.53.

[63] See, e.g., Katherine Pence, "'You as a Woman Will Understand': Consumption, Gender and the Relationship between State and Citizenry in the GDR's Crisis of 17 June 1953," *German History* 19 (2001): 218–52; Ina Merkel, "Leitbilder und Lebensweisen von Frauen in der DDR," in Hartmut Kaelble, Jürgen Kocka, and Hartmut Zwahr, eds., *Sozialgeschichte der DDR* (Stuttgart, 1994), 359–82.

[64] The number of registered housing applicants in the town rose from 953 in January 1948 to 1,882 in the first quarter of 1971. See the statistics for the entire period in StA-S, Abt. Wohnungspolitik 5938, 5948, 8918; StA-S Sekr. des BM 2254. On housing developments elsewhere in the GDR, see Hannsjörg Buck, *Mit hohem Anspruch gescheitert: Die Wohnungspolitik der DDR* (Munster, 2004). Also see Hartmut Mehls, "Arbeiterwohnungen und Wohnerfahrungen in Hoyerswerda zwischen 1955 und 1965," in Peter Hübner, ed., *Niederlausitzer Industriearbeiter, 1935 bis 1970: Studien zur Sozialgeschichte* (Berlin, 1995), 233–62; Hübner, *Konsens*, 130–77; Kopstein, *Politics*, 173–94; Winkler, *Sozialpolitik*, 43–9, 96–7, 129–32.

often "without any consideration for those involved."[65] This meant, in practice, that local occupants were required to take in boarders or exchange their quarters with others in order to make more efficient use of available space and thus provide for those with supposedly greater needs.

Forced transfers frequently affected the families of individuals who had recently fled to the West, with political retribution apparently playing a role in such decisions (practical considerations did so as well, of course: Reports of illegal flight alerted officials to units that could now be categorized as underoccupied). The gradual exhaustion of underoccupied space as well as the steady influx of new arrivals from other areas in the GDR – prompted by the frenetic growth of local industry beginning in the mid-1950s – quickly offset any temporary gains resulting from compulsory transfers and emigration to the West, however. The failure to satisfy local housing requirements also reflected the sluggish pace of construction of new units due to severe labor and material shortages. In fact, the situation worsened considerably over the course of the decade: By early 1961, the number of housing applications on file in the town of Saalfeld alone surpassed 1,400, one-third of which were now classified as urgent. Though less acute, shortages also began to crop up in the countryside, especially in the larger villages.[66]

Local officials were especially preoccupied at this time with finding housing for members of the intelligentsia, whose numbers steadily dwindled following Nikita Khrushchev's 1958 ultimatum. To encourage doctors and other medical personnel to remain in Saalfeld, urban officials ordered that the health sector now be given "the greatest priority." For similar reasons, the district legislature issued a decree in March 1961 that called for the construction of special apartment buildings just for those in the education sector (this came in response to a new East German law requiring local authorities to provide all teachers with apartments within a year of arrival at a given locale). The erection of the Berlin Wall later that year helped stem the flow of these and other highly trained specialists to the West but, in so doing, created new difficulties by significantly reducing the amount of space previously made available by illegal flight. This unintended consequence underscored the way in which official policies aimed at solving one problem often gave rise to others.[67]

Besides focusing on members of the intelligentsia, authorities remained especially concerned about providing industrial workers with adequate lodging.[68]

---

[65] StA-S, Abt. Wohnungspolitik 8924, Wie wird die Wohnungspolitik in der Stadt Slf durchgesetzt, 15.5.65. See Chapters 1–3 on housing shortages and official responses during the first postwar decade.

[66] See StA-S, E 11, Prot. der Sitz. des Rates der Stadt, 28.2.61. More generally, see the various reports and analyses in StA-S, Sekr. des BM 2254, 3481, 6623; StA-S, Abt. Wohnungspolitik 5938, 5945, 5946, 8924; ThStA-R IV/4/10/117, 136, 164, 240. For a useful overview of housing construction in the town of Saalfeld between 1953 and 1964, see Werner, "Chronik," 52–3.

[67] See the reports from this period in StA-S, Sekr. des BM 2225, 2226, 2254, 3481, 3459; ThStA-R, FDGB KV Slf 3567, 6186, 6302.

[68] On the distribution of local housing according to social group and occupation, see the statistics in StA-S, Abt. Wohnungspolitik 5938, 8918; StA-S, Sekr. des BM 2254, 3481.

This was motivated by economic and ideological reasons as well as purely numerical ones, and prompted a decision several months after the June 1953 upheaval to set up so-called worker housing societies (AWGs) throughout the GDR. To encourage participation and help ensure the success of this new scheme aimed at alleviating the desperate housing situation, the state offered members a variety of benefits, including large sums of credit, substantial tax breaks, and, when possible, a generous supply of construction material. For their part, and to help offset production costs and exploit the advantages of collective labor, AWG members were required to pay 2,500 marks over a five-year period and actively participate themselves in the construction of their future dwellings.[69]

Despite the many benefits offered by the state, the AWGs got off to a slow start in Saalfeld because of little initial interest. As of late 1955, fewer than 200 workers had joined the three societies formed one year earlier in the district's largest factories. Progress was further impeded by chronic material shortages, a lack of commitment on the part of construction workers (who received substantially less pay for AWG projects), and "unsatisfactory work intensity" on the part of those who had agreed to sign up. Because the beneficiaries were obliged to work an average of thirty hours each month, many members simply refused to volunteer their services because of the substantial overtime they were often forced to perform in addition to their normal forty-eight-hour work-week. Pointing out that most had only agreed to participate in the construction of their own apartments, if at all, officials lamented that "collective thinking" had not advanced very far and that there were only scattered instances of limited "solidarity."[70]

A series of reforms introduced in 1957 – which included more favorable financial conditions and the formation of AWGs in smaller factories and public institutions – helped spur greater interest. So, too, did the creation two years later of a Central Worker Housing Society (ZAWG). District membership almost doubled by the end of 1959 as a result, and the societies subsequently accounted for 85 percent of all new dwellings built at the time.[71] But burgeoning demand quickly surpassed the district's limited resources, which meant that the growing popularity of the movement soon overwhelmed local officials, leading to severe backlogs:

The ZAWG planned on accepting 250 new members in 1960 [but received] 150 applications in the first two months alone. Once the 250 applications are received, the ZAWG will be filled to capacity.... That means that all who apply later will first get an apartment after 1965; those who handed in their applications in the last few months will have to wait four to five years before they can finally move in.[72]

---

[69] See Frerich and Frey, *Handbuch*, 430ff.

[70] MxA-U, BGL 466, Bericht über die AWG, 20.6.56. Also see the reports in ThStA-R IV/4/10/132, 137; Werner, "Chronik," 60.

[71] StA-S, Sekr. des BM 3481, Bericht der Abt. Wohnraumlenkung, 4.8.60. See the figures in StA-S, Sekr. des BM 2256, Niederschr., 24.5.59; ThStA-R, FDGB KV Slf 6148, Prot. der Sekretariatssitz. des FDGB KV Slf, 23.11.59.

[72] See StA-S, Sekr. des BM 3481, Referat, n.d., and Bericht der Abt. Wohnraumlenkung, 4.8.60.

FIGURE 8. The district's first major "cement-slab"(*Plattenbau*) complex was built in the 1960s in Gorndorf, a village located on the outskirts of the town of Saalfeld. © Bildarchiv des Stadtmuseums Saalfeld.

In response to this problem, in response to the continuing needs of the Maxhütte, and in response to the planned expansion of Zeiss and Wema, high-level authorities decided in the early 1960s to invest 77 million marks – "no chickenfeed" (*kein Pappenstiel*), as one official put it – in a large housing project in Gorndorf, a village located on the northeastern outskirts of the town of Saalfeld and within close proximity to the steel mill.[73] Almost 500 apartments were distributed in the district's first major "cement-slab" (*Plattenbau*) complex by the end of 1964, primarily to those employed at Saalfeld's three largest factories.[74] Despite plans to build more than 2,000 additional units in Gorndorf by 1970, construction more or less came to a halt during the latter part of the decade because of the diversion of resources to projects taking place elsewhere in the region. As a result, no new apartments were built for the steel mill during the last two years of the decade, and none was planned for the foreseeable future.[75]

73 StA-S, Sekr. des BM 3459, report, 5.62.
74 See the statistics in StA-S, Abt. Wohnungspolitik 8924.
75 On the Gorndorf project as well as the subsequent construction freeze, see ThStA-R IV/4/10/210, Plan für den Wohnungskomplex Slf–Gorndorf, 8.6.62; StA-S, Abt. Wohnungspolitik 8924, Wie wird die Wohnungspolitik in der Stadt Slf durchgesetzt, 15.5.65; BStU ASt-G 0552, Lagebericht II. Halbjahr 1964, 4.1.65; StA-S, Sekr. des BM 6623, report, 15.2.66; ThStA-R IV/B-4/10/112, Information über die Beratung der Frauenkommission, 28.5.70.

The ambitious promise made in the Seven-Year Plan of 1959 to provide every family with suitable housing by 1965 thus remained an elusive goal in Saalfeld – and elsewhere – well past that deadline.[76] The progressive decay of older buildings only made matters worse: One-third of all apartments in the town were more than seventy years old at the time, and approximately 70 percent were in urgent need of restoration – which limited the possibility of enlarging existing units because they generally fell into disrepair several years after renovation. In addition, local officials were forced to cordon off an increasingly large number of apartments because of security concerns.[77] As a result, the total number of apartments in the town increased by less than 500 between late 1965 and early 1971, which meant that the number of housing applications would reach almost 2,000 by the year Walter Ulbricht fell from power – an even higher figure than those reported in the late 1940s. Noting that dozens of families were still living in wooden barracks, urban officials concluded that they could not solve the problems involved in constructing new apartments on their own and that the only practical solution was a thorough search for underoccupied living quarters and another series of forced transfers.[78]

In essence, then, little had changed in Saalfeld during the first two postwar decades. The number of apartments may have increased by approximately 150 percent during this period, but many still had no modern amenities: Only half had their own bath or shower in 1971, and fewer than 500 apartments had central heating, washing facilities, *and* an interior toilet – and most of these were located in the unattractive housing projects built in the 1960s.[79] Western observers might have looked with disdain on the concrete jungles that began to dot the GDR's landscape at the time even though they could have just as easily found similar buildings on the peripheries of their own cities. The drab uniformity of the East German *Plattenbau* nevertheless came to symbolize for many in the West an inhumane system with no regard for human individuality. Yet, for those Saalfelders forced to live in older, substandard units with few or no modern comforts, these were desirable dwellings well worth fighting for. And fight they did – in a constant struggle waged against fellow citizens as well as against local representatives of the regime.

[76] On the role that housing played in the Seven-Year Plan, see Buck, *Wohnungspolitik*; Petra Gruner, "'neues leben – neues wohnen': Das Wohnungsbauprogramm des Siebenjahrplans," in Neue Gesellschaft für Bildende Kunst, ed., *Wunderwirtschaft: DDR–Konsumkultur in den 6oer Jahren* (Cologne, 1996), 90–5.

[77] See the reports, analyses, and statistics in StA-S, Sekr. des BM 3481, 6623; StA-S, Abt. Wohnungspolitik 8918, 8924; BStU ASt-G, KD Slf 2311. Local landlords complained that the low rents enforced by the state made it impossible for them to pay for necessary repairs, which was "why houses in the town and in the villages had such intolerable façades." See ADL, KV Slf 25556, Bericht, 9.3.62.

[78] See StA-S, Abt. Wohnungspolitik 8924, Bericht zur Stadtverordnetenversammlung über Wohnungspolitik, 28.4.66; StA-S, Abt. Wohnungspolitik 8918, Analyse über die Wohnungssituation der Stadt Slf, 27.4.70, and Auswertung der Eingaben–Analysen für das I. Quartal 1971, 22.4.71; StA-S, Sekr. des BM 7761, Textanalyse über die Eingabentätigkeit im II. Halbjahr 1971, 17.12.71.

[79] See the statistics on modern housing amenities in StA-S, Abt. Wohnungspolitik 8918.

An Apartment of One's Own

Apart from a small minority who chose to build their own homes using private means or move illicitly into empty apartments, most Saalfelders continued to rely on the state for their needs – which was why many held *it* primarily responsible for the district's desperate housing situation. As one disgruntled party member complained, those on high "only make demands of us" but failed to provide any real assistance (he had been forced to live with his ex-wife in the same apartment for more than a year after remarrying because officials could not provide him with new lodgings).[80] Local housing authorities, as the most immediate representatives of the state, naturally bore the brunt of much of this criticism. Frustrated applicants frequently accused them of being rude, lazy, and deceptive, of failing to keep their promises, and of unfairly favoring certain groups and individuals. Verbal abuse as well as occasional threats of physical violence prompted a number of functionaries to resign (the fact that several also quit once their own housing problem had been solved did nothing, of course, to improve their reputation).[81]

Authorities usually replied to such criticism by reminding housing applicants that the current situation was an unfortunate remnant of capitalism and the war – an excuse that wore increasingly thin a decade after the end of hostilities.[82] The large number of formal grievances lodged against local housing authorities nevertheless prompted several investigations of their performance, which concluded that their failure to remedy the situation, introduce proper measures, and satisfy the "thoroughly realizable demands of our workers" was a result of chaotic, inefficient, and unsystematic work methods.[83] Such criticism occasionally devolved into personal attacks on individuals accused of improper behavior or a "lack of class consciousness." In 1959, for example, the SED District Secretariat roundly denounced leading housing officials as "petty-bourgeois elements" who either drank and gambled to excess or provided apartments only to members of the "bourgeois circles" with whom they supposedly caroused.[84]

In severity, then, criticism from above more than matched the vehemence of attacks from below. But assigning blame to mid-level officials was nothing

---

[80] ThStA-R IV/7/220/1003, Prot. der MV der SED GO–Kraftverkehr, 3.8.61.

[81] See, e.g., the reports, correspondence, and minutes in StA-S, Sekr. des BM 2226, 2254; also see the minutes of the town hall gathering in StA-S, Allg. Verw. 178.

[82] See, e.g., StA-S, Sekr. des BM 3481, Bericht der Abt. Wohnraumlenkung, 4.8.60. For similar excuses in the Soviet Union during the interwar period, see Wolfgang Leonhard, *Die Revolution entlässt ihre Kinder* (Cologne, 1962), 19.

[83] See StA-S, Abt. Wohnungspolitik 5946, Gesamtbericht der Zweigkontrolle in der Stadt Slf über die Arbeit mit den ehrenamtlichen Kräften im Allgemeinen und die Wohnungspolitik im besonderen, n.d., and Prot. der Sitz. des Wohnungsausschusses, 22.6.51. For similar complaints and investigations, see the reports in ThStA-R IV/4/10/117, 132, 164; StA-S, Sekr. des BM 2254, 6623.

[84] ThStA-R IV/4/10/164, Bürovorlage über die Überprüng der Arbeitsweise des Rates der Stadt Slf auf dem Gebiet der Wohnraumlenkung und der Grundstückverwaltung, 2.1.59.

more than a typical response from on high, for it was much easier to censure these whipping boys than to admit that the constraints of state socialism had effectively impeded a satisfactory resolution of the local housing crisis. In their own defense, housing authorities reminded their superiors that they were simply overwhelmed by the sheer volume of work because of understaffing, poor training, and high turnover rates. Many also complained about the often immoderate or unreasonable demands made by many of the applicants themselves: The regime's pledge in 1959 to provide all East Germans with an apartment by 1965 had "unfortunately led to a misunderstanding on the part of many in search of housing. They have transformed the goal of 'an apartment for everyone' (*jedem eine Wohnung*) into 'an apartment of *one's choice* for everyone' (*jedem seine Wohnung*)."[85] As a result, many Saalfelders supposedly rejected official offers because they did not meet their high standards or conform to their unreasonable wishes.

Officials were generally sympathetic when those in search of lodging refused to accept apartments that were either too small or in poor condition. They were considerably less tolerant, however, of the excessive demands purportedly made by members of the intelligentsia, especially when they insisted on special treatment because of their professional status:

[I]t's hard to have much understanding when, for example, a young doctor who just arrived from the university demands ... a study, living room, bedroom, children's room, kitchen, bathroom, garage (even though he doesn't own a car) and garden – and especially when he considers an apartment without a boiler not to be modern. ... Sometimes one can't avoid having the impression that these citizens have forgotten who paid for their studies.[86]

Social resentment and class antagonism were clearly alive and well in Saalfeld, and were not limited to local officials. In fact, one of the most common complaints voiced by housing applicants – besides lengthy waiting periods and the poor condition of existing units – focused on the privileged treatment of certain groups and individuals, especially those at the Maxhütte.[87] Though most pronounced during the years leading up to the June 1953 upheaval, the sense of injustice engendered by official favoritism became especially widespread once authorities decided in the mid-1960s to allocate half of the newly constructed apartments in Gorndorf to those employed at the steel mill. In response to announcements at the time that smaller factories would not receive any additional housing before 1970, functionaries at the washing-machine factory pointed out that some of their colleagues had already been waiting ten years for an AWG apartment: "In the meantime their children have grown up and left home. ... There are colleagues in the Maxhütte who aren't even in the AWG

---

[85] See StA-S, Sekr. des BM 3481, Bericht der Abt. Wohnraumlenkung, 4.8.60.
[86] Ibid.
[87] See, e.g., the minutes of the town hall gathering in StA-S, Allg. Verw. 178.

for half a year and already have an apartment."[88] Clearly recognizing the frictions created by such preferential policies, the SED District Secretariat had
decided a decade earlier not to announce until after completion that four-fifths
of all apartments to be built in 1953 were to go to the Maxhütte – in the
hope that all local residents would participate in the planned project: "That
the distribution would then take place according to the previously decided
ratio goes without saying."[89] By resorting to such deceptive ploys, local officials were clearly playing with fire – as the events of June 1953 made all too
clear.

The housing benefits enjoyed by those employed at the steel mill were not
the only source of indignation, however. Many Saalfelders also carped about
the preference given to Soviet troops and state security officials, as well as to
individuals who had earlier left for the West and then returned – especially
since those who had chosen to remain in the GDR had already been waiting
much longer for an apartment. But how were distribution decisions ultimately
made in practice? Emphases continually shifted but, as the foregoing suggests,
economic, political, and security considerations continued to play a determi-
native role. Responsibility for assigning apartments generally fell to two main
bodies: the district housing office (*Wohnungsamt*) and the urban housing committee (*Wohnungsausschuß*). Despite bureaucratic rivalries between the two
agencies, the latter was primarily charged with locating underoccupied quarters and recommending assignments based on urgency lists. Its decisions were
made at public meetings that gave committee members the opportunity to discuss, announce, and justify assignments to urgency categories, transfers, and
the allocation of available lodging. Formal objections lodged by disgruntled
individuals were also addressed at these meetings, where supplicants had the
opportunity to argue in support of their requests.

The housing committee was usually required to choose among several peti-
tioners and, as a rule, tended to make decisions based on the number of persons
in a given household as well as the size of the apartment under consideration.
Because of concerns about popular reaction as well as a desire to maintain
a united front, especially sensitive cases – e.g., those involving decisions that
were politically motivated, that "could create considerable damage to the public
good if discussed openly," or that might have led to disputes among members –
were normally handled behind closed doors. Although the sparse minutes of
these meetings suggest that decisions were usually made according to the actual
needs of the individual or family in question, the committee apparently decided
in favor of those who either regularly attended its sessions or who came with a
specific apartment in mind. In other words, applicants who made nuisances of
themselves or who kept their eyes and ears open for available lodging usually

---

[88] See ThStA-R, FDGB KV Slf 8010, IB der KV IG Metall Slf, n.d.; ThStA-R, FDGB KV Slf 6205,
Bericht über die Frauenversammlung im VEB Waschmaschinenwerk, 21.1.65; BStU ASt-G 0552,
Lagebericht II. Halbjahr 1964, 4.1.65.
[89] ThStA-R IV/4/10/95, Vorplanung Wohnungsbau 1952, 30.4.52.

had the best chance of success: As one official admitted, his coworkers only tended to handle the cases of those who continuously came to their office.[90]

The competitive nature of this system prompted many applicants to argue that they – for a variety of reasons – had a more legitimate right to a certain unit. To improve their chances even further, they occasionally backed up such arguments by denouncing rivals or by informing against neighbors and colleagues who supposedly inhabited underoccupied quarters.[91] Such betrayals were not always motivated by purely selfish designs, however: Perceived inequities also led to denunciation even in cases where it would not have led to an improvement in one's own housing situation. In the summer of 1971, for example, one local resident voluntarily informed the mayor of Saalfeld that a large family in his neighborhood was forced to live in a single overcrowded room while a couple in his own building – whom he mentioned by name – occupied a much larger apartment. He requested that an official investigation be conducted in order to determine whether or not something could be done about this gross "injustice."[92] Authorities actually encouraged snitching, in fact, as a way in which to locate underoccupied quarters and assure a more equitable distribution of available space, despite – or perhaps because of – its divisive effects.

Whatever the reason, when local officials proved unable or unwilling to satisfy requests, frustrated applicants often turned instead to higher-level authorities for succor and support. This usually involved the submission of written complaints to district and regional authorities or to state and party officials in Berlin – such as the SED Central Committee or even the president of the GDR, Wilhelm Pieck. Although such appeals were almost always forwarded to local officials with a request that the matter be given immediate attention, this effort to put pressure on district functionaries met with varying success. In 1959, for instance, only twenty-nine of the fifty-five complaints sent to the capital were favorably resolved. Irritated employees at the district housing office were quick to point out that these cases had been settled only because the individual in question had already been placed on an urgency list: The request would have been granted anyway, they claimed, and its subsequent resolution had supposedly had little to do with the fact that a complaint had been lodged with a central agency.[93]

---

90 ThStA-R IV/4/10/132, Bericht über die Arbeit des städtischen WA und der Wohnungskommissionen, 2.11.55. The applicant's chances were usually best when he or she approached the committee with a particular apartment in mind. See, e.g., StA-S, Abt. Wohnungspolitik 5946, Prot. der Sitz. des Wohnungsausschusses, 23.5.52, and Prot. der Sitz. des Zentralen Wohnausschusses, 19.3.53.

91 See, e.g., the minutes of these meetings in StA-S, Abt. Wohnungspolitik 5945–7.

92 StA-S, Sekr. des BM 7761, memorandum, 6.7.71.

93 StA-S, Sekr. des BM 3481, Bericht der Abt. Wohnraumlenkung, 4.8.60. For examples of such appeals and petitions, see StA-S, Abt. Wohnungspolitik 5938, 5946; StA-S, Sekr. des BM 2254, 3459, 7762. On petitions for aid more generally, see Steffen Elsner, "Flankierende Stabilisierungsmechanismen diktatorischer Herrschaft: Das Eingabenwesen in der DDR," in Christoph Boyer and Peter Skyba, eds., *Repression und Wohlstandsversprechen: Zur Stabilisierung von Parteiherrschaft in der DDR und der CSSR* (Dresden, 1999), 75–86; Jonathan

Local housing authorities not only resented outside interference, as this suggests, but also steadfastly refused to bow to pressure from above. In the spring of 1952, members of the urban housing committee stubbornly – and successfully – rejected a request by the newly appointed chairman of the SED District Secretariat for the immediate transfer of a woman to another apartment in order to make room for his own family.[94] Housing officials proved especially intransigent when members of the district legislature tried to intervene on behalf of supplicants who had appealed to them directly for assistance: As one plucky functionary complained, many representatives harbored the "false opinion" that their requests were to be handled with priority.[95]

Such disputes were most common and usually most acrimonious between housing authorities and factory officials, who tenaciously advanced the demands of their own staff members – in large part because of justifiable fears that inadequate lodging would lead to further labor shortages or to unrest on the shop floor. According to the head of the district housing office, this "local patriotism" was a form of "bourgeois nationalism" that only served to "weaken or paralyze" the work of his agency. For their part, factory functionaries regularly censured housing officials for the "bureaucratic and heartless" way in which they dealt with applicants from their firm.[96] They complained, moreover, that it was exceedingly difficult to work productively with those in charge of distribution decisions. Always quick to point out the economic importance of their own VEBs, many nevertheless continued to write letters, make phone calls, and issue threats as well as so-called urgency certificates in support of their staff.[97]

When housing officials remained inflexible, many factories turned instead to the local mayor for support. The surviving correspondence of these high-level urban officials – a flurry of letters and in-house memoranda – not only attested to their high degree of personal involvement in housing matters, but also to their remarkable ability to cut through red tape and resolve particularly difficult cases, especially ones involving state and party cadres or members of privileged social groups. Though most solicitous of the frequent requests and complaints passed along by the District Secretariat and the District Council (as one town councilor admitted in 1965, she always had "a good laugh seeing the mayor shake" when such cases remained unresolved), they also devoted a

Zatlin, "Eingaben und Ausgaben: Das Petitionsrecht und der Untergang der DDR," ZfG 45 (1997): 902–17.

94 Supported by members of the CDU faction, the chairwoman of the committee rejected the first secretary's request that the woman (who suffered from tuberculosis) be transferred to another apartment while waiting for emigration officials to decide on her application to leave the GDR. See StA-S, Abt. Wohnungspolitik 5946, Niederschr. über die außerordentliche nichtöffentliche Sitz. des städtischen Wohnungsausschusses, September 1952.

95 See StA-S, Sekr. des BM 3481, Bericht der Abt. Wohnraumlenkung, 4.8.60; ThStA-R IV/4/10/164, Bürovorlage, 2.1.59.

96 See StA-S, Abt. Wohnungspolitik 5946, Gesamtbericht der Zweigkontrolle, n.d.; MxA-U, BGL 430, Prot. der Sitz. der AGL–Verw., 22.6.55.

97 For such tensions as well as such requests, see, e.g., the correspondence, reports, and minutes in StA-S, Sekr. des BM 2254, 3481, 6261; StA-S, Abt. Wohnungspolitik 5946–7.

great deal of attention to direct appeals from ordinary citizens.[98] These written or oral requests were frequently abject or servile in tone and often contained heartrending accounts of personal misfortune – such as the following plea submitted by a cleaning lady employed by a local coal distributor:

> Excuse me for personally turning to you. I have no strength left and don't see any other way.... Since October 1970 my son lives with his family (wife and two children) as our tenant.... The empty apartments we reported to the housing department were given to others.... There are fights in our home almost every day.... My husband and son are both hot-tempered.... I address to you, most honorable mayor, an urgent request: Let my son have an apartment so that we can all carry out our work again in peace.[99]

Taking a somewhat different tack, other applicants underscored their steadfast loyalty to the regime – along with the expectation that the party and state would now respond in kind. In a similar request at the time, another resident emphasized that both of her sons had voluntarily performed their "honorable NVA service" and that she had "already often proven her trust in the state": A "good" member of the SED for fifteen years, she had even served as the superintendent of her building since 1954 because "the landlady... shows no interest and neglects her duties.... Now please help me for once." Such appeals often had the desired effect: Richard Pohle, the mayor at the time, found an amenable solution within the month.[100]

A decade after he had left office, many Saalfelders continued to speak highly of Pohle, who served as mayor from 1964 to 1986. A native of the nearby Thuringian town of Greiz, where he was trained as an embosser, Pohle was born to working-class parents in 1921.[101] He joined the Social Democrats in 1945 and became the deputy chairman of the local SED six months after its founding. After attending a vocational school in Leipzig, Pohle entered the town administration as an energy official in the late 1940s and eventually worked himself up the ladder to become mayor of Greiz in 1960. He was transferred to Saalfeld four years later to replace Feodor Pfeffer, an old acquaintance who had recommended him for the post and who had stepped down himself because of personal frictions with the district *Landrat*.

Reflecting on his lengthy tenure as mayor, Pohle noted that the desperate housing situation had always created the most problems in Saalfeld. He hastened to add, however, that no one was forced to live under a bridge – "as in the West" – and emphasized that he and his wife had occupied the same "modest" apartment since their arrival in the mid-1960s. As mayor, he usually spent one

---

[98] Quotation from BStU ASt-G 0552, Halbjahranalyse II. Halbjahr 1965, 17.12.65. For examples of state, party, and factory officials requesting that the mayor intervene on behalf of certain individuals, see the correspondence in StA-S, Sekr. des BM 3459, 6261, 6805, 7761, 7762.

[99] StA-S, Sekr. des BM 7762, correspondence, 14.12.71.

[100] See StA-S, Sekr. des BM 7762, correspondence, 23.2.71. For other examples of how Pohle responded to individual requests, see the additional correspondence in this file as well as in StA-S, Sekr. des BM 2256, 3481, 7761.

[101] Richard Pohle, in discussion with the author, May 1995.

day each weekend walking around the town to see how "things really were" so that he could respond accordingly and be prepared for the periodic reports he was required to make to the District Secretariat and District Council. In addition to his success in dealing with many of Saalfeld's most pressing housing and supply issues, Pohle noted that he was most proud of two accomplishments: the creation of a sister-city arrangement with the French town of Stains and his work on an East German commission charged with improving the way in which officials responded to private petitions for assistance.

Clearly solicitous of citizens in need, Pohle was especially willing to help the elderly and needy as well as those who had demonstrated their fidelity to the GDR. But available evidence also suggests that he was less than forthcoming when it came to those who had acted in ways that were somehow politically suspect: In a letter explaining why it was impossible to satisfy one demand for an apartment, for instance, he cryptically noted that the family in question had "placed itself outside the legal norms of our socialist society because of its behavior." After receiving a similar rejection, one indignant resident wrote a lengthy letter to the producers of *Prisma*, a popular television show that dealt with complaints submitted by ordinary East Germans about their everyday frustrations.[102]

A large number of housing applicants resorted to more active forms of protest, in fact, when their requests were not granted by local functionaries; these included refusals to pay party or union dues, participate in paramilitary training, or perform other sociopolitical activities. Many also threatened to leave for the West if they were not given immediate satisfaction. After the construction of the Berlin Wall made this a less viable option, refusal to vote in upcoming elections became an increasingly popular strategy.[103] Instead of leading to disciplinary measures or other sanctions, such protests often resulted in a positive outcome – as in the case of one party member at the VEB Wema, who poignantly explained to his superiors why he would no longer perform any political or "educational" activity on the shop floor: "[I]t simply breaks my heart when I compare my apartment to other ones." Sympathetic officials promised to investigate and do all that they could to find him a larger dwelling.[104]

---

[102] StA-S, Sekr. des BM 7761 and 7762, correspondence, 19.8.71, and Beschwerde, 16.11.71. Also see Ina Merkel, *"Wir sind doch nicht die Meckerecke der Nation": Briefe an das Fernsehen der DDR* (Cologne, 2000).

[103] See, e.g., ThStA-R, FDGB KV Slf 6186, Agitationseinsatz anläßlich der Wahl am 17.9.61 in Oberwellenborn, Information, 17.9.61, and Agitation zur Wahl der örtlichen Volksvertretung, 18.9.61; ThStA-R IV/7/220/1003, Prot. der MV der SED GO–Kraftverkehr, 23.3.61, 28.4.61, 3.8.61. Also see the information reports in ThStA-R IV/7/226/1137 (2.11.56); ThStA-R IV/A-4/10/092 (20.9.63, 11.10.63); ThStA-R, FDGB KV Slf 6302 (30.9.65); ThStA-R IV/B-4/10/104 (5.12.70).

[104] ThStA-R IV/7/230/1160, IB der SED GO–Wema, 28.7.54. For similar incidents at Zeiss, see ThStA-R IV/7/231/1164 and 1166, Prot. der LS der SED GO–Zeiss, 19.11.54, and Prot. der MV der SED GO–Zeiss, 26.5.55.

There were a number of reasons why local functionaries were usually willing to reach an amicable agreement in housing disputes involving rank-and-file
party members or low-level officials: Besides the fact that these individuals were
often close friends or acquaintances, it would have been disadvantageous to
alienate loyal cadres who were supposed to set a positive example for their colleagues. But what, apart from humanitarian considerations, accounted for their
general willingness to resolve disputes involving ordinary Saalfelders, especially
those who threatened to flee or not vote in an election? The district could have
ill afforded to lose even more workers, given the chronic labor shortages that
already plagued local factories. And even though elections were rigged, officials
clearly placed great emphasis on symbolic shows of public acclamation: Those
who refused to vote not only expressed their disapproval of the regime in a
very public manner that could give rise to unwelcome discussion but also set a
dangerous example for their peers. Local officials were apparently motivated as
well by concerns about censure from their own superiors, to whom disgruntled
residents sometimes turned in desperation. But in the end, the desire to maintain
harmony and preserve domestic peace was arguably the greatest impetus for
solving local housing problems. Whether consciously pursued with this intent
in mind, the strategy proved largely successful: Despite the threats made in the
late summer of 1953 with regard to housing and other supply shortages more
generally, there would be no repeat performance of June 17 in Saalfeld – or
anywhere else in the GDR, for that matter.[105]

The everyday responses to endemic scarcity on the part of local officials and
residents bring to mind the concept of *communist neotraditionalism* first used
to describe China and the Soviet Union during the post-Stalinist era. In an
attempt to characterize the "patterns of authority" that helped to stabilize
these regimes, Andrew Walder and Ken Jowitt have emphasized the emergence
of social networks that enabled ordinary individuals to procure a variety of
goods and services that were in short supply. They focus in particular on the
"clientelist" relationships that developed (especially between low-level officials
and their immediate subordinates) in which favors and rewards were selectively distributed in return for loyalty, consent, cooperation, and other desired
forms of social, political, and economic behavior. In a throwback to more traditional forms of rule, all of this supposedly helped ensure stability by coopting
privileged individuals and groups and, more generally, by making those who
lived under Soviet–style regimes highly dependent on those in charge for the
satisfaction of their everyday material needs.[106]

---

[105] On the threats made that summer, see ThStA-R IV/4/10/105, Vorlage, 21.8.53.
[106] See Kenneth Jowitt, "Soviet Neotraditionalism: The Political Corruption of a Leninist Regime,"
    Soviet Studies 35 (1983): 275–97; Andrew Walder, *Communist Neo-Traditionalism: Work and
    Authority in Chinese Industry* (Berkeley, 1986). Also see Frank Ettrich, "Neotraditionalis-
    tischer Staatssozialismus: Zur Diskussion eines Forschungskonzeptes," *PROKLA* 22 (1992):
    98–114; Martin Kohli, "Die DDR als Arbeitsgesellschaft? Arbeit, Lebenslauf und soziale Dif-
    ferenzierung," in Kaelble, Kocka, and Zwahr, *Sozialgeschichte*, 37–8.

But what about those who were not privy to various forms of privilege? And what were the potential consequences for stability when – as was often the case – the congenital constraints of state socialism made it impossible for local and factory officials to satisfy the demands and meet the expectations of those under their charge? Why did that failure, in other words, not lead to more concerted challenges from below? Walder provides one persuasive answer to this question by concentrating on the ways in which the privileged treatment of shop-floor activists helped to divide the Chinese workforce and thus prevent collective forms of behavior. Along similar lines, he emphasizes the way in which the use of personal connections to gain access to scarce goods through the proverbial back door reinforced individual action at the expense of more collective ones.[107] As we have seen, similar patterns of behavior emerged in the GDR as well – for these as well as for a variety of other reasons discussed in the preceding chapters: The preferential treatment of activists was one, but only one, factor in this regard.

In an attempt to explain widespread acquiescence, those who have looked at East Germany in particular have argued that the many social benefits offered by the state – affordable housing, child care, and inexpensive goods – helped maintain stability by fostering a similar sense of loyalty to the regime among large segments of the population. This, in turn, supposedly compensated for the regime's lack of political legitimacy. It was true that, in many respects, the German state social model took on new dimensions in the GDR. But because Father State was a poor relation with limited means, it was often forced to resort to juggling acts in which one segment of society received some benefit or privilege at the exclusion and expense of another – just as in China and the Soviet Union. As a result, most Saalfelders could – and did – point to another person or group that was, at least in their eyes, in some way or other better off than they. Whether intended or not, the favoritism and material disparities that resulted from such policies sowed discord among Saalfelders by promoting envy and mutual resentment. This effectively undermined social solidarity and, in so doing, forestalled collective challenges to the regime that could have had highly destabilizing effects in the long run.

[107] See Walder, *Neo-Traditionalism*, 162–89.

Conclusion: A Divided Society in a Divided Nation

Schluß mit der Spaltung des schaffenden Volkes!
An end to the division of the working people!

–Appeal by the German Communist Party (June 1945)

The winter months of late 1969 and early 1970 were among the coldest and snowiest on record in the eastern half of Germany in almost a century. Shortages of food and energy reached alarming levels – even by GDR standards – as a result of the severe weather conditions and accompanying production backlogs, giving rise once again to a great deal of popular discontent. In an ironic allusion to the celebratory festivities that had just marked a milestone in the history of the postwar socialist state, disgruntled East Germans mocked at the time, "No coal in the basement, no potatoes in the sack. Long live the twentieth anniversary" of the GDR.[1] Such widespread anger about a material situation reminiscent of the immediate postwar years was entirely understandable, especially in light of the modest improvements associated with the recent economic reforms of the mid-1960s. The preceding period may have been a "golden age," relatively speaking, but it was a short-lived one. In fact, the crisis that came at the close of the decade turned out to be one of the final nails in the coffin of Walter Ulbricht's reform program as well as that of the Communist leader himself, who was unceremoniously removed from office a year and a half later.[2]

The upheaval that took place at the highest level of the East German political spectrum had no equivalent at the grass roots – despite claims made by one of the first source-based studies to appear after the fall of the Berlin Wall that the GDR was on the verge of revolution in 1970 because of a desperate supply situation not unlike the one that had helped trigger the disturbances of June

---

[1] Stefan Wolle, *Die Heile Welt der Diktatur: Alltag und Herrschaft in der DDR, 1971–1989* (Berlin, 1998), 33–5.
[2] See footnote 2 in the Introduction for works on the fall of Ulbricht.

1953.[3] The violent clashes that occurred at the time between striking workers and security officials in Poland because of similar supply difficulties – and that later helped spawn the Solidarity trade union movement – had no counterpart in the GDR either. In Saalfeld itself, there were no unusual signs of unrest that winter apart from the customary grumbling and habitual acts of nonconformity long familiar to local officials.

The same had been true during every other potential flash point since June 1953: from the destalinization campaign of 1956 to its abrupt end following the disturbances in Poland and Hungary later that year, from the alarming international developments and unpopular domestic measures that prompted the complete closure of the border in 1961 to the highly confrontational policies adopted soon thereafter in the protective shadow of the Wall. Forced collectivization, compulsory military conscription, new and more rigorous campaigns aimed at boosting productivity, recurring shortages of the most basic supplies and services: These and many of the same explosive ingredients that had led to the earlier upheavals in Saalfeld continued to create serious tensions and engender widespread discontent throughout the district. Yet, there was no repeat performance of August 1951 or June 1953. Why that was the case is the question that has lain at the heart of this study, which began by identifying some of the more common explanations for the long-term stability of the SED regime: repression and obedience, legitimacy and loyalty, apathy and withdrawal, conciliation and compromise. To what extent do its findings about the district of Saalfeld support such claims?

One major contention of this book is that repression did not in itself preclude large-scale protest or violent insurrection. Even if the domestic security apparatus was still in its infancy during the first postwar decade, the series of mass arrests that took place in the late 1940s and early 1950s nevertheless marked the high point of Stalinist terror in the eastern half of Germany. Yet, the two most spectacular challenges to the regime during the Ulbricht era both took place at this time (repression may have been relaxed after the announcement of the New Course in early June 1953, but that did not mean that memories of the recent past had simply disappeared overnight: Fear cannot, after all, be shut off like a light switch).

Harrowing recollections of the strong-arm responses to those upheavals, as well as the subsequent buildup of the infamous state security apparatus, obviously made most Saalfelders and other East Germans more circumspect about taking to the streets once again in order to express their discontent. The construction of the Berlin Wall less than a decade later created an entirely new situation even less conducive to mass protest. There was, for all intents and purposes, no longer a relatively easy escape route to the Federal Republic, as there had been in 1951 and 1953, and the sobering effect of this new state of affairs should not be underestimated. Yet, the fact remains that the two early

---

[3] Gerhard Naumann and Eckhard Trümpler, *Von Ulbricht zu Honecker: 1970, ein Krisenjahr der DDR* (Berlin, 1990).

upheavals both occurred during the most repressive period in the history of the GDR – and that the demonstrations that would later bring down the regime in 1989 also took place at a time when the possibility for exit was still limited and when the Stasi was arguably at the height of its power. All of this clearly underscores the limits of repression and fear as a *sufficient* explanation for East German stability and the absence of mass unrest over so many years.

The very fact that the first major uprising in the Soviet bloc took place in the GDR – as well as the fact that the mass protest movement that gripped much of the region in 1989 and 1990 began there as well – similarly give the lie to shallow claims that the regime was so stable because East Germans qua Germans were passive and obedient. So, too, does the overwhelming regularity with which many Saalfelders – including low-level officials and rank-and-file party members – resolutely resisted the sundry demands placed on them by the party and state, openly criticized the policies of the SED, and willingly expressed their disapproval about unpopular political, social, and economic developments.

That there was so much discontent at the grass roots was not in itself surprising. But what was astonishing, given the repressive nature of the dictatorship, was the readiness with which many expressed their displeasure, either verbally or in more furtive forms. The frequency, similarity, and very nature of the most common grievances and patterns of resistant behavior – across time and space, gender and generational cohort, as well as social and occupational milieu – cast considerable doubt, in short, on any suggestion that the legitimization strategies pursued by the regime helped it to win the support of large segments of the population and thus shore up its long-term stability.

Given the dictatorial practices of East German authorities, few would argue that the GDR enjoyed legitimacy in the classic sense described by Max Weber: It was neither traditional nor legal-bureaucratic nor charismatic (as others have pointed out, Walter Ulbricht was, in short, no Adolf Hitler).[4] And for that very reason, those who do contend that the regime enjoyed widespread loyalty have generally looked elsewhere to support their case: to the way in which its antifascist rhetoric supposedly resonated with many East Germans, for example, or to the supposed popularity of the social benefits that it provided. Yet, the many Saalfelders who openly compared the methods of the SED to those of the Nazis, or who vehemently criticized remilitarization and the absence of basic political freedoms, obviously remained immune to official claims that the GDR represented a dramatic break with and positive alternative to National Socialism.

---

[4] See Max Weber, *Economy and Society: An Outline of Interpretive Sociology*, vol. 1, eds. Guenther Roth and Claus Wittich (Berkeley, 1978), 31–8. Also see Mary Fulbrook, *Anatomy of a Dictatorship: Inside the GDR, 1949–1989* (Oxford, 1995), 272–3; Martin Sabrow, "Der Konkurs der Konsensdiktatur: Überlegungen zum inneren Zerfall der DDR aus kulturgeschichtlicher Perspektive," in Konrad Jarausch and Martin Sabrow, eds., *Weg in den Untergang: Der Innere Zerfall der DDR* (Göttingen, 1999), 89–90.

Along similar lines, those social benefits that were purportedly most popular were, if anything, among the most important sources of *discontent* during the entire Ulbricht era because of insufficient availability and chronic scarcity. Only after the fall of the Berlin Wall would they become a nostalgic source of longing for many.

That said, social benefits did improve after Erich Honecker came to power in 1971, the only period in which the GDR could perhaps be accurately characterized as a "welfare dictatorship" (*Fürsorgediktatur*). Yet, the Honecker years ended with the collapse of the regime, in part because it was increasingly unable to satisfy expectations that it had helped raise and make good on the social promises upon which it had staked its very legitimacy.[5] But it had failed to do so under Ulbricht as well, which suggests the need for caution when making claims about the potential effect that this failure had on the viability of the regime: The inadequacy of official legitimization strategies aimed at securing support did not, in other words, automatically translate into mass unrest at the grass roots.[6]

All of this should not suggest that the regime was universally abhorred or that the GDR teetered for decades on the brink of a "latent civil war" just waiting to break out between the rulers and ruled.[7] In fact, the written sources produced by the regime and upon which much of this study is based provide a rather distorted portrait of prevailing opinion: Because local officials tended to highlight critical commentary and undesired behavior in their reports – and to allude only briefly to popular support in empty-sounding, formulaic phrases – the undiscerning observer could easily gain the impression that the overwhelming majority of Saalfelders simply rejected the regime root and branch. In the absence of reliable public opinion surveys, any claims about the state of popular opinion remain inexact and impressionistic.[8]

It would nevertheless be wrong to surmise from this a complete absence of loyalty. As an important series of interviews conducted during the waning years of the GDR with East Germans born in the 1920s and early 1930s clearly suggests, many members of the so-called reconstruction (*Aufbau*)

[5] For the concept of welfare dictatorship, see Konrad Jarausch, "Realer Sozialismus als Fürsorgediktatur: Zur begrifflichen Einordnung der DDR," *APuZ* B20 (1998): 33–46. For a useful (though ideologically tainted) overview of social policy in the GDR, see Gunnar Winkler, ed., *Geschichte der Sozialpolitik der DDR, 1945–1985* (Berlin, 1989). For more critical views, see Beatrix Bouvier, *Die DDR – ein Sozialstaat? Sozialpolitik in der Ära Honecker* (Bonn, 2002); Hans Günter Hockerts, "Grundlinien und soziale Folgen der Sozialpolitik in der DDR," in Hartmut Kaelble, Jürgen Kocka, and Hartmut Zwahr, eds., *Sozialgeschichte der DDR* (Stuttgart, 1994), 519–44; Wolle, *Heile Welt*.

[6] For a different view, see Arnd Bauerkämper, *Die Sozialgeschichte der DDR* (Munich, 2005), 66.

[7] Compare Armin Mitter and Stefan Wolle, *Untergang auf Raten: Unbekannte Kapitel der DDR–Geschichte* (Munich, 1993).

[8] On official efforts to measure popular opinion, see Heinz Niemann, *Hinterm Zaun: Politische Kultur und Meinungsforschung in der DDR: Die geheimen Berichte an das Politbüro der SED* (Berlin, 1995); idem, *Meinungsforschung in der DDR: Die geheimen Berichte des Instituts für Meinungsforschung an das Politbüro der SED* (Cologne, 1993).

generation – and especially those who enjoyed social mobility and career advancement – remained devoted to a regime that had rewarded them for their loyal behavior in the past. Such devotion has not been a central focus of this book, largely because of the constraints imposed by the available documentary evidence: As Michael Burleigh has written about the Nazi period, "consensus, like love, requires no written expression," and that was apparently true in the GDR as well.[9] Yet, some degree of attachment to the regime, "grudging" or otherwise, undoubtedly played an important role in its long-term stability.[10] Along similar lines – and whatever their misgivings – industrial workers *did* continue to accept piecework wages, farmers *did* continue to hand over their products to the state, and individuals from all social groups *did* continue to carry banners, march in parades, and vote in fraudulent elections. That was not in itself necessarily indicative of enthusiastic support, but it did suggest that most came to terms with the exigencies of the regime in one way or another. The various forms of apathy and nonconformist behavior described at length in this study arguably made concessions at other times and in other areas somewhat more bearable for them.[11] And to that extent, refusal and withdrawal – no matter how selective – contributed, at least in part, to regime stability.

Yet, such strategies and responses, like repression and loyalty, provide only an incomplete explanation for the longevity of the GDR and the absence of more aggressive challenges from below despite overwhelming evidence of widespread discontent. Based on everyday developments in the district of Saalfeld, this book has argued that one major key to stability lay primarily elsewhere, namely, in the general willingness of local officials to try to accommodate those under their charge – above all workers and farmers.

Local functionaries generally tried to avoid confrontations with the two groups in whose name the party claimed to rule by endeavoring when possible to satisfy their demands and find solutions to their grievances, by negotiating some sort of settlement that often involved concessions, or by turning a blind eye to noncompliance and insubordination when it came to enforcing the more unpopular dictates of high-level authorities – all in an assiduous attempt to defuse conflict, achieve consensus, and thus maintain harmony on the shop floor and in the countryside. What else might have accounted for such solicitous behavior? In the first place, many functionaries shared – or were at least sympathetic

---

[9] Quotation from Michael Burleigh, *The Third Reich: A New History* (London, 2000), 157. Also see the interviews in Lutz Niethammer, Alexander von Plato, and Dorothee Wierling, *Die Volkseigene Erfahrung: Eine Archäologie des Lebens in der Industrieprovinz der DDR* (Berlin, 1991).

[10] The idea of *grudging loyalty* is a variation on *loyal reluctance*, a term coined in Klaus-Michael Mallmann and Gerhard Paul, "Resistenz oder loyale Widerwilligkeit? Anmerkungen zu einem umstrittenen Begriff," *ZfG* 2 (1993): 99–116. There is little evidence to suggest that the SED regime enjoyed the widespread support that supposedly existed under the Third Reich. On the latter, see Robert Gellately, *Backing Hitler: Consent and Coercion in Nazi Germany* (Oxford, 2001).

[11] See Ehrhart Neubert, *Geschichte der Opposition in der DDR, 1949–1989* (Bonn, 1997).

to – the more common complaints voiced by ordinary Saalfelders. Just as important, the SED justified its leadership by emphasizing its role as the vanguard of the laboring classes, and for that very reason, its representatives at the grass roots could not simply afford to ignore their complaints or wishes. Their reactions to everyday unrest and discontent were not solely dictated by ideological imperatives, however: The almighty plan, upon which the functioning of the East German economy ultimately hinged, could not be fulfilled without the compliance of the laboring masses.

But such strategies of appeasement did not alone account for the absence of mass unrest. After all, local officials had sought harmonious arrangements and been careful not to antagonize unduly those who lived and labored in the district even before the two upheavals of the early 1950s – as the failure to introduce more stringent production norms had made abundantly clear, to name only one prime example. The various formal and informal mechanisms that helped ensure domestic peace, as well as the conciliatory efforts adopted to that end, were by no means a product of June 17, in other words. Yet, the uprising arguably made local functionaries even more reticent about testing the patience of those under their charge and further reinforced their willingness to reach consensus through leniency, negotiation, and compromise.

The upper echelons of the party and state became more attentive to everyday material grievances as well – however ineffectually, given the continuing economic constraints of state socialism. The corrective measures and carrots of social pacification introduced after August 1951 and June 1953 nevertheless deserve emphasis because they demonstrated that repression was not the only – or even the principal – way in which socialist authorities responded to protest, especially when industrial workers were involved. Moreover, they would never again introduce unpopular policies directed solely against this most volatile of all East German social groups, or provoke its members by revoking a series of unpopular measures except for those that adversely affected them alone. That was perhaps the most valuable lesson learned on June 17.

The main sources of social, economic, and political dissatisfaction nevertheless remained largely the same in Saalfeld long thereafter – without giving rise to another mass upheaval. And that is where a consideration of the horizontal relations *among* East Germans themselves becomes as important as the vertical relationship between the regime and the so-called masses when trying to account for regime stability.

More popular treatments of the GDR have emphasized the much-vaunted cohesiveness of East German society, pointing, for example, to the strategic consumption networks that evolved in response to endemic scarcity.[12] Along similar lines, a number of scholarly investigations have focused on the cooperation

---

[12] On the alleged solidarity of the East German *Notgemeinschaft* ("community created by necessity"), see, e.g., Peter Bender, *Fall und Aufstieg: Deutschland zwischen Kriegsende, Teilung und Vereinigung* (Halle, 2002), 128–9.

and cohesion of industrial workers, especially within factory collectives.[13] This study has shown just the opposite, namely, that relations among workers – as well as relations among and *within* other social groups – were marked by serious frictions and fundamental divisions. It was those very divisions, in fact, that effectively prevented serious challenges to the regime and that, in so doing, accounted for so many years of domestic stability.

This fundamental argument flies in the face of prevailing claims about the high degree of solidarity that supposedly characterized East German society. Yet, most protest in Saalfeld was clearly limited to individuals. The upheavals of August 1951 and June 1953 were prominent exceptions – but even there, the degree of solidarity exhibited during these short-lived eruptions should not be exaggerated: The general lack of coordinated activity, the relatively short duration of the disturbances, and the failure of most individuals to join the strikes and demonstrations all underscored the absence of collective behavior and extended forms of solidarity beyond the most immediate

That was not unique to the GDR, of course. Over the past decades, the difficulty of bringing about collective action has attracted a great deal of scholarly attention and has led to the development of many theoretical frameworks that describe the requirements for and obstacles to mass mobilization. Most tend to agree that the most basic requirements are shared common interests, as well as the ability and opportunity to organize and mobilize.[14] Many Saalfelders – regardless of their age, gender, and social background – clearly shared a number of social and economic grievances that should have led them to join ranks against the regime, at least in theory. But given the repressive nature of the East German dictatorship, the absence of independent and effective institutional forms of representation, and the tendency of low-level officials to respond to conflict by searching for individual solutions on an ad hoc basis, the paucity of collective forms of activity was not very surprising.

That was not the only explanation, however: The divisions created by organized competition and the activist movement, the selective distribution of bonuses and premiums, the policy of wage differentiation across economic sectors and regions, and the scramble for limited goods, services, and housing were another important structural factor hindering collective action – and one that goes beyond a monocausal emphasis on repression alone. Strained relations between the genders and among different generational cohorts played an important role here as well. So, too, did the social and material disparities produced by the preferential treatment of certain groups more generally, a result

---

[13] This is especially true of Peter Hübner and Jörg Roesler; see Chapter 8.
[14] On collective action, see, e.g., the classic studies by Charles Tilly, *From Mobilization to Revolution* (Reading, MA, 1978); Sidney Tarrow, *Power in Movement: Social Movements, Collective Action, and Politics* (Cambridge, 1994); Mark I. Lichbach, *The Rebel's Dilemma* (Ann Arbor, MI, 1995); Mancur Olson, *The Logic of Collective Action: Public Goods and the Theory of Groups* (Cambridge, MA, 1971).

of the juggling acts that the regime performed because of its limited means – or in order to coopt those considered most essential to the economy and reward the politically faithful and ideologically acceptable. All of this understandably promoted deep-seated resentment on the part of those less privy to official largesse.

From the perspective of an outside observer, material differences among East Germans were certainly far less pronounced than they were in the West: Pay differentials between factory directors and low-level staff members were less extreme, and workers and members of the intelligentsia did often live side by side in the new cement-slab housing projects begun in the 1960s. But the "fine distinctions" that continued to exist created widespread perceptions of inequity and inequality that were a source of great frustration and anger for most Saalfelders – in large part *because* of the expectations engendered by the constant flow of official rhetoric about social justice and equality.[15] Most individuals could and did point to another person or group that was, in some way or other, better off than they: other colleagues in one's brigade, other brigades in one's department, other departments in one's factory, other factories in one's town or district. The same was true of farmers in other collectives as well as consumers in other regions.

In a different way, comparisons of one's own situation to that of Germans in another Germany created just as much discontent. And according to the theory of relative deprivation, the way in which people evaluate their own circumstances usually depends on whom they compare themselves to.[16] It is certainly true that the propensity of many Saalfelders to measure their own situation unfavorably against that of other reference groups was one of the major reasons for the high levels of discontent in the district. And it is also true that feelings of relative deprivation or injustice can lead to opposition or active protest – as it often did in the factories and villages of Saalfeld. But – and this is something that proponents of the theory have not stressed sufficiently – relative deprivation can also explain the *absence* of large-scale collective action because of the divisions it helps create. This was clearly the case in Saalfeld, where such frictions largely accounted for the absence of collective behavior that would have allowed the disgruntled to present a broader united front to authorities when pressing their demands. At the same time, these very divisions made it easier for authorities to impose – and ensure that ordinary East Germans would succumb to – a wide variety of highly unpopular policies. If a "latent civil war" was waged in the GDR, it was one that pitted Saalfelders against themselves.

[15] "Fine distinctions" refers, of course, to the title of the German translation of Pierre Bourdieu, *La Distinction: Critique sociale du jugement (Die feinen Unterschiede)* (Paris, 1979).

[16] On the concept of relative deprivation, see Walter Runciman, *Relative Deprivation and Social Justice: A Study of Attitudes to Social Inequality in Twentieth-Century England* (Berkeley, 1966). Also see Ted Gurr, *Why Men Rebel* (Princeton, NJ, 1970); Barrington Moore, Jr., *Injustice: The Social Bases of Disobedience and Revolt* (White Plains, NY, 1978). For a helpful overview, see Iain Walker and Heather Smith, eds., *Relative Deprivation: Specification, Development, and Integration* (Cambridge, 2002).

And that is why the administrative town's coat of arms provides such a fitting symbol for the nature of communal relations there during the postwar socialist era: It depicts two fish that appear completely identical, looking away from one another, arranged back to back on a field of muted green – highly symbolic of a divided society in a divided nation on a divided continent.

Harmony achieved through discord is, admittedly, something of a paradox. Yet, social fragmentation – as well as official accommodation – were nevertheless the most important keys to East German stability and the longevity of the socialist regime. It could be objected that there is an inherent contradiction in this argument, however: If most local officials were willing to appease those under their charge, why should one expect the latter to have joined together to resist the demands placed upon them by the party and state or to press their own demands for change more forcefully? In the first place, attempts at conciliation did not necessarily mean that low-level functionaries were able to rectify or eliminate the many deficiencies that gave rise to discontent and grumbling; in fact, and as we have seen, most of the same grievances continued to resurface regularly throughout the Ulbricht era. Secondly, the behavior of most Saalfelders was primarily *passive* and not *proactive* in nature. In other words, industrial workers and farmers were surprisingly adept at adopting a defensive posture; their ability to actively bring about desired change was much more limited. In response to piecework wages, for instance, workers were generally able to secure production quotas that could be easily filled and overfilled; they were unable, however, to bring about the abolition of this unpopular wage system. Most may have been remarkably *eigensinnig* in the way in which they pursued their own interests, in other words, but they were not in a position to burst the parameters set by the party and state.[17] East Germany was, in short, like a large procession – not unlike the one portrayed on the cover of this book – in which the SED piped the tune: Most workers and farmers marched forward to that music, but the steps that they danced to were very often of their own design.

The extent to which all of this represented fundamental opposition to the regime as such, a question that has motivated much work on the Third Reich, is difficult to determine. One should avoid heavy-handed comparisons between the two dictatorships, of course, yet the ongoing debate about resistance and opposition under the Nazis has generated a broad range of scales and spectrums that provide a useful guide to similar behavior in East Germany. A number of scholars have even developed comparable ones for the GDR: By attempting to identify and categorize various expressions of defiance, they underscore both the difficulty and the necessity of differentiating among forms of behavior ranging from apolitical nonconformity to outright political opposition.[18]

---

[17] On the concept of *Eigen–Sinn*, see Alf Lüdtke, *Eigen–Sinn: Fabrikalltag, Arbeitererfahrungen und Politik vom Kaiserreich bis in den Faschismus* (Hamburg, 1993).

[18] Useful overviews of this vast literature include Mallmann and Paul, "Resistenz"; Ian Kershaw, "'Widerstand ohne Volk?' Dissens und Widerstand im Dritten Reich," in Jürgen Schmädeke

How one classifies acts of defiance in East Germany ultimately depends on
the type of behavior in question. Although it has been subject to much criticism,
Martin Broszat's concept of *Resistenz* (i.e., behavior, *regardless of motives or
intentions*, that effectively blocked, limited, or contained Nazi power and the
demands of the regime) nicely characterizes poor sociopolitical participation
in the GDR because it emphasizes the ability of many East Germans to with-
stand the demands placed on them from above while at the same time underscor-
ing the difficulty of determining motivation.[19] But what about poor discipline
and high absenteeism at the workplace, for example? Following a useful distinction suggested by Tim Mason for the Third Reich, much of this behavior
belonged under the rubric of "workers' opposition," i.e., opposition in the *limited* sense of the struggle for basic economic interests – as opposed to political
resistance or "politically self-conscious behavior ... the illegal, conspiratorial
activities of those groups and individuals, who sought to weaken or overthrow
the nazi [sic] dictatorship. ..."[20]

Given the regime's total claims as well as the notorious difficulty of neatly separating the political from the social or economic in a society as deeply politicized
as the East German one, any form of resistance or nonconformity nevertheless
ran the risk of assuming political overtones – regardless of intent and no matter
how ambiguous. It could be argued, moreover, that all nonconformist behavior

and Peter Steinbach, eds., *Der Widerstand gegen den Nationalsozialismus: Die deutsche
Gesellschaft und der Widerstand gegen Hitler* (Munich, 1985), 779–98. On the various scales
of resistance developed for the GDR, see, e.g., Rainer Eckert, "Widerstand und Opposition
in der DDR: Siebzehn Thesen," *ZfG* 44 (1996): 49–67; Ilso-Sascha Kowalczuk, "Artiku-
lationsformen und Zielsetzungen von widerständigem Verhalten in verschiedenen Bereichen
der Gesellschaft," in Enquete–Kommission, *Aufarbeitung von Geschichte und Folgen der
SED–Diktatur in Deutschland: Widerstand, Opposition, Revolution*, vol. 7/2 (Baden-Baden,
1995), 1203–84; Hubertus Knabe, "Was war die 'DDR–Opposition'? Zur Typologisierung des
politischen Widerspruchs in Ostdeutschland," *DA* 2 (1996): 184–98. For a nuanced comparative approach to developments in the GDR and the Third Reich, see, e.g., Günter Heyde-
mann and Heinrich Oberreuter, eds., *Diktaturen in Deutschland – Vergleichsaspekte: Strukturen, Institutionen und Verhaltensweisen* (Bonn, 2003); Klaus Schönhoven, "Drittes Reich und
DDR: Probleme einer vergleichenden Analyse von Diktaturerfahrungen," in *JHK* (Berlin, 1995),
189–200.

[19] On the concept of *Resistenz*, see Martin Broszat, "Resistenz und Widerstand: Eine Zwischenbilanz des Forschungsprojektes," in Martin Broszat, Elke Fröhlich, and Anton Grossmann, *Bayern
in der NS–Zeit: Herrschaft und Gesellschaft im Konflikt*, vol. 4 (Munich, 1981), 691–709. Much
of the criticism of this term reveals a careless instrumental reading of Broszat's work. That said,
the term does fail to differentiate adequately among various forms of defiant behavior because
it is all-encompassing. For this reason, the effort by Broszat's critics to develop spectrums that
more carefully distinguish among the varying degrees of resistant behavior has been an important corrective. For a review of this criticism, see Mallmann and Paul, "Resistenz," 107–10. A
study that questions the applicability of the term *Resistenz* to the GDR in particular is Gary
Bruce, *Resistance with the People: Repression and Resistance in Eastern Germany, 1945–1955*
(Lanham, MD, 2003). For a balanced assessment, see Christoph Kleßmann, "Opposition und
Resistenz in zwei Diktaturen in Deutschland," *Historische Zeitschrift* 262 (1996): 453–79.

[20] Tim Mason, "The Workers' Opposition in Nazi Germany," *History Workshop Journal* 11
(1981): 120. Also see Fulbrook, *Anatomy*, 156.

was perforce "political" because most East Germans knew that it would or could be interpreted as such by those in positions of authority. Yet, the considerable difficulties involved in determining with any precision the underlying motivation should warn us against automatically politicizing such behavior or equating rebellious acts with fundamental protest. By doing so, we would commit the same egregious mistake made earlier by most East German officials and ideologues and run the risk of misleadingly transforming the GDR into a society of heroic resistance fighters. Those engaged in active political resistance consciously aimed at overthrowing the regime were clearly a tiny minority. Yet, the various forms of noncompliant behavior examined at length in this study demonstrate at the very least the *Eigen–Sinn* of many Saalfelders, as well as their ability to resist successfully many of the unwelcome demands placed on them by the party and state. That was no small feat, given the repressive nature of the second German dictatorship.

What does all of this say about the fundamental nature of the SED regime? The history of the GDR has become a growth industry since the opening of the archives, and for more than a decade, scholars working in this field have developed a wide variety of terms aimed at pithily characterizing the regime and its defining elements.[21] The most popular have involved some sort of variation on the totalitarian model, which reflects the resurgence of scholarly interest in this theory since the collapse of the Soviet bloc.[22] The discussion has been especially vitriolic in Germany, where those on the left have tended to stress the differences, and those on the right the similarities, between bolshevism and fascism. The debate is highly politicized, and has sparked fears that any comparison will lead to a relativization of the crimes committed by the National Socialists. However justified these concerns may be, and despite the fact that the totalitarian model often served as an ideological tool in the Cold War, it does have some heuristic value for an investigation of the GDR: Because of the way in which it tries to characterize the basic features of modern dictatorships, it can be used as an ideal type with which to compare the empirical evidence, leading to questions about why the regime corresponded – or failed to correspond – to that ideal. In other words, the model helps to frame important analytical questions about the nature of state socialism as well as the character of

---

[21] These are conveniently summarized in Bauerkämper, *Sozialgeschichte*, 59–60; Torsten Diedrich and Hans Ehlert, "'Moderne Diktatur' – 'Erziehungsdiktatur' – 'Fürsorgediktatur' oder was sonst? Das Herrschaftssystem der DDR und der Versuch seiner Definition," *Potsdamer Bulletin für Zeithistorische Studien* 12 (1998): 17–25.

[22] Two classic accounts of totalitarian theory are Carl J. Friedrich and Zbigniew Brzezinski, *Totalitarian Dictatorship and Autocracy*, 2nd ed., rev. (New York, 1966); Hannah Arendt, *The Origins of Totalitarianism* (New York, 1951). Useful overviews include Eckhard Jesse, ed., *Totalitarismus im 20. Jahrhundert: Eine Bilanz der internationalen Forschung* (Bonn, 1996); idem, "War die DDR totalitär?" *APuZ* B40 (1994): 12–23; Achim Siegel, ed., *Totalitarismustheorien nach dem Ende des Kommunismus* (Cologne, 1998); Wolfgang Wippermann, *Totalitarismustheorien: Die Entwicklung der Diskussion von den Anfängen bis heute* (Darmstadt, 1997). For persuasive arguments rejecting the application of this concept to the GDR in particular, see Ralph Jessen, "DDR–Geschichte und Totalitarismustheorie," *Berliner Debatte INITIAL* 4/5 (1995): 17–24.

state–society relations in East Germany. This book has implicitly addressed one of these questions: the extent to which the regime was able to achieve its total claims to reshape society and control the so-called masses.

One Polish intellectual has compared totalitarianism with a movie script in which every action and every utterance is carefully laid out.[23] This is clearly an exaggeration: Not even the most dogmatic proponents of the theory would suggest that any regime was in a position to achieve such total control. Without trying to create a straw man or parody totalitarian theory, this study has nevertheless demonstrated the distinct limits to the SED's total claims in all areas of political, economic, and social life – something that the proponents of the theory do not emphasize sufficiently. The inability of the party and state to prevent wages from rising faster than productivity, to enforce shop-floor discipline in the factories and collective work in the countryside, to mobilize sociopolitical participation, even on the part of low-level functionaries and rank-and-file party members – all of this, and these are only some of the more prominent themes examined in the preceding chapters, suggest the very real limits of the East German dictatorship and of its ability to "direct" society.

As a result, official party policy did not always translate into reality but instead often produced a number of unintended consequences. Piecework wages were specifically designed to stimulate productivity, for example, but often served instead as a brake on output by leading workers to hold back labor reserves in order to maintain low production quotas and boost earnings. What proponents of totalitarian theory have failed to take sufficiently into account is, in short, the wide-ranging ability of those living under Soviet-style regimes to defy the dictates of those in power and, in some circumstances, even manipulate policy to their own benefit. To put it somewhat differently, they have focused almost exclusively on the authority of those who ruled while essentially ignoring or discounting agency on the part of those who were ruled.[24]

The extreme fragmentation of East German society nevertheless brings to mind the sort of mass social atomization, caused by repression or the fear of repression, that proponents of totalitarian theory have identified in their work on Soviet-style or fascist regimes. This is not an attempt to smuggle in totalitarian theory through the back door, for the term *atomization* is far too strong: The unity and camaraderie that characterized relations within at least some factory or agricultural collectives, as well as the readiness of many Saalfelders to create personal consumption networks in response to endemic scarcity, call attention to the fact that forms of cooperation and collaboration continued to exist in the GDR. But these small pockets of solidarity underscored at the same

---

[23] See Ralph Jessen, "Die Gesellschaft im Staatssozialismus: Probleme einer Sozialgeschichte der DDR," *GG* 21 (1995): 97.

[24] The regime did not, to put it somewhat differently again, enjoy an absolute monopoly on power, which had many sources and which moved in multiple directions in Saalfeld. Michel Foucault's ideas about power are especially instructive in this respect. For a useful introduction, see Michel Foucault, *Power*, ed. James Faubion, trans. Robert Hurley and others (New York, 2000).

time the absence of greater cohesion among larger groups of East Germans. Fear of denunciation may have led to cautious behavior and discretion in personal and professional relationships, and the exposure of friends and family members as Stasi informers since the fall of the Berlin Wall clearly suggests that such prudence was well advised.[25] Yet, the many structural factors discussed at length in this study arguably played an even greater role than fear in creating social divisions. Totalitarian theorists were largely correct, then, in positing the divisive nature of state socialism; they got it right, but not necessarily for all of the right reasons. Moreover, they suggest a degree of conscious design on the part of officials not supported by the available evidence.[26]

Saalfeld was, of course, only one of approximately 200 administrative districts in East Germany, and its 60,000 inhabitants were only a small percentage of the population as a whole. What can developments and trends there say about the Communist experience in the GDR as a whole – or, for that matter, about the Communist experience elsewhere in the socialist bloc? In the first place, some of the specific findings in this study are similar to those discovered by scholars who have looked at other regions – suggesting that much of what it has to say about this small Thuringian district undoubtedly holds true for the rest of East Germany as well.[27] Whatever Saalfeld's peculiarities, the very fact that the *same* kinds of complaints and modes of behavior, the *same* kinds of disputes and outcomes, and the *same* kinds of reactions by local officials continued to arise in *different* factories and communes across the district and *throughout* the period from 1945 to 1971 does as well. In fact, many of the findings presented here recall patterns of authority and resistance identified in other socialist societies as well. There is also much about Saalfeld reminiscent of the work done by those who have looked at autocratic regimes of the *non*socialist

---

[25] See, e.g., Erich Loest, *Die Stasi war mein Eckermann: Oder, Mein Leben mit der Wanze* (Göttingen, 1991); Timothy Garton Ash, *The File: A Personal History* (London, 1997).

[26] In the absence of such evidence, it would be imprudent to suggest that the regime intentionally pursued such strategies in an effort to divide East Germans and thus maintain domestic harmony. Many of the measures that its leaders adopted (such as organized competition) were clearly intended to ensure stability, of course – but in a different way: by improving the overall economic performance of the GDR, for example, or by winning the support of certain groups. Those measures nevertheless created social strains and conflicts that clearly posed a potential threat to stability. But at the same time, it was those very conflicts that helped *preserve* stability by hindering concerted challenges to the regime from below. This paradox alerts us to yet another: With the onset of modernity, fear of social conflict and the breakdown of society became a widespread preoccupation in Germany and elsewhere. The *Burgfrieden* of 1914, the Nazi *Volksgemeinschaft*, and later Walter Ulbricht's *sozialistische Menschengemeinschaft* all attested to a pervasive desire for social unity. Yet, if this study is correct, it was the social *disunity* of East German society that ultimately accounted for so many years of domestic peace.

[27] Useful overviews of the vast literature on the GDR include Bauerkämper, *Sozialgeschichte*; Rainer Eppelmann, Bernd Faulenbach, and Ulrich Mählert, eds., *Bilanz und Perspektiven der DDR–Forschung* (Paderborn, 2003); Beate Ihme-Tuchel, *Die DDR* (Darmstadt, 2002); Corey Ross, *The East German Dictatorship: Problems and Perspectives in the Interpretation of the GDR* (London, 2002).

variety, neatly synthesized in James Scott's sweeping look at domination and the "arts of resistance" across the globe and throughout much of modern history.[28]

Anger about unsatisfactory material conditions and supposedly unfair social differentiation was not and is not limited to autocracies, of course. But in East Germany and other Soviet-style regimes, most citizens held the party and state personally accountable for their own material prosperity and social welfare – not only because of the wide-ranging control that the latter exercised in areas regulated elsewhere by the market, but also because of their very claim about the right to rule totally. As a result, their systematic failure to deliver the goods, so to speak, and make good on their promises went a long way toward accounting for the low levels of support enjoyed by these regimes – as well as the shaky foundation of stability on which they tottered for many decades.

In his classic study of the Nazi seizure of power in a single town, William Sheridan Allen noted that the years from 1933 to 1945 had a "curiously static quality" about them.[29] In many respects, that was true of the Saalfeld district as well. Once the foundations of the socialist state were laid in the late 1940s, the essential structures of SED rule remained essentially the same over the remaining years of the regime. There were important changes, of course, many of which have been examined in the preceding chapters: These included notable improvements in provisioning and supplies, for example, the transformation of production relations in the countryside, and the reliance on increasingly refined methods of state surveillance. As Peter Bender has noted – even if one does not entirely accept his terminology – there was a qualitative difference between the "totalitarianism of the 1950s" and the "authoritarian boredom of the 1980s."[30]

Yet, one of the most striking aspects of Saalfeld's history during the Ulbricht era was the remarkable degree of continuity that characterized many of the major themes explored in the preceding chapters: the various sources of collective dissatisfaction and the ways in which discontent was expressed,

---

[28] See, e.g., Padraic Kenney, *Rebuilding Poland: Workers and Communists 1945–1950* (Ithaca, NY, 1997); Sheila Fitzpatrick, *Everyday Stalinism: Ordinary Life in Extraordinary Times: Soviet Russia in the 1930s* (New York, 1999); idem, *Stalin's Peasants: Resistance and Survival in the Russian Village after Collectivization* (New York, 1994); Andrew Walder, *Communist Neo-Traditionalism: Work and Authority in Chinese Industry* (Berkeley, 1986); James Scott, *Domination and the Arts of Resistance: Hidden Transcripts* (New Haven, CT, 1990). For an overview of his own work on Hungarian workers as well as other studies on workers in the rest of postwar Eastern Europe, see Mark Pittaway, "Control and Consent in Eastern Europe's Workers' States, 1945–1989: Some Reflections on Totalitarianism, Social Organization, and Social Control," in Clive Emsley, Eric Johnson, and Pieter Spierenburg, eds., *Social Control in Europe, 1800–2000*, vol. 2 (Columbus, OH, 2004), 343–67; Mark Pittaway, ed., "Labor in Postwar Central and Eastern Europe," special issue, *ILWCH* 68 (2005). Also see Peter Hübner, Christoph Kleßmann, and Klaus Tenfelde, eds., *Arbeiter im Staatssozialismus: Ideologischer Anspruch und soziale Wirklichkeit* (Cologne, 2005).

[29] William Sheridan Allen, *The Nazi Seizure of Power: The Experience of a Single German Town, 1922–1945*, rev. ed. (New York, 1984), 282.

[30] Bender, *Fall und Aufstieg*, 198.

nonconformist behavior and the widespread refusal to comply with party and state demands, and official strategies aimed at dealing with popular grievances and open conflict. That is why the second part of this study has taken a more thematic approach. Most of the social, economic, and political complaints voiced by Saalfelders during the upheavals of the early 1950s continued to surface regularly – though in a less concentrated form – throughout the next two decades. And the ways in which local officials responded to conflict and tried to defuse tensions were largely the same both before and after the twin explosions of 1951 and 1953 as well. Their methods became increasingly refined after those two events, however, as they discovered how to calibrate their responses and negotiate harmony more effectively. Conciliatory efforts aimed at maintaining harmony were by no means a result of August 16 and June 17, then, but the upheavals did reinforce a widespread willingness to reach consensus through negotiation and compromise. For their part, and even if their efforts did not always meet with success, ordinary Saalfelders learned over time how to deal with the regime in order to advance their demands and defend their everyday interests more adroitly as well.

According to one scholar, an "approach that primarily takes into account social dissimilarities, individual strategies of refusal or even the weakness of the repressive system may contribute to explaining the collapse of GDR society, but cannot account for its continued existence for decades."[31] This study has argued just the opposite. But the regime nevertheless imploded in the fall of 1989. Had something fundamentally changed during the final two decades that might have accounted for this unexpected development?

An attempt to explain the demise of the GDR lies beyond the scope of this investigation, which focuses on the first twenty-five years of its history. But even a study that consciously limits itself to investigating the long-term stability of a regime that ultimately falls apart cannot skirt entirely the question of eventual collapse. Since the fall of the Berlin Wall and the opening of the archives, scholars who have addressed this important question have posited a variety of explanations: a failing economy on the brink of collapse, a loss of confidence on the part of a sclerotic ruling elite, the rise of a grass-roots opposition following the signing of the Helsinki Accords in 1975, the growing frustration of a younger generation blocked from career advancement, and, last but not least, the so-called Gorbachev factor.[32] There is another possibility as well: After the

---

[31] Detlef Pollack, "Modernization and Modernization Blockages in GDR Society," in Konrad Jarausch, ed., *Dictatorship as Experience: Towards a Socio-Cultural History of the GDR* (New York, 1999), 28. This is a translation of the article cited in footnote 29 of the Introduction.

[32] For a useful overview of the literature, see Ihme-Tuchel, *DDR*, 73–89; Ross, *Dictatorship*, 126–48; see also Archie Brown, *The Gorbachev Factor* (Oxford, 1997). According to Jeannette Madarász, isolated social groups managed to come together during the final two year of the regime and help bring about its collapse. She does not explain clearly, however, why the divisions that had previously separated them (largely the result, in her view, of uneven access to privileges doled out by the regime) suddenly and supposedly receded in the late 1980s. See her *Conflict and Compromise in East Germany, 1971–1989: A Precarious Stability* (Houndmills, UK, 2003).

arrest or flight of those involved in the June 1953 uprising, it took another generation before a group of individuals would emerge that was willing to challenge the authority of the regime and energetically call into question its legitimacy.

But those who initiated the crucial events that led to the breaching of the Wall in the fall of 1989 were not industrial workers and collective farmers, the two largest social groups in the GDR and the main focus of this study: They were primarily artists, intellectuals, and religious figures in large cities such as Leipzig and Berlin. Ordinary East Germans living on the periphery would later join in the protest movement, but they were not the ones who jump-started it – and they were certainly not the ones who would eventually lead it.[33] Accommodation and fragmentation effectively forestalled large-scale unrest by these groups until the very end.

Since the absorption of the GDR into the Federal Republic more than a decade ago, the initial euphoria unleashed by the fall of the Berlin Wall has given way to disappointment and bitterness – *Anschluß* followed by melancholy, as Charles Maier has aptly put it.[34] High levels of unemployment, widespread feelings of social and economic insecurity, and a sense of being misunderstood and even ridiculed by their brethren in the West have led many East Germans to look back with derision on Chancellor Helmut Kohl's optimistic promise that most of them would be better off after unification. Much of this study has focused on the role that feelings of injustice and relative deprivation played in accounting for the longevity of the GDR. Such sentiments have not dissipated in the new Germany; they have instead taken on new forms of expression, as many former East Germans continue to compare their situation unfavorably with that of others – this time especially with those in the West. Up to now, much of this discontent has been channeled into electoral support for parties on the extreme left and right of the political spectrum. But could it be that the social frictions and jealousies that helped account for the long-term stability of the GDR will – under entirely different political conditions more open and more conducive to popular protest – lead at some point to instability in the new German state? This would be one of the great paradoxes of German unification.

---

[33] See, e.g., Karsten Timmer, *Vom Aufbruch zum Umbruch: Die Bürgerbewegung in der DDR 1989* (Göttingen, 2000); Christian Joppke, *East German Dissidents and the Revolution of 1989: Social Movement in a Leninist Regime* (New York, 1995). Also see Linda Fuller, *Where Was the Working Class? Revolution in Eastern Germany* (Urbana, IL, 1999). Compare the contrary claim that workers "played the decisive part in toppling the regime" in 1989 in Gareth Dale, *Popular Protest in East Germany, 1949–1989* (London, 2005), 186.

[34] Charles Maier, *Dissolution: The Crisis of Communism and the End of East Germany* (Princeton, NJ, 1997), 285–329.

Primary Sources

I. Archives

Thüringisches Staatsarchiv Rudolstadt (ThStA-R)
Kreisleitung der SED Saalfeld
Kreisparteikontrollkommission der SED Saalfeld
Bezirksleitung der SED Gera
Rat des Bezirkes Gera
Thüringisches Kreisamt Saalfeld
Kreisrat Saalfeld
Freier Deutscher Gewerkschaftsbund, Bezirksvorstand Gera
Freier Deutscher Gewerkschaftsbund, Kreisvorstand Saalfeld
Freie Deutsche Jugend, Kreisleitung Saalfeld
Kreisblock der Antifaschistischen Parteien Saalfeld
Volkspolizeikreisamt Saalfeld
Bezirksbehörde der Deutschen Volkspolizei Gera
Zentralverwaltung für Statistik, Kreisstelle Saalfeld
VEB Maxhütte Unterwellenborn
Grundorganisation der SED VEB Maxhütte Unterwellenborn
Grundorganisation der SED VEB Rotstern Saalfeld
Grundorganisation der SED VEB Wema Saalfeld
Grundorganisation der SED VEB Pumpspeicherwerk Hohenwarte
Grundorganisation der SED VEB Kraftverkehr Saalfeld
Grundorganisation der SED VEB Carl Zeiss, Fertigungsstätte Saalfeld
Grundorganisation der SED VEB Carl Zeiss Jena

Stadtarchiv Saalfeld (StA-S)
Sekretariat des Bürgermeisters
Allgemeine Verwaltung
Ratssitzungen
Abt. Handel und Versorgung
Abt. Organisation
Abt. Sozialwesen

Abt. Wohnungspolitik
Kaderabteilung/Personalakten
Statistische Angelegenheiten
Standesamt
Umsiedleramt

Kreisarchiv Saalfeld (KrA-S)
Vorsitzender des Kreisrates
Büro des Rates/Sekretariat des Rates
Abt. Inneres
Abt. Handel und Versorgung
Abt. Landwirtschaft
Abt. Wohnungspolitik
Kreisplanungskommission
Kaderabteilung
Org.–Instrukteurabteilung
Örtliche Versorgungswirtschaft
Amt für Arbeit
Gesundheitswesen und Sozialwesen

Thüringisches Hauptstaatsarchiv Weimar (ThHStA-W)
SED–Landesleitung Thüringen
Kreisrat Saalfeld[1]
Land Thüringen–Büro des Ministerpräsidenten
Thüringisches Ministerium des Innern
Landesbehörde der Volkspolizei Thüringen
Land Thüringen–Ministerium für Volksbildung
Personalakten thüringischer Behörden und Einrichtungen

Maxhütte Archiv Unterwellenborn (MxA-U)[2]
Werksleitung
Betriebsdirektion
Betriebsgewerkschaftsleitung

Unternehmensarchiv der Carl Zeiss Jena GmbH (UACZ)
Fertigungsstätte Saalfeld (Saalfelder Betriebsleitung)

Bundesbeauftragte für die Unterlagen des Staatssicherheitsdienstes der ehemaligen DDR, Außenstelle Gera (BStU ASt-G)
Kreisdienststelle Saalfeld
Bezirksverwaltung Gera

Stiftung Archiv der Parteien und Massenorganisationen der DDR im Bundesarchiv Berlin (SAPMO–BA)
Politbüro des Zentralkomitees

---

[1] This holding is now located in the Thüringisches Staatsarchiv Rudolstadt.
[2] This archive has been liquidated and its holdings transferred to the Thüringisches Staatsarchiv Rudolstadt.

Sekretariat des Zentralkomitees
Tagungen des Zentralkomitees
Nachlass Walter Ulbricht
Büro Ulbricht

Bundesarchiv, Abteilung Potsdam (BA-P)
Ministerium des Innern–Hauptverwaltung Deutsche Volkspolizei

Sächsisches Staatsarchiv Chemnitz (SStA-C)
SED–Gebietsleitung Wismut

Archiv der sozialen Demokratie in der Friedrich-Ebert-Stiftung, Bonn (AdsD)
Bestand Ostbüro

Archiv des Deutschen Liberalismus in der Friedrich-Naumann-Stiftung, Gummers-bach (ADL)
Kreisverband der LDPD Saalfeld
Bezirksverband der LDPD Gera
Ostbüro

Archiv für Christlich–Demokratische Politik in der Konrad-Adenauer-Stiftung e.V., Sankt Augustin (ACDP)
Bezirksvorstand der CDU Gera

Statistisches Bundesamt, Zweigstelle Berlin[3]
Statistisches Zentralamt der Staatlichen Plankommission
Statistisches Zentralamt der Deutschen Wirtschaftskommission

Institut für Sozialdatenanalyse e.V., Berlin
unpublished studies by the Akademie für Gesellschaftswissenschaften beim Zentralkomitee der SED

II. Interviews

Frieda Appelt (born 1924; clerk at district police bureau)
Hans Becher (born 1925; school administrator)
Gerd Friedrich (born 1939; engineer at VEB Wema)
Hans Gruner (born 1913; union chairman at VEB Zeiss)
Friedrich Jung (born 1926; vocational school teacher)
Horst Kämmer (born 1927; master craftsman, deputy union chairman at VEB Zeiss)
Horst Müller (born 1940; engineer at VEB Wema)
Richard Pohle (born 1921; mayor of Saalfeld)
Leopold Rölig (born 1921; mason, communist functionary)
Walter Schilling (born 1925; skilled worker at VEB Zeiss)
Bertold Ziener (born 1939; engineer at VEB Wema)

[3] These holdings are now located in the Statistisches Bundesamt in Bonn.

Index

Note: The names of all East German institutions, organizations, and political parties are listed under their full English translation and not under their German or English acronyms.